Can Language Be Planned?

Contributors

S. TAKDIR ALISJAHBANA

JYOTIRINDRA DAS GUPTA

JOSHUA A. FISHMAN

CHARLES F. GALLAGHER

MUHAMMAD ABDUL HAI

EINAR HAUGEN

BJÖRN H. JERNUDD

HERBERT KELMAN

JOHN MACNAMARA

CHAIM RABIN

JOAN RUBIN

BONIFACIO P. SIBAYAN

THOMAS THORBURN

WILFRED H. WHITELEY

Can Language Be Planned?

Sociolinguistic Theory and Practice for Developing Nations

EDITED BY JOAN RUBIN AND BJÖRN H. JERNUDD

An East-West Center Book
The University Press of Hawaii

Copyright © 1971 by The University Press of Hawaii

All rights reserved

International Standard Book Number: 0–8248–0100–8

Library of Congress Catalog Card Number: 70–129618

Printed at Heritage Printers, Inc., U.S.A.

Bound by Haddon Craftsmen, Inc., U.S.A.

First edition

CONTENTS

PREFACE

During the academic year 1968–69, four scholars, Jyotirindra Das Gupta, Joshua Fishman, Björn Jernudd, and Joan Rubin, met together at the East-West Center, Institute of Advanced Projects, Hawaii, to consider what the nature of language planning might be, what problems it might be expected to solve, and how it might shed light on some of the problems that some social sciences have been trying to consider. The inspiration for, and funding and administration of, this year belongs to Joshua Fishman. As one of the first sociolinguists, Dr. Fishman has in the past ten years succeeded in focusing attention on the importance of this new field and in promoting scholarship into its many aspects. An earlier conference (Airlie House, Virginia, November, 1966) organized by Charles Ferguson and Joshua Fishman considered language problems of developing nations; the year of research in Hawaii provided an opportunity to consider in depth some of the questions brought to light at this conference.

One of the special features of the year in Hawaii was a four-day meeting on language-planning processes. At the meeting, held in Hawaii during April 7–10, 1969, some ten participants (Alisjahbana, Ferguson, Gallagher, Hai, Haugen, Kelman, Macnamara, Rabin, Sibayan, and Thorburn) were invited on the basis of their previous personal experience with, or study of, language planning and policy or on the basis of a disciplinary focus that might shed light on language planning in the future. Together the participants represented several academic disciplines (anthropology, linguistics, sociolinguistics, political science, sociology, economics, economic planning, social psychology) and had knowledge about language policy and planning in several areas of the world (Indonesia, Philippines, Ireland, Kenya and Tanzania, Israel, Pakistan, and Turkey). Einar Haugen, one of the fathers of the study of language planning, was unable to attend. However, the editors are extremely pleased that he agreed to submit a paper, which has been included in this volume. Unfortunately, Abdul Hai was ill at the time of the meeting and could not attend. His recent death is a loss to the field.

The meeting proved highly successful as all the participants came away having seen language planning in a new light, having considered the potentialities of both the practical and theoretical products that language planning might offer and having had the pleasure of some highly stimulating discussions. The papers in this book represent a revised version of those presented to this meeting. The book itself represents only a beginning in what we feel must become a significant part of the field of sociolinguistics. Although the term language planning is to be found in the literature, this is the first time that a consideration of the potentialities and limitations of language planning as a sociolinguistic study and pursuit is taken up. It is also the first time that a multidisciplinary approach is brought to bear on the problems of language planning. All of these considerations are, of course, only a beginning; and our conclusions are only hypotheses to be used for further research.

This book is intended to serve several purposes: to demonstrate the need for a multidisciplinary approach to language planning, to awaken the interest of all the social sciences to the role of language in modernization, to interest social scientists in the theoretical gain to be had from the study of language planning, to help widen the field of sociolinguistics by interesting linguists in people's attempts to influence their own speech and the social and economic environment of deliberate language change, and to encourage participant language planners to scrutinize the processes that occur as they proceed to make and carry out language decisions. It is also meant to serve as a stimulus to research in language planning.

The year at the East-West Center for the above-mentioned four scholars was indeed only a beginning of their interest in language planning. Drs. Fishman and Ferguson have sought and obtained a three-year research grant from the Ford Foundation starting in September 1969 for the study of language-planning processes in four to five countries. Serving as country coordinators for this research will be Jyotirindra Das Gupta, Björn Jernudd, Joan Rubin, Joshua Fishman, and Charles Ferguson. As of this writing, Joan Rubin was already working in Indonesia with the full cooperation, participation, and interest of her Indonesian colleagues. Dr. Harsja Baktiar, dean of the Fakultas Sastra, Universitas Indonesia is serving as country director of the study.

Although this book rightly should have been edited by Joshua Fishman, he modestly declined in favor of the current editors in a generous gesture to further encourage their interest in the subject. We are both most indebted to Joshua for his support. Publication of this book and the year at the East-West Center would not have been possible without the grant that the Ford Foundation made for 1968–69. We wish to thank the Foundation for its continuous support and for its encouragement of our research and publication. We would also like to thank the East-West Center's Institute of Advanced Projects for providing salaries, offices, and logistic support during our year in beautiful Hawaii. Finally, we would like to thank the editorial staff for its patience with us as we gathered the revised papers from literally all four corners of this round world (which from a postal point of view does not always seem to have gotten much smaller).

January 2, 1970

Joan Rubin
Stanford University
Björn Jernudd
Monash University

INTRODUCTION: LANGUAGE PLANNING
AS AN ELEMENT IN MODERNIZATION

JOAN RUBIN
  Department of Anthropology, Tulane University
BJÖRN H. JERNUDD
  Department of Linguistics, Monash University

LANGUAGE PLANNING AS PRACTICED TODAY

The terms of reference defining the functions of Malaysia's Language and Literature Agency are as follows: (1) to develop and enrich the national language; (2) to promote literary talents, especially in the national language; (3) to print or publish or assist the printing or publication of books, magazines, pamphlets, and other forms of literature in the national language as well as in the other languages; (4) to standardize the spelling and pronunciation and to coin appropriate terminologies in the national language; and (5) to compile and publish a national language dictionary.

The Malaysian "language-planning agency" tries to meet these objectives by engaging in a wide variety of language activities, such as publishing textbooks, novels, and journals; convening meetings of subject specialists for terminology development; compiling dictionaries; and promoting language courses.

Such objectives and strategies relating to language problems are by no means unique to Malaysia. Other countries that face problems of rapid modernization and, perhaps, simultaneously seek national consolidation have also established similar agencies (for a survey of Southeast Asian agencies, see Noss, 1967; some others are listed in Tauli, 1968). The study of *language planning* describes decision-making about language. The recurrence, salience, and significance of language problems in developing societies press for overt techniques of solution and create a demand for a theory of action that would offer ways of finding and evaluating alternative solutions to given problems (Fishman, 1968). The formulation of such a theory has historic experience as a prerequisite. But historic experience alone is not enough; nor are established academic disciplines alone equipped to formulate such a theory. In the present volume, language planning is seen from the vantage point of sociolinguistics, sociology, social psychology, political science, and economics; for language planning cannot be seen in isolation from social planning. The coordination of people's views regarding language, the gathering of data as background to language decision-making, the technical tools for choosing among several alternatives, and the like are all problems that require the knowledge and methods of many and seemingly diverse disciplines.

Strong government concern with language, expressed by creating a national language-planning agency that has wide-ranging responsibilities, characterizes primarily the developing and new nations. Such a "policy approach" to language and communications development contrasts with the "cultivation approach" of many Western nations, where language problems are being solved through a variety of public and private institutions (Neustupný, 1968a; see also Fishman, paper 1, this volume; Das Gupta, 1968; Alisjahbana, 1965), rather than in a simple administrative framework. Whereas in developed countries people seldom speak about standardizing and modernizing an entire language system as a conscious or organized activity because these processes are now incrementally continued after a very long period leading toward consolidation, in African and Asian countries that have newly achieved nationhood, language planning is often considered as just one more task in the development plans of their countries.

LANGUAGE PLANNING AS A TOPIC OF STUDY

Most people, upon hearing the term language planning, assume that the appropriate specialist concerned is a linguist. In fact, many of the writers on this topic have been linguists. However, owing to their professional bias, the scholarly language-planning literature has not concerned itself with an obvious fact; namely, that language planning as part of social change is subject to the rules of this kind of change. The linguistic literature on language planning, instead of emphasizing the *change process,* has rather focused on the *linguistic product.* Moreover, since many linguists of the present generation generally believe that language is an "autonomous system" and therefore is not subject to deliberate modification by variables outside this system, they themselves have not been willing to participate in language planning. On the other hand, many persons who have concerned themselves with language planning have suffered from either of two other biases: they have looked for absolute and universally true answers to language problems in terms of linguistic variables alone; or they have been insufficiently aware of the social implications of their decisions.

Practitioners of actual language planning often attempt to solve language problems in purely linguistic terms either without considering the social environment in which a selected alternative is to be implemented or without attempting to predict outcomes. Thus they can never tell whether their activity has been successful. At the same time, however, they know a great deal first hand—and are at least unconsciously influenced by this knowledge—about the full chain of the decision-making process—a process, say, that starts with themselves, as originators of a new set of terms, and leads to the subject specialists, as users of such terms.

Much of language planning has also been relatively restricted because of the minor role that some practitioners have accepted for themselves—practitioners who are either unwilling or unable to consider the full importance that their work might have for a developing society. Interest in studying proposed solutions to language problems as a branch of the more general discipline of planning has only recently become of sufficient scope so that a discipline called language planning could be seriously considered.

The present interest has been sparked largely by the pioneering work of the linguist Einar Haugen, who not only used the term in his article (1966b) but also contributed an important study of actual language planning in Norway (1966a). More recent academic attention to general language-planning problems includes the work of Guxman (1960); Ray (1961 and 1963); Havránek (1963); Alisjahbana (1965); Tauli (1968); and Fishman, Ferguson, and Das Gupta (1968). Two countries that have studied their language-policy problems extensively to make concrete recommendations are Canada (1965, 1967, and 1968) and Ireland (1965, 1966, and 1968). A vast literature is available mainly locally, describing the organization and activities of various national academies (see, for example, the afore-mentioned Malaysian Language and Literature Agency, 1967; publications of the National Language Research Institute, Japan, for instance, 1966; or of a Swedish language agency, Allén, 1967).

The German literature on *"Sprachkultur"* is well known (see, for instance, the journals *Sprachpflege* and *Sprache im technischen Zeitalter*). In addition, there are articles and books that describe either the results of planning (Heyd, 1954) or the development of a given (set of) languages (Kurman, 1968; or Chatterji, 1926); or there are books that describe the principles to be used in solving specific language problems (see items listed under language problems in the suggested reading list at the end of this volume). Our point here is that, although the discipline of language planning as it is conceived by us is even more recent, in the embryonic stage, there are national traditions of language cultivation and development and that there are in the literature many descriptions of language problems, products, policies, and agencies awaiting systematization.

DEFINITION OF LANGUAGE PLANNING

Language planning is *deliberate* language change; that is, changes in the systems of language code or speaking or both that are planned by organizations that are established for such purposes or given a mandate to fulfill such purposes. As such, language planning is focused on problem-solving and is characterized by the formulation and evaluation of alternatives for solving language problems to find the best (or optimal, most efficient) decision. In all cases it is *future-oriented*; that is, the outcomes of policies and strategies must be specified in advance of action taken. Since such forecasting implies uncertainty or risk, planning must allow for reformulations as new situations develop (see below). Although change of language use and linguistic rules are the objects of language planning, such change does *not* take place *in vacuo*. Thus, language planning as a discipline must consider the facts of language within the fuller social context: it must consider the relevance of economic variables and interests (for a discussion of language as a resource, see Jernudd and Das Gupta, paper 11, this volume); the relevance of social variables and interests (for example, attitudes towards language and towards users of a language and the motivational links that relate the sociolinguistic systems to other social phenomena, Neustupný, 1968a); the relevance of political variables (such as the expression of vested interests through problems of language); and the relevance of demographic and psychological variables. As a discipline, language planning requires the mobilization of a great variety of disciplines because it implies the channeling of problems and values to and through some decision-making administrative structure.

LIMITATIONS AND UNKNOWNS
OF LANGUAGE PLANNING

Language planning, thus defined, can be a very useful tool; still there are limitations in the general planning theory that need to be kept in mind (for a fuller discussion, see Rubin, paper 12, this volume).

First of all, there is always the problem that there will be uncertainties even when there is a careful plan. These uncertainties can be classified into two types: those that are unknown (risk cases) and those that are only predictable within certain probability limits. While the former may be unknown at the beginning of the implementation process of the plan, it is possible to modify the plan as these appear, depending on their relevance to the goals to be attained. Moreover, although all of the environmental variables may not be forecast with a high degree of accuracy, it may still prove useful for the planner to isolate the various events that might occur and the actors or strategies appropriate for each plan (see Alderson and Halbert, 1968; and Thorburn, paper 13, this volume).

Second, there is still a discussion within a planning theory as to how big a goal one can or, prescriptively speaking, should tackle. Braybrooke and Lindblom (1963) discuss the difficulties of a plan that is too comprehensive. They list some eight reasons why this sort of approach—although used currently—is likely to fail. Yet at what point the goals are to be understood as being too general to be properly planned has not yet been clearly described.

Another practical limitation of planning is the costliness of making plans. It takes a good deal of time and energy to acquire the necessary information to make a good plan. Therefore, the cost of planning may not necessarily be felt to be rewarded by sufficient benefits. Alderson and Halbert (1968) suggest the following criteria to be used to assess the possibilities of planning: if the decisions are interdependent, if the cost of error is high, or if the environment is reasonably predictable. Other criteria might also serve as measures of the prognosticative utility of planning for a given set of circumstances.

While language behavior is subject to planning efforts (as well as to all of the constraints that political, social, economic, and cultural parameters place on any planning activity), language per se has certain characteristics that will color the kind of planning that is appropriate (see, for example, Alisjahbana, paper 9, this volume). Since language is partly innate behavior and something that is with us all the time, attempts at changing such behavior will have to take this fact into account. Thus, it may be that language-change processes will be slower than those of many other kinds of behavior, or it may be that language change requires a more intensive type of implementation.

If used in the right contexts, language planning can help to eliminate wastage (including, of course, human wastage); enhance communication, both within and between nations; and encourage feelings of unity and democracy.

A growth of scholarly concern with conscious language change and an accompanying intensification of a discussion concerning general aspects of such language determination would undoubtedly lead to more efficient decision-making with regard not only to the implementation of given language policies but also to the formulation of these policies themselves. Such concern would allow a greater realism to be injected into (1) the more technical matters of codifying and implementing terminologies, spellings, and the like; and (2) the politics of formulating national language programs. The growth of knowledge about language planning would aid new nationalism and internationalism alike: from the point of view of scholarly commitment to truth, it may remain entirely a matter of chance whose ideology is the benefactor. Although the individual scholar may prefer to work in situations and with data that mirror his own values, this does by no means exclude the use of his findings towards other goals; nor should such preferences prevent the registering of "undesirable" knowledge. Whether language planning contributes "more" to the consolidation of nationalism than to internationalism, we hope that the positive values of bridging communication gaps will outweigh the dangers of narrowly nationalistic attempts at isolating a speech community.

The question of what kinds of language planning can be useful remains open. Certainly the language problems to be solved are multiple, and the wastage of human resources owing to the many current *ad hoc* solutions are rather obvious. But several questions remain. One of these is: how much standardization is useful? To answer this question, we must specify and quantify differences in communication effects owing to unification (Thorburn, paper 13, this volume). Another question is: which part of language can you decide to do something about and which part must be left alone? Some aspects of language may be intractable, or there are, at least, some that cannot be changed easily. What kinds of elaboration are most effective? One may ask, for example, whether the specification of general rules for word-formation within a particular language is, under similar circumstances, more effective than the recommendation of specific words. Still another question is: what should be the speed at which novelty is introduced? Are some language features better introduced and enforced all at once while there are others that need to be implemented over a long period of time? Rabin (paper 5, this volume) discusses the pros and cons of rapid versus slow introduction of spelling reform.

To be meaningful and productive, the theory of language planning would need to specify in detail what kinds of language planning would be useful under what circumstances for what kinds of people speaking what kinds of languages. Haugen (1966a) has demonstrated how, unless the planners are clear about their goals and the strategies to achieve them, attempts at changing language may start an avalanche that may get out of hand. On the other hand, he has also demonstrated that many aspects of language have been subjected to manipulation by language planners and that control of language behavior has been exercised.

THE RELATION OF LANGUAGE PLANNING TO OTHER DISCIPLINES

While language planning borrows from other disciplines, it may also be expected to contribute to them. The focusing on people's attitudes about language and on their actions towards language should aid the understanding of the role of consciously induced change as a part of the theory of language change. Generalizations about the causes and possibilities of language change are often made in abstraction without sufficient emphasis on the social context of language structures (see the articles on linguistics by Hymes, Malkiel, and Gumperz in the *International Encyclopaedia of the Social Sciences*). Language planning will contribute towards an understanding of deliberate language change and its sociolinguistic environment, as well as help evaluate under what particular conditions deliberate change is likely to succeed or not.

Since an important set of goals of language planning concerns the improvement of communications, it must not remain isolated from the wider social concern of improving the entire communicative system. The theory, therefore, must state the relations of language factors to other aspects of communication, such as the graphic means of communicating versus the linguistic means, for example, and their interaction.

Language planning shares methodologies with other disciplines.

Hence, not only may it promise a contribution to the theory of language change but it will also share with this theory several sociolinguistic techniques in approaching language data. Thus, we have, for example, diachronic-linguistics theory and language-planning theory both of which employ sociolinguistic methods in recording and studying the areal and social propagation of linguistic innovations.

Perhaps more important than the above in the immediate future, however, is the link of language-planning theory to standardization theory, since the latter has developed primarily with regard to engineering problems and also through engineering organizations with regard to technical terminologies (see Wüster, 1966, about technical terminology; and Struglia, 1965, for bibliographical information about standardization).

In this volume, several papers view language as a resource, according to the methodology of economics. Language offers an object for economic study, which sharply illustrates the possibilities and difficulties of applying economic methods to less obviously pecuniary and sometimes non-quantifiable variables. The "cost-benefit" method (Thorburn, paper 13, this volume) may itself benefit from meeting the challenge of evaluating and systematizing consequences of proposed language change. Similarly, problems of educational measurement and educational-program formulation are brought out in Rubin's paper. Other examples could be added from the fields of sociology, social psychology, and many more.

THE PAPERS

Some of the contributions to the conference focused primarily on the motivational or rationalizing behavior behind language policy. Fishman relates nationalist ideology (subdivided into unification, authentification, and modernization) to the types of emphases that language planning may take, whereas Das Gupta focuses on religious ideology in the formation of language policy. Kelman suggests that, to enhance national mobilization, language planning ought to focus on the instrumental functions of language rather than on the sentimental functions. Ferguson in the discussion (paper not included) examined the relation between attitudes and patterns of usage suggesting that usage changes first, with attitudes and rationalization following thereafter. Whiteley's comparison of Kenyan and Tanzanian language policy suggests that, in Tanzania, Ferguson's sequence of usage first, then attitudes, is reversed. Gallagher suggests that language planning is most successful when it goes along with other kinds of social change. He also points out that Turkey has a tradition of thorough linguistic reorientation, which in turn suggests that we may need to explore the features of, and distinguish between, societies with and without such readiness to accept foreign linguistic influence.

Several contributors described in detail aspects of planning in their own countries. Each highlights some deficiencies that their language planners did not—and should have—attended to. In Israel, Rabin focuses on (1) the gap between suggestions for spelling reform and the strategies used to carry out these reforms; (2) the importance of the goals and interests of the planners themselves in agreeing to and promoting spelling reforms; and (3) the many vested interests that have impeded the promotion of such a reform. Sibayan describes the experiments used to evaluate language use in education, the policies that were adopted as a consequence of the results of these experiments, and some of the social factors behind the subsequent discussion. He discusses in detail a survey conducted to evaluate current attitudes towards language-teaching policies. Macnamara suggests that one reason why Irish language planning has been so unsuccessful is the lack of knowledge of the people's desires in kind: no clear objectives of language policy were ever specified; no attempt (with the exception of his own work, we would like to add) has ever been made to forecast what the outcome might be of a particular policy as well as of the important fact that to promote Irish was to go against the instrumental need that English already satisfied. Alisjahbana, who has a great deal of personal experience in Indonesian language planning, emphasizes the need to include psychological, cultural, and social constraints in language planning to insure some measure of success. He describes some of the problems of grammar standardization and vocabulary elaboration, which the planners had to face in Indonesia.

Jernudd and Das Gupta in their joint paper take the view that language is a resource, and they develop a rationale for the study of language planning on this basis. Rubin demonstrates how evaluation procedures could be a useful part of the language-planning process. Thorburn and, through his inspiration, Jernudd show an approach to choosing an optimal planning alternative by using cost-benefit models for decision-making. Das Gupta focuses on the kinds of pressure groups that operate in language decision-making, while Rabin studies the linguistic goals that planners may have. Haugen's paper scrutinizes Tauli's idealistic view of the possibility of finding universally valid answers to particular linguistic problems.

The list of selected references tries to direct scholars and language-planning practitioners to a literature that exemplifies the work of language-planning agencies, of government proposals for planning, of attempts to define language planning, and of discussions of language problems both from a general and a specific point of view.

CONCLUDING REMARKS

Although our desire in this book is to begin to establish constraints on theory based on practice and to enhance practice through a more coherent theory, we are aware that this volume is just a beginning to fulfilling this desire. We still do not know how language planning *actually* operates: what are the goals that planners have considered, what motivates their considerations of particular goals and their acceptance of certain goals, what are the alternative strategies that the planners consider, how do these express given goals, how do they evaluate the strategies, what outcomes do planners predict for various strategies, and what does in fact happen? We do not know in any detail just how well the abstract notions thus far delimited correspond to realities of language planning. We need to know what kinds of decisions are made, what influences these decisions, what limitations must be taken into account, and in what areas of language-behavior planning can be meaningful, feasible, and even profitable. To meet these questions, practitioners of language planning should be encouraged to publish details of their decision-making so that others may profit from their first-hand knowledge and experience. They should in turn be encouraged to look at their own decisions to improve them. We hope that the efforts in this book will help. We also hope that academicians will find language planning an interesting way to gain insight into human motivations, rationalizations, and decision-making within the process of social change.

REFERENCES

Alderson, Wroe and Halbert, Michael H. 1968. *Men, Motives and Markets.* Englewood Cliffs: Prentice-Hall.

Alisjahbana, S. Takdir. 1965. New National Languages: A Problem Modern Linguistics Has Failed to Solve. *Lingua,* 15: 515–530.

————. This volume. Some Planning Processes in the Development of the Indonesian-Malay Language. Paper 9.

Allén, S.; Dahlstedt, K-H.; Fant, G.; Marc-Wogau, K.; and Teleman, U. 1967. *Språk, Språkvård och Kommunikation* [Language, Cultivation of Language and Communication]. Verdandi-orientering no. 5. Lund: Prisma.

Braybrooke, David and Lindblom, Charles E. 1963. *A Strategy of Decision:*

Policy Evaluation as a Social Process. Glencoe: Free Press.

Bright, William, ed. 1966. *Sociolinguistics. Proceedings of the UCLA Sociolinguistics Conference, 1964.* Janua Linguarum, Series Maior, 20. The Hague: Mouton.

Canada. Royal Commission on Bilingualism and Biculturalism. 1965. *A Preliminary Report.* Ottawa: The Queen's Printer.

————. 1967. *General Introduction, Book I: The Official Languages.* Ottawa: The Queen's Printer.

————. 1968. *Book II: Education.* Ottawa: The Queen's Printer.

Chatterji, S. K. 1926. *Origin and Development of the Bengali Language.* Calcutta.

Das Gupta, Jyotirindra. 1968. Language Diversity and National Development. *In* Fishman, Ferguson, and Das Gupta, 17–26.

Dewan Bahasa dan Pustaka [The Language and Literature Agency]. 1967. *A General Outline of Its First Ten-Year Progress and Achievement.* Kuala Lumpur.

Fishman, Joshua A. 1968. Sociolinguistics and the Language Problems of the Developing Countries. *In* Fishman, Ferguson, and Das Gupta, 3–16.

————. This volume. The Impact of Nationalism on Language Planning: Paper 1.

Fishman, Joshua A.; Ferguson, Charles A.; and Das Gupta, Jyotirindra, eds. 1968. *Language Problems of Developing Nations.* New York: John Wiley and Sons.

Guxman, M. M., ed. 1960. *Voprosy Formirovanija i Razvitija Nacional'nyx Jazykov* [Formation and Development of National Languages]. Moscow.

Haugen, Einar. 1966a. *Language Conflict and Language Planning: The Case of Modern Norwegian.* Cambridge: Harvard University Press.

————. 1966b. Linguistics and Language Planning. *In* Bright, 50–71.

Havránek, Bohuslav. 1963. *Studie o Spisovném Jazyce* [Studies on the Literary Language]. Prague: Naklad ČSAV.

Heyd, Uriel. 1954. *Language Reform in Modern Turkey.* Oriental Notes and Studies, 5. Jerusalem: Israel Oriental Society.

Ireland. Commission on the Restoration of the Irish Language. 1965. *The Restoration of the Irish Language.* Dublin: Stationery Office.

————. 1966. *White Paper on the Restoration of the Irish Language. Progress Report for the Period Ended March 31, 1966.* Dublin: Stationery Office.

————. 1968. *White Paper on the Restoration of the Irish Language. Progress Report for the Period Ended March 31, 1968.* Dublin: Stationery Office.

Jernudd, Björn H. and Das Gupta, Jyotirindra. This volume. Towards a Theory of Language Planning. Paper 11.

Kokuritsu Kokugo Kenkyūzyo [National Language Research Institute]. 1966. *An Introduction to the National Language Research Institute.* Tokyo.

Kurman, George. 1968. *The Development of Written Estonian.* Indiana University Publications, Uralic and Altaic Series, 99. Bloomington: Indiana University Press.

Neustupný, Jiří V. 1968a. Language Problems of National Development. Paper presented at the *Symposium on Current Frontiers in Linguistic Anthropology* held at the Eighth International Congress of Anthropological and Ethnological Sciences, Tokyo and Kyoto, September 3–10. Mimeo.

————. 1968b. Some General Aspects of "Language" Problems and "Language" Policy in Developing Societies. *In* Fishman, Ferguson, and Das Gupta, 285–294.

Noss, Richard. 1967. *Language Policy and Higher Education.* Higher Education and Development in South East Asia, 3:2. Paris: UNESCO and the International Association of Universities.

Ray, Punya S. 1961. Language Planning. *Quest,* 31: 32–39.

————. 1963. *Language Standardization.* The Hague: Mouton.

Rabin, Chaim. This volume. Spelling Reform—Israel 1968. Paper 5.

Rubin, Joan. This volume. Evaluation and Language Planning. Paper 12.

Struglia, Erasmus J., ed. 1965. *Standards and Specifications: Information Sources.* Detroit: Gale Research.

Tauli, Valter. 1968. *Introduction to a Theory of Language Planning.* Acta Universitatis Upsaliensis, Studia Philologiae Scandinavicae Upsaliensia, 6. Uppsala: University of Uppsala.

Thorburn, Thomas. This volume. Cost-Benefit Analysis in Language Planning. Paper 13.

Wüster, E. 1966. *Internationale Sprachnormung in der Technik* [International Standardization of Technical Language]. Bonn.

The Motivation and Rationalization
for Language Policy

1. THE IMPACT OF NATIONALISM ON LANGUAGE PLANNING[1]

JOSHUA A. FISHMAN
Ferkauf Graduate School, Yeshiva University

Both modern nationalism as a mass movement and language planning as an aspect of national modernization are Western influences in South and Southeast Asia. At the same time, they are also reactions against Western influences. In either case they have been only selectively accepted or followed when compared to their original, European models. It is the purpose of this chapter to indicate the major similarities and differences between earlier European manifestations of nationalism and its impact on European language planning (these manifestations being themselves rather variegated and, therefore, ripe for picking and choosing on the part of Asian and African modernizers) and the subsequent recurrences of nationalism and language planning in South and Southeast Asia to this very day.

NATIONALISM

Three broad emphases characterize the manifestations of modern mass nationalism in Europe since the days of the French Revolution and its Napoleonic aftermath:

Unification

Nationalism as an integrative movement seeks to go beyond the primordial ties to family and locality (which defined the affiliative horizon of the common man in predominantly pre-industrial and pre-urban times) and to forge wider bonds that can draw the rural, the urban, and the regional into a broader unity: the nationality. In its birth throes nationalism stresses the inherent unity of populations that have never been aware of such unity before. In its further development nationalism may stress uniformation rather than unification alone.

Authentification

Nationalism is uniqueness-oriented. The avowed rationale for the unification of hitherto particularistic and diverse subgroups and the manifest
dynamism both for the unificatory as well as for the purposive goals of
nationalism are the ethnic uniqueness and cultural greatness of the nationality. This uniqueness, it is claimed, was, in the past, responsible for
glorious attainments. If it can be recaptured in all of its authenticity,
then, it is predicted, surely greatness will once again be achieved and,
this time, permanently retained.

Modernization

Nationalism is a response to the problems and opportunities of modernity.
Under the leadership of new proto-elites[2] that are oriented with respect
to the challenges involved, nationalism brings to bear the weight of unified
numbers and the dynamism of convictions of uniqueness upon the pursuit
of organized cultural self-preservation, the attainment of political independence, the improvement of material circumstances, or the attainment
of whatever other purpose will enhance the position of the nationality in
a world in which social change is markedly rapid and conflictive.

All three ingredients mentioned above are essential for differentiating
between nationalism and other social movements.[3] Without recognizing
the ingredient of broader unification, nationalism cannot be differentiated
from millenial sectarianisms, which, though alienated from most of their
contemporaries, nevertheless, stress uniqueness as a response to the corruptions of modern life. Without recognizing the stress on ethnic or
indigenous uniqueness, nationalism cannot be differentiated from cross-
national movements for political, economic, or cultural planning, including international socialism and various regional confederations.
Without recognizing the stress on accepting and overcoming the obstacles
of modernization, nationalism cannot be differentiated from nativistic
and traditionalistic movements that seek a genuine return to the ways of
the past rather than (as in the case of nationalism) a selective and
purposive orientation thereto.[4]

Dialectic

It is quite apparent from the foregoing that there is a built-in dialectic
within nationalism, a quite inevitable tension between its major components. Most obvious is the tension between the requirements of modernization and those of authentification. The one emphasizes the instrumental

uniformities required by modern politico-operational integration and is constantly straining toward newer, more rational, more efficient solutions to the problems of today and tomorrow. The other emphasizes the sentimental uniformities required by continuity based on sociocultural integration and is constantly straining towards purer, more genuine expressions of the heritage of yesterday and of long ago.

A potential conflict also exists between the goal of authentification and that of unification since, in reality, pre-nationalist authenticity is highly localized. As a result, the supralocal authenticity sought by nationalism must, to a large extent, be elaborated and interpreted rather than merely returned to or discovered ready made. The more stress on real authenticity, therefore, the more danger of regionalism and ultimate secessionism. The more stress on unification/uniformation, the less genuine authentification.

Even unification/uniformation and modernization are frequently at odds with each other. Some modern goals might well be more fully or easily attained through the encouragement of diversity (e.g., relations with important neighboring sources of supply might well be improved if ethnic minorities speaking the same languages as those used in the sources of supply were encouraged to maintain their distinctiveness), while some pre-existing uniformities are actually weakened rather than strengthened by industrialization, urbanization, and other modernity tendencies (e.g., the weakening of religious bonds).

It is part and parcel of the essence of nationalism to incorporate these potentially conflicting themes in its basic ideology. Similarly, it is part and parcel of the essence of nationalism to engage the dialectic that is caused by the tension between these themes and to derive from this dialectic a constant procession of solutions to the problems engendered by its own ideological commitments. It is this dialectic between potentially conflicting elements that constantly recharges the dynamism of nationalist causes. Their business is always unfinished because none of the goals of nationalist ideology is ever fully attained or even substantially assured, not only because of possible outside opposition, but also because of the internal instability of any resolution between its own contending components.

TYPES OF EUROPEAN NATIONALISM

Modern European nationalisms were generally responses to the same co-occurrences that prompted other major mass modernization movements of the past two centuries (widespread dislocations and disorganization of recently urbanized populations brought on by the impact of industrialization, the appearance of proto-elites offering action-oriented solutions to mass problems related to social change, and the massification of political and cultural participation in response to the pressures exerted by both the masses and elites referred to). While nationalism proved to be combinable, perhaps, in view of the similarity in its origins, with all major co-occurring ideologies (*viz.*, democratic nationalism, socialist nationalism, facist nationalism, etc.), it contributed a very special emphasis of its own: *its stress on the ethnic authenticity of the nationality*. This stress appears to have been recognized in two different (but interrelated) fashions throughout the course of the nineteenth century.

The State into Nationality Process

Nationality in the older and more firmly established European states was considered to be a by-product of the common political-operational institutions that had evolved in these states over the centuries. By the early nineteenth century, these states had already gone through lengthy and successive processes of expansion and unification, which, on the one hand, had produced a rather widespread sentiment of common nationality among their urban upper and middle classes and which, on the other hand, made it easier for them to cope with the problems of continued social change. These were the so-called (and self-called) historic nations of Europe who could claim in the nineteenth century that their primary institutions (their royal houses, their governmental traditions, their educational systems, their well established commercial and industrial patterns, and, above all, their centuries of "shared experiences") had produced the unified and authentic nationalities that populated them. Common nationality, therefore, was a derivative, a by-product, of common institutions rather than anything that could exist prior to or without such institutions. The "historic nations" of Europe were, by consensus, England, France, Spain, Portugal, Holland, Denmark, and Sweden and, at least potentially, also the Russian, Austro-Hungarian, and Ottoman empires. The fact that these latter three were still digesting various ethnic groups was well recognized, but it was assumed not only that they would succeed in doing so but also that it was only natural and proper that they continue to do so. Had not England digested the Welsh, the Scots, and the Irish? Had not France digested the Bretons, the Normans, the Gascons, the Occitans; and Spain the Galicians, the Catalons, the Basques, and the like? The same process of unification and re-authentification on a broader base would doubtlessly occur in the still multiethnic empires as well, given time and the improvement of their primary institutions. This then became the target of nationalism in the "historic nations" of nineteenth century Europe: the institutional liberalization and modernization of the established states, for only such liberalization and modernization could alleviate the suffering of the masses, could further the unity of states, and could constructively harness the genius of nationalities that the common institutions had created. The nationalism of the "historic nations" of the early nineteenth century was, therefore, liberal nationalism. It was the nationalism of those who already had their own historically evolved and recognized states and state institutions. It was also the nationalism of the colonizers, for the "historic nations" of Europe were, simultaneously, the nations that held, and were to continue to seek, political and economic colonies, both close at hand as well as in new territories beyond the seas, in the Americas, in Asia, and in Africa. It was this supralocal brand of nationalism (with its stress on the integrative capacity of political-operational institutions from which is derived a more abstract level of sociocultural authenticity) that they exported willy-nilly to their far-flung outposts.

Nationality into State Processes

The Napoleonic wars and the widespread but successful revolutions of 1830 and 1848 increased the awareness of European liberal intellectuals that there *were* apparently *some* nationalities who *were* such even in the absence of states of their own. Could anyone deny that the Greeks, the Poles, the Germans, the Italians, the Hungarians, and the Irish were nationalities? Although they had no states of their own at the time, and, therefore, no integrating state institutions under their own control, they nevertheless once had had them, long ago; and these, it was believed, had left such an imprint on the life of the people that they had continued as nationalities, as "defeated historic nationalities," on the strength of their common past memories.

The theory of the primacy of established institutions and of the derivative nature of nationality was salvaged by the subcategory of "defeated historic nations," and liberal nationalists of the "historic nations" frequently championed the causes of such nationalities, both for altruistic and for balance-of-power reasons.

The "Peoples without Histories"

Down to the very end of the nineteenth century and even into the twentieth, the intellectuals and spokesmen of the "historic nations" of the Atlantic coastline of Europe continued to argue, and then to plead, on behalf of the validity and the morality of the primacy of state-into-nationality process. Their efforts, however, were largely in vain because the very populations whom they sought to contain (and, in contrast, with whom they had termed themselves "historic nations") could not be contained.

The outmoded political-operational institutions of the multiethnic empires of Central, Eastern, and Southern Europe could not begin to fashion sufficiently integrative sociocultural bonds to compensate for the severe dislocation of their ethnically variegated rural populations. Proto-elites, trained in Western Europe, incessantly appeared to organize the mass demand for material improvement and for popular participation along ethnic lines. In organizing, in activating, and in focusing the masses, the proto-elites proceeded not only to capitalize and elaborate upon widespread sociocultural integrative themes of prior stability, justice, glory, and independence but also to fashion from them a view of nationality that was particularly appropriate for their own needs.

Among the submerged peoples of Europe, nationality was espoused as a primary, natural phenomenon, which, in turn, gave rise to the state as a secondary, instrumental by-product. Nationalities represented God-given demarcations or unities, and, as such, their uniqueness deserved to be prized, defended, liberated, and enhanced. These uniquenesses—and first and foremost among them, their respective vernaculars—were not only reflections of the limitless ingenuity and bounty of the Divine Force but also, each in its own right, directly responsible for the past period of greatness and glory that each submerged nationality had at one time experienced. The nationalist mission, therefore, was to recover or reconstruct the authentic uniqueness of the nationality (which had been contaminated by foreign models) and, thereby, to recover for the *present* as well as establish for the future the greatness that had existed in the *past*.

By means of this interpretation of nationality, the peoples of Central, Eastern, and Southern Europe sought to attain two goals. They did not want to be "peoples without histories" or even new nationalities; rather, they wanted to view themselves as continuations of old and once-illustrious traditions. However, neither they nor their leaders wanted to return to the past. Therefore, their slogan was "We must be ———— and Europeans." The past was a key to the spirit of greatness, but, once unlocked, this spirit was to be used to overcome current hardships and to gain the good things of the world today. Thus, more recent European nationalism emphasized the ethnic uniqueness and authenticity of the nationality. Nationalities created states for their own protection and enhancement—for the recovery, cultivation, and enhancement of linguistic and cultural treasures. The nationality is primary and eternal. The state is derivative and unstable.[5]

Although their nationality-into-state view of nationalism contributed mightily to the trials and tribulations that destroyed the multiethnic empires of the Habsburgs, the Czars, and the Sultans, it had but faint echoes throughout most of Africa and Asia. Between the two of them, however, the state-into-nationality processes and nationality-into-state processes reflect the two kinds of integrative bonds upon which all nations depend and which constantly reinforce each other, converge with each other, and give birth to each other. Just as the state-into-nationality nations stress(ed) their common sociocultural bonds, particularly in times of stress, so did (and do) the nationality-into-state nations stress politico-operational institutions as soon as they gain(ed) independence and face(d) the functional problems of modern nationhood.[6]

TWO EXAMPLES OF LANGUAGE PLANNING IN EUROPE

Even if (as would be useful for other purposes) we restrict language planning[7] to the elaboration, codification, and implementation that go on once language-policy decisions have been reached and, furthermore, even if we restrict our attention to language planning on behalf of varieties being put to newer and "higher" purposes than those to which they hitherto had normally been put, we nevertheless find ample illustrations of such planning in each of the two types of European nationalisms that we have reviewed.

In France

The classical example of language planning in the context of state-into-nationality processes is that of the French Academy. Founded in 1635—i.e., at a time well in advance of the major impact of industrialization and urbanization—the Academy, nevertheless, came after the political frontiers of France had long since approximated their current limits. Nevertheless, sociocultural integration was still far from attained at that time, as witnessed by the facts that in 1644 the ladies of Marseilles Society were unable to communicate with Mlle. de Scudéry in French; that in 1660 Racine had to use Spanish and Italian to make himself understood in Uzès; and that even as late as 1789 half of the population of the South did not understand French. The unparalleled literary creativity in French under the patronage of Louis IV could aim, at most, at a maximal audience of two million literates (out of a total estimated population of twenty million). However, actually, no more than two hundred thousand participated in the intellectual life of the country, and many of these considered Italian, Spanish, and Occitan far more fitting vehicles for cultured conversation, whereas for publications Latin, too, was a common rival. All in all, the French Academy assumed an unenviable task—and one much ridiculed throughout the centuries—when it presumed to codify French vocabulary, grammar, and spelling to perfect refined conversation and written usage.[8]

Several aspects of the Academy's approach show its premodernization goals and views. Far from seeking to provide technical nomenclatures for industrial, commercial, and other applied pursuits, the Academy steadfastly refused to be concerned with such "uncultured" and "unrefined" concerns. Instead of attempting to reach the masses with its products, the Academy studiously aimed its publications (at least for three centuries, if not longer) at those already learned in the French language. Finally, instead of appealing to anything essentially French in "spirit," in "genius," in "essence," or in "tradition," it defended its recommendations via appeals to such purportedly objective criteria as euphonia, clarity, and necessity (redundancy). More than two hundred years after its founding, when the Academy's continued lack of concern for the technical vocabulary of modernization had come to be accompanied by attacks on *anglomania* and the tendency to *angliciser*, the worst that was said about overly frequent English borrowings was that they were unnecessary rather than that they were un-French.[9]

From the point of view of its members, the Academy was an institution—one of several—whose goal was to fashion and reinforce French nationality. The Academy existed prior to, and independently of, the French nationality. Indeed, French nationality was but a by-product of the work of the Academy and of similar institutions and, therefore, logically could not and morally should not be invoked to carry out the Academy's goals. A similar disinclination to appeal to nationalist authenticity marks the largely informal efforts on behalf of language planning in England and the much more formal efforts of the (Royal) Academy in Spain.

In the nationality-into-state context, the links between the authenticity component of nationalism and language planning, on the one hand, and the modernization-unification components of nationalism and language planning, on the other hand, are much more prominent and much more conscious. As a result, institutions and guidelines for language planning come into being very early in the mobilization process and remain in the foreground at least until authenticity, modernization, and unification seem reasonably assured. Here we are dealing with more highly pressured situations in which language planning is of high priority not only because of ideological considerations but also because without it the new elites can neither communicate with each other about specialized elitist concerns while remaining within the limits of authenticity nor move the masses towards greater unification, authentification, and modernization.

In Turkey

The case of Turkish language planning[10] is justifiably well known for the speed and the thoroughness with which it pursued modernization. As part of its over-all post World War I program of seeking a *new* Turkish identity (in contrast with its old Ottoman-Islamic identity), governmentally sponsored language planning conscientiously and vigorously moved to attain script reform (Roman in place of Arabic script), to attain Europeanization of specialized nomenclatures (rather than the Arabic and Persian loan words hitherto used for learned or cultured purposes), and to attain vernacularization or simplification of vocabulary, grammar, and phraseology for everyday conversational use (discarding the little understood and ornate flourishes patterned on Arabic or Persian).

Obviously, Turkish language planning was a part of Atatürk's over-all program of modernization. No nationalist movement, however, can continue to push modernization without regard for authenticity. Thus the break with the holy Arabic script soon came to be defended on the ground that it was unsuited for the requirements of authentic Turkish phonology. Since even the prophet had clearly been an Arab before he was a Mohammedan, he could hardly dispute the desire of Turks to put the needs of their Turkish authenticity first. The vast Europeanization of Turkish technical vocabulary had to be rationalized on the basis of the Great Sun Language theory. On the basis of this authenticity-stressing theory, it was claimed that all European languages were initially derived from Turkish. In that case, all recent borrowings could be regarded as no more than reincorporations into the Turkish language of words or morphs that it had originally possessed but lost under the foreign impact of Arabic and Persian. Thus, the process of borrowing from European sources was ultimately not rationalized as a modernizing step, but, rather as an authenticating step! So, too, and even more clearly, was the vernacularization and simplification of non-technical Turkish. Here the language of the Anatolian peasant was held up as a model of purity and authenticity on the ground that it had been least contaminated by foreign influences and least corrupted by foreign fads.

Thus, on every front, decisions about language modernization in Turkey were finally rationalized and legitimatized through sentiments of authenticity and a way was found for these two components of nationalist ideology to reinforce common nationalist goals rather than to conflict with them or with each other. Such dialectic skill is by no means rare in the annals of language planning within highly nationalist contexts. On occasion, modernization may appear to have the upper hand and, on other occasions, authentification is stressed. In the longer run, however, what needs to be grasped is not so much the seesawing back-and-forth as the need to retain both components (actually all three components since uniformation, too, must not be lost); and what needs to be found is a *modus vivendi* between them. Many examples of arriving at resolutions to the contradictory pressures built into nationalist language planning are to be found in the Estonian, Czech, Ukrainian, Greek, Turkish, and other relatively recent European language-planning experiences. These examples deserve at least as much attention as do those drawn from more uncompromising periods in which one or another component of the "holy trinity" was stressed.

SOUTH AND SOUTHEAST ASIAN NATIONALISM

If we review the past half century of South and Southeast Asian nationalism[11] (combining approximately three decades of pre-independence and two decades of post-independence history), we find that it is overwhelmingly of the state-into-nationality variety. Its emphases are still primarily instrumental, with a stress on the building of modern and unified politico-operational institutions, out of which, it is hoped, will develop a new and broader level of sociocultural integration and authenticity as Indians, as Pakistanis, as Malaysians, as Indonesians, as Filipinos, and the like. In this sense, South and Southeast Asian nationalisms follow directly in the tradition of the nationalisms of their former colonial masters (as well as in the footsteps of their own selectively reconstructed and interpreted Great Traditions), although, of course, without anything like the long experience with autonomous politico-operational integration available to the Euro-American state-nationalities by the time they began to face the stresses of modernization. As a result, South and Southeast Asian nationalisms present a combination of state-into-nationality *ideologies* plus nationality-into-state *urgency and inexperience.*

Although South and Southeast Asian nationalism focuses upon modernization and upon unification (the latter component requiring particular attentions since the actual ethnic diversity encountered is often far greater than that which existed in the multiethnic states of pre-World War I Central, Eastern, and Southern Europe), there *is,* nevertheless, attention to the rediscovery and re-creation of unifying authenticity. To some extent, such authenticity is found in great pre-Western traditions and glories; to some extent, it is found in more recent experiences of struggling against *political* (pre-independence) and *economic* (post-independence) colonialism. In either case, however, the authentification themes in South and Southeast Asian nationalism are supraethnic. Indeed, all attempts to revise the ethnically meaningless political boundaries inherited from colonial rule (i.e., all attempts to pursue nationality-into-state nationalism) have been assiduously resisted and decried as "colonialism in disguise" and as "artificially contrived by Western economic interests."

Had similar developments come to pass in Europe, then the Austro-Hungarian, Russian, and Ottoman Empires not only would have remained intact territorially but also would have converted into new politico-operational structures in which ethnic Austrians (Germans), Hungarians, Russians, and Turks would no longer have been undisputed masters relative to Czechs, Slovaks, Croates, Poles, Ukrainians, Armenians, Arabs, and countless others. Instead, as we know, these multiethnic empires were burst assunder, and their fragmentation was legalized, justified, and protected by the Versailles and Trianon treaties. In South and Southeast Asia, on the other hand, as well as in all the other new nations of Africa and Asia, there has been relatively little redrawing of colonial boundaries, either along ethnic or other sociocultural integrative lines, neither at the time of independence nor since. Save for Ceylon, Burma, Pakistan, Cambodia, Laos, and Vietnam, there have been no ethnic secessions or divisions;[12] and save for the unification of West Irian with Indonesia (and the unification of British and Italian Somaliland, as well as the short-lived unification of Egypt and Syria, outside of the area that we are discussing), there have been no (quasi-)ethnic unifications.

Certainly, this represents one of the major differences between the somewhat earlier national independence movements in Europe and the somewhat later ones in Asia, a difference which harks back to the differing models of nationalism under which they were conducted.

LANGUAGE PLANNING IN SOUTH
AND SOUTHEAST ASIA

The lesser stress on ethnic authenticity in South and Southeast Asian nationalism thus far is reflected in the correspondingly greater roles of both indigenous and imported Languages of Wider Communication (rather than of vernaculars alone) as languages of central government and higher education. The well-nigh-complete and rapid displacement of Latin, French, German, Russian, and Arabic that marked the end of Austro-Hungarian, Czarist, and Ottoman hegemony in Central, Eastern, and Southern Europe has had no parallel in South and Southeast Asia.[13] Even the displacement of Dutch in Indonesia was conducted with a regional Language of Wider Communication in mind (a variety of Malay), rather than on behalf of a vernacular. Although some vernaculars have gained a level of recognition since independence that they never had in colonial days, the positions of English and French, on the one hand, and of Hindi, Urdu, Malay, Indonesian, and Pilipino, on the other hand, are definite signs of the continued supraethnic stress of South and Southeast Asian language planning.

Indeed, the most central symbols and institutions of nationhood, the very processes of modernization and unification per se, are generally not related to vernaculars at all. Thus, as the nations of South and Southeast Asia progress along the path towards politico-operational integration, we may expect that the new sociocultural integration that they must seek to develop and the authenticity that they must seek to stress will also be supraethnic. In the language-planning field, this has taken the direction of protecting and increasing the authenticity of the non-Western Languages of Wider Communication that have come to be adopted for national unificatory purposes. In this sense, the views of the language-planning agencies of South and Southeast Asia[14] are constantly becoming more and more similar to those of early twentieth century Central, Eastern, and Southern Europe (even though they are not dealing as exclusively with vernaculars); and less and less like those of state-into-nationality contexts that originally provided them with models.

Romanization of Script

Wherever classical literary traditions existed in pre-independence South and Southeast Asia, Romanization of script has usually been rejected. Although a modicum of Romanization is practiced in conjunction with highly technical and advanced scientific work conducted in India, Pakistan, and Ceylon (e.g., the proposals to introduce Romanization of script of a wider front)—as an aid to literacy, modernization, or interregional communication—it has been resisted as vigorously in those countries as it has been in China, Japan, or Israel outside of the area under consideration. The mass ideologization of this resistance is consistently in terms of indigenous authenticity as opposed to foreign artificiality.[15]

Purification

The tendency to reject European or, more generally, "international" lexical or morphological items, even for rather technical scientific or governmental work, is increasing throughout South and Southeast Asia. So, too, is the tendency to limit the various influences of the vernacular on the national languages, even though such influences would tend to make these languages more widely understood. With respect to Hindi, these tendencies take the direction successively of more extreme Sanscritization, ignoring the pleas of educators and statesmen alike that such treatment severely restricts the functional utility of the language. A similar process of Arabo-Persianization (and Islamization) is transforming High Urdu. In Malaysia, Indonesia, and the Philippines, it leads to a growing emphasis on Austronesian derivatives, rather than on Graeco-Latin roots, in developing the specialized nomenclatures that Malay, Indonesian, and Pilipino increasingly require. In most of the earlier twentieth century European cases of language planning, the purification efforts were directed at one or another neighboring vernacular rather than at internationalisms as such.[16] In South and Southeast Asia, given the general identification of internationalisms with Euro-American colonialism, purification shows tendencies of combating "cultural colonialism" much more than neighboring vernaculars, all the more so, since the latter have little if any national significance.[17] The interest in indigenizing the national languages of South and Southeast Asia is a definite sign of the new and broader sociocultural integration that they must succeed in developing to the end that a new supraethnic authenticity will develop that will correspond to the new unification and modernization that has been emphasized thus far.[18]

CONCLUSIONS

South and Southeast Asian nationalism is slowly but predictably being transformed from complete reliance on state-into-nationality processes into increasing attention to (supraethnic) nationality-into-state processes as well. In this transition we may expect a growing ideologized stress on indigenousness in general and on the sociocultural integration evolved, during the period of independence, in particular. The national languages, although initially regional Languages of Wider Communications, are important symbols and media of the new authenticity of these states.

Language planning in South and Southeast Asia may be expected to be increasingly subjected to supraethnic authenticity goals on the part of governmental and intellectual elites. Whereas language planning thus far has been concerned primarily with such unification and modernization goals as mass literacy, participation, and productivity, the very focus on these goals has and must contribute, ultimately, to a redistribution of attention so that authenticity will also receive the recognition it has always required as one of the three equal-but-opposite partners in the inevitable triangle that nationalism represents.

NOTES

1. An abstract (prepared for the Proceedings of the Consultative Meeting on Language-Planning Processes, East-West Center, Institute of Advanced Projects, University of Hawaii, April 7–10, 1969) of a forthcoming volume *Nationalism, Language, and Language Planning* (Fishman). Detailed documentation of the historical processes and trends reviewed in this abstract will be found in the aforementioned volume. Only a few bibliographic landmarks will be cited in this abstract. This abstract was written while the author was a Senior Specialist (1968–69) at the Institute of Advanced Projects, East-West Center, University of Hawaii, Honolulu, Hawaii.

2. *Proto-elites:* the leadership of nationalist groups in their early and formative period, before they are fully and formally organized.
   Elites: the leadership of later, more organized periods in the history of nationalist movements.

3. Of the huge literature on (European) nationalism the major presentations which devote some attention to all three of these components are (Deutsch, 1953; Gellner, 1964; and Znaniecki, 1952).

4. Nationalism shares with all of the foregoing the characteristic of being a protest movement related to social change and the dislocation resulting therefrom. It is illustrated by Despres (1967).

5. The feverishness with which the so-called peoples without history proceeded to recover, to reconstruct, and, where necessary, to design their histories is interestingly reviewed in Jaszi (1929); Kolarz (1946); and Kahn (1950).

6. The distinction between the state-nationality and nationality-state forms of nationalism is implicit in Zangwill (1917) and Talmon (1965); and

explicit in Pflanze (1966) and Rustow (1968). The cyclical interaction between these two stages of nationalism is implicit in Zangwill (1917) and explicit in Fishman (1968). By contrast, the number of scholars who have argued that only one or another of these processes is possible or desirable is extremely great and is reviewed in Fishman's manuscript.

7. For a brief but enlightening introduction to language planning, given these very restrictions, see Ferguson (1968). The basic references are Haugen (1966a and 1966b).

8. Though somewhat quaint and quite out of date by now, the only extensive account of the linguistic efforts of the French Academy are those of Robertson (1910). For interesting and little-known facts concerning the unenviable condition of French in France before the revolution, no one can rival Brunot. The few illustrations cited here are those recently enumerated by Gache (1969) in his review of the changed relative strengths of English and French.

9. The following poem of 1853 by Viennet is an example of French elitist rejection of "anglomania," without nationalist animus of any kind.

> On n'entend que des mots à déchirer le fer,
> Le railway, le tunnel, le ballast, le fender,
> Express, trucks, wagons; une bouche française
>   Semble broyer du verre ou mâcher de la braise . . .
> Certes, de nos voisins, l'alliance m'enchante,
> Mais leur langue, à vrai dire, est trop envahissante!
> Faut-il pour cimenter un merveilleux accord
> Changer l'arène en turf et le plaisir en sport,
> Demander à des clubs l'aimable causerie,
> Flétrir du nom de grooms nos valets d'écurie,
> Traiter nos cavaliers de gentleman-riders?
> Je maudis ces auteurs dont le vocabulaire
> Nous encombre de mots dont nous n'avons que faire
>   (cited by Gache, 1969)

10. The most detailed account of Turkish language planning under the impetus of the Atatürk revolution is that of Heyd (1954). Less well known is Heyd's study of Gökalp—a somewhat earlier and less revolutionary Turkish nationalist who more clearly indicated the need to Europeanize certain domains of the national language and culture—to Turkify other domains, while leaving a few relatively untouched in their pre-nationalist Perso-Arabic garb (Heyd, 1950). Gallagher (paper 8, this volume) indicates that such is currently the case, some forty years after the modernizing excesses of Atatürk's reforms.

11. Two informative introductions to Asian nationalisms and to the differences and similarities that characterize them vis-à-vis European nationalisms are those of Kautsky (1962) and Kennedy (1968).

12. The recent secession of Singapore from Malaysia might be considered

another example of an ethnic secession, although economic factors were probably more salient considerations.

13. The reestablishment of Russian hegemony, first, in the Soviet Union and, then, after World War II, in most of Eastern Europe, has led to the reestablishment of Russian as a Language of Wider Communication throughout the area. The point here, however, is the extreme rapidity with which Russian vanished as a language of government and of higher education in Poland, the Baltic States, Bessarabia and even the Ukraine after the defeat of the Czarist forces, as opposed to the continued role of English in India, Pakistan, and the Philippines and the continued role of French in Vietnam, Laos, and Cambodia after independence from colonial rule was obtained.

14. The most extensive list of the language-planning agencies of Southeast Asia is that reported by Noss (1967), who also discusses the language policies and problems of each country in the area. No similar list or discussion is available for South Asia.

15. The rationales for suggesting—and for rejecting—the use of a common Roman script in India are clearly and repeatedly presented in India (1963). Before their victory, Chinese communists consistently espoused Romanization schemes. As late as 1958, this was still official policy (Reform, 1958), although it has since then been quietly abandoned. In the Chinese case, Romanization would lead to the loss of the unifying supra-ethnic (and supraphonic) written language and to possibly dangerous encouragement to local vernaculars. Thus, whereas Romanization would be a step away from (oft sanctified) indigenousness in India—and would render understandable written texts that differ more in script than they do in vocabulary and grammar—it would tend to have the opposite effect in China, where the common supraphonic script masks the very great differences that exist between the various local languages.

16. German is the prime European exception to this generalization, and even there the use of internationalisms continued down into the Nazi period without being entirely displaced (Koppelman, 1956). The origin of the antiinternationalist tendency in German language planning goes back to the violently anti-French sentiments of Fichte, Herder, and even earlier fathers of German nationalism, all of whom struggled against and suffered from the Francomania of German princelings and courtiers (Kedourie, 1961).

17. For ample evidence of the ideologies of indigenization effecting South and Southeast Asian language planning, see several of the papers (other than those of the editor) in Alisjahbana (in press). Very marked rationales of this kind are advanced and defended by Del Rosario (1968).

18. Sociocultural integration on the basis of post-independence authenticity is also appealed to in campaigns that aim at decreasing reliance on imported Languages of Wider Communication (such as English) in India, the Philippines, and elsewhere.

REFERENCES

Alisjahbana, S. Takdir, ed. In press. *The Modernization of the Languages of Asia*. Kuala Lumpur.

Bright, William, ed. 1966. *Sociolinguistics. Proceedings of the UCLA Sociolinguistics Conference, 1964*. Janua Linguarum, Series Maior, 20. The Hague: Mouton.

Brunot, Ferdinand. 1924–53. *Histoire de la Langue Française des Origines a nos Jours*. 1–9 (in 14 pts.). Paris: A. Colin.

Del Rosario, Gonsalo. 1968. A Modernization-Standardization Plan for the Austronesian-derived National Languages of Southeast Asia. *Asian Studies*, 6: 1: 1–18.

Despres, Leo A. 1967. *Cultural Pluralism and Nationlist Politics in British Guiana*. Chicago: Rand McNally.

Deutsch, Karl W. 1966. *Nationalism and Social Communication: An Inquiry into the Foundations of Nationality*. 2nd ed. (revised tabular and bibliographic material). Cambridge, Mass.: MIT Press.

Ferguson, Charles A. 1968. Language Development. *In* Fishman, Ferguson, and Das Gupta, 27–36.

Fishman, Joshua A.; Ferguson, Charles A.; and Das Gupta, Jyotirindra, eds. 1968. *Language Problems of Developing Nations*. New York: John Wiley and Sons.

Gache, Paul. 1969. Langue Française et Langue Issue de l'Angleterre. *Le Travailleur*, 39: 15: 1, 5.

Gellner, Ernest. 1964. *Thought and Change*. Chicago: University of Chicago Press.

Haugen, Einar. 1966a. *Language Conflict and Language Planning: The Case of Modern Norwegian*. Cambridge: Harvard University Press.

———. 1966b. Linguistics and Language Planning. *In* Bright, 50–71.

Heyd, Uriel. 1950. *Foundations of Turkish Nationalism: The Life and Teachings of Ziya Gökalp*. London: Luzac and Harvill.

———. 1954. *Language Reform in Modern Turkey*. Oriental Notes and Studies, 5. Jerusalem: Israel Oriental Society.

India. Ministry of Scientific Research and Cultural Affairs. 1963. *A Common Script for Indian Languages*. Delhi: Republic of India.

Jazsi, Oscar. 1929. *The Dissolution of the Habsburg Monarchy*. Chicago: University of Chicago Press.

Kahn, Robert A. 1950. *The Multinational Empire: Nationalism and National Reform in the Habsburg Monarchy, 1848–1918*, 2 vols. New York: Columbia University Press. (Also note his one vol. abridgement, 1957. *The Habsburg Empire: A Study in Integration and Disintegration*. New York: Praeger.)

Kautsky, John H. 1962a. An Essay in the Politics of Development. *In* Kautsky (1962b), 1–122.

————, ed. 1962b. *Political Change in Underdeveloped Countries: Nationalism vs. Communism.* New York: John Wiley and Sons.

Kedourie, Elie. 1960. *Nationalism* (Rev. 1961). New York: Praeger.

Kennedy, Joseph. 1968. *Asian Nationalism in the Twentieth Century.* New York: Macmillan.

Kolarz, Walter. 1946. *Myths and Realities in Eastern Europe.* London: Lindsay Drummond.

Koppelman, Heinrich L. 1956. *Nation, Sprache und Nationalismus.* Leiden: Sijthoff.

Noss, Richard. 1967. *Language Policy and Higher Education,* Higher Education and Development in South-East Asia, 3:2. Paris: UNESCO and the International Association of Universities.

Pflanze, Otto. 1966. Characteristics of Nationalism in Europe, 1848–1871. *Review of Politics,* 28: 129–143.

Reform of the Chinese Written Language. 1958. Peking: Foreign Languages Press.

Robertson, D. Maclaren. 1910. *A History of the French Academy 1635 [1634]–1910.* New York: Dillingham.

Rustow, Dankwart. 1968. Language, Modernization and Nationhood. *In* Fishman, Ferguson, and Das Gupta, 87–106.

Talmon, J. L. 1965. *The Unique and the Universal.* London: Secker and Warburg.

Zangwill, Israel. 1917. *The Principle of Nationalities.* London: Watts.

Znaniecki, Florian. 1952. *Modern Nationalities.* Urbana: University of Illinois Press.

2. LANGUAGE AS AN AID AND BARRIER TO INVOLVEMENT IN THE NATIONAL SYSTEM

HERBERT C. KELMAN
Department of Social Relations, Harvard University

The basic thesis that I would like to develop in this discussion is that language is a uniquely powerful instrument in unifying a diverse population and in involving individuals and subgroups in the national system. However, some of the very features of language that give it this power under some circumstances may, under other circumstances, become major sources of disintegration and internal conflict within a national system. These considerations should have some definite implications for language policy not only in developing nations but also in long-established nations marked by diglossia—whether officially recognized (as in Canada or in Belgium) or unrecognized (as in the United States). Specifically, I will try to argue that, while the development of a national language may be highly conducive to the creation and strengthening of national identity, the *deliberate* use of language for purposes of national identity may—at least in a multiethnic state—have more disruptive than unifying consequences.

Let me be clear from the outset that I bring to this discussion no background whatsoever in the field of linguistics—socio- or otherwise—nor have I engaged in any systematic empirical studies of language problems in various societies. Whatever qualifications I may have for discussing this issue are based on the fact that I have made some systematic efforts in recent years to deal with the more general question of individual and subgroup involvement in the national system. This paper, then, is essentially a theoretical exercise—an attempt to draw out the implications of my scheme for defining the role of language and for developing national language policies. If my conclusions appear reasonable as they are confronted with the data of sociolinguistics, then the exercise will have been worthwhile. It would reinforce the theoretical scheme itself, and it might, at the same time, contribute to language planning by bringing a different perspective to bear on the problem—a perspective that might suggest some questions to be asked and perhaps some directions to be followed in the search for answers.

SOURCES OF POLITICAL LEGITIMACY OF THE NATIONAL SYSTEM AND OF PERSONAL ATTACHMENT TO IT

In this section and the next, I shall briefly review a scheme distinguishing different patterns of individual and subgroup involvement in the national system and indicate how one might assess these patterns and empirically explore their antecedents and correlates. I shall then turn to the implications of this theoretical scheme for the role of language in fostering involvement in the national system.[1]

One of the ways of conceptualizing the involvement of individuals and subgroups in the national system is to examine the degree and nature of their acceptance of the system's ideology. The ideology of the modern nation-state (which is, essentially, my definition of nationalism[2]) has at least three generic features, shared by all its variants: (1) The ultimate justification for maintaining, strengthening, or establishing a political system that has jurisdiction over a particular population—that is, an internationally recognized nation-state—is that this system is most naturally and effectively representative of that population; in principle, the political entity corresponds with an ethnic, cultural, and historical entity with which at least large portions of the population identify. (2) The nation-state is the political unit in which paramount authority is vested and which is entitled to overrule both smaller and larger political units. (3) Establishing or maintaining—or both—the independence, integrity, and effective functioning of the nation-state is an essential task to which all members of the system are expected to contribute.

These three elements provide the basic set of assumptions that govern the relationship of a nation-state to other states in the international system and the relationship of the political leadership to the individual citizen. In addition, the ideology of any given nation-state has certain unique features, corresponding to the particular functions that it must perform in the light of its level of development, its international position, its power and success in the international arena, and its internal structure.

The way in which the national ideology is interpreted and incorporated into the belief systems of individuals and subgroups within a population may vary widely. Depending on their demographic and personality characteristics and on their positions within the social and political structure, individuals may vary in the components of the ideology that they emphasize or deemphasize, the intensity of their commitment to the nation-state, their definition of the citizen role and the expectations that go with it, and the way in which they enact this role. It is essential to the effective functioning of the nation-state, however, that the basic tenets of the national ideology or at least its behavioral implications be widely accepted within the population. Acceptance of the ideology implies that the individual regards the authority of the state and hence its specific demands (within some broadly defined range) as legitimate. The state's ability to mobilize citizens in its support and to demand sacrifices from them in times of national crisis depends, in the final analysis, on its perceived legitimacy in the eyes of the population.

Two ultimate sources of legitimacy for the national system can be distinguished: (1) the extent to which it reflects the ethnic-cultural identity of the national population and (2) the extent to which it meets the needs and interests of that population. In the long run, a political system cannot maintain its legitimacy unless, at least, a significant proportion of the population perceives it as meeting their needs and interests (although it can, of course, retain power by relying on coercive means, even if only a small elite are adequately integrated into the system). In shorter runs, however, a system can maintain its legitimacy—even if it is not working effectively, is facing serious economic difficulties, or is torn by internal conflicts so that it can adequately provide for the needs and interest of only some segments of the population at the expense of others—as long as it is seen by wide segments of the population as representing their national (ethnic-cultural) identity.[3]

At the social-psychological level, the legitimacy of a political system is reflected in the sense of loyalty that its members have towards it. Perceived legitimacy implies that the individual member is in some fashion personally involved in the system—that he feels attached to it and is integrated into its operations. We can distinguish between two sources of loyalty or attachment to the nation-state, which correspond to the two sources of legitimacy at the system level: sentimental attachment and instrumental attachment. These two sources of attachment constitute the rows of Table 1 (taken from Kelman, 1969). This table summarizes the present scheme, which has yielded six patterns of personal involvement in the national system. It should be noted that these patterns are by no

Table 1: Patterns of Personal Involvement in the National System

Manner of Integration into the System

	Consolidation	Mobilization	Conformity
System requirements conducive to this type of integration	Consolidation	Mobilization	Conformity
Influence process characteristic of this type of integration	Internalization of system values	Identification with system roles	Compliance with system demands seen as legitimate

Source of Attachment (Loyalty) to the System

	Ideological	Role-Participant	Normative
Sentimental	Commitment to cultural values reflective of national identity	Commitment to the role of the national linked to group symbols	Acceptance of demands based on commitment to the sacredness of the state
Instrumental	Commitment to institutions promotive of the needs and interests of the population	Commitment to social roles mediated by the system	Acceptance of demands based on commitment to law and order (principle of equity)

After Kelman, 1969, p. 280, by permission of the publisher and the editor.

means mutually exclusive; although different individuals, subgroups, and systems may differ in the emphasis they place on one or another of these patterns, various combinations of them are possible and indeed likely.

An individual is sentimentally attached to the national system to the extent that he sees it as representing him—as being, in some central way, a reflection and an extension of himself. The system is legitimate and deserving of his loyalty because it is the embodiment of a people in which his personal identity is anchored. Sentimental attachment may be channeled in three different ways, as given in the three columns of Table 1: (1) The individual may be committed to the values basic to the national culture, taking interest and pride in the special qualities of his people, its characteristic way of life, its cultural products, its national and often its religious tradition, and the goals for which it has stood in its historical development. (2) He may be identified with the role of the national in the sense that it enters importantly into his self-definition and that it constitutes a genuine emotional commitment for him, whenever group symbols bring that role into salience. (3) He may be committed to the state as an embodiment of the people, and, hence, as a sacred object in its own right, entitled to unquestioning obedience of its authoritative demands.

An individual is instrumentally attached to the national system to the extent that he sees it as an effective vehicle for achieving his own ends and the ends of members of other systems. For the instrumentally attached, the system is legitimate and deserving of his loyalty because it provides the organization for a smoothly running society, in which individuals can participate to their mutual benefit and have some assurance that their needs and interests will be met. Instrumental attachment, again, may be channeled in three different ways, depending on the manner in which the individual is integrated into the system: (1) The individual may be committed to the ideology underlying the particular social and economic institutions through which the society is organized, typically because he regards these institutional arrangements as maximally promotive of the needs and interests of the entire population. (2) He may be committed to a variety of social roles (occupational roles, community roles, and roles in various other subsystems), whose continued and successful enactment depends on the maximally effective functioning of the larger national system. (3) He may be committed to law and order as an end in itself, being primarily concerned with keeping the fabric of ordinary life undisturbed.

Whether an individual's sentimental or instrumental attachment is mediated primarily through system values, roles, or normative demands depends in large part on his position in the society. I would hypothesize, for example, that individuals high in socioeconomic status, education, and political power are more likely to be ideologically integrated, while those low in these areas are more likely to be normatively integrated. For the long run, the legitimacy of the system depends on the extent to which at least its major elites are ideologically integrated. This implies a periodic renewal of the system's cultural values and a periodic reassessment of the adequacy of its social institutions in meeting the needs and interests of the general population, particularly at times of internal division and intrasocietal conflict. Although legitimacy ultimately rests on ideological commitments, normative commitments are in a sense the most reliable in the short run. If these are shared by the masses of the population, political leaders can expect relatively automatic acceptance of their authoritative demands. Finally, role-participant integration provides the major basis for mobilizing a population—particularly its middle classes—for special efforts or sacrifices. It produces commitments that are more active and enthusiastic than those based on normative integration, but less selective and conditional than those based on ideological integration. In a well-integrated system, political leaders have at their disposal national symbols and subsystem roles that they can use for purposes of mobilization. National symbols can be brought into play to heighten emotional arousal, since emotional responses to such symbols are typically conditioned in the course of the child's socialization in the home, the school, and the church. Subsystem roles can be co-opted in the service of the state, since in the complex, bureaucratically structured, modern nation-state these roles are highly dependent on the central authorities.

Sentimental and instrumental attachments can, within limits, substitute for one another. Thus, if sentimental attachments are strong, the system can maintain its legitimacy even though it does not adequately meet the needs and interests of the population or does so only for a small proportion of the population. By appealing to the common national identity of the people, the leadership may be able to elicit their loyalty despite internal divisions and inequities. This is a particularly valuable resource in the initial stages of political development, when elites typically have to mobilize mass support without being able to offer many concrete benefits to the majority of the population. Similarly, if instrumental attachments are strong, the system can maintain its legitimacy even though it does not adequately reflect the ethnic-cultural identity of the population or does so only for a small proportion of the population.

Furthermore, sentimental and instrumental attachments can have a mutually reinforcing and facilitative effect on one another. If a population perceives the system as being genuinely representative and reflective of its identity, then it is inclined to place trust in the system for meeting its needs and protecting its interests. Supported by this initial confidence of the citizens and by their willingness to give them the benefit of the doubt, political leaders are in a stronger position to push for economic development and to organize the society in a way that will meet the needs and interests of the population. Similarly, a well-functioning society, which provides meaningful roles for its citizens, will develop a set of common values and traditions and a sense of unity that are tantamount to a national identity, even if the population was originally diverse in its ethnic and cultural identifications. This national identity need not displace the original ethnic-cultural identities of the component groups but can exist alongside of them. In the former case, then, we have a type of nationalism in which the primary push is from nation to state: an existing national consciousness is used in the process of state-building. In the latter case, we have a type of nationalism in which the primary push is from state to nation: an existing sociopolitical structure is used in the process of nation-building.[4]

Assessing Personal Attachment to the National System

Before we turn to the implications of the theoretical scheme for the role of language, it would be useful to concretize it somewhat by describing ways of measuring the different patterns it distinguishes and by citing variables to which these patterns are empirically related. Unfortunately, the scheme as outlined in the preceding section has not yet been put to an empirical test. It is possible, however, to illustrate the ways in which one might operationalize and validate such patterns by drawing on empirical studies of earlier versions of the present scheme.

In a study of national role involvement in an American community, DeLamater, Katz, and Kelman (1969) distinguished three types of commitment to the national system—symbolic, normative, and functional. Two of these correspond fairly closely to two of the cells of Table 1 and can, therefore, serve to illustrate the empirical possibilities of the present scheme: Symbolic commitment is more or less equivalent to the sentimental role-participant cell in Table 1; and functional commitment, to the instrumental role-participant cell. Differences between symbolic and functional commitments in the earlier study are, thus, relevant to the sentimental-instrumental distinction (rows of Table 1), on which the present discussion focuses. That is, in terms of the scheme of Table 1, symbolic and functional commitments represent a difference in the source of the person's attachment to the system, keeping his manner of integration constant.

Data in the study by DeLamater et al. were obtained through intensive interviews, consisting of a variety of questions about the respondent's conception of his national role, as well as a series of attitudinal and demographic items. The interview included a number of items that were specifically designed to tap each of the three types of national commitment. Responses to the items deemed relevant to a given type of commitment were then intercorrelated, and a scale for that type of commitment was constructed out of those items that seemed to hang together statistically.

The scale for symbolic commitment included eight items that tapped the respondent's emotional involvement with national symbols—his personal attachment to these symbols and his sensitivity to any indication that they are being slighted. Thus, a respondent would receive positive points on this scale if he indicated (1) that anyone who criticizes the government in time of national crisis is not a good American; (2) that anyone who does not stand during the playing of the national anthem is not a good American; (3) that he owns an American flag and that he displays it on national holidays; (4) that he feels the American public pays insufficient respect to the flag; (5) that he disapproves of Americans who take no pride in America's armed forces; (6) that he would consider it an insult if a foreigner laughed at the Peace Corps; (7) that he would be insulted or angry if a foreigner criticized racial segregation in the United States and attacked the free enterprise system; and (8) that he feels that he is "first, last, and always an American." In terms of the present conceptual scheme, a high score on this scale would indicate a strong sentimental attachment to the national system, channeled through an identification with the national role and triggered by the presentation of national symbols.

The scale for functional commitment included six items that tapped the respondent's orientation to the economic benefits of American society and his emphasis on citizen participation. Thus, a respondent would receive positive points on this scale if he indicated (1) that the things that particularly remind him of being an American include factors relating to opportunity; (2) that, to be a good American, a person ought to participate in public affairs; (3) that apathetic persons are among those whom he regards as "not good Americans"; (4) that people refer to affluence and related matters when they talk about "the American way of life";

(5) that one of the most important things that makes America different from other countries is its level of opportunity; and (6) that one of the most important things that makes America different from other countries is its level of affluence. In terms of the present conceptual scheme, a high score on this scale would imply a strong instrumental attachment to the national system, channeled through the person's entanglement in various social roles that depend on the effective functioning of that system.

The symbolic and functional scales that I have just described do not represent the most appropriate measures of sentimental and instrumental role-participation, since they were, of course, derived from a different, though related, conceptual scheme. Nevertheless, they offer a concrete illustration of how we might go about operationalizing these two (as well as the other four) cells of Table 1. Moreover, differences between symbolically and functionally committed individuals on other attitudinal and demographic items, observed in the study by DeLamater et al. provide some suggestive evidence about the antecedents and correlates of sentimental and instrumental attachment, at least when these are channeled through identification with system roles.

Comparisons were made in that study between "pure groups," consisting of individuals with high scores on one of the three types of commitment and low or medium scores on the other two. The "high symbolic" group and the "high functional" group turned out to differ in many areas. Thus, in terms of their demographic characteristics, the functionally committed were younger than the symbolically committed; they were better educated; they had higher incomes; they were more often in professional or technical occupations; they had fathers who were better educated and more often in professional or technical occupations; they were more likely to describe themselves as "middle class" (rather than "working class"); and they were more bureaucratically oriented. The symbolically committed were more likely to have grown up in farming families, to have lived on a farm for ten years or more, and to have lived in the area for ten years or more.

The two groups also differed on a variety of attitudinal items. Thus, the functionally committed showed, in a number of different ways, their greater openness to other cultures and systems, their greater tolerance for deviant political positions, and their greater support for liberal causes. The symbolically committed tended to favor a more militant stance in American foreign policy and were much less willing than the functionally committed to turn over power to international organizations.

These findings are generally consistent with some of the hypotheses regarding sentimental and instrumental attachment that can be derived from the present formulation. Thus, on the antecedent side, we would expect sentimental attachment (in an established society) to be strongest among those individuals and subgroups who are geographically stable, who are rooted to the soil or to a particular region of the country, and whose occupations are traditional and local in focus. We would expect instrumental attachment to be strongest among those who are geographically and occupationally mobile, whose occupations are linked to bureaucratic and national organizations, and whose perspective is cosmopolitan. On the consequent side, we would expect sentimental attachment to lead to a more exclusive definition of nationality (e.g., of what it means to be an American or a good American), to a sharper dichotomy between own nation and other nations and a more suspicious and less open attitude towards other nations or international institutions, and to a tendency to conceive international conflicts in zero-sum terms. Instrumental attachment, on the other hand, should lead to a more inclusive definition of nationality, a greater openness to other nations and international institutions, and a greater readiness to conceive international conflicts in non-zero-sum terms.

These hypotheses about sentimental and instrumental attachments must be viewed as nothing more than first approximations. They do not take into account the primary mode of integration that characterizes a particular individual or group (i.e., the columns in Table 1). It is quite likely that the latter variable and the source of attachment interact in such a way that differences between sentimental and instrumental attachments differ, depending on whether these attachments are channeled through values, roles, or norms. Such more refined interaction hypotheses have not yet been developed. Furthermore, the hypotheses presented above do not deal with the case—which may indeed be quite prevalent in some systems —where strong sentimental as well as instrumental attachments coincide in the same person or group.

LANGUAGE AS A UNIFYING FORCE

Having explicated our conceptualization of personal involvement in the national system, particularly the distinction between sentimental and instrumental attachments, we can now turn specifically to the role of language in these processes. I would propose that a common language is a potentially powerful unifying force for a national population because it

strengthens both sentimental and instrumental attachments and, furthermore, because it plays a major role in the mutual reinforcement of these
two processes.

At the sentimental level, a national language serves as a major object
and symbol of attachment by bridging immediate loyalties with transcen-
dent ones. It is through his mother tongue that the child is exposed to the
songs, the heroic tales, and the traditional wisdoms of his people. The very
language in which he communicates with his mother and with his immediate environment also serves to link him with a wider group, most of whose
members are distant in time and place. Language thus provides a continuity and scope without which a sense of overarching nationality could
not be constructed; it provides concrete, emotionally significant products
that the individual received from previous generations and will pass on
the future ones and that, in the present, link him to a widely dispersed
population, most of whose members he does not, and never will, know
personally. Beyond that, those primordial bonds that tie the child to his
mother and immediate kin are now extended to all those who share the
same mother tongue. Thus, the attachment to a distant group takes on
some of the emotional intensity and irreducible quality that are normally
restricted to primary relationships.

Language may strengthen sentimental attachment to the national
group by enhancing not only the continuity but also the authenticity of
the national tradition. Here we are dealing with language in the form of a
sacred tongue, rather than a mother tongue. It is the vehicle for transmit-
ting the sacred documents of the people, in which its history and mission
are spelled out. It is the raw material of poetry, in which the achievements
of the people and the beauties of its land are described. It thus provides
not only authentic evidence for the greatness of the people but also concrete cultural products that can be cherished and studied in their own
right.[5]

The sacred tongue and the mother tongue, of course, are often different even for what Fishman (1968b) calls "Type B Nations"; i.e.,
nations characterized by a single great tradition. Typically, however, they
represent two varieties (classical and vernacular) of the same basic language and may therefore have a cumulative effect on sentimental attachment. Alternatively, there may be differences within the population, with
sentimental attachment for some elements being primarily rooted in the
classical language; for others, in the vernacular; and for still others, in
both.

At the instrumental level, a common language helps to integrate the system and to tie increasing numbers of individuals into it. In a society that does not have a common language—more precisely, a society characterized by diglossia without widespread bilingualism (cf. Fishman, 1967)—we are likely to find not only impairments in social planning and in the efficiency of institutional arrangements but also a limited access to the system for wide segments of the population and an allocation of resources that discriminates against minorities or other subordinate groups. On the other hand, with a national language, it is easier to develop political, economic, and social institutions that serve the entire population. Central authorities are in a better position to plan with greater scope and greater efficiency. Since the entire country can be treated as a single arena for purposes of economic planning, for example, there is less likelihood of unnecessary duplication of effort and there are more possibilities for working out a beneficial division of labor between different regions of the country. If there are several separate language groups, it may be necessary to develop separate administrative units for each, both to avoid language difficulties and to minimize suspicions of discrimination: the resulting arrangement is likely to be more wasteful and less flexible than one that is possible in a linguistically unified population. Furthermore, a common language facilitates the development of an educational system that offers mobility and opportunities for participation to all segments of the population.

From the point of view of individuals, familiarity with the dominant language is a key to genuine participation in the system, to social mobility, and to enactment of a variety of social and economic roles. When there is a single national language, opportunities for integration of individuals are likely to be more evenly distributed within the population. Since there are no systematic barriers to participation on the basis of linguistic group, there is also likely to be less discrimination on the basis of ethnic and social-class differences, which are typically correlated with linguistic differences. In sum, a common language contributes to the development of social institutions that meet the needs and interests of the entire population and to the participation of all segments of the society in meaningful social roles. In so doing, it helps to create widespread instrumental attachment to the system.

A common language not only strengthens sentimental and instrumental attachments but also contributes to the mutual reinforcement of these two processes. I mentioned earlier that a well-functioning society is conducive to the development of sentimental attachments, despite initial ethnic divisions. Language can greatly facilitate this development. Even in the absence of a common language, the functional interdependence that derives from successful instrumental interactions may have a "spill-over" effect. That is, when different segments of a population engage in productive and equal-status interactions around instrumental concerns, they are likely to discover common values and customs and to develop common traditions and communication habits. In the absence of a common language, however, this process becomes more difficult, and there is, thus, a greater tendency to restrict communication to its instrumental purposes. The existence of a common language, on the other hand, allows and encourages communications to extend beyond their strictly instrumental focus and to include the sharing of old and the development of new cultural values and orientations. In effective instrumental interactions between elites and masses, a common language is likely to have a similar binding effect, enhancing citizens' sentimental attachment to the system.

Conversely, I have proposed that sentimental attachment—based on the feeling that the system reflects the identity of the people—may promote the development of instrumental attachments and, in fact, of a well-functioning system that meets the needs and interests of the population. Specifically, citizens who are sentimentally attached are more ready to place trust in the system's ability to meet the needs and protect the interests of the population, even if this has not yet been demonstrated; and to participate in the society's political and economic processes, even in the absence of immediate payoffs. Again, a common language is useful in this process, since it is, to a large extent, through language that the gap between present reality and future promise must be bridged. Political leaders who share a common language with all segments of the population are in a better position to draw on traditional symbols of trust in their communications. The shared nuances of the common language make it possible to convey more readily not just the message itself but also the way in which this message is to be understood and the kind of credence that can be given to it. Similarly, interactions between different segments of the population are likely to benefit from the existence of a common language because of our general inclination to trust more readily those who "speak the same language" as we do.

In short, a common language helps to maintain a continuous cyclical process of reinforcement between sentimental and instrumental attachments. By enhancing trust in political leaders and other subgroups within the population, a common language strengthens instrumental attachments to the system. These instrumental attachments, in turn, facilitate the development of sentimental ones by encouraging—again with the aid of a common language—the discovery of cultural commonalities. As sentimental attachments increase, a common language—by enhancing trust—can help to draw on these for the further strengthening of instrumental ones; and so the process continues to feed on itself.

LANGUAGE AS A DIVISIVE FORCE

The very factors that make language such a powerful, unifying force in nation-states that have a common language make it a potentially divisive force in multilingual states. It goes without saying that a common language is not a necessary condition for a unified state and that one or more major language groups can coexist in a system with minimal conflict between them. Switzerland, of course, is the example *par excellence*—though Kloss (1967) predicts that even there language problems "may some day become apparent in Ticino" (p. 43), since, in Switzerland, Italian does not have equal status with German and French. But even if we take Switzerland as an example of a successful multilingual system, there are many more examples of conflict in multilingual societies, with varying degrees of intensity in different states at different historical junctures.

The historical conditions and the language policies pursued in a state often conspire to cause one or more of the language groups to feel aggrieved—to feel that their rights are being violated and that their language and those who speak it are denied the opportunities and protection to which they are entitled. Differences in language are almost always correlated with other ethnic differences, sometimes with religious differences and often with socioeconomic differences between the groups, which may strongly affect the nature and intensity of the grievance. Typically, the aggrieved group is the one that speaks the minority language, irrespective of whether this language is officially recognized. Grievances may also focus, however, (1) on a language spoken by groups that are socioeconomically disadvantaged, even though they be in the majority; or (2) on a language that is spoken by a majority within the country but is lacking international status or a language shared with a lesser power in the international arena than the power that shares one of the minority languages.

Depending on the language policy, it is even conceivable that the group speaking the dominant language may feel aggrieved, for example, because it is persuaded that too much allowance is being made for the lesser languages.

In any event, given a language-related conflict within a national system, it may be greatly exacerbated by the fact that both sentimental and instrumental considerations are likely to become involved and, in particular, are likely to reinforce one another. First, the aggrieved group is likely to feel that its sense of group identity is being threatened—that its national (in the nationality rather than the state sense) language is being derogated, its cultural self-development and literary expression inhibited, and its educational efforts undermined. Secondly and probably most importantly, the group is likely to feel that, because its language is not given due recognition, it experiences discrimination at the instrumental level—that its members are denied equal opportunities, that they are excluded from full participation in the system, and that their socioeconomic mobility is stymied.

In most of the cases of which I am aware, in which language conflict in a multilingual society has become an explosive issue, the aggrieved group is by and large in a disadvantaged position. It tends to be less economically developed, and its access to many opportunities for participation and mobility is indeed limited—at least, in part, by the fact that political and economic power are concentrated in the hands of those who speak the more favored language. Cause and effect, of course, cannot be readily disentangled here. The group may be disadvantaged because it does not speak the dominant language, but it may be equally true that its language has remained subordinate because of the group's relatively lower level of development. Most probably, a cyclical process has been operating: As the society develops economically and becomes more centralized, the language of the dominant group takes on greater and greater importance, and the subordinate group—lacking facility in the dominant language—finds it more and more difficult to gain entry into the system. Typically, as Fishman (1967) has pointed out, the subordinate group is also internally split in such cases; its upper classes tend to be bilingual and thus able to participate fully in the system, while the masses are left behind. "Such polities are bound to experience language problems as their social patterns alter in the direction of industrialization, widespread literacy and education, democratization, and modernization more

generally. . . . The educational, political, and economic development of
the lower classes is likely to lead to secessionism or to demands for
equality for submerged language(s)" (p. 34).

Typically, then, it is instrumental considerations of this sort, linked
to linguistic divisions, that lead to such massive disruptions as language
riots and separatist, nationalist movements. Sentimentally based grievances in and of themselves are unlikely to lead to major upheavals; they
tend to arouse only a small proportion of the population who are particularly devoted to the maintenance of the group's cultural and educational
institutions. The call for renewal of group identity and for cultural self-
development in the face of external threat may, however, give added
impetus to an instrumentally based struggle. It may help to mobilize and
unify the group to engage in that struggle, by increasing its self-awareness
as a separate entity with interests of its own. It would appear, for example,
that the Gaelic League, as described by Macnamara (paper 4, this
volume), played such a role in the Irish revolution—and it is interesting,
in this connection, that the success of the revolution drastically weakened
the League and the Irish language movement.

Assuming that the primary impetus for major linguistic conflicts is
an instrumentally based grievance—a response by the weaker language
group to discrimination, to exclusion, and to denial of its rightful share
of power and resources—the conflict readily becomes intensified by sentimental elaborations. Since language is so closely tied to group identity,
language-based discrimination against the group is perceived as a threat
to its very existence as a recognizable entity and as an attack on its sacred
objects and symbols. The issue is no longer merely a redistribution of
power and resources, but it is self-preservation of the group and defense
against genocide. The conflict becomes highly charged with emotion
and increasingly unmanageable. Genocide, after all, is not a matter for
negotiation but for a last-ditch defense.

This is not to say that these sentimentally based grievances are
always devoid of any basis in fact. My point is simply that, since language
is embedded in both sentimental and instrumental issues, language conflicts are readily susceptible to this kind of escalation—to a tendency to
raise the level of the conflict to a battle about ultimates—not only in
rhetoric but also in reality. This phenomenon, of course, can also be observed in ethnic conflicts, such as the Biafran independence struggle or
the current black revolution in the United States, in which language plays
a less obvious role, though not an entirely negligible one.

In short, the cyclical process of reinforcement between sentimental and instrumental attachments engendered by a common language has its negative counterpart in the case of language conflicts in a multilingual society. Language divisions increase the likelihood that, in an instrumental conflict between different groups, fundamental identity differences will be brought into focus, converting the conflict into a sentimental one. As the conflict is carried on at the sentimental level, language divisions increase the likelihood that mutual trust will be further eroded, thus making negotiated settlements ever more difficult to achieve.

SOME IMPLICATIONS FOR LANGUAGE POLICY

It is clear from what I have said that a common language offers many advantages to central authorities in their attempt to develop and con- solidate a unified and cohesive political system. It does not follow, how- ever, that central authorities in multilingual systems ought to direct their language policies towards the development or establishment of a common language. Because of the sentimental and instrumental considerations that I have discussed in the last section, such policies may well create inequities and meet with resistances and may hamper, rather than enhance, the unity and integration of the system. The wisdom of a policy aimed at establishing a common language depends on the needs of the particular society and on the possibilities for establishing such a language that are available to it. In assessing the available possibilities, it is of course necessary to take into account the cost of establishing a common language in terms of the probable loss in the regime's perceived legitimacy and the probable increase in social unrest.

I bring to this discussion a general bias against *deliberate* attempts by *central* political authorities to create a sense of national identity, whether by a policy of establishing a national language or by any other means. I bring such a bias not because I wish to minimize the importance of a sense of national identity to the effective functioning of a nation-state or to question policies designed for other purposes that, as a consequence of their operation, contribute to the development of national identity. What I am arguing is that a sense of national identity ideally ought to— and, in fact, is most likely to—emerge out of a well-functioning national system that meets the needs and interests of the entire population, rather than out of deliberate attempts to create it directly. Let me qualify my statement further by saying that I refer to the central political authorities, not to various agencies within the society—public or private—that have a special interest in promoting one or another type of cultural or linguistic development. It is when such activities are carried out by (or are under the direction of) the agencies holding the primary political power and when they are tied in with the process of building the basic socioeconomic institutions that I become suspicious.

Clearly, I am expressing a value position here. In my view, the primary role of the central authorities is to promote and ensure the functional integration of the system. To that end, it is essential that they (1) establish and maintain institutional arrangements that adequately meet the needs and interests of the entire population and (2) provide maximal opportunities for all elements of the society—regardless of ethnic origin, language, religion, or social class—to participate in the running of the system and in its benefits. Policies following this principle can be expected to create instrumental attachments to the system, out of which sentimental attachments can gradually emerge. I am afraid that a concentration by central authorities on the direct manipulation of sentimental attachments may serve as a substitute for the work they should be doing at the instrumental level and as a cover for failures to create adequate socioeconomic institutions and to provide meaningful roles for all segments of the society. Although my bias against deliberate attempts to create national identity derives from my value position, I also believe that this is not a very effective way of promoting national identity. I would propose —and this, of course, is a proposition that can and must be put to an empirical test— that a sense of national identity is more likely to develop when it is not forced but allowed to emerge out of functional relationships within the national society.

So far, I have been speaking of national systems—particularly newly emerging systems—in general. My argument becomes clearer and stronger, however, when we focus on the effort to create a nation-state, not merely out of a population that is largely tied to local communities and not at all oriented towards a national center, but out of a population that is divided into separate ethnic groups, each engendering strong sentimental attachments and often with a history of intense conflict among them. In such a situation, deliberate attempts to create a common national identity are likely to face particularly great obstacles and may well increase the disintegration rather than the unity of the society. Such policies are likely to be perceived as attempts to force individuals to choose between loyalty to their own group and loyalty to the central authorities, who represent, at least in part, a foreign group. This threat to ethnic identity is likely to arouse sentimental attachments to the group in their fullest emotional intensity and to create tremendous resistances to the policies designed to promote national identity. In short, I am hypothesizing that direct efforts to create national identity may bring the ethnic subgroup identities to the fore and lead to a structuring of the situation in competitive terms, in which the more primordial attachments are more likely to prevail.

Beyond mobilizing such resistances, direct efforts at creating national identity may actually strengthen the divisions within the society. The weaker ethnic groups may perceive them as attempts, not at creating an overarching national identity, but at imposing the identity of the dominant group on the rest of the society. An obvious example can be found in the reactions of weaker (though still major) ethnic groups, within a population, to a policy of establishing the dominant group's language as the national language; language policy, however, presents special complications to which I shall return shortly. More generally, direct attempts to create a national identity in a multiethnic state may have divisive consequences by reinforcing the ideal of correspondence between political units and cultural units. If, indeed, political authority is to be linked to the sense of group identity, then each ethnic or linguistic group is inclined to vest this authority, not in the central leadership, but in its own leaders, who reflect its identity in a more self-evident way. In other words, in a multiethnic society, a direct appeal to national identity may merely serve to focus attention on group identity and thus encourage polarization along ethnic lines.

If national policies in a multiethnic society are to keep from arousing and mobilizing subgroup identities, they may have to go beyond the mere avoidance of direct manipulation of national identity. In situations in which one or more of the weaker ethnic groups are suppressed, central authorities may actually have to take positive steps to protect their subgroup identity—to assure their freedom to develop their own cultural institutions, maintain their own schools, and preserve their own language. Such actions, interestingly, would enhance these citizens' instrumental attachment to the central system by servicing their sentimental attachment to their subgroups. Furthermore, the central authorities, in a situation in which certain ethnic groups are or feel suppressed, must assure that ethnic status does not limit any group's access to the power and the resources of the system. If polarization along ethnic lines is to be avoided, they must see to it that ethnic variations are not correlated with variations in socioeconomic status and in political power—in other words, divisions based on sentimental and on instrumental loyalties cut across each other. This may create the anomalous situation in which ethnic characteristics may, in fact, have to be taken into account deliberately in order to assure access to the system by groups that have in the past been systematically excluded—as has been true, for example, for Negroes in the United States.

The implications of the above remarks for language policy are fairly straightforward. I would be inclined to raise serious questions about the deliberate use of language policies for the purpose of creating a national identity. Macnamara's discussion (paper 4, this volume) of the failures of the Irish language movement provides an excellent illustration of the difficulties in restoring a national language for purely sentimental reasons, in a situation in which such a language served no functional purpose. These difficulties arose despite the fact that there is no major ethnic division within the country and that the movement aroused no sentimentally based resistances. In multilingual societies, such an effort may create far stronger resistances and contribute to internal conflict and disintegration for the reasons that I have already spelled out.

In terms of general principles, I would argue, very simply, that language policies ought to be based entirely on functional considerations. That is, in selecting languages for various purposes, in influencing the population's language behavior, and in planning the educational system, central authorities ought to be concerned primarily with two issues: (1) how to establish and facilitate patterns of communication (both internally and internationally) that would enable its socioeconomic institutions to function most effectively and equitably in meeting the needs and interests of the population; and (2) how to assure that different groups within the society, varying in their linguistic repertoires (for either ethnic or social-class reasons), have equal access to the system and opportunities to participate in it. Out of these processes, a national language, evoking sentimental attachments, may gradually emerge. I would seriously question, however, any policy designed to promote such a language on a sentimental basis and to suppress other languages in the hope of establishing the national one in their stead.

Stating these general principles, however, leaves unanswered the most important questions in developing a language policy. Although one may agree that a common language should not be promoted for strictly sentimental (national identity) reasons, there remains the fact that a common language usually has a great deal of instrumental value as well.

It may well be true, in a given situation, that the best way to assure the adequate functioning of socioeconomic institutions and to provide equal opportunities for participation in the system to all segments of the population is to institute a common national language. Thus, even if we subscribe to the principle that language policies should be based on functional considerations, we must ask, in each case, whether these purposes can be best served by establishing a common language and, if so, on what basis such a language is to be selected. In making such decisions, of course, one must weigh the instrumental value of a common language—and any particular common language—against the costs entailed by the establishment of such a language. One must take into account the sentimentally based resistances that such a policy would generate. One must consider the extent to which this policy—compared to various possible alternatives —can assure subgroups of the protection of their ethnic identities and of access to the system. In each individual case, of course, different issues are involved and different policies are, therefore, indicated.

Let me look briefly at the kinds of considerations that are likely to arise in the three types of new nations distinguished by Fishman (1968b). The problems would appear to be least complicated in the case of Type B nations. The solution of modernizing the traditional language—usually in its classical version—so that it can replace whatever Language of Wider Communication may have been in use for administration, higher education, and other purposes; and such a solution would seem, in most cases, to have the greatest functional utility and, at the same time, to contribute to national identity. It would clearly be easier to spread this language among wide segments of the population than it would be to spread the European language that it would be replacing, thus making communication between the central authorities and the population more effective, facilitating the educational process, involving more citizens in the system, and giving the masses of the population greater access to system roles. Such a policy does have several possible disadvantages from a functional point of view, which—though usually outweighed by the advantages—ought to be kept in mind:

(1) The use of a European language as the national language would have an advantage in terms of facilitating international contacts, which are crucial to the development of all new states. Giving up this advantage, however, would usually seem to be a price worth paying for the contribution of an indigenous national language to the functional integration of the larger society and to bridging the gap between elites and masses. The

elites, particularly those with extensive international involvements (including the scientists and scholars), will have to continue to use a Language of Wider Communication for many purposes, but their problems in this respect are no greater than those found in the smaller European states, whose national languages are not widely spoken—such as the Netherlands or the Scandinavian countries. Elites of these countries inevitably have some disadvantage in that they have to do much of their work in a language not their own. For example, in Scandinavia, I have felt considerable empathy with my fellow social scientists because they have to do most of their reading, much of their scholarly discussion, and a good deal of their writing in a language in which they normally do not do their thinking. I have been impressed, however, with the way in which the large majority have managed to overcome this obstacle. In some respects, I feel that they have an advantage in that they are less likely to allow their professional jargon to invade their everyday language. They have learned their jargon in English and their own languages, therefore, remain relatively uncontaminated by it. The shift in language may make them more effective in communicating scientific ideas to wider audiences in their own societies. Perhaps this is one of the reasons (though I know it is not the only one) why Scandinavian academics seem to be more likely to write and speak for the mass media in their own countries than, for example, their American counterparts.

(2) The use of the classical version of the indigenous language still accrues to the advantage of the more upper-class, more urbanized segments of the population, who are more likely to have had contact with it and whose children have far more opportunities to master it. Thus, such a policy helps to perpetuate existing discrepancies by making it more likely that those who are already well off—and their offspring—will have greater access to system roles. This is indeed a serious problem, but it probably cannot be solved by way of language selection. The selection of a national language must be accompanied by other deliberate efforts to open up educational, occupational, and political opportunities to those segments of the population that are not already in favored positions. If these other steps are taken, language is unlikely to be a major barrier when the national language is not a completely foreign tongue but merely a more classical variety of the language everyone speaks.

(3) Fishman (1968b) and others have pointed out that efforts to modernize the classical language may arouse resistance from its traditional caretakers, who regard the language as sacred and want to keep its original

form intact. This may be particularly troublesome where the classical language is associated with religious traditions, as in the Arab world. Here, of course, we are dealing with one aspect of the larger struggle between modernizing and traditional elites, which inevitably accompanies the modernization process. It seems to me that language is probably among the less intractable aspects of this struggle, since it should be possible to modernize the language and yet maintain a field of classical scholarship centering on the traditional literature.

Type A nations, in terms of Fishman's distinctions, present, in my view, a somewhat more difficult problem. There the population has neither a single "great tradition"—as in Type B nations—around which they can rally nor several such traditions—as in Type C nations—that make conflicting demands. In such nations, Fishman points out, the European language of the former colonial power is usually selected as the national language, under conditions that are relatively free of conflicts. The great advantage of this state of affairs, from a functional point of view, is that it permits continuity and facilitates international activities, which are so vital to the developmental process. In other words, on the one hand, the disadvantages of selecting an indigenous language that I mentioned under point (1) above are avoided in this situation. On the other hand, the disadvantages discussed under point (2) are greatly exacerbated. The use of a Western language as the national language clearly points in an elitist direction and makes it even more likely that the discrepancies and the distance between the educated, urbanized, Westernized few and the masses of the population will be perpetuated and perhaps increased. The very distant Western language would set up a formidable barrier to the participation of wide segments of the population in modern system roles.

It seems to me that this is a problem of such dimensions that it may outweigh the functional advantage of selecting a European language. If a "compromise" *lingua franca* with indigenous roots—such as Swahili in Tanzania (cf. Whiteley, paper 7, this volume)—is available, it would, in my view, have much to recommend itself, since it would be more accessible to the masses of the population. Of course, if such an option is not available, a European language may be the only solution; but constant attention to the problem of bridging the gap between elites and masses would, in that case, be more than ever imperative.

Fishman's Type C nations present the most perplexing problems for language planning, as I have already pointed out in some of my earlier remarks about multiethnic states. Type C nations contain several ethnic groups, each with its own language and with strong sentimental attachments to it. The appropriate language policies in such situations depend, among other things, on the number of major languages that enter into the competition. In discussing the possible ways of handling multiple languages, Kloss (1967) points out that "complete equality of status seems possible only in countries that have two or at most three languages. No country could conduct its affairs in four or more languages without becoming hopelessly muddled" (p. 42).

From a functional point of view, of course, a single national language has many advantages, but the selection of such a language is beset with innumerable problems. Selection of one of the competing indigenous languages as the national language arouses resistance on both a functional and a sentimental basis, since the other language groups feel that this choice places them at a disadvantage (as it very likely does) and, at the same time, degrades their own "great traditions." The problem may be eased when the languages involved are closely akin (see Kloss, 1967, p. 44), most probably because the disadvantages experienced by the minority language groups are less severe when a language related to their own is adopted as the national language. But even this is not necessarily true. For various sentimental reasons, small differences between two languages that are objectively very similar may be magnified (just as, on occasion, large differences may be ignored). Such reactions are often linked to the names assigned to languages: two highly similar languages may be given different names and perceived as quite distinct, while two very different languages may bear the same name and be perceived as versions of the same language.

One possible solution in a situation marked by competition between a number of indigenous languages, each cherished by its own group, is to choose as the national language one that places all groups at a more or less equal disadvantage. This criterion can be met by selecting a European language for that purpose. Such a choice, however, presents its own problems, as I have already indicated. While it may not create unequal advantages on an ethnic-linguistic basis (at least for the elites), it exaggerates inequalities on a class basis. It is likely to perpetuate elitism and a lopsided class structure and to weaken the links of the population with the center. In Type C nations the problem is further complicated by the fact that use of a European language is resented on sentimental grounds, since—unlike Type A nations—they have "great traditions" with which various segments of the population are strongly identified. Thus, to take a major example, neither Hindi nor English has proven satisfactory as a national language for India—the former, because of the violent objections of non-Hindi speakers (particularly Tamil speakers, whose language belongs to a different family from Hindi and who have generally been further removed from the centers of power); the latter presumably because it went counter to an evolving sense of national self-awareness.

The choice of Swahili as a common national language in Tanzania, which seems to be meeting with some success (see Whiteley, paper 7, this volume), represents another example of a solution that is widely accepted, at least in part, because it places almost everyone at an equal disadvantage. Since Swahili is the indigenous language of only a very small proportion of the population, none of the groups that might otherwise be in competition are unduly disturbed by its selection. At the same time, Swahili does not have some of the drawbacks that English, as a Western language, would have. This may be an instructive example in that it suggests that a minority language may, under certain circumstances, represent a more functional choice than a dominant language. Of course, it must be kept in mind that Swahili, though it is the first language for only very few Tanzanians, is the second language for many and, in any event, is closely related to the Bantu languages spoken by the majority of the population. Thus, it has the advantage of facilitating communication and participation without the disadvantage of giving undue benefits to one or some of the major language groups as compared to others. Whiteley also discusses some of the structural factors in the pre-independence period—involving both the political structures of the peoples living in Tanganyika and the administrative structure established by the British—that inhibited the development of strong language loyalties. These historical conditions, again, created a receptive atmosphere for instituting Swahili as the national language.

In sum, in situations in which the vast number of competing languages makes it impossible to assign official status to all of them, there may be no alternative to instituting a single national language. It is essential that the language selected be such that the majority of the population can readily master it and that it does not give an undue advantage to some groups at the expense of others. Of course, if the majority of the population is sentimentally attached to a single language for historical, ideological, or perhaps religious reasons, as is true for Hebrew in Israel, then the task of selecting a national language is made easier, despite the fact that the population speaks many unrelated languages. Often, however, it is precisely the language to which there are no strong sentimental attachments that provides the optimal compromise because, although its selection may not arouse tremendous enthusiasm, it also does not arouse threat and resentment. If no satisfactory way can be found to equalize advantages and disadvantages across the population, then the major solutions may have to be sought not so much in language planning as in educational and political planning. Educational planning would have to be directed at systematically compensating for the disadvantages of the excluded groups; political planning may have to be directed at reducing the significance of linguistically based disadvantages by appropriate arrangements to decentralize power.

In those multilingual states in which the number of competing languages is two or three—to adopt the cut-off point suggested by Kloss (1967)—it may well be reasonable from a functional point of view to abandon the goal of a single national language. The mere decision, however, to assign official status to two or three languages does not necessarily eliminate language conflicts with potentially very disintegrative effects. Such a policy seems to be working well, for example, in Switzerland, but not at all well in Belgium. Thus, it is not enough to assign official status to two or three languages; it is also necessary to consider the specific conditions that will make such a policy effective and equitable.

A major source of complication is that two languages that are equally official do not necessarily occupy the same status within the society. One of the languages may well be dominant, partly because it is spoken by a larger proportion of the population but more importantly because of differences in the level of economic development of the two groups. Language may help perpetuate and magnify long-standing discrepancies between the groups. The problem may become exacerbated by the fact that the elites of the subordinate group, fluent in the dominant language, achieve mobility for themselves and become increasingly alienated from their own group. It is this kind of correlation between language and the level of development that contributes to the language problems of Belgium and Canada, and its apparent absence that partly accounts for the relatively problem-free situation in Switzerland (cf. Fishman, 1967, p. 34). It is apparent, from these considerations, that language planning must be closely linked with economic planning. Educational efforts—including systematic learning of the dominant language within the subordinate group—can help in bringing larger proportions of that group into the system. Beyond that, however, language problems are likely to persist until that group *as a group* is brought into the system through its economic development.

Another condition that plays a major role in the integration of an officially multilingual society is the nature of the political structure. In Switzerland, for example, power is highly decentralized, which makes control of the center a less desperate issue. The relative dominance of different language groups has fewer political implications. Moreover, the subdivisions are not based on language per se. Although each canton does have a dominant language (and this is probably more readily accepted by the minority because it is the majority in other cantons), the operative units in the system are the cantons rather than linguistic groups. Thus, there is little tendency for polarization along linguistic lines. The division does not exactly cut across linguistic lines (although there are some linguistically mixed cantons), but it does not follow linguistic lines either. There are obviously many special circumstances in the Swiss case, but it at least suggests the importance of language planning in the context of political planning. One direction that certainly merits attention by those who are concerned with the integration of multilingual societies is the search for political arrangements in which power is decentralized (thus reducing the magnitude of potential conflict) but not distributed along strictly linguistic lines (thus reducing the drift toward polarization).

CONCLUSION

I have presented a framework for analyzing the involvement of individuals and subgroups in the national system, which distinguishes, among other things, between two sources of attachment to the system: sentimental and instrumental. These two types of attachment can potentially reinforce and facilitate each other. By the same token, the correspondence of the two may well have dysfunctional consequences. For example, a state that has adequate resources to meet the needs and interests of its entire population and, thus, to generate instrumental ties for its various subgroups may be prevented from doing so by the existence of powerful, sentimentally based divisions within the population.

A common language may help to unify a population because it strengthens both sentimental and instrumental attachments to the system and, moreover, contributes to the mutual reinforcement of the two. Conversely, the lack of a common language in a multiethnic society may increase divisiveness and conflict by producing resistance and threats at both the sentimental and instrumental levels and by contributing to the mutual reinforcement of these two types of friction.

What are the implications of this analysis for language policies in multilingual societies? Although a common language would obviously make for a more unified and cohesive society, efforts to create such a language where it does not already exist may have precisely the opposite effect. In determining whether a common language would be helpful and, if so, what form it ought to take, policy makers and language planners must consider not only the potential of such a language in binding the population to the nation-state, sentimentally and instrumentally, but also the sentimentally and instrumentally based resistances that the proposed policy would call forth in different subgroups within the population.

My speculations about criteria for language planning—and I must stress that they are only speculations—start with the proposition that the deliberate use of language policies for the purpose of creating a national identity and of fostering sentimental attachments is usually not desirable. Rather, language policies ought to be designed to meet the needs and interests of all segments of the population effectively and equitably, thus, fostering instrumental attachments out of which sentimental ones can then gradually emerge. This proposition is based in part on my value preferences and my concern that the direct manipulation of sentimental attachments may serve as a substitute for efforts at the instrumental level of creating adequate socioeconomic institutions and of providing meaningful roles for all subgroups within the society. The proposition, however, is also based in part on certain empirical assumptions, such as the assumption that a sense of national identity is more likely to develop out of functional relationships within the society than out of deliberate attempts to promote it; or that direct efforts to promote a national identity in multiethnic societies will bring subgroup identities to the fore and thus generate resistance and strengthen internal divisions. These assumptions can and should be put to an empirical test. The validity of my recommendations clearly depends on how well these assumptions stand up to such a test.

Even if one accepts the proposition that language policies should be designed to meet the needs and interests of all segments of the population in the most effective and equitable way, he has to determine what specific policy is most likely to be conducive to this end in a given society at a given point in time. In some situations, a common national language may be most appropriate; in others, the recognition of two or more official languages; and in yet others, the combination of a national administrative language, with officially recognized local languages. Where a common language is indicated, the particular language most appropriate for that purpose may be the language spoken by the majority of the population, or a language spoken by a minority group, or a Language of Wider Communication, or a modernized version of a classical language. Whatever language policy is developed, its success may depend on careful coordination with educational planning and with economic and political development.

In evaluating these and other alternative policy options, it is important to assess the integrative and disintegrative effects that each policy is likely to have on both the sentimental and instrumental levels. These effects, in turn, will depend on the strength and nature of the attachments of various segments of the population to the national system and to their own subgroups. Thus, for example, so far as resistances to national language policies are based primarily on instrumental considerations, planners have greater freedom to select the most efficient solution, provided such a solution is combined with educational, economic, and political arrangements designed to overcome systematic inequities between different ethnic groups. If, on the other hand, resistances are largely based on sentimental attachments to the separate ethnic groups, it may be preferable to adopt a less efficient solution that is designed to protect the integrity of cultural minorities. It should be possible to derive more specific hypotheses about the probable effects of different policies under various conditions as the theoretical framework presented in this paper is refined and subjected to empirical tests.

ACKNOWLEDGMENT

This paper was prepared for the Conference on Language Planning Processes, East-West Center, Honolulu, April 7–10, 1969. The work was supported by U.S. Public Health Service Research Grant MH 07280 from the National Institute of Mental Health.

NOTES

1. The approach is presented in more detail in Kelman (1969), and some of its additional features and implications are discussed in Kelman (1968). The assumptions behind this approach bear striking resemblance to Fishman's formulations (see, for example, Fishman, 1968a, 1968c, and paper

1, this volume). Although his approach and mine, in my view, are fully compatible with one another and are intended to highlight the same phenomena, there are some differences in the precise distinctions that are drawn and in the way certain terms—like "nation"—are defined. I shall use the distinctions and definitions that I have been working with, but I hope that the similarities in the basic approach and purpose will be apparent.

2. Fishman (1968a) suggests the term "nationism" for this purpose, which has many advantages and avoids certain ambiguities. On the other hand, my usage is consistent with my argument that the correspondence between state and nationality is central to the ideology of the modern nation-state.

3. The sources of legitimacy distinguished here are similar to, though not completely isomorphic with, Fishman's distinction between sociocultural integration and political-operative integration (cf. Fishman, paper 1, this volume).

4. Compare Fishman's distinction between nation-state and state-nation (Fishman, paper 1, this volume).

5. I am grateful to Professor Chaim Rabin for pointing out to me that sentimental attachment may be intensified not just by the existence of a common language per se (in the structural sense) but also by the existence of a common "manner of being addressed." He cites the Austrians and the German-speaking Swiss as an example: They speak the same language as the Germans, but they attach a great deal of importance to the uniquely Austrian or Swiss way of using that language. Thus, it is the use of the language rather than its structure that serves as a national symbol and object of sentimental attachment. Perhaps the continuity of national tradition is enhanced by a common language in the sense of the accustomed manner of being addressed, while the authenticity of the tradition is enhanced by a common language in the structural sense.

REFERENCES

DeLamater, John; Katz, Daniel; and Kelman, Herbert C. 1969. On the Nature of National Involvement: A Preliminary Study in an American Community. *Journal of Conflict Resolution*, 13.

Fishman, Joshua A. 1967. Bilingualism with and without Diglossia; Diglossia with and without Bilingualism. *Journal of Social Issues,* 23: 2: 29–38.

———. 1968a. Nationality-Nationalism and Nation-Nationism. *In* Fishman, Ferguson, and Das Gupta, 39–51.

———. 1968b. National Languages and Languages of Wider Communication in the Developing Nations. Paper presented at the Regional Conference on Language and Linguistics, Dar es Salaam, Tanzania.

———. 1968c. Sociolinguistics and the Language Problems of the Developing Countries. *International Social Science Journal,* 20: 211–225.

———. This volume. The Impact of Nationalism on Language Planning. Paper 1.

Fishman, Joshua A.; Ferguson, Charles A.; and Das Gupta, Jyotirindra, eds. 1968. *Language Problems of Developing Nations.* New York: John Wiley and Sons.

Hymes, Dell. 1967. Models of the Interaction of Language and Social Setting. *Journal of Social Issues,* 23: 2: 8–28.

Kelman, Herbert C. 1968. Education for the Concept of a Global Society. *Social Education,* 32: 661–666.

―――. 1969. Patterns of Personal Involvement in the National System: A Social-Psychological Analysis of Political Legitimacy. *In* Rosenau, 276–288.

Kloss, Heinz. 1967. Bilingualism and Nationalism. *Journal of Social Issues,* 23: 2: 39–47.

Macnamara, John. This volume. Successes and Failures in the Movement for the Restoration of Irish. Paper 4.

Rosenau, James N. ed. 1969. *International Politics and Foreign Policy,* 2nd ed., rev. New York: Free Press.

Whiteley, Wilfred H. This volume. Some Factors Influencing Language Policies in Eastern Africa. Paper 7.

3. RELIGION, LANGUAGE, AND POLITICAL MOBILIZATION

JYOTIRINDRA DAS GUPTA
Department of Political Science, University of California, Berkeley

The pervasive impact of religion on South Asian politics is commonly recognized. The influence of the great traditions of Hinduism, Buddhism, and Islam on political orientations, organizations, and processes has been noted in many studies.[1] However, the specific manner in which religious traditions of the people have been utilized by the mobilizing leaders and groups in the course of political modernization has not yet been studied with the care it deserves. In South Asia, religion is both a factor of division and unity. As a factor of social division, its potentiality for generating social conflict can be better appreciated when it is considered in the context of other forms of social division. In this connection, the divisions in South Asian societies based on language, culture, religion, caste, and class assume great importance. This paper will take into account the relation between religious and language divisions, their translation into political divisions, and, particularly, the interaction between the politics of religion and language.[2]

The purpose of this paper is to examine the specific manner in which religious loyalties have been utilized by the mobilizing groups and leaders to influence the course of language politics in selected areas of South Asia. The time period we are considering stretches from the middle of the nineteenth century to our own day. We begin our account from the time of the consolidation of the British rule in India, which was also the time when modern political organizations, based on nationalist convictions, began to emerge. The gradual spread of Western education in English and Indian languages was turning the attention of the educated elite increasingly to search for an authentic national identity.

Segmented Memory

Although the emergence of national awareness was based on a feeling of resentment against the alien colonial authority, it was not easy to discover a positive image of the nation to serve as a generally acceptable symbol of the nationalist movement. It was expected that the new elite would look to the past for deriving support for the national idea. Looking backward, however, many Hindu leaders and intellectuals recalled the resentment of their religious community to the centuries of Muslim rule, which preceded the British conquest. They could not forget that their loss of freedom did not begin with the British conquest and that in their day nationalism would imply struggle against the British authorities and the vestiges of the Muslim rule in the social and cultural fields as well.[3] Many Muslim leaders and intellectuals, on the other hand, recalled with great pride how they subjugated the overwhelming number of Hindus for several centuries, imposed their culture on many sectors of Indian life, and also succeeded in converting a substantial number of Hindus to their superior religious community.[4] The differential recall of the country's tradition suggested to these leaders the alternative possibilities of organizing separate and rival strands of nationalist movements.

But these leaders did not exhaust the newly emerging elite. Another set of leaders and intellectuals drawn from all religious groups in looking back at the same tradition discovered that a composite Indian culture, drawing from several religious traditions, including Hinduism and Islam, has developed as a fact of social history. It is useless to try to separate its components in religious terms. Rather, it is the duty of the nationalist movement to further this process. This way it would also be possible to achieve secular modern politics transcending religious affiliations and thus to mobilize the entire population of the country around a single symbol of a unified community.[5] The appeal to a secular national symbol obviously demanded a high degree of detachment from the religious conflicts of the past and the present and an equally high degree of intellectual composition of the possibilities of a cooperative community. Heroic leaders like Rammohun Roy or Dadabhai Naoroji could gather around them a bold group of modernists who could transcend the segmented memory arising from religious affiliations. It was not easy, however, even for the most educated men either to erase the impact of partisan history or to resist the temptation of the relatively easier identification of their own religious community with the nation. But what seemed to be socially so difficult was, to an extent, made politically possible by the advocates of composite nationalism.

Mass Politics

From the beginning of the twentieth century, nationalist elites in India attempted increasingly to recruit the masses for political action. The desire to enlarge the popular base of the movement raised the question of casting the nationalist appeal in a popular form. This question was mainly composed of two parts: how best to evoke a sense of solidarity by means of popularly persuasive symbols and how to communicate this appeal to the masses in a manner comprehensible to them. The established factors of loyalty that produce group cohesion were highly segmentary, as in the cases of caste, kinship, status, and class. It is here that the appeal to the great traditions of religion offered a crucial mobilizing possibility. On the one hand, the evocative power of the symbols of religious identification in the Indian society was beyond question; on the other hand, religion cut across the various segmental cohesive ties of the smaller range. The efficacy, however, of religious symbols to integrate various social groups also signified the possibility of dividing the nation along religious lines.

The leaders of the era of mass politics used religious symbols in a number of ways. The secular nationalists sought to utilize Hindu, Muslim, and other symbols in order to mobilize the common people of these communities into a wider national movement represented by the Indian National Congress. The Hindu and the Muslim particularist movements used religion to create exclusive solidarity of their own communities.[6] But in spite of the variation of purpose, the very use of religion to attract the masses signified the necessity of interpreting religious loyalty in a language that would be persuasive to the masses. The nationalists of the earlier decades had relied on the English language. Now they had to use the languages of the people.

Religion and Language Division

Each religious community was divided into several language groups, and the latter cut across religious communities. For example, Hindus and Muslims of India as a whole were divided in at least sixteen major language groups, with no language identified exclusively with either of the religious groups. In North India, the picture was more complicated because educated Hindus and Muslims used two styles of the same language that they preferred to call Hindi and Urdu respectively. Yet, there was considerable religious overlap between the speakers of these two styles. It should be noted here that Hindi is written in Devanagari script, while Urdu uses Persian script. In spite of a common core of vocabulary, learned writing in Hindi uses more Sanskrit words, and Urdu uses more Persian words.[7]

The linguistic similarity of Hindi and Urdu was gradually overshadowed by the deliberate exaggeration of the difference between these languages by leaders of religious groups for mobilizational purposes. The Hindu particularist leaders of North India seized upon the legacy of Persian and Urdu dominance (resulting from Muslim rule) as their target of attack. Political consciousness in North India made the Hindus realize that because of their vast superiority of numbers, they ought to elevate Hindi to a status of prestige and wide use. In the early phase of the twentieth century, even those Hindu leaders who used Urdu for all purposes began to claim that they in fact spoke Hindi. Similarly, Muslim leaders of North India urged all their co-religionists to declare their speech as Urdu, though they might in fact speak either Hindi or some village dialects indistinguishable from their Hindu neighbors. Gradually, the nomenclature of languages in North India followed more the politically motivated names suggested by leaders of religious groups than the ones that they had actually been using for identification previously. As a result, census-reporting of the numbers of speakers of languages in North India was dictated more by religious affiliation than by established names.[8]

Politics of Language Identification

A deliberate attempt was made by the partisans of linguistic identification according to religious affiliation to draw countrywide support for Hindi and Urdu from the wider Hindu and Muslim communities in India. By the second decade of this century, some leaders of the Hindi language associations tried to promote Hindi as the common language of all Hindus.[9] The success of this campaign was limited partly because the Hindus belonging to non-Hindi language communities were opposed to such an identification. This campaign failed also partly because of the secularist outlook of most nationalists led by Gandhi, Nehru, and others who were interested in promoting Hindi as a national language, cutting across religious affiliations and regional ties. Their success in persuading the Indian National Congress to adopt this view revealed that neither the

Hindi speakers nor the Hindu people as a whole substantially cared for a policy of Hindi-Hindu identification.

On the Muslim side, the identification of religion and politics was more integral and widely pervasive. From the very beginning of the rise of Muslim modernist consciousness, the bulk of the leadership made a heavy investment in the symbolic capability of Islamic solidarity. They identified not merely nationalism with religious solidarity but also the latter with linguistic solidarity. They were not aware that the majority of the Muslims in India did not speak Urdu and that this majority in fact shared with the Hindus the languages and literature of many different areas in India. They persistently claimed that Urdu was the language of the Muslims. The vast number of Muslims who spoke Bengali, Gujarati, Punjabi, and other languages did not substantially resist this claim. This happened in spite of the fact that, for the majority of the non-Urdu-speaking Muslims, Urdu was not even a significantly preferred second language.

It is worth noting that the identification of Muslim interest with the cause of Urdu was proposed primarily by the Muslim leadership of North India. Till the day of partition of the subcontinent, the religious and political leadership of the North Indian Muslims increasingly became a reference standard for the bulk of the Muslims in most parts of India. It did not matter that apart from symbolic deference most Muslims had nothing to do with Urdu. It was equally irrelevant that the most persuasive leader of Muslim religious nationalism in India himself happened to be a non-Urdu speaker.[10] What ultimately mattered was the call for identification and the capability of this call to persuade the relevant audience.

After Independence

The partition of India and the advent of independence initially carried forward this process of identification. The leaders of Pakistan reiterated their claim that Urdu was in fact the language of the Muslims. The immediate aftermath of independence in Pakistan witnessed consistent efforts to enshrine this claim in the Constitution. It should be noted that the partition of the subcontinent left the Urdu-speaking area out of Pakistan. Ironically, in Pakistan there was less reason to identify Urdu with the Muslim community than there was in undivided India. Even in the 1961 census, Urdu is reported to be the mother tongue of less than 4 per cent of the total population, more than 52 per cent being speakers of Bengali. The other major regional languages of Pakistan are Punjabi, Sindhi, and

Pushto. Deprived of a regional base and numerical rationale, Urdu never-theless continues to be one of the two state languages of Pakistan, the other being Bengali.[11]

The declaration of Bengali as the other state language was a result of intensive agitation on the part of the Bengali Muslims, who attacked the very notion of absolute identification of Urdu with the Muslim com-munity.[12] In India, after independence, the limited Hindi-Hindu identi-fication was under considerable attack from the Dravidian language speakers and also from the Hindi speakers of secular persuasion. Even at the level of national language policy, a number of Hindu leaders from the non-Hindi-speaking areas, who had fought for Hindi in the pre-independence days, now became bitter adversaries of Hindi.

Two decades after independence, it seems that the rationale for a linguistic unity reinforcing religious solidarity is on the decline in the Indo-Pakistan subcontinent. But this decline is more visible on the national level than at the state levels of contemporary Indian politics. The decline of the symbolic capability of Urdu in Pakistan owes itself mainly to the disappearance of the internal threat to Muslim nationalism coming from the non-Muslims. In India, however, the religious back-ground of the Hindi-Urdu conflict is still alive in the North Indian states. There are fifty million Muslims in post-partition India, and about half of them speak Urdu, the bulk of whom are in North India.

Urdu Demands and Muslim Politics

The pattern of Muslim politics in independent India is, of course, bound to be different from pre-partition days. Before 1947, Muslims claimed to be a nation by virtue of their religious solidarity. When Pakistan was created as a Muslim nation, the Muslims of India were caught in a con-tradiction. Now that they were left in a secular state, they were supposed, at least formally, to detach politics from religion and religion from lan-guage. The major Urdu-speaking region remained in India, but Urdu could not hope to become the political focus of a religious nationalism. At best it could be the symbolic focus of Muslim religious culture and minority rights. This is the role Urdu has tended to appropriate in spite of the fact that about half the Muslim population of post-partition India do not speak Urdu.

One of the problems of Indian politics after independence has been the conflict between the Hindu and Muslim religious groups in North

India regarding the place of Urdu. At the national level, Urdu is included in the list of languages of the Union; at the state level, it is one of the official languages of Jammu and Kashmir. In Uttar Pradesh, Bihar, and Andhra Pradesh, there are sizeable concentrations of Urdu speakers. Even in these states, however, the proportion of speakers remains close to 7 per cent of the state population. In Andhra Pradesh, Urdu is recognized as an additional language for the Telengana area. In Bihar and Uttar Pradesh, there have been persistent movements to make Urdu the second official language. With the exception of the tragic 1967 movement in Bihar, the major center of the Urdu movement has been Uttar Pradesh. The legacy of Muslim nationalism in Uttar Pradesh and the counter-legacy of the revivalist Hindu nationalism in the same area have added to the complexity of language rivalry.

A series of movements continued in Uttar Pradesh after 1948. The representation of Urdu interest in these movements has mainly been provided by the Anjuman Taraqqi-i-Urdu. This organization of language interest transformed its objective from religious nationalism to the promotion of minority-group rights after independence. Its national leaders are recruited from secular Muslim groups.[13] At the lower levels of leadership, however, the basic Urdu demands are kept alive by the less secular Muslim religious associations. In the sixties, these organizations came together in a common united front.[14] Gradually, the leadership supplying mobilizational resources for the Urdu movement has been coming more and more from exclusively Muslim religious associations. The basic demands of the Urdu movement are educational, political, economic, and administrative. But there is something more to it in the sense that all these demands are welded together in a conscious attempt to mobilize Muslim support for Muslim leadership belonging to various parties. In this case, language serves as a symbol; religion provides the mobilizational base; and the latter is used for realizing the political objectives of the Muslim leadership of North India.

Hindu Reaction

In Uttar Pradesh, the more organized the language demands of the Urdu speakers have tended to become, the greater has been the hostility from the Hindu religious associations.[15] Just as the Muslim associations cut across various political parties, the same is true for the Hindu associations. Since 80 per cent of the state population are Hindus, however, they have an almost overwhelming command over political and other resources of the state. A substantial section of those who command the resources view with suspicion the organized moves of the Muslim associations, even when their demands are legitimate. In fact, this suspicion enables the more particularist Hindu organizations to expand their Hindu support-structure and to cast doubts on the value of the secular norms of the state.

As a result, language politics increasingly takes the form of religious rivalry in which contending religious groups and their political leaders play their game of power. The obvious casualty of this process happens to be the legitimate components of the language demands of the minority groups. The organizational effects of this process are indicated by the fact that Hindu and Muslim religious particularist forces have made substantial progress in this area. One mitigating factor in this process, however, is that, whenever religious rivalry has tended to submerge the rational claims of the minority language groups, the national political authority has tried to intervene and its secular intervention has often offset the power of the regional Hindu extremist forces.

Indications

This brief survey indicates how political groups and leaders utilizing religious loyalty as a mobilizational resource have sought to influence the course of language politics and policy in the Indian subcontinent in general and in North India in particular. In a developing area, it is the political elite that has attempted to define the language interest of a community. Neither religious divisions nor language divisions of a society provide any clear indication about the "natural" interests of the religious or the linguistic communities, especially in a situation where such divisions cut across each other. Deliberate investment of religious identity to a particular language can succeed or fail, depending on the power of the leaders to persuade people and on the interaction of multiple social and historical factors. Before the partition of the subcontinent, Urdu succeeded in muting intra-Muslim language rivalry, but after the creation of Pakistan the same was not possible. This shows the fluidity of cleavage lines based on language and the flexibility of language interest. In India the use of Hindi by the particularists and the secularists for their political purposes reveals similar elasticity of language interest and its variable ties with religious interests, which are determined by the needs and capabilities of the political mobilizers in the form of groups or leaders. This survey also shows that, to the extent that language and religious interests are kept separate, it is relatively easier for various groups to rationally negotiate with each other, especially when the political framework approximates a secular democratic model.

NOTES

1. See, for example, the collection of papers edited by Donald E. Smith, *South Asian Politics and Religion* (Princeton: Princeton University Press, 1966).
2. For a detailed study of these aspects, see Jyotirindra Das Gupta, *Language Conflict and National Development* (Berkeley and Los Angeles: University of California Press, 1970).
3. This view of a long chain of Hindu leaders, beginning from the middle of the nineteenth century, still continues to be upheld by the leaders of Hindu particularist organizations like the Jana Sangh and the Hindu Mahasabha. For early elaboration of such views, see C. H. Heimsath, *Indian Nationalism and Hindu Social Reform* (Princeton: Princeton University Press, 1964).
4. For this view, see Hafeez Malik, *Moslem Nationalism in India and Pakistan* (Washington, D.C.: Public Affairs Press, 1963).
5. Perhaps the best representative of this view was Mahatma Gandhi. See his *Thoughts in National Language* (Ahmedabad: Navajivan, 1956).
6. The leading Hindu movement was represented by the Arya Samaj, which was especially important in North India. Muslim particularism began with the Aligarh movement, which was later carried forward by the Muslim League.
7. See John J. Gumperz, Language Problems in the Rural Development of North India, *Journal of Asian Studies* 16, no. 2 (February 1957): 251–259.
8. In North India political influence determines whether an individual reports his mother tongue to be Hindi, Hindustani, Urdu, or one of the major dialects.
9. The most important association promoting Hindi at this time was the Hindi Sahitya Sammelan, founded in 1910. The leadership included secularists and Hindu particularists. The reference here is to the latter group. For details concerning the politics of the language associations, see note 2.
10. The reference is to M. A. Jinnah.
11. For a general discussion of the language composition of Pakistan, see Donald N. Wilber, *Pakistan, Its People, Its Society, Its Culture* (New Haven: HRAF Press, 1964), pp. 71–83.
12. The Bengali language agitation is analyzed in Hasan Hafizur Rahman, ed., *Ekushe February* (Dacca: Punthipatra, 1965), especially pp. 15–30 and 209–232 (in Bengali).
13. Until 1969, its most prominent leader was Dr. Zakir Hussain.

14. The Muslim Majlis-i-Mushawarat.
15. This is a cumulative process that has continuously sharpened the Hindu-Muslim conflict of this area. After the division of India, the Hindu leaders of Uttar Pradesh and elsewhere blamed Muslim separation as a tragedy. Consequently, their attitude towards the Muslims seemed to have hardened. They refused to grant any special status to Urdu and brushed off most charges of discrimination against Urdu. Whether the Hindu-dominated government was actually guilty of deliberate discrimination has been a subject of controversy. See the *Report of the Uttar Pradesh Language Committee* (Lucknow: Superintendant, Printing and Stationary, 1963).

Case Studies of Language Planning

4. SUCCESSES AND FAILURES IN THE MOVEMENT FOR THE RESTORATION OF IRISH

JOHN MACNAMARA
Department of Psychology, McGill University

The majority of Irish people seem to have dropped Irish in favor of English somewhere between 1750 and 1850, though the process of change went on for a period far longer than a hundred years. The seventeenth century saw the crushing of a culture that was in certain of its elements well over a thousand years old. English rule from then on was solidly established, and, though Irish continued in some landed families,[1] it gradually became mainly the language of an impoverished and disinherited peasantry. English had for long been strong in the towns. With the passage of time, the peasantry adopted the language of the towns and of the upper classes, and the language switch seems to have been for the most part complete by 1851, when the first census to take account of language was held. In that year, only about 5 per cent of the population described themselves as monolingual Irish speakers, and a further 23 per cent described themselves as bilingual. Although these figures are probably underestimates,[2] it is clear that by 1851 the proportion of monolingual speakers was very small, indeed.

Of course, the old order did not go under without a cry. As early as the late seventeenth century, Dáivi O Bruadair, the Munster poet, satirized those of his contemporaries who affected to speak *gósta gairbh-Bhéarla* ("a feeble imitation of the harsh English tongue").[3] Nevertheless, the generations that succeeded him decided that there was no future in Irish and that, if they were to better themselves, they needed to know English. So they learned it. The process of replacing Irish by English continues to the present when less than 3 per cent of the school-going population speaks Irish as a home language,[4] many of whom are bilingual. Furthermore, the Irish-speaking population is located mainly in three pockets on the west coast, which, until the coming of the motorcar, were relatively remote from the rest of the country.

Although the Irish language was replaced by English, Ireland never lost the feeling that it was Irish and different. First, there was the geographical fact that the country was an island. There were other factors: the Catholic majority in the country as a whole and the Presbyterian minority in the north-east corner had maintained their religious independence through a checkered history of religious discrimination and persecution, especially during the eighteenth century; the Irish Catholics for the most part perceived themselves as ethnically and historically distinct from the English. Until the year 1800, there was the parliament in Dublin; after the Act of Union had abolished the Dublin parliament, there was a series of political struggles—religious, economic, and agrarian—to sustain among Irishmen the sense that they were different. The middle of the nineteenth century saw the rise of the Young Ireland movement and with it the propagation of a distinctly Irish nationalism. Subsequently, Isaac Butt formed an Irish parliamentary party to press for the repeal of the Act of Union and for Home Rule for Ireland. Charles Stewart Parnell forged the party into an effective instrument that was to play a large part in Irish politics for well over a generation.[5] Moreover, there was, throughout the nineteenth century and especially during the early years of the present century, an Anglo-Irish literary movement that became more and more consciously national (Sullivan, 1969). One of the principal ways in which the movement fostered its national characteristics was by drawing on themes from old Irish literature and from folklore collected in the Irish-speaking areas. Several of the writers, too, notably Lady Gregory and John M. Synge, attempted to capture in their English some of the flavor and rhythm of the Irish language. Thus, although the Irish language had declined, many forces contributed to the maintenance and perhaps growth of the feeling that Ireland was a nation distinct from and different from England.

Indeed, one of the interesting aspects of nineteenth-century Irish nationalism is that it flourished after the decline of the indigenous language. Language-revival literature apart, nineteenth-century nationalist sentiment has not been expressed in Irish (Breathnach, 1956). There is much truth, then, in Fishman's (1968, footnote 16) suggestion that English has been "completely indigenized [in Ireland] and associated with a new indigenous Great Tradition." Indeed, a large part of the literary work of the past 150 years has been translation and re-creation. The sense of continuity with the past has been maintained; the Catholic religion has survived the switch of languages; the Irish farmers now own the land; a native government has been established; the principal works of Irish literature have been translated into English,[6] and a new "Irish" literature in English has been created.

The Gaelic League

The decline of Irish was noted with regret by many Irishmen, and, from the end of the eighteenth century, sporadic efforts were made to stem, and even reverse, the flow.[7] It was not until the end of the nineteenth century, however, that a language-revival movement that was strong enough to make an impact on the country as a whole began. The movement was inspired and promoted mainly by an organization known as the Gaelic League, whose first president, Dr. Douglas Hyde, called, in the address that led to the foundation of the League (in 1893), for a return to the language, manners, and customs of the Gaelic past and for a concerted effort to "de-Anglicize" Ireland. Although the Irish language was always central to the League's programs, the initial linguistic plan as found in the league's constitution was quite modest—*an Ghaedhealg do choimeád dá labhairt i n-Eirinn* ("to maintain Irish as a spoken language in Ireland"). In its propaganda and in its public image, however, the League's linguistic aims were wider and agree more closely with the aims attributed to it by the Commission on the Revival of Irish (Coimisiún um Athbheochan na Gaeilge, 1964): to foster Irish as the national language of Ireland and to spread its use as a spoken language.[8]

After an inconspicuous beginning, the Gaelic League suddenly caught the popular imagination and attracted wide support for its cultural and educational program. From a mere idea in 1893, it reached 120 branches by 1901 and 593 branches by 1904.[9] Its main strategy was to establish a network of adult classes, but it also used such means as the public lecture, the pamphlet, the parade, the popular competition, and the satire.[10] Its success lay in no small measure in that it united the support of persons from every political group, from every religious denomination, and, to a lesser extent, from every social class.[11] With this support, the Gaelic League was able to collect money, employ persons full-time, undertake publication, and press forward its plans for the language.[12] By 1905, the League's successes were already impressive. Attending the League's classes had become a popular thing to do; a weekly newspaper, *An Claidheamh Soluis,* had been started; the foundations of a modern literature in Irish had been laid; popular interest in Gaelic literature, music, and customs had been aroused; a public protest had been staged in which the British Postmaster General had been forced to accept mail addressed in Irish; the Dublin County Council had been prevailed upon to favor in its appointments candidates who knew Irish (a pattern that was to become much more general); and many primary schools, some secondary schools, and teacher-training colleges had been persuaded to introduce Irish.[13] The years which followed were to see further progress, the climax of which, perhaps, was the League's success after an acrimonious struggle in having Irish included as a necessary subject for matriculation in the new National University of Ireland.

The Gaelic League was closely related, though not perhaps caus-ally,[14] to the revolutionary movement that culminated in 1922 in the estab-lishment of the Irish Free State. I suspect, however, that the very vigor and success of the political movement weakened the League, and, with it, the language movement. The return of the Liberals to power in West-minster in 1905 meant that Ireland came to life politically once more and began to discuss the prospects of Home Rule. Later, in 1913, when Home Rule was passed by the House of Commons and when Presbyterian Ulster had responded by founding the Ulster Volunteers to defend themselves, the rest of the country countered by founding the Irish Volunteers, a mili-tary body that had no sharply defined policy or purpose but a body that could be put to use by men who had a mind to use it. These men turned out to be the members of the Irish Republican Brotherhood, who from 1913 forward were to grow in number and play an increasingly important role in the shaping of events. The leaders of the revolutionary movement were almost to a man prominent members of the Gaelic League, and as they became more active politically the League inevitably declined.[15] Nevertheless, something of the old enthusiasm survived until the estab-lishment of the Irish Free State in 1922. From then on, the League felt that the main responsibility for the restoration of Irish devolved on the young government. The League, though it still exists, in effect bowed out. What happened is well put by the Commission on the Revival of Irish (Coimisiún um Athbheochan na Gaeilge, 1964); the translation of it is given below:

> It stands to reason that people's enthusiasm should have waned as soon as the war with England was ended, and since the cultivation of the language was seen as part of that war it was natural that their devotion should diminish. That left the language movement short of members and short of money,

particularly because many people felt that in an Irish state there would be no necessity for the League to engage in work for the language. But the language movement was weakened in many other ways too; some of its most effective leaders lost their lives in the war of independence; some of its supporters devoted their lives to politics as ministers or members of parliament, and others entered the civil service or local authorities. Due to the political divisions which resulted from the civil war, enmities arose within the language movement itself; some lost heart; others were disgusted by the bitter language and the cruelty of the civil war, and others became indifferent and cynical. There was an end, to a great extent, to zeal for the language; some branches [of the League] were wound up; in a lot of places *feiseanna* ("conventions") were given up (pp. 24–25).

It must be remembered, too, that the Gaelic League's policies disturbed many of the northern Presbyterians whose ancestors had never spoken Irish, and thus these policies contributed something to the political division of the country (O Cuív, 1966, p. 159) and, hence, to the causing of the civil war that ensued upon the division. Indeed, the main issue on which the civil war was fought was whether to accept the political division of the country. Entanglement in such an issue probably took from the ingenuous idealism with which the League began, but other tragedies also played their part. The civil war was followed in due course by the depression of the 1920's and the 1930's and later still by the world war. During those years, the restoration movement seemed on the surface to make great progress. Professor Denis Gwynn (1928), writing in the late twenties, felt, however, that the enthusiasm had "evaporated." After listing many seemingly stringent requirements aimed at making Irish an essential part of Irish life, he goes on to say: "But the country has quickly adapted itself to these formal requirements, and in practice they have not involved any serious hardship" (p. 228). At present, the situation remains largely unchanged. Both the officials engaged in operating many (but not all) language regulations—such as those relating to certain appointments, to oral examinations in Irish for university students and those relating to the approval of secondary teachers—and the persons to whom they apply quietly conspire to set the regulations aside. Indeed, in applying most language regulations, the prevailing attitude has been *pas trop de zèle*.

EDUCATION

The Primary School

The Gaelic League and its language program have at all times been openly opposed by a certain number of Irishmen[16] in the South whose patriotism could scarcely have been doubted, but the number of such men was small. The disenchantment and apathy of which I spoke in the previous section were mainly tacit, for the mass of the people acquiesced in the official restoration policy, which the state has maintained since 1922. Official policy could be seen at work in many sectors of public life but nowhere more clearly than in education. One of the first acts of Irish government after it took charge of the country was to lay down that "the Irish language be taught, or used as a medium of instruction, for not less than one full hour each day in all national [primary] schools where there was a teacher competent to teach it."[17] The order was an immediate result of a National Programme Conference, representative of many Irish organizations, called in summer 1921 by the Irish National Teachers' Organization (INTO). The Conference had proposed that, in addition to Irish as a subject in its own right, all the work in the infant classes and the teaching of history, geography, singing, and physical training in higher classes should be conducted where possible through the medium of Irish. A second National Programme Conference, convened in 1925 by the Minister of Education at the request of INTO, reiterated—with some reservations—these proposals and advocated that the use of Irish as a teaching medium be extended "as far as possible."[18] The Department of Education adopted the resolutions of the second Conference and in 1934 made them obligatory on all national school teachers.

How were teachers to be found who could implement these policies? First of all, though the language policy of the native government was more extensive and more vigorous than anything proposed by the earlier British government, the British government, under pressure from the Gaelic League and since the turn of the century, had been quietly fostering the teaching of Irish.[19] For twenty years before the establishment of the Free State, then, the number of primary-school teachers who knew Irish was increasing. To meet the demands of the new policies, however, the Free State took two measures: (1) teachers under the age of forty-five were required to take summer courses and (2) provision was made to recruit primary-school teachers from the Irish-speaking areas. In order to help native Irish speakers become teachers, the government established in 1926 the first of six *preparatory colleges* that were run exclusively through the medium of Irish. To these colleges, which followed the normal program for secondary schools, students were admitted mainly on state scholarships. Half the places were reserved for native Irish speakers, and half, for English speakers who showed promise, especially in Irish. These students made their way in time to teacher colleges where all was again taught in Irish. When the system was in full swing, the preparatory colleges provided about one-third of the yearly intake to the body of primary teachers (O Catháin, 1967); their alumni had a good grasp of Irish. There was one unnecessary but major drawback attached to these colleges. If a student at any time decided that teaching was not for him, he had to repay the government all the money spent on him; it was a condition so crippling to the majority of preparatory-college students that withdrawal from teaching was virtually impossible. These colleges were discontinued by the Department of Education in the early 1960's partly to obviate the moral pressure that I have just mentioned and partly to insure that teachers would be drawn from a wider sector of the community. Their disappearance, however, marks the end of any concerted effort to draw teachers from the Irish-speaking districts.

At the time when I went to primary school in the middle 1930's, it was forbidden to teach English or to use English in the infant classes of the state-financed national (primary) schools. Irish as a subject was compulsory in all classes, and English as a subject was compulsory in the second class (roughly second grade) and all higher classes. Further, the rule was that Irish was to be used as the medium of instruction in all classes and subjects where the teacher was competent to do so and where the children were competent to learn in this manner. In practice, the decision whether to teach through the medium of Irish depended mainly on the principal teacher in the school, on the local inspector, and, to a lesser extent, on the school manager (i.e., in nearly all cases, the local parish priest). The position of Irish as a subject remains the same today, but the position of English has changed somewhat. In 1948 permission was given to teach English to infants for half an hour a day (Ireland, Department of Education, 1954, p. 70). There has also been a change in official attitude towards teaching through the medium of Irish. A minute of the Department of Education (1965, p. 115) in 1960 discouraged the use of Irish as a teaching medium for the younger classes in national schools.

The schools I attended as a boy were with one exception[20] typical in that they taught most subjects in English above the level of infants, though Irish was to a limited extent used as a teaching medium. Indeed, teaching through Irish reached its peak during my school days. There were about 5,000 national schools in the country, of which some 230 were in the *Gaeltacht* (Irish-speaking district);[21] in the latter, all subjects were taught in Irish. During the 1930's the *total* number of schools that taught all subjects in Irish increased until in 1939 it reached 704. But after that the number declined.[22] By 1944 the number was down to 601; by 1956 it was 389, and by 1966 it was down to 309.[23]

The typical primary teacher when I was a boy was, naturally, middle-aged and had learned Irish for the most part in summer courses. He had at his disposal a small number of Irish primers, readers, conversation source books, and songbooks. For the more advanced classes he had a much larger range of short-story books and novels from which to choose. For the more formal aspects of the language, he could have used any of a number of simple grammars (the one prepared by the Irish Christian Brothers was widely used), a large Irish-English dictionary compiled in a rather haphazard fashion by Father Patrick Dineen,[24] and an equally large but chaotic English-Irish dictionary compiled by Father Lambert McKenna, S. J. The orthography, stabilized by Dineen's dictionary, was archaic and agreed more or less with that of early modern Irish (1250–1600). Books were almost exclusively printed in a beautiful font based on one presented by Queen Elizabeth I to Trinity College, Dublin.

It is difficult for me to assess the typical primary teacher's command of Irish in those days. Like his counterpart today his Irish probably revealed strong influence from English in phonology, syntax, and vocabulary.[25] He had probably some mixture of dialects in his speech and writing, though the Munster dialect was likely to have the upper hand, and he probably preferred schoolbooks in that dialect. The influence of Munster Irish, the most southerly of the three dialects and with the smallest number of speakers, can be attributed to the influence of Coláiste na Mumhan, which was founded in west Cork in 1904. It was the first of a series of colleges founded by the Gaelic League for the purpose of preparing teachers for the League's classes. Coláiste na Mumhan set the pattern in a number of ways, and this included a penchant towards Munster Irish. An additional powerful support for that dialect was Canon Peter O'Leary, whose prolific writings were very widely used in schools and evening classes. He was the great champion, against a lot of learned opposition, of *caint na ndaoine*; that is, Irish based on the plain speech of country people rather than on literary sources. The phrase that was quite a slogan in the heyday of the Gaelic League had the effect of inclining people to accept the "direct method," an oral method in which the teaching of formal grammar was delayed until the pupil had made some progress in speaking the language. The language was vigorously taught, and we made rapid progress in it. The lion's share of the schoolday was given to it; in the early 1960's over his first six years at school, a child spent some 37 per cent of his time learning Irish, and only 20 per cent learning English (Macnamara, 1966, p. 132). The likelihood is that in my primary-school days the proportion of time for Irish was even higher.

Perhaps the impact on the primary-school child of all the hopes and all the effort can be summed up in a personal reminiscence, which is a little sad to recall. When I was about eight years old, I went into a shop to buy sweets with my sister who was three years older than I. The lady behind the counter, to my great surprise, asked us why we were not talking Irish. We just hung our heads, as children do. But outside I asked my sister what the lady meant. She explained to me that we were learning Irish at school so that we would talk it all the time. And I asked her quite honestly: "Is Irish for talking?" This episode represents to me the inevitable effect when society at large disclaims responsibility for a social enterprise and leaves it to the schools.

Since my schooldays the Irish language has been changed considerably and so, too, have the methods of teaching it. At the request of Mr. de Valera, then *taoiseach* (prime minister), the Dáil (counterpart of the House of Commons in London) translation office produced a simplified spelling in 1945. A circular issued in the same year by the Department of Finance to all other government departments established the new spelling as official, and it has since been well-nigh universally accepted. In 1953 the translation office produced a first version of a new simplified and standardized grammar. A revised version was published in 1958, together with the simplified spelling, and a circular issued by the Department of Finance in that year made the grammar official. The standardization of grammar was confined to morphology and was guided by four principles:

1. to adopt no form or rule that is not well authenticated in the living speech of the *Gaeltacht*;
2. to choose those forms that are most widely used in the *Gaeltacht*;
3. to pay due attention to the history and literature of Irish;
4. to seek regularity and simplicity.[26]

In general the standardized morphology has been welcomed and accepted, though it has drawn the fire of some scholars.[27]

McKenna's English-Irish dictionary has been replaced by a businesslike dictionary compiled, under the auspices of the Department of Education, by Professor Tomás de Bhaldraithe (1959) and a staff of collaborators. Adopting Harrap's *Shorter English and French Dictionary* as basis and model, de Bhaldraithe (1959) set about providing "Irish equivalents for English words and phrases in common use" and also Irish equivalents for a large sample of modern technical terms. "The dictionary," says the preface, "however, is primarily based on current usage, and draws on the older literary language or on neologisms only where the living speech of the *Gaeltacht* is found wanting" (p. v.). In the introduction of technical terms, the dictionary sometimes had to choose between a large number of coinings that had been collected from experts in the various fields; at other times it had to coin new terms. For the most part the dictionary favored Greco-Latin borrowings of the sort that have become common in many European languages, English included.[28] In short, de Bhaldraithe's dictionary marks an important step in the standardization of Irish, namely, the standardization of the lexicon and of the style of lexical extensions.

There has been a widespread swing to Connacht Irish, which has the largest number of speakers and is intermediate between the Munster and the Donegal dialects. The swing is especially pronounced in the work of Father Colmán O Huallacháin and his collaborators at Institúid Teangeolaíochta Eireann (linguistic institute) who have completed a frequency count of Irish vocabulary and of Irish syntactic structures (Roinn Oideachais, 1966). They have used the results to prepare tapes for use in language laboratories, a course in the phonology of Irish, courses for use in primary schools, and materials for use in broadcast courses on television and radio.[29] In all these materials the Connacht dialect has been favored, so its pre-eminence is now assured.

Secondary Schools

In vocational schools at the secondary level, Irish tends to be just a compulsory subject. In secondary (grammar) schools, too, Irish is a compulsory subject, and no more time is given to it than to other subjects. For many years, however, a large proportion of secondary-school students were taught all subjects except English through the medium of Irish, and they wrote their public examinations in Irish. The schools are privately owned and run mainly by religious communities of men and of women; so the decision about the medium of instruction lies with the school authorities. The decision about which language to use in answering public examination questions lies with the student. To encourage the use of Irish as a teaching medium, there was and still is an elaborate system of financial and academic rewards. For example, schools that taught all subjects

in Irish received an increase of 25 per cent on the capitation grants paid
to them by the government for each student.[30] On the other hand, if students wrote their public examinations in Irish, they received a bonus of 10
per cent of their total mark in some subjects and 5 per cent in others (Ireland, Department of Education, 1968). The number of schools that taught
in Irish has varied over the years. In 1941, 64 per cent of grammar-school
students were taught exclusively or partly in Irish. As in primary schools,
however, there has been a great drop since the late 1940's in the amount
of teaching through Irish. In 1951 only 54 per cent of grammar-school
pupils were being taught wholly or partly in Irish. The decline is evident
in both the relative and the absolute figures. In 1944, out of a total of 377,
there were 98 grammar schools in which all subjects except English were
taught in Irish; in 1956 there were 87 such schools out of a total of 474;
in 1966 there were 72 out of a total of 585; and in 1968 there were 51
out of 596 schools.[31] The reasons for the decline are difficult to establish.
Unquestionably, they include an acute shortage of textbooks and reference
books in Irish, but presumably they also include a changing attitude to
the restoration of the language or at least to the place of education in such
a restoration.

Third-Level Education

In higher education the place of Irish is much more confined than in secondary education. All university colleges offer courses in Irish language
and literature, but only Galway (UCG), the smallest in the country,
seriously attempts to offer, in the arts and sciences, courses that are taught
and examined in Irish.[32] Appointments to teaching posts in those departments in UCG in which Irish is used and appointments to a wide range of
teaching posts in University College Cork (UCC)[33] are subject to the condition that the persons appointed are able to teach their subjects through
the medium of Irish. There is a loophole, however. If the university college advertises a post and fails to find a suitable candidate who is competent in Irish, it can then fill the post without any reference to Irish.

In the colleges of advanced technology, Irish is not used, so far as
I am aware, as a teaching medium. Training colleges for primary-school
teachers do carry out a limited amount of their teaching in Irish; ten years
ago, however, practically all such work was conducted in Irish. In the
training college that I am most familiar with, the change came about as
much at the wish of the students as of the staff.

What strikes one as one surveys the educational scene is the reduction in restoration effort as one passes from primary- to secondary-level and again from secondary to higher education. The difference between the levels can be attributed in part to the pedagogical principles of those who planned our education since 1922, in part to the increasing demands on students' time as they grow older, in part to the fact that hitherto the state exercised more control in primary- than in secondary- , and in secondary- than in third-level education, and in part to the increasing shortage of text-books in Irish as one ascends the educational ladder. The arrangement clearly embodies the belief that the time to teach a second language is when children are young. Explanations apart, however, the effect is that the main burden for the restoration of Irish has been placed on the shoulders of that section of the school population that is weakest and is least likely to resist.[34] Furthermore, the educational provision for the restoration calls into question the seriousness of the whole effort to restore Irish.

OTHER ASPECTS OF IRISH LIFE

Officialdom

The constitution (Ireland, Stationery Office, 1937) states: "The Irish language as the national language is the first official language. The English language is recognized as the second official language" (Article 8, §§ 1 and 2). It is clear, however, that in reality the roles of the two languages are reversed and that hitherto English has been the dominant language. In 1958 the government set up a commission to examine progress and ad-vise on how the restoration might best be effected. The commission's re-port,[35] a document of close to 500 pages, appeared in 1964. To the objectives of the restoration movement, of which the following is a trans-lation, it devotes less than one page:

> What we understand by the Revival [restoration] is that the [Irish] lan-guage should once again be a normal means of conversation and commun-ication among Irish people. This has been the objective of the Irish language movement from its inception and of the political movement which stemmed from it [sic], and this has been the linguistic objective of every government since the foundation of the State (p. xiii).

The commission's report gives a realistic account of the place of Irish in various aspects of Irish life, public and private, at the time. It also makes numerous proposals that have formed the basis of subsequent government programs to promote Irish. Among the recommendations that the government acted upon was one to establish a consultative council regarding the Irish language. In the years since the commission's report, the government has issued a white paper on restoration policy and two progress reports (Ireland, Commission, 1965, 1966, 1969). However, if we are to believe the consultative council (Comhlacht Comhairleach na Gaeilge, 1969), although some of the commission's proposals have been put into operation, many have not, and progress has been rather disappointing. I feel that most people would agree that the commission's report has hitherto had little effect on the linguistic trends in the country. In the rest of this subsection and in the next, I can do little better than follow the lead of the official documents through different sectors of Irish life, adding what comments seem appropriate.

Almost all parliamentary business is transacted in English, but all legislation is printed in both languages. The commission's recommendation that a system of simultaneous translation be established in parliament has not been carried out. The three major political parties officially support the restoration of Irish, but since 1963 the largest opposition party, Fine Gael, has opposed the policy of compelling secondary students to learn Irish and of requiring knowledge of Irish as an essential qualification for appointment to public posts.[36] The party in power, Fianna Fáil, stands by the policy of compulsion. In recent elections, Fine Gael attempted to raise the issue of compulsory Irish, but it was not taken up seriously by the other parties and seemed to have little effect on the outcome of the election.

All civil servants are required to know Irish at the time of their recruitment, but, apart from the Department of Education and the Department for Irish-speaking Districts, few civil servants use Irish to any extent in their daily work (Ireland, Commission, 1966, p. 8). The commission made twenty-six proposals for increasing the use of Irish in the civil service of which the principal one was that in each department a nucleus should be established in which work would be carried out in Irish. This proposal has been adopted in most, but not all, departments (Comhlacht Comhairleach na Gaeilge, 1969, p. 16). I have been informed, however, that the nucleus in many departments is a section whose work is either mostly with other civil servants or merely with records and accounts. Time will tell whether the civil service in arranging matters thus has merely accommodated to pressures or has accepted the changes enthusiastically.

The small Irish army trains its officers mainly in Irish, maintains an

Irish-speaking company of 175 men, and gives drill orders in Irish. Apart
from this, however, Irish scarcely has wider currency in the army than in
the rest of the community. Recruits for the state police force are required
to have some knowledge of Irish, but as long as they work in the English-
speaking districts they will scarcely ever need Irish in the course of their
duties. The commission proposals for these two bodies were not very far-
reaching, and neither the army nor the police force seems to have changed
materially since the report (Coimisiún um Athbheochan na Gaeilge, 1964,
chapters 9 and 10; Ireland, Commission, 1969, p. 8).

All lawyers before qualifying are required to give evidence that they
know Irish, but it is almost unheard of that in an English-speaking district a court should conduct its business in Irish. One prominent Dublin
solicitor told me that to qualify he had to memorize the Irish equivalents
of a great number of legal terms and undergo a stiff examination in Irish;
but that, in the course of his career, he had only once been asked to draw
up a legal document in Irish and he had refused because he had long since
forgotten his Irish. Curiously, the 1966 and 1969 progress reports, which
discuss other aspects of public life, omit any mention of the law.

Local government has proved recalcitrant. The commission proposed increased use of Irish in local authority meetings and documentation but hitherto little change has been effected (Comhlacht Comhairleach
na Gaeilge, 1969, p. 17).

The state runs television and radio and requires both to present some
programs in Irish. With the assistance of an official from RTE (the body
that runs television and radio), I checked through the program for the
week, February 8–14, 1969 and found that 7.8 per cent of the time on
television and 3.8 per cent of the time on radio was taken up with programs exclusively in Irish. The first figure represents not too inaccurately
the status of Irish on television; the second figure does not really represent
the place of Irish on radio. RTE is at present experimenting with a plan
for running numerous bilingual programs on radio, and already the Irish
radio audience has grown quite accustomed to frequent switches in language. The good will of the audience towards such a venture was suggested by the public response to a new-fashioned radio and television
program, *Buntús Cainte,* designed to teach basic Irish to adults. Of the
first part of the accompanying booklet, over two hundred thousand copies
were sold (total population of Ireland equals 2.8 million), and of the
second part, just under two hundred thousand copies were sold. Audience
research has further revealed that as many as three out of four persons

will look at the television news in Irish if they happen to be in a position to view the telecast.

Business

Many of the large business organizations are what are called "state-controlled" or "semistate" bodies (e.g., the organizations responsible for transport, electricity, peat, sugar, fishing, and tourism). As a result of the commission's report and subsequent government directives, many of them have made an effort to foster Irish, especially by displaying notices in Irish and by providing bilingual forms. However, the new provisions in most cases have been quite limited and amount to little more than a token of good will. The difficulty in going further, apparently, is partly that the personnel do not know Irish sufficiently well, partly that the business and commercial world in which they operate is almost completely English-speaking, and partly that the public has given little encouragement for such a move (Ireland, Commission, 1969, pp. 8–10; Comhlacht Comhairleach na Gaeilge, 1969, p. 17).

To business outside the semistate bodies and to trade unions, the commission devotes in all six-and-a-half pages of its some 480-page report (Coimisiún um Athbheochan na Gaeilge, 1964, pp. 383–387, 439–441). It is the weakest section of the report, though it deals with what may be, from the point of view of the restoration, the most important sector of all. The recommendations to business men are mainly concerned with public displays and with advertising; those to trade unions and similar institutions are mainly about patronage of Irish. Although some businesses have done some advertising in Irish, the remark of the latest progress report (Ireland, Commission, 1969) is fully justified:

> It has not been possible, however, to take any significant step forward because of limited interest by the general public in using Irish in the commercial domain (p. 32).

The Catholic Church

What has been the attitude of the Catholic Church to the restoration movement? In seeking an answer to this question it is important to bear in mind that while 95 per cent of the people in the Republic of Ireland are Catholics, the modern church in Ireland grew up in independence of—at times in opposition to—the British government. The separation of church and state is to this day complete at least from the point of view of organization. The Catholic Church, as an institution, then, could and did for a long time remain aloof from the restoration issue. In general it has rested content with providing services in Irish in Irish-speaking districts and services in English in English-speaking ones, though there have been instances where this general rule has been transgressed in both directions. When church services were mainly in Latin the church's position was largely unquestioned, but now that the vernaculars have replaced Latin in the liturgy, the calm has been disturbed. Dublin alone among English-speaking areas provides masses in Irish regularly. The substance of the Dublin regulation is one "Irish" mass in each church each Sunday.

The feebleness of the restoration movement has frequently been attributed to lack of ecclesiastical support. It seems to be the case that through the years the Catholic Church, following the people as a whole, has favored English. Maynooth, the central seminary for the country, has since its foundation in 1795 conducted all its work in English or in Latin. Furthermore, the church, when it felt itself threatened, could take severe measures to defend its independence. In the early years of the present century when the church was attacked by the journal, *The Irish Peasant*, for not pressing forward with Irish in the primary school, Cardinal Logue had the journal suppressed (Inglis, 1960). Towards the end of the first decade of the century during the dispute about the place of Irish in the National University of Ireland (then being founded), the hierarchy dismissed Father O'Hickey from his post as professor of Irish in Maynooth on grounds of intemperate language. Father O'Hickey had certainly been unrestrained in his condemnation of the responsible body, which included several distinguished ecclesiastics, for opposing the plan to make Irish an essential subject for matriculation (McDonald, 1967, p. 232 ff). The Gaelic League won, but the victory was a Pyrrhic one (Horgan, 1948, p. 191). Father O'Hickey was a broken man, and the League seems to have been divided by the case.

To return to the Catholic Church's position concerning Irish, the church has for many years directed that children should be taught their catechism in the language of their homes. Thus by implication the church has opposed the whole movement to teach through the medium of Irish. The direction was again repeated by the most recent plenary synod in 1956 (Catholic Hierarchy, 1960, *decretum* 242, § 3). At the same synod, however, the hierarchy for the first time officially favored the restoration movement. It directed priests in catechetical instruction, in preaching, and in public prayers to use the language that their hearers understood but "to favour Irish where prudence permitted."[37]

These remarks refer to the Catholic Church as an organization; they do not refer to subsidiary bodies or to individuals within the church. It would hardly have been possible to mount the state's educational policies for Irish without the support of several of the teaching religious communities, in particular the Irish Christian Brothers (Martin, 1967). In addition, of course, many individual Catholics, lay and clerical, have given their full support to the restoration movement, and I suspect that the proportion of clerics has been higher than that of laymen. Indeed, it is rather unlikely that official approbation on the part of the hierarchy would have added significantly to the strength of the movement. The Irish people are accustomed to distinguishing the church's competence in the area of faith and morals from her competence in other areas, and they resent any attempt on the church's part to control what they consider as non-religious. And while there have been numerous attempts to make the restoration of Irish a spiritual issue, the majority of Irish people, I feel, class it as a temporal one.

Gaeilgeoirí—Supporters of the Restoration Movement

When one moves away from the official worlds of church and state, one finds numerous organizations whose object is to promote Irish. Besides the Gaelic League, which still has two hundred branches, there is Gael Linn, a wealthy, highly organized, and purposeful business organization. Its aims include practical projects to promote the economic welfare of Irish-speaking districts and to bring Irish into the business world. In recent years, however, it has expanded its business enormously in the English-speaking parts of the country, and it will be interesting to see whether it will be able to retain its commitment to Irish as well as an expanding interest in the world of business. An Comchaidreamh, the parent of Gael Linn, caters to the graduate community. There is Cumann na Sagart, a thousand-strong clerical group, which promotes the use of Irish by awarding prizes to the towns in English-speaking districts that use Irish the most. There is An Réalt, a religious organization, which has between 750 and 1,000 members, whose meetings are conducted in Irish. There is Comhar na Meanmhúinteoirí, a society of secondary-school teachers, with about 500 members, who, among other things, aim to strengthen the position of Irish in secondary education. There are numerous other bodies of whom the most interesting is Na Teaghlaigh Ghaelacha, a group of families that have banded themselves together to lend each other support in making Irish the language of their homes. To coordinate the activities of all such organizations, there is the Comhdháil Náisiúnta na Gaeilge; in all, it has fifteen affiliated bodies. Finally, there is An tOireachtas, an annual convention of language enthusiasts; among other ceremonies at this convention, prizes are awarded for different types of literary work.[38]

What is there to read in Irish? Apart from a literature that extends backward over more than a thousand years there are the literary works that owe their existence to the language movement itself. Perhaps the movement's greatest success has been the important literary revival which it stimulated.[39] Some of Ireland's best novelists, short-story writers, poets, and, to a lesser extent, dramatists have written either exclusively or in part in Irish. Unfortunately, most of these writers are little known outside a small circle of *Gaeilgeoirí*. Some of them have certainly sacrificed a larger audience for the privilege of working in their ancestral tongue. However, An Club Leabhar, a book club that has about two thousand members (O Néill, 1969), has guaranteed by Irish standards a good sale for their work. Besides books there is a small range of periodical literature. The nearest to a general newspaper is Inniu, published by Glún na Bua, though there is also a weekly, *Amárach*, which addresses itself only to the people of the *Gaeltachtaí*. The two liveliest and most intellectual periodicals are *Comhar*, published monthly by An Comhchaidreamh, and *Feasta*, published monthly by the Gaelic League. Taken as a whole, the literary output has been impressive and today anyone who wishes to understand modern Ireland and above all the full range of its literary activity should learn Irish.

Apart from the organizations I mentioned whose *raison d'être* is the restoration of Irish, there are numerous other organizations that have varied aims and give general support to the language movement. First among these is the Gaelic Athletic Association, which is very popular, especially in rural areas: it always had strong nationalist tendencies, and it puts its facilities at the disposal of the Oireachtas. There is also the Muinter na Tíre, a widespread but rather formless organization that aims at bettering the lot of the rural population. In addition, there is The Irish Countrywomen's Association, the Comhaltas Ceoltoirí Éireann (a body of Irish musicians), and the Union of Students of Ireland (O Néill, 1968). With the exception of the Gaelic Athletic Associations' contribution to the Oireachtas, however, the support of such bodies for Irish counts little.

CONCLUSION

The major problem of any group committed to the restoration of Irish is that the task has proved far more difficult than was imagined seventy years ago. As a result, there is much inter- and intra-societal division about the proper ends of the revival movement and about the means to attain these ends. It is by now agreed by most people that Irish will not become the principal language of the country in the sense that it will not be the language spoken by most persons for most purposes. In 1964, the Irish Marketing Surveys, Ltd.,[40] released the findings of a poll of attitude towards Irish. They found that about 83 per cent of the population did not believe that Irish could be restored as the most widely spoken language, and, revealingly, the younger the person questioned, the less likely he was to believe that it could be. Subsequent to this, the government's white paper on Irish appeared, and in it we find a subtle change that did not escape the public at the time. Although the white paper cites the Constitution, which states that Irish is *the* national and *the* first official language, it goes on shortly to say: "The national aim is to restore the Irish language as a *general* medium of communication (Ireland, Commission, 1965, p. 4). The white paper further goes on to recognize—perhaps for the first time in such a document—that the country is dependent and will continue to be dependent on a knowledge of English. Although the terms of both the Constitution and the white paper are so vague that they rule out a firm conclusion that the official policy had changed, many people felt that a significant change had been signaled.

It would be wrong to conclude, however, that the Irish people wish to drop Irish altogether. On the contrary, we have already seen that they gave a warm welcome to broadcast programs aimed at teaching basic Irish to adults. Furthermore, some 76 per cent of persons questioned by the Irish Marketing Surveys, Ltd., said that they would like to see Irish widely spoken as a "second language"; 53 per cent felt that this was not an unrealistic objective. In addition, 76 per cent approved of Irish being taught in national (primary) schools.

There is little agreement on the means that ought to be used to achieve any of the restoration objectives. This arises in no small measure from the confusion about the objectives themselves, but, even among people who agree on a particular set of objectives, there is often sharp disagreement on methods. One point emerges with reasonable clarity from all the discussion: the Irish people are opposed to a policy that aims to achieve its objectives by compulsion, at least in the secondary schools; the Irish Marketing Survey, Ltd., reports that 72 per cent were opposed to compulsory Irish in secondary schools. On the other hand, opinion was almost evenly divided on whether Irish should be "essential" for appointment to clerical posts in state-sponsored bodies, while a majority (52 per cent as opposed to 41 per cent) favored the view that Irish should be "essential" for admission to clerical and administrative posts in the civil service. Interestingly, however, the younger groups were less inclined to favor Irish as being essential for these posts. In recent years an organization, the Language Freedom Movement (LFM), has been formed to secure that the restoration is effective by free choice rather than by compulsion. LFM's avowed aims do not, however, include any opposition to the idea of restoring Irish. Its position has been a delicate one, and it has not always effectively defended itself against charges of being "opposed to the language." At present it claims 6,700 members. Then, too, in a small number of areas, parents have objected to Irish being used as the teaching medium for primary-school children, and at the time of writing the majority of parents have withdrawn their children from two small schools in the west of Ireland for the purpose of having the teaching medium changed to English.

Evaluation of Progress

No serious attempt has been made by any official organization to determine what the people want in regard to Irish and to English, and none to determine what the people are prepared to work for. This has meant that linguistic objectives have been stated in relative ignorance of how the people felt about them. Under the circumstances, politicians have had no alternative but to leave the objectives obscure and undefined. Furthermore, apart from my own study, to which I have previously referred in another context, no attempt has been made to measure progress towards any specified goal or to compare the relative effectiveness of alternative strategies.[41] Various persons, acting in a private or in an official capacity, have from time to time put forward different ideas. Some of the ideas have been adopted by the government or by voluntary bodies, and others have been dropped; at best the choice has been guided by a shrewd guess. Since those who launch a new enterprise have not at the outset determined a

level of success below which the enterprise would not be permitted to
sink, ideas have tended to continue in operation after they have lost any
usefulness. Today, there are numerous ideas and numerous bodies to
back them, but between them these bodies divide and share an energy
that is all too limited for the main task. Quite simply, the movement is
floundering.[42] Furthermore, in the absence of long-term and short-term
objectives and of thorough evaluation, there is no machinery for deciding
when the movement as a whole is successful, when it should be dropped
when failing, or when a major change in objectives or in methods is indicated. Thus, the movement will probably continue to flounder.

The reason for the present state of affairs in the restoration movement is not solely the lack of clear purpose among its supporters. The
forces against the movement have been enormous at all times. By adopting English, Irish people have allied themselves to the most powerful
political interests in the world. English is of inestimable value to an Irish-
man as a language of culture and of commerce and also as a means to
earn his bread in the English-speaking world, which lies to the east and
west of him. From this English-speaking world come his news, his books,
his films, and a great proportion of his television and radio programs.
Against all this, Irish can call to its support only cultural and nationalistic
arguments that have hitherto not stood up to those which, without any propaganda, have supported the case for English. The two cases perhaps are
not necessarily opposed to each other in the sense that bilingualism might
not prove an unrealistic solution. However, it seems clear that the Irish
people have not gone for bilingualism with any real heart. By and large,
they have settled for English and have been satisfied with a cultural and
ceremonial role for Irish, not unlike that role which Latin enjoyed until
recently in the Catholic Church and in the academic community.

The people who have championed the restoration of Irish have for
the most part been middle class. Learning Irish is to the material advantage of the middle classes in that it is required in certain important examinations and for appointments to certain posts. By and large, Irish has
not meant a similar material advantage to the working class, and, most
significant of all, the material advantages that the *Gaeltacht* people have
seen in Irish have not outweighed those that they could see in English.
Both of these groups have demonstrated, and continue to demonstrate,
that the Irish society is essentially English-speaking and that the material
advantage in the long run lies with English. Indeed, every effort that has
been made to improve the lot of the *Gaeltacht* people and to use the

Gaeltacht as the great school in which to learn Irish has lured the inhabitants towards the English language or towards the English-speaking world (O Danachair, 1959). The *Gaeltacht* people, and the working classes, then, have, by their behavior, cut through a deal of middle-class wishful thinking and exposed it for what it is. And no efforts of the government have been able to reverse the tide. It seems unlikely, indeed, that the native government could ever have secured a substantial material advantage for Irish at any level of society without methods so dictatorial that Irish democracy would have been destroyed. And in the final analysis, neither Irish politicians nor the Irish people wanted that.

ACKNOWLEDGMENT

Two people were particularly helpful to me when I was preparing this paper, Séamus O Mórdha, of the Irish department in St. Patrick's College, and Donal McCartney, of the history department in UCD. I gratefully acknowledge their help, and I would also like to thank the following persons who helped in various ways: George Byrne, R. Dudley Edwards, Tadhg Kelly, Christopher T. Morris (L.F.M.), Eamonn O Murchú, and Oisín O Siochrú. These people do not, of course, all agree with all the opinions expressed in the paper; I accept full responsibility for all opinions expressed in it.

NOTES

1. Murphy (1949), for example, points out that the family of Daniel O'Connell, the great Irish politician, was bilingual in the late eighteenth century and that the family seemed to be diglossic—Irish for use in the home and neighborhood; English for contact with the world of fashion and with officialdom.
2. While most scholars agree that the figures are underestimates, there is some disagreement concerning the extent of the inaccuracy. O Cuív (1951), in general, seems to place slightly more credence in them than do Wall (1969) or O hAilín (1969). It seems unlikely, however, that we shall ever be able to go much beyond the statement in the text.
3. O Fiaich (1969) captures well the bitterness and indignation of those who, together with O Bruadair, resisted the change and called their more malleable contemporaries such names as *bodaigh an Bhéarla, fian an Bhéarla,* or *bruscar an Bhéarla,* all meaning something like "the English-speaking rabble."
4. The 1961 census (Ireland, Central Statistics Office, 1963–66, vol. 9) gives 64,275 as the number of "Irish speakers" aged three years and over within the *Gaeltachtaí,* or Irish-speaking districts, as officially designated in 1956. This figure is 2.44 per cent of the total population aged three

years and over. There are certainly native speakers of Irish who live outside the *Gaeltachtaí* and who were not, therefore, included in this count. Nevertheless, the number of native speakers of Irish in the population has continued to decline. Caoimhín O Danachair (1969), who knows Irish-speaking districts as few others do, considers that the number today is less than fifty thousand, or about 2 per cent of the population. On the other hand, some 27 per cent of the population described themselves in the same census as able to speak Irish, an increase of 6 per cent on the 1946 census; i.e., the most recent previous census—*loc. cit.*, Table 2. The increase may be related to the rapid extension of secondary schooling during the interval.

5. Beckett (1966) gives a concise but authoritative account of the events covered in the text.

6. The work of translation has been carried on by scholars and poets from the end of the eighteenth century to our own time. The roster of workers' names is very long, indeed, and includes many of the great names associated with the Anglo-Irish literary movement.

7. For accounts of these, see Ryan (1939), O hAilín (1968 and 1969), O Buachalla (1968), and O Cadhain (1969).

8. Translated from Coimisiún um Athbheochan na Gaeilge (1964, p. 14).

9. This information and several of the details that follow are taken from Hyde's (1937) autobiography. See also O'Brien (1960), Dillon (1960), McCartney (1967a and 1967b), O Cadhain (1969), O hAilín (1969), and O Tuama (1969).

10. Douglas Hyde wrote a humorous play, *The Bursting of the Bubble* (published in 1903, in which he pilloried his opponents, especially academics who inclined towards ascendency. In the art of satire, however, Hyde was a mere infant beside his contemporary and strong supporter, D. P. Moran, editor of *The Leader*. See Inglis (1960) and McCartney (1967b).

11. See, for example, the evidence given by Miss Nellie O'Brien to the American Commission on Conditions in Ireland (1921). I have asked some elderly people who knew the League before the Great War; they believe that its main support came from the middle- and lower-middle income groups—the small shopkeepers, the primary-school teachers, and the local functionaries—rather than from the working classes or from the more well-to-do professional classes.

12. McCartney (1967a) records that in one year the Gaelic League collected £6,000 and employed twenty-two people full-time. O Cadhain (1969), picking a month at random, found that in November 1906 the League sold 12,672 copies of its publications, an enormous figure for Ireland at that time.

13. See Hyde (1937), in which he takes the narrative only up to 1905.

14. It is extremely difficult to determine the relationship between the Gaelic League and the revolutionary political movement. The League deliberately maintained a position of political neutrality until 1915, when the revolutionaries took control. Hyde then resigned the presidency, and the

League's constitution was altered to support the policies of the revolutionaries. Hyde (1937) later claimed that the League was largely responsible
for the success of the independence movement; he has the support of some
later scholars—see Beckett (1966, p. 417). It is probable, however, that
the League's influence was more subtle and indirect, that it created a
climate that could ultimately be turned to good account by the revolutionaries, and above all that it provided the revolutionaries with the most
acceptable justification for their endeavors: see especially McCartney
(1967a and 1967b) but also Martin (1967). Certainly, the leaders of
the independence movement had been, almost to a man, members of the
League, and when the embryonic native government met in Dublin in
1919, its first meeting was conducted largely in Irish, and it established a
ministry of the Irish language to which it appointed the then president of
the Gaelic League.

15. See McCartney (1967b), who also points out that the period of the 1914–
    18 war was hardly a propitious time for nationalist societies such as the
    Gaelic League. In 1919, when it was already harmless, it was suppressed
    by the British government.

16. See for example: Webb (1904); Ryan (1905); Sheehy-Skeffington (1905);
    O'Donnell (1910); Moore (1911–14), though the sincerity of his patrio-
    tism might be questioned; Tierney (1927); Irish National Teachers' Orga-
    nization (1941); Murphy (1948); and Breathnach (1956 and 1964).
    These writers varied from total rejection of the restoration movement to
    rejection of part of the associated educational policy.

17. For this and many of the following observations on the educational aspects
    of the restoration movement, I rely on Ireland, Department of Education
    (1954, p. 62). O Huallacháin also surveys this area.

18. The real force at both these Conferences seems to have been Father T.
    Corcoran, S. J., professor of education in University College, Dublin. His
    power came in part from his position and in part from the fact that the
    first two ministers for education were his colleagues on the staff of UCD.
    His views, which today have a distasteful autocratic ring, are to be found
    in Corcoran (1925). Among other things, he held that the restoration of
    Irish could be effected in a single generation by the schools alone: "They
    can do it even without positive aid from the homes."

19. The initial step was to have Irish taught in Irish-speaking districts. In per-
    suading the government to accept this, the Gaelic League had a powerful
    supporter in William Walsh (1900), archbishop of Dublin.

20. This was the national school in Ballyvaughn, Co. Clare; at the time, Bally-
    vaughn was included in what was called *an breach-Ghaeltacht* (bilingual
    district), though only one boy in the school was a native Irish speaker.

21. This figure is taken from Ireland, Department of Education (1958), the
    first *Report* after the *Gaeltacht* had been legally redefined and the first to
    give a reasonable estimate of the number of schools in what might without
    semantic violence be called *Gaeltachtaí*. The official definition of the *Gael-
    tacht* is to be found in Ireland, Stationery Office (1956).

22. McCartney (no date) points out the trend. Among the reasons that he gives for the decline is a pamphlet of the Irish National Teacher's Organization (1941), which reported widespread dissatisfaction among teachers regarding the practice of teaching English-speaking children through the medium of Irish. The Department of Education ignored the pamphlet, but it seems to have had its effect. McCartney points out further that, during the early 1940's, primary-school teachers quarrelled continuously with the Department, and he suggests that the decline in question was a manifestation of the teachers' dissatisfaction.

23. For these figures, see, respectively, Ireland, Department of Education (1945, 1957, 1967).

24. There were also abbreviated editions of Dineen, on whose influence, see O Cuív (1969). For a popular but authoritative history and description of the Irish language, see Green (1966).

25. Speaking about students who had been through the secondary schools, two professors of Irish, Murphy (1948) and Breathnach (1956), state that the educational system sacrificed quality and accuracy for quantity and fluency. The same could probably be said of primary-school teachers who had learned Irish in school.

26. Translated from *Gramadach na Gaeilge agus litriú na Gaeilge: An caighdeán oifigiuil* (1958, p. viii).

27. See, for example, Breathnach (1956).

28. MacEoin (1961) gives a fuller description of the principles upon which the dictionary is based. Although the dictionary regularly has recourse to Greek for technical terminology, it is guilty of occasional inconsistencies. Thus for "hypermetropia," it gives the Irish *hipearmeatróipe*, whereas for "myopia," it gives *gearr-radharc* (short-sight).

    In the matter of legal terms, the dictionary had less freedom. Since 1945 there exists a statutory Irish Legal Terms Advisory Committee, whose function is to advise the Minister for Justice about the suitability of Irish equivalents for English legal terms. Irish terms chosen by the minister, with the advice of his committee, have by law the same "force and effect" as the English terms that they translate. Cf. Ireland, Stationery Office (1945).

29. For the course in Irish phonology, see Annunciata le Muire agus O Huallacháin (1966). The course for schools is known as *Buntús Gaeilge*; that for broadcast is known as *Buntús Cainte*.

30. See Ireland, Department of Education (1957). The regulations are being changed at the moment.

31. The last set of figures was given to me by the Department of Education; the earlier ones are taken from Ireland, Department of Education (1945, 1958, and 1967 respectively).

32. The subjects in which UCG offered courses in Irish in 1963 were: Irish, history, archaeology, Latin, Greek, mathematics, geography, education, economics, commerce, accountancy, experimental physics, mathematical physics, botany, chemistry, and part of philosophy. See Coimisiún um

Athbheochan na Gaeilge (1964, p. 307). For an early discussion of some of the problems involved, see Tierney (1927), Mulcahy (1927), O Briain (1927), Browne (1927), and Bergin (1927).

33. These are the departments: archaeology, ancient classics, German, Romance languages, history, geography, philosophy, education, mathematics, music, economics and commerce, and accountancy. See Coimisiún um Athbheochan na Gaeilge (1964, p. 307).

34. This point, which was made many years ago by the great Irish scholar Osborn Bergin (1927), is repeated in Coimisiún um Athbheochan na Gaeilge (1965, § 447) and in the most recent progress report, Ireland, Commission on the Restoration of the Irish Language (1969, p. 38).

35. Coimisiún um Athbheochan na Gaeilge (1964). An English synopsis of the report will be found in Ireland, Commission on the Restoration of the Irish Language (1964).

36. See *The Irish Times*, 22 March 1963 for a report of a speech by the then party leader, Mr. James Dillon, to the Fine Gael *Ard Fheis*. See also Fine Gael (1966).

37. Catholic Hierarchy of Ireland (1960, *decretum* 239): "*usum linguae Gadelicae prudenter promoveant.*" One is reminded of Percy French's band, which "was playing cautiously a patriotic tune."

38. I received most of the details of information in this paragraph from Comhdháil Náisiúnta na Gaeilge. For Gael Linn, see O Móráin (1958).

39. See MacEoin (1969) and O Cadhain (1969). MacCana (1969) briefly discusses the literary tradition in the Irish language prior to the revival.

40. I am quoting from a press release from Irish Marketing Surveys, Ltd., (1964). A recent report, Ernest Dichter International Institute for Motivational Research (1968), comes to roughly the same conclusions in a rather obscure manner.

41. On the whole topic of evaluation in relation to language planning, see Rubin (paper 12, this volume).

42. This opinion, which is not uncommon among the *Gaeilgeoirí*, has recently been expressed with great force by Desmond Fennell (1969).

REFERENCES

American Commission on Conditions in Ireland (ACCI). 1921. *Evidence on Conditions in Ireland.* Washington, D.C.: ACCI.

Annunciata le Muire agus O Huallacháin, Colmán. 1966. *Bunchúrsa foghraíochta.* Dublin: Stationery Office.

Beckett, James G. 1966. *The Making of Modern Ireland 1603–1923.* London: Faber and Faber.

Bergin, O. 1927. Comments on the Foregoing Article (Tierney, 1927), no. 3. *Studies,* 16: 17–20.

Breathnach, R. A. 1956. Revival or Survival? An Examination of the Irish Language Policy of the State. *Studies,* 45: 129–145.

———. 1964. Irish Revival Reconsidered. *Studies,* 53: 18–30.

Browne, P. 1927. Comments on the Foregoing Article (Tierney, 1927), no. 2. *Studies*, 16: 15–17.

Catholic Hierarchy of Ireland. 1960. *Acta et decreta concilii plenarii quod habitum est apud Maynooth die 7 Augusti et diebus sequentibus usque ad diem 15 Augusti 1956.* Dublin: Gill.

Coimisiún um Athbheochan na Gaeilge. 1964. *An tuarascáil dheiridh.* Dublin: Stationery Office.

Comhlacht Comhairleach na Gaeilge. 1969. *Tuarascáil don tréimhse 1 Aibreán, 1966 go dtí 14 Meitheamh, 1968.* Dublin: Stationery Office.

Corcoran, T. 1925. The Irish Language in the Irish Schools. *Studies*, 14: 377–388.

de Bhaldraithe, Tomás. 1959. *English-Irish Dictionary.* Dublin: Stationery Office.

Dillon, M. 1960. Douglas Hyde. *In* C. Cruise O'Brien, ed. *The Shaping of Modern Ireland.* London: Routledge and Kegan Paul, 50–62.

The Ernest Dichter International Institute for Motivational Research. 1968. *A Motivational Research Study for the Greater Use of the Irish Language,* 2 vols. New York: Croton-on-Hudson.

Fennell, D. 1969. Language Revival: Is It Already a Lost Cause? *A Supplement to "The Irish Times", 21 January.* Dublin: Irish Times.

Fine Gael. 1966. *Fine Gael Policy for a Just Society: 3 Education.* Dublin: Fine Gael Headquarters.

Fishman, Joshua A. 1968. National Languages and Languages of Wider Communication in the Developing Nations. Paper presented at the Regional Conference on Language and Linguistics, Dar es Salaam, Tanzania.

Gramadach na Gaeilge agus litriú na Gaeilge: An caighdéan oifigiúil. 1958. Dublin: Stationery Office.

Green, D. 1966. *The Irish Language.* Dublin: Cultural Relations Committee of Ireland.

Gwynn, D. 1928. *The Irish Free State, 1922–1927.* London: Macmillan.

Horgan, J. J. 1948. *Parnell to Pearse: Some Recollections and Reflections.* Dublin: Browne and Nolan.

Hyde, Douglas (De hIde, D.) 1931. *Mise agus an Connradh (go dtí 1905).* Dublin: Stationery Office.

Inglis, B. 1960. Moran of the *Leader* and Ryan of the *Irish Peasant. In* C. Cruise O'Brien, ed. *The Shaping of Modern Ireland.* London: Routledge and Kegan Paul, 108–123.

Ireland. Central Statistics Office. 1963–66. *Census of Population of Ireland, 1961,* 9 vols. Dublin: Stationery Office.

Ireland. Commission on the Restoration of the Irish Language. 1964. *Summary, in English, of Final Report.* Dublin: Stationery Office.

———. 1965. *The Restoration of the Irish Language.* Dublin: Stationery Office.

———. 1966. *White Paper on the Restoration of the Irish Language: Progress Report for the Period Ended March 31, 1966.* Dublin: Stationery Office.

———. 1969. *White Paper on the Restoration of the Irish Language: Progress*

Report for the Period Ended March 31, 1968. Dublin: Stationery Office.

Ireland. Department of Education. 1945. *Report 1943–44*. Dublin: Stationery Office.

——. 1954. *Report of the Council of Education: Primary School*. Dublin: Stationery Office.

——. 1957. *Rules for the Payment of Grants to Secondary Schools*. Dublin: Stationery Office.

——. 1958. *Report 1956–57*. Dublin: Stationery Office.

——. 1965. *Rules for National Schools under the Department of Education*. Dublin: Stationery Office.

——. 1967. *Report 1965–66*. Dublin: Stationery Office.

——. 1968. *Rules and Programme for Secondary Schools, 1968–69*. Dublin: Stationery Office.

Ireland. Stationery Office. 1937. *Constitution of Ireland*. Dublin.

——. 1945. *Irish Legal Terms Act, 1945: Number 18*. Dublin.

——. 1956. *Ionstramaí Reachtúla I. R. Uimh 254 de 1956: Ordú na limistéirí gaeltachta, 1956*. Dublin.

Irish National Teachers' Organization (INTO). 1941. *Report of Committee of Inquiry into the Use of Irish as a Teaching Medium to Children Whose Home Language Is English*. Dublin: Central Executive Committee, INTO.

MacCana, P. 1969. Irish Literary Tradition. *In* B. O. Cuív, ed. *A View of the Irish Language*. Dublin: Stationery Office, 35–46.

MacEoin, G. S. 1961. Reviews of T. de Bhaldraithe, ed. *English-Irish Dictionary* and *Graiméar Gaeilge na mBráithre Críostaí*. In *Studia Hibernica*, 1: 218–223.

——. 1969. Twentieth-Century Irish Literature. *In* B. O. Cuív, ed. *A View of the Irish Language*. Dublin: Stationery Office, 57–69.

Macnamara, John. 1966. *Bilingualism and Primary Education: A Study of Irish Experience*. Edinburgh: Edinburgh University Press.

Martin, Francis X. 1967. 1916—Revolution or Evolution? *In* F. X. Martin, ed. *Leaders and Men of the Easter Rising: Dublin 1916*. London: Methuen, 239–252.

McCartney, Donal. 1967a. From Parnell to Pearse (1891–1921). *In* T. W. Moody and F. X. Martin, eds. *The Course of Irish History*. Cork: Mercier Press, 294–312.

——. 1967b. Hyde, D. P. Moran, and Irish Ireland. *In* F. X. Martin, ed. *Leaders and Men of the Easter Rising: Dublin 1916*. London: Methuen, 43–54.

——. n.d. Education and Language 1938–51. Unpublished paper, Department of History, University College, Dublin.

McDonald, W. 1967. *Reminiscences of a Maynooth Professor*. Paperback edition. Cork: Mercier Press.

Moore, G. 1911–1914. *Hail and Farewell*, 3 vols. London: Heineman.

Mulcahy, R. 1927. Comments on the Foregoing Article (Tierney, 1927), no. 1. *Studies*, 16: 10–15.

Murphy, G. 1948. Irish in Our Schools: 1922–1945. *Studies*, 37: 421–428.

———. 1949. The Gaelic Background. *In* M. Tierney, ed. *Daniel O'Connell: Nine Centenary Essays*. Dublin: Browne and Nolan, 1–24.

O Briain, L. 1927. Comments on the Foregoing Article (Tierney, 1927), no. 4. *Studies*, 16: 20–22.

O'Brien, C. Cruise. 1960. 1891–1916. *In* C. C. O'Brien, ed. *The Shaping of Modern Ireland*. London: Routledge and Kegan Paul, 13–23.

O Buachalla, B. 1968. *I mBéal Feirste cois cuan*. Dublin: An Clóchomhar.

O Cadhain. 1969. Conradh na Gaeilge agus an litríocht. *Inniu*, 31 January and 7 February.

O Catháin, S. 1967. Education in the New Ireland. *In* F. MacManus, ed. *The Years of the Great Test 1926–39*. Cork: Mercier Press, 104–114.

O Cuív, Brian. 1951. *Irish Dialects and Irish-speaking Districts*. Dublin: Institute for Advanced Studies.

———. 1966. Education and Language. *In* D. Williams, ed. *The Irish Struggle, 1916–1926*. London: Routledge and Kegan Paul, 153–166.

———. 1969. The Changing Form of the Irish Language. *In* B. O. Cuív, ed. *A View of the Irish Language*. Dublin: Stationery Office, 23–34.

O Danachair, Caoimhín. 1969. The Gaeltacht. *In* B. O. Cuív, ed. *A View of the Irish Language*. Dublin: Stationery Office, 112–121.

O'Donnell, F. H. 1910. *History of the Irish Parliamentary Party*, 2 vols. London: Longmans, Green.

O Fiaich, T. 1969. The Language and Political History. *In* B. O. Cuív, ed. *A View of the Irish Language*. Dublin: Stationery Office, 101–111.

O hAilín, T. 1968. The Irish Society agus Tadhg O Coinnialláin. *Studia Hibernica*, 8: 60–78.

———. 1969. Irish Revival Movements. *In* B. O. Cuív, ed. *A View of the Irish Language*. Dublin: Stationery Office, 91–100.

O Huallacháin, Colmán. Bilingualism in Education in Ireland. Georgetown University Monographs, Language and Linguistics Series.

O Móráin, D. 1958. Gael-linn: Principle and Practice. *Threshold*, Autumn.

O Néill, E. 1968. The Language Revival in Ireland. *In* F. G. Thompson, ed. *Maintaining a National Identity*. Dublin: The Celtic League, 54–63.

O Tuama, S. 1969. The Gaelic League in the Future. Lecture given on Radio Eireann in Thomas Davis Lectures series.

Roinn Oideachais. 1966. *Buntús Gaeilge: Reamhthuarascáil*. Dublin: Stationery Office.

Rubin, Joan. This volume. Evaluation and Language Planning. Paper 12.

Ryan, D. 1939. *The Sword of Light: From the Four Masters to Douglas Hyde 1636–1938*. London: Arthur Barker.

Ryan, F. 1905. On Language and Political Ideals. *Dana*, 1: 273–279.

Sheehy-Skeffington, F. 1905. Review of *Thomas Moore* by Stephen Gwynn. *New Ireland Review*, 23: 39.

Sullivan, D. J. 1969. The Literary Periodical and the Anglo-Irish Revival 1894–1914. Unpublished doctoral dissertation, University College, Dublin.

Tierney, M. 1927. The Revival of the Irish Language. *Studies*, 16: 1–10.
Wall, M. 1969. The Decline of the Irish Language. *In* B. O. Cuív, ed. *A View of the Irish Language*. Dublin: Stationery Office, 81–90.
Walsh, W. J. 1900. *Bilingual Education*. Gaelic League pamphlets, 8. Dublin: Gaelic League.
Webb, A. 1904. The Gaelic League and Politics. *Dana*, 1: 141–144.

5. SPELLING REFORM—ISRAEL 1968

CHAIM RABIN
   Hebrew University, Jerusalem

LINGUISTIC BACKGROUND

Spelling of Consonants

The Hebrew script is essentially consonantal; that is, the basic transliterated values of its twenty-two characters are: ' (glottal stop), *b, g, d, h, v, z, ḥ, ṭ, y, k, l, m, n, s,* ᶜ (pharyngal), *p, tz, q, r, sh,* and *t.* These values are historical, and in actual speech some of these are pronounced the same, varying according to the various traditional reading dialects still preserved by Jewish communities, especially in prayer, and in the two principal pronounciations now current in Israel: that of Jews originating from Asia and Africa (Sephardim) versus that of those whose parents came from Europe and America (Ashkenazim), to simplify the division somewhat.

Some of the above characters also have more than one sound: *b, k,* and *p* are in both Israeli dialects under certain conditions also pronounced [v], [x], and [f]; *sh* is in a number of words pronounced[s]; and ' and in Ashkenazi dialect also ᶜ are often silent.

As far as the consonants are concerned, the spelling is thus strictly historical and requires considerable skill both in reading and writing.

Spelling of Vowels

Originally, long vowels were indicated within the consonantal spelling as follows: *v* stands sometimes for /o/, sometimes for /u/; *y* stands for /i/ and, on comparatively rare occasions, for /e/. At the end of a word, *h* indicates the presence of a vowel, mostly /a/, but sometimes /e/, rarely /o/. However, for over a thousand years vowel quantity has not been distinguished in pronunciation, and the short /o, u, i, e/ sound just the same as the former long vowels. This means that the vowel indication is in fact simply part of the historical spelling, just as is the knowledge when to pronounce *v* and *y* as consonants and when as vowels.

In Bibles, prayer-books, poetry, and books for young children and language learners, such as dictionaries and grammars, full vowel-indication is achieved by a system of symbols placed above, below, and inside the letters, as it is in so many Asian scripts. In Hebrew this system is called *pointing*. There is no difficulty in reading a pointed passage, except for one symbol that indicates both /a/ and /o/; but it is very difficult to learn how to point words correctly because, although there are fourteen vowel symbols representing original long, lengthened, short, and reduced vowels, today only five, or in some pronunciations six, different vowels are sounded. The original quantity of the vowels was regulated by syllable structure and other features; thus, in order to place them correctly, one has to know Hebrew grammar very well: in fact, grammar teaching in schools today is largely concerned with inculcating correct pointing. In spite of this, only very few people attain the ability to point any word or form at sight. The preparation and proofreading of texts with full vocalization is done by specialists, and they are well paid. Besides, there are no fixed rules for pointing the many foreign words in present-day Hebrew, even though their pronunciation is quite clear.

Vowel-Indication as a Language Problem

The main problem about this system of vowel-indication is its cost. While the setting of an average sixteen-page text of straight non-vocalized print cost $75 in 1969, the same text would cost over $150 if fully pointed. The symbols above and below the letters are set as separate lines and require justifying. A system for linotyping a much simplified pointing by having the vowel symbols cast on the same body requires approximately 250 keys and is used only for immigrant newspapers, which, as a result, are heavily subsidized. The pointing cannot be typed. Although a typewriter enabling the vowels to be typed in a separate operation (that is, each line being typed twice) has been designed, not enough orders were received to justify having the letters cast.

Long before the pointing was invented, it had become common practice to help the reader by inserting *v* and *y* not only where they are grammatically justified but also in places where /u, o, i/ were originally short vowels. This is called full (plene) spelling, as opposed to the grammatical (defective) spelling described above. The effect of this procedure can be gauged by stating that /i/ constitutes 6 per cent of the sounds in a running text; /o/, 5.7 per cent; and /u/, 2.3 per cent; while the unrepresented vowels are /a/, 17.1 per cent; and /e/, 13.5 per cent. Moreover, the method does not help to distinguish between /u/ and /o/. A further help is provided by writing *vv* for consonantal /v/ and *yy* for consonantal /y/. In spite of its comparatively small statistical incidence, the full spelling does help a great deal in distinguishing, for instance, the active and passive modes in many verbs or in identifying the correct form of nouns, since Hebrew, like Arabic, extensively employs vowel patterns for grammatical purposes (for instance, *spr* can be read /safar/ "he counted," /siper/ "he told," /supar/ "it was told," /sapar/ "barber," /sefer/ "book," and /sfar/ "frontier". Full spelling will differentiate the verbal forms as *spr*, *sypr*, and *swpr*, but it still leaves the nominal forms undifferentiated).

Full spelling has never been employed consistently to indicate all cases of /u, o, i/. In practice it has always been used with extreme irregularity, the very same forms being sometimes spelled in full and sometimes grammatically, the general tendency being to insert the helping letters when the writer becomes aware of the possibility of an alternative reading. Since the majority of words in a text can be read in alternative ways (sometimes in quite a number of different ways) but since only in a limited percentage of cases the alternative reading makes sense, it is rather a matter of chance whether the writer becomes aware of the alternative and takes precautions. The full spelling thus becomes a source of irregularity in spelling by introducing an arbitrary personal and momentary factor of choice. A survey of Israeli newspapers in 1966 showed that they differed somewhat in degrees of fullness but that none of them had anything like a consistent system of its own. The same word might appear with different spellings within a few lines. This applied both to Hebrew and borrowed words and to non-Hebrew proper names. In the telephone book, a name may appear in different places, according to how its owner chooses to spell it.

In principle, full spelling should never be used when a text is pointed, as the distinction between the different vowel symbols involves also the *v* and *y* of the grammatical spelling; therefore, any extra *v* or *y* leads to a grammatical mistake. In practice, however, already in the middle ages, pointing was quite frequently inserted in a fully spelled text. On the other hand, educated writers in letters and the like will often insert one or two vowel symbols to make the meaning clear; and such "partial pointing" is often used in the more expensive type of book. In theory, words thus treated should be grammatically spelled, but in informal writing this rule is often ignored.

Indeed, it is very doubtful whether the normal adult accustomed to full spelling is at all able to use grammatical spelling, except with a great deal of cogitation and frequent faults. Children and young people, on the other hand, employ grammatical spelling even when they do not point what they write. This is because of the insistence of the schools, where grammatical spelling is considered an indispensable pre-requisite to correct grammar.

The young child nowadays learns to read and write by a syllable technique of consonant plus vowel symbol, reads for one to three years only pointed texts, and then gradually passes to unvocalized texts, still spelled in such a way that they could be pointed, that is, in grammatical spelling. This is also the way many books intended for children's private reading are printed. As the child goes on to reading newspapers and books printed for adults, he acquires the ability to read full spelling but continues to write grammatical spelling. Young typists and university students in most cases still adhere strictly (at least in theory) to this type of spelling. In his early twenties a person gradually abandons the school spelling and adapts to the irregular full-spelling habits of the adult world.

Summary of Spelling Problems

The problems offered by the situation here described can be set out as follows:

1. The existence of two spellings and the resulting need for re-learning spelling at some time in every person's life.
2. The lack of regularity in the spelling most commonly used.
3. The insufficient indication of vowels in either system of spelling that leads to:
   a) false identification of words, which have to be rectified in the light of the context in the sentence (on the other hand, it is rather rare that a sentence remains completely ambiguous to the end);
   b) mispronunciations of correctly identified words and forms. It is claimed by educators that this is the source of the widespread use of non-grammatical speech forms, even in the language of educated people, as they have no visual corrective for the forms used in everyday language;

c) children are virtually cut off from reading anything not specially printed for them. This includes public notices, newspapers, and even private letters;

d) the transition from vocalized (pointed) texts to non-vocalized ones creates an additional difficulty for the child in a system of writing which in any case presents the common difficulties of historical spelling. It is claimed that this transition problem is partly responsible for the low reading achievements of part of the school population. (Other causes are no doubt the great difference in vocabulary and sentence structure between spoken and written Hebrew and the paucity of reading material couched in simple popular style.);

e) the situation much increases the difficulties experienced by the immigrant, the casual visitor, and the interested person abroad in learning Hebrew. The transition from pointed to normal spelling is much harder for the foreign learner than it is for the Israeli child, who is familiar with the language. Observation proves that quite a proportion of new immigrants continue, for many years, to cling to the special newspapers printed for immigrants (supplementing the meager content of these by newspapers in their own language or in English), and few get as far as reading Hebrew literature. Some claims have been made that the spelling difficulties frighten off potential settlers; it is of course impossible to check such an assertion.

Proposals for Reform

During the past few decades, there have been dozens of proposals for reforming the Hebrew writing system by creating an adequate representation of vowels that can be written or printed within the line, or at least that can be printed more cheaply and easily than full pointing. There have been several proposals to rationalize partial pointing by restricting it to one or two vowel symbols only, which would be inserted whenever the vowel appears. It is claimed by the authors of these proposals that the consistent indication of this one vowel (or of the absence of a vowel) will enable the reader to supply the remaining vowels unequivocally. These proposals involve doubling (or trebling) the number of keys for printing or typing.

Another type of proposal consists in designing additional letters to represent the vowels, instead of placing them above and below the line. This would make is possible to set, print, and type fully vocalized texts by machines designed in the ordinary way and would involve fewer additional letters than partial pointing. Suggestions range from sets of symbols to represent all items of the traditional pointing to restricted sets for the five or six vowels actually heard (this means supplying letters for /a, e, i/ (and perhaps /é/), as /o/ and /u/ can be indicated by the traditional dot accompanying *v* in pointing).

Some have proposed using the letters ', *h, v, y,* ᶜ, systematically to indicate vowels, as is done in Yiddish (and was done in another Semitic language, Mandaean).

There have also been several suggestions for adopting a roman script. In the late twenties and thirties, even a short-lived newspaper, a book, and a book for teaching Hebrew were published in different systems of romanized Hebrew by well-known public figures. One scientist proposed romanization for scientific publications in order to avoid the difficulty of recognizing international scientific terms in unvocalized Hebrew transliteration. These proposals fall into two classes: those that transliterate the traditional spelling and, therefore, necessitate the addition of new letters, diacritic points, or digraphs; and those that represent a present-day Israeli pronunciation. It should be noted that the Hebrew Language Academy (see below) created an official system of roman transliteration for names and the like that have extra letters to be indicated by underlining (I am not aware of any proposal to introduce this particular system for printing continuous texts); and that various methods of romanization are currently employed in scientific linguistic texts and in beginners' teaching.

Difficulties of Implementing Spelling Reform

Two research projects in which the present writer was involved have shown that the experienced reader who speaks Hebrew as his native or everyday language has no particular trouble with the process of reading by elimination, which the unvocalized Hebrew script demands. Tests have shown that fourteen-year-olds read unvocalized texts at the same speed and with the same degree of comprehension as they do pointed texts. It is true that when reading aloud at sight, almost every reader will misread words and have to correct himself when the continuation of the sentence shows him that he erred, but in silent reading this constant self-correction is apparently not noticed by the reader. The average educated person is thus quite unaware of the problems of reading Hebrew; but if he thinks about the matter, he would see the advantages of the system: a Hebrew text is approximately 25 per cent shorter than its translation into a European language; because of the absence of capitals and italics, Hebrew books can be produced much more cheaply than equivalent works in European languages (and this in spite of the comparatively tiny number of Hebrew speakers, 2.25 million); the absence of vowels is even felt to speed up comprehension by throwing into relief the consonantal root of words; an educated reader can understand with little effort texts written as much as two thousand years ago in their original spelling (not to speak of the Bible, which he always reads with pointing). The spelling difficulties I have enumerated earlier affect marginal and largely inarticulate groups: children, the uneducated, and new immigrants. The educated reader tends to feel that these people should make the same effort that he made himself in order to learn to read fluently, rather than cause him difficulties by changing his ingrained reading habits. Some even resent the very idea that others should have things made easier than they had themselves.

To this natural educated conservatism are added two specific features connected with the state of Hebrew as a language revived only ninety years ago from books—a language that is held by many to be still in the process of revival. The average person fully identifies himself with the ideology (1) that present-day Hebrew should be kept as close as humanly possible to the language of the "Sources"; that is, the classical works written between 1200 B.C. and A.D. 500; and (2) that linguistic continuity must not be broken by allowing changes in structure to penetrate into correct usage. It is only natural that the system of writing is viewed as part of this continuity and that its abandonment, or changes that affect the appearance of the text, as betrayal of the Language Revival, if not of the National Revival. In a cultural atmosphere where books written about A.D. 200 or in A.D. 1100–1200 are currently read by non-specialists, the problem of having to reprint a large number of books in case of a change in spelling has quite a different relevance than it does in a Western society where the average reader mainly reads contemporary works.

As stated above, Hebrew is spoken in Israel according to two pronunciation norms, both well established and standardized. The young Israeli betrays in his accent nothing of the language his parents spoke, which in many cases he himself still can speak to some extent. His speech marks him in Israeli society as a member of the Ashkenazi or the Sephardi group, whether or not his parents' Hebrew pronunciation belonged to the type that sounded the pharyngals (Sephardi of today). But the two dialects show no signs of coalescing, and Israeli Hebrew is impartially represented by both of them. Both correspond in a sense to the present historical spelling. A more perfect spelling would have to represent particularly either the one or the other of the two dialects and thus lend the dialect an authority it does not have today. Moreover, many, if not most of the users, of the non-pharyngal (Ashkenazi) pronunciation theoretically admit that the pharyngal pronunciation is "better" because it is closer to the spelling and that, in fact, they "ought" to pronounce not only the pharyngals h and c but also the t, the doubled consonants, and the neutral vowel [ə]. This so-called Semitic pronunciation, which goes far beyond the Sephardi dialect in the matter of spelling-pronunciation, is used by radio announcers and taught in many schools, though only a few individuals use it in daily life. At present it is possible to pay lip-service to this ideal, without bothering to adhere to it in practice (just as it is possible to admit that one should speak grammatically, without adhering to all grammar rules in one's speech); but a spelling reform might force a choice between the pronunciation as it is and the theoretical "Semitic" form of pronunciation.

INSTITUTIONAL BACKGROUND

The revival of spoken Hebrew in Palestine began in 1881. Already in 1890, a "Language Committee" was formed for the purpose of planning vocabulary extension and other matters. Although short-lived, it was re-established in 1904 under the same name and has been functioning uninterruptedly since, but with a change in its status in 1953 to an official organ of the new state of Israel, under the name of "Academy for the Hebrew Language."

The Academy was established by a Law promulgated in 1953 as "Supreme Institution for the Science of the Hebrew Language" for the purpose of "directing the development of the Hebrew language on the basis of research into the language in all its periods and branches" (paragraph 2). "Decisions of the Institution in matters of grammar, spelling, terminology, or transcription that have been published in the *Official Gazette* by the Minister of Education and Culture are binding upon educational and scientific institutions, upon the government, its departments and institutions, and upon organs of local government" (paragraph 10). This is interpreted to mean that such publications in the *Official Gazette* must bear the signature of the said Minister. "The participation of the

State in the budget of the Institution shall form part of the budget of the Ministry of Education and Culture" (paragraph 11), and the "Minister of Education and Culture is responsible for the carrying out of this Law" (paragraph 13). The members of the Academy number between fifteen and twenty-three (paragraph 4a); but the maximum number of twenty-three does not include members that have reached the age of seventy-five years, although such members continue to take part and to vote (amendment, 1969); in addition, there are up to twenty-three advisory members, who can vote on all linguistic matters, but not in the election of new members or in changes of the Constitution. Members receive no pay. As constituted at present, the membership (including advisory members) comprises ten teachers of linguistics at universities, fifteen other university teachers, eleven writers, and eight from other professions (teachers, style-correctors, etc.). The Academy employs a number of so-called Scientific Secretaries who are highly trained and experienced Hebrew linguists and who participate in committees and in the plenary meeting with voting rights.

The language-planning work of the Academy is carried on through committees. The majority of these are terminology committees, appointed *ad hoc* for the purpose of dealing with a specific subject and dissolved when the requisite dictionary has been completed. If, after a number of years, it is decided that the same subject be dealt with once more, a new committee is formed. These terminology committees usually have a majority of non-academicians, people who are experts in the subject discussed and who have a leaning towards Hebrew terminology; and the Academy is represented by one or more of its members and by one of the secretaries (who also keeps the protocol), its chairman always being an Academy member. A smaller number of committees deals with general language matters: grammar, day-to-day grammatical problems, grammatical terminology, style and usage, transcription, and the like. These consist of Academy members and scientific secretaries only who are usually appointed for two years at a time. A completely separate staff is engaged in the preparation of the Historical Dictionary, under the direction of the Vice-President (Acting President) of the Academy, Professor Z. Ben-Ḥayyim.

All decisions of committees require confirmation by the plenary meeting, which takes place five times a year. Such decisions are first circularized (sometimes at several stages of the work) to all members of the Academy, and may, if any member so desires, be discussed in the plenum.

In practice, terminology is largely confirmed *en bloc*, with only some doubtful points being raised in the plenum, while decisions on general questions are re-discussed in detail by the plenum. All decisions are voted on. The gist of every speaker's remarks and the proportions of votes for and against are published in the Academy's *Memoirs*. Protocols are kept of the discussions in the non-terminological committees but are not published in print. Committees and the plenum are the only forums the Academy offers for discussion on matters of language planning. The Institution also publishes two periodicals, *Our Language* and *Our Language for the People*. At first both publications carried articles by members and non-members on principles and details of language planning, but since the Academy took over from the Language Committee both periodicals carry only scientific articles concerned with research into the language (in the past and in the present).

The question of spelling was treated as a matter for the direct attention of the plenum, and at the time of writing no permanent committee has yet been set up for this branch of the Academy's activities, which, as we have seen above, had been specifically included in its tasks by the Constitutive Law. Such a committee is to be set up (see below).

THE EVENTS

The 1948 Rules

The earliest record of a discussion about spelling in the Language Committee is in the Minutes (Zikhronot) of 1913, when a lecture on the subject was delivered by David Yellin (1864–1941). In 1920–21 the same Yellin opened a discussion on the subject, advocating a strict grammatical spelling. The Language Council never officially decided on this, but Yellin's immense influence with the teachers led to the adoption of the grammatical spelling by all schools. This settled the matter temporarily but had little influence on the practice outside schools, and pressure grew for the Language Council to take up the challenge of regulating the adult unpointed spelling. "At the request of various interested parties," the Council appointed towards the end of 1938 a special committee to make proposals for "full" spelling and for a system of transliteration of foreign words into Hebrew. The consultations opened with a major lecture, which was published in the Council's quarterly journal, and were also remarkable for a new departure in the field of communications and public relations: Professor N. H. Torczyner (Tur-Sinai), who afterwards became, and still is, president of the Council (and the Academy), delivered a series of lectures on the spelling problem on the newly established Palestine Radio. In summer 1940, the spelling proposal was sent out for consideration to all members of the Language Council and met with violent opposition, especially from the members in Tel Aviv. Finally, the Council decided to set up another special committee in Tel Aviv "to examine the proposal," but this second committee turned out to be more sharply divided into extremist factions of innovators and conservatives, and some even demanded changes in Hebrew grammar before deciding on a spelling. After the Tel Aviv committee had returned its mandate without arriving at any agreed proposals, the plenary meeting of the Council discussed the original Jerusalem proposals and made some additions to them but resolved that no final decision could be made and that the proposals should be placed before the general public for discussion: "It was incumbent upon the Language Council to give an opportunity to all those circles in the community who were interested in spelling reform to study the proposals in detail and to express their opinion about them before the Council could adopt any binding decision whatever."

In spring 1942, the proposals were published in the Council's quarterly journal, *Leshonenu* (11:232–41). They were preceded by a preamble setting out the principles on which all members of the original Jerusalem committee were in full agreement. These are: to leave in force the co-existence of two spellings, "grammatical" when pointed and "full" when unpointed; the spelling must be based upon the Sources of the language (the Bible and early Rabbinic literature) and its recognized grammar; be adapted to present-day educational and practical needs; and, above all, be acceptable to the public. It must therefore not be revolutionary in any way, and especially not add new letters or introduce new principles in the use of the existing letters. In fact, it should only regulate existing usage and hence cannot be expected to be consistent; rules could only give general guidance and would have to be complemented by a spelling dictionary to be worked out by the Language Council.

In view of these principles, we need not wonder that the proposed spelling was curiously asymmetrical. It rules that /u/ would be written throughout with a *v*, but /o/ would be indicated by *v* only when it corresponded to one of the three symbols sounded [o] in the pointing and not already marked by an added *v* (the so-called *ḥolam*), but not when it corresponded to one of the other two. While in this matter there was still a direct connection with the pointing, the regulation of the spelling of /i/

by *y* was further made dependent on whether the vowel stood in a closed syllable (in which case it was not to be marked) or in a syllable preceding a consonant doubled in the pointing orthography (but now no more pronounced double). As for consonants /v/ and /y/, these were to be indicated by a single *v* and *y* in the beginning of a word, but a double *vv* and *yy* when not in the beginning of a word.

The additions made by the plenary meeting required the distinction of /b/ from /v/, /k/ from /kh/, and /p/ from /f/ by inserting a dot into *b, k,* and *p*; of /sh/ from /s/ by placing a dot over the latter; and of /u/ from /o/ by placing a dot into the *v* when indicating /u/—all these being taken over from the pointing system.

The proposed spelling made a large number of common words clearer but still allowed for much uncertainty in reading, since it indicated neither /a/ nor /e/ nor absence of vowel and since it left the majority of the occurrences of /i/ unmarked. Its use also required a command of grammar hardly to be expected from the general public.

After the publication of these proposals, the Council convened two public scientific conferences to discuss them. Since those from outside the Council who participated in these meetings appeared to agree to the general principles, though differing on matters of detail, the Council resolved in spring 1944 to set up a new "Committee for Formulating the Spelling Rules," which included, apart from members of the original committee of 1938–40, some of the most outstanding opponents of the proposals. The new body took a much longer time over its consultations, from January 1945 to summer 1947. Its members also took part in consultations with bodies such as the editorial boards of encyclopedias to investigate some of the practical aspects of their problem. In autumn 1947, they presented their proposals to the Central Committee of the Language Council. This body authorized the publication of the proposals after detailed discussion. They were published in *Leshonenu* (16:82–7) in spring 1948 and reissued with a preface by the Council's President as a small booklet in spring 1949, this still being the principal official form in which these rules are circulated. As a sign of the times, the popular edition not only illustrates the rules by an excerpt from a well-known article on the evils of Jewish cultural assimilation in the diaspora but also adds a transcription of the Proclamation of Independence. The establishment of the independent State of Israel on May 14, 1948 gave these rules a new aspect; while so far the Language Council had legislated for a voluntary school system of the Jewish population of Mandatory Palestine, it was now called upon to regulate an important aspect of the cultural activities and the communication needs of the sovereign state.

The new rules only very slightly modified those of 1942, and all observations on the latter also apply to the new rules. The preamble once more stresses that the rules only regulate and standardize spelling habits already current and admits that in some matters the individual user will have to decide between alternatives permitted by the rules. The compilation of a complete spelling dictionary is envisaged as a desirable but somewhat remote possibility. On the other hand, it is stated, for the first time, that "the Language Council hopes that, if only teachers, authors, and the educated public will conscientiously observe these rules, much experience will be gathered in a few years, and will enable us to re-examine the rules and to improve them." In another passage, the aim of the rules is referred to as "progress towards complete vowel indication." It thus appears that at least some of those active on the Council envisaged a continuous process of spelling reform by easy stages.

The wording of the two pages of introduction to the rules of 1948, from which relevant passages have been quoted, seems to indicate quite clearly that it was intended to be binding upon the public ("teachers, authors, and the educated public") in the same way as other decisions of the Language Council had generally been accepted as binding, in spite of the absence of any sanctions. The phrase used for the authorized "publication" (*pirsum ba-rabbim*, literally, "making them known to the general public") is one used for promulgations of legal decisions also. The Council indeed made an attempt to get the rules adopted by the Hebrew school system, but this was prevented by the personal opposition of the director-general of the educational network, and the schools have since then continued to cling to the grammatical spelling for all grades. It is not clear whether any real effort was made to persuade the editorial boards of newspapers to adopt the Council's spelling rules. In practice, no newspaper follows these rules to any marked extent. The majority of educated Israelis are quite unaware that a body of rules for full spelling exists at all. It is thus true that apart from the publications of the Council and later of the Academy, the above spelling rules are applied consistently by the country's most prestigious publishing firm *Mosad Bialik* (supported by the Jewish Agency for Palestine), yet while that firm's publications are found on the shelves of all educated people and have been a model for other publishers, their spelling seems to have failed to arouse a desire for imitation.

There can be little doubt that one of the reasons for the lack of attention in the country to the 1948 rules was their timing. Their publication took place in the middle of the War of Independence, and this was followed by years of economic and political difficulties, while the country was in the throes of absorbing a massive immigration. Few people had their minds on such a minor matter as spelling rules. By the time people could apply themselves again to such matters, the rules had lost their novelty, and the very fact that they had not gained public acceptance made people suspicious of them. The main reason, however, was the lack of any legal authority for the Language Council's decisions, which had been responsible for the failure of imposing the rules upon the schools. It was to remedy this flaw that the leaders of the Language Council applied themselves vigorously to persuading the government to set up the Language Academy and to give it authority by law.

The 1962 Committee

When the Academy was established in 1953, it took over the Council's spelling rules for its own publications but did not immediately proceed to submitting those rules for official ratification by the Minister of Education and Culture. It was felt that the opportunity should be used for improving the rules before having them made law. Until the end of 1956, the Academy was busy with making rules for transcribing Hebrew names and the like into roman script for public notices and for many other needs of the State. Only after the rules for romanized transliteration had been passed did the Academy set up a committee for spelling, which besides the members of the Academy's grammar committee also included three appointees of the Ministry of Education and Culture (one of these was also a member of the Academy). One of the Ministry representatives withdrew after the first meeting. The spelling committee sat for two years in a body and in subcommittees and presented its proposals to the plenum of the Academy on April 8, 1962.

Owing to pressure of work in the plenum and the need to have the proposals styled by the Academy's scientific secretariate, about six months passed between the completion of the committee's work and their presentation. In the meantime, rumors had begun to circulate among members of the Academy and among the public about the revolutionary character of the proposals. Some six weeks before the date of the plenary meeting in which the proposals were to be presented, one of the larger newspapers published a preview, based on information said to come from people in the know and implying that there already was adverse criticism. In order to prevent further leakage of information before the official release, the meeting of the plenum was arranged for a Sunday afternoon, and the letter containing the proposals delivered to the houses of the Academy members on Friday afternoon—Saturday being the weekly holiday on which no newspapers appear and no business is transacted. Nevertheless, the same newspaper carried an article on Sunday morning with all the more sensational details of the proposals. This rather weakened the effect of the unprecedented step—unprecedented for the Academy—that the press had been invited to attend both the meeting at which the proposals were to be announced and the meeting set for the following morning at which they were to be discussed. The papers, on the whole, reported briefly on the proposals and collected views, mostly adverse, from the academicians. One paper announced that 90 per cent of the members would vote against the proposals.

The proposals were in two parts, one unanimous and the other put forward by one-half of the committee only. Even the unanimous proposal went quite a way beyond the 1948 spelling rules in marking the vowels: every /u/ was to be marked by a *v* with a dot in it; every /o/ by a *v* with a dot over it; every /i/ by a *y* with a dot or line over it; while the letters *v* and *y* without diacritics denote the consonants. Only few, well-defined exceptions were admitted. Also the other diacritic symbols in the consonants of the 1948 spelling were to be used.

The other, non-unanimous proposal advocated the introduction of two new symbols to mark the vowels /a/ and /e/. It was left open whether these would appear above the line (though between the letters) or would be of the size of ordinary letters. The exact form was to be determined by a competition among graphic artists. For the purpose of presenting the proposal, /a/ was provisionally indicated by a raised ˘ and /e/ by a raised ^. (The choice of these symbols proved unfortunate, as the newspapers identified the a-symbol as "roman v" and claimed that the proposal introduced roman letters into the Hebrew alphabet). If accepted, this would have provided—in combination with the unanimous proposals —an unambiguous representation of all vowels according to present-day Israeli pronunciation, since absence of vowel would now have been clearly distinguished, and the vowel [ə] is non-phonemic and conditioned by the phonetic context.

In the introductory lecture by Professor Z. Ben-Ḥayyim, chairman of the committee, it was made clear that the proposals involved the retention of the pointing, including its different, grammatical spelling, but only for "passive" use, especially in religious books, as the new spelling would remove the need for the use of the pointing in school-books and poetry. This was indeed the most complete solution for the spelling problem that was ever placed before the Academy by one of its appointed committees. It would have made the reading of all words unambiguous (except, of course, for true homonyms); since it left the consonants unchanged, however, it still perpetuated the difficulties experienced in writing Hebrew correctly.

While many of the speakers in the three meetings devoted to the discussion of the committee's proposals agreed to the first part, on which the whole committee had agreed, only one or two advocated acceptance of the principle of new symbols for the /a/ and the /e/. A number of speakers proposed solutions of their own, generally in the direction of some systematized partial pointing. One famous novelist among the members expressed the view that "this generation was not yet prepared," that the time had not yet come for reforming the spelling. In the end, the chairman posed the question "whether the Academy sees any necessity for dealing with the problem of reforming the spelling." A vote was taken, and the reply was a unanimous "yes." As a result of this vote, a new special committee was appointed, including two of the members of the former committee, and four new members, among them two of those who had spoken most vigorously against the full spelling as such. According to the practice of the Academy, this meant that the proposals of the 1962 committee were still before the assembly. This was on January 8, 1963.

The 1964 Committee

Already on February 12, 1964, the new committee reported to the plenum. Its six members proposed six different solutions to the spelling problem. One was the proposals of the 1962 committee; the other five were not fully worked-out systems but general directives for working out proposals. The only one that had any novelty in it was to design an easier, "popular" system of pointing, to be used concurrently with the established and inherited pointing system. In the discussion, the chairman of the committee declared that they were in fact seeking the guidance of the plenum before proceeding to the elaboration of any of the proposals that were put forward.

Several members now proposed that the Academy should for the present put off the discussion of the spelling reform *sine die,* seeing that there was so little common ground. A vote taken on this, however, revealed that only two were for it and fifteen against. Another proposal, to put off discussion *sine die* but to declare the 1948 spelling rules of the Language Council to be binding until further notice was also rejected by a slightly smaller majority. A similar majority rejected the proposal, put forward by one of the linguist members, that a new committee should first institute a program of research before embarking on new proposals.

The 1967 Committee

In order to give some directive to the new committee, which was now to be appointed, a vote was passed on the question whether the solution should be on the lines of perfecting the unpointed spelling while retaining the pointed spelling ("two spellings"). This was decided by a large majority (eleven to four). Finally a new committee of five was elected, ironically under the chairmanship of the member who had proposed that a new committee should proceed only after a period of research. Only one of the 1964 committee members was included, and he had not been on the 1962 committee.

On February 28, 1967, three years later, the new committee reported with a proposal agreed by three of its five members but with far-reaching reservations (but no positive proposals) from the remaining two. The new proposals were basically identical with those agreed by the whole of the 1962 committee: to indicate throughout /u, o, i/ (with some exceptions for /i/), but to retain the double writing of the consonantal /v/ and /y/.

This proposal was discussed at two meetings, but as the discussion proceeded it became increasingly clear that an important body of members objected to the basic principle contained in the directive to the committee when it was elected: that its task was to develop and elaborate the unpointed spelling. These members again and again proclaimed that the only feasible solution lay in the direction of partial pointing. In the end it was decided to close the discussion and to hold, after some time, a meeting only for the purpose of voting for whichever of the systems so far proposed would be able to command the necessary majority. The advocates of partial pointing were asked to place detailed proposals before the Academy secretariate and, if possible, to get together on a joint system of partial pointing.

Already before the end of 1966, some educators who were not members of the Academy had placed before the Pedagogical Council of the Ministry of Education and Culture a plan to teach children to read by a system that would relieve them of the necessity to learn the full spelling after having read for a number of years nothing but the grammatical spelling. This was to combine the pointing with the full spelling, except that this would be accompanied by the pointing symbols as a kind of phonetic help. This, in fact, was the very system that had been used for some years already in the newspaper for new immigrants, which was widely used in courses for the latter. Since the whole pointing system is linked with the grammatical spelling, the proposal meant the violation of many grammatical rules that were currently taught in schools. One of its authors announced his intention of writing a new Hebrew grammar, based on the combined spelling. Since there were no binding rules for full spelling, it was also proposed at one point that the Ministry's Pedagogical Council should decide on rules as applied to the combined spelling for schools. The plan was discussed for a number of months, and while some educators were inclined to accept it, members of the Academy were opposed to it. At no point in the discussions was the Academy officially approached, although several of its leading members were individually invited to participate in the discussions.

THE REFORM

The Academy members who had advocated partial pointing announced after some time their inability to arrive at an agreed proposal. On the other hand, a number of members, despairing of getting any agreement on one of various spelling proposals of the past six years, decided to ask the assembly to confirm the 1948 spelling of the Language Council. A proposal for a resolution was signed by ten members. It is quoted here in full:

For many generations, two systems of spelling have been current in Hebrew, namely, pointed and unpointed. Though in each of the two systems we can discern in our literature various shades of usage, the pointed spelling is today employed in school teaching according to one well defined system of rules. This system, which in its time was regulated by the Language Council, has evident advantages for learning the language, and is rightly called Grammatical Spelling. However, side by side with the pointed spelling, there is in use an unpointed spelling system, which has never been displaced by the use of pointing. Its use, in fact, is wider than that of pointed script. However much the Language Council and the Academy were concerned—as is their task and as they were authorized—to arrive at a decision, they did not see their way to establishing one of the two systems as the exclusive one for writing Hebrew. The various systems for unification made by the Council and the Academy were unsuccessful. Today, too, the Academy does not consider the time ripe to do away with one of the two systems.

The use of the pointed spelling is absolutely necessary today, for instance, in teaching and children's education, in prayerbooks and poetry, as well as in various kinds of popular publications. Its use should be enlarged to include all written documents addressed to the general public, because through it the reading of Hebrew words becomes clear beyond doubt, and the language is guarded from the corruptions in speaking which have their cause in the spelling. In all cases where the pointing system is used, it must be according to the spelling rules established for the last few generations, and every deviation from these rules will be considered a mistake.

For generations now the unpointed system has been employed in a number of varieties, each of which seeks to compensate for the absence of vowel indication by using added *v* and *y* to various extent. After many discussions and experiments of over a number of years, the Language Council established rules for unpointed spelling, which were designed to systematize it.

The Academy resolves to reaffirm and to recommend for adoption the system of the Academy in its final formulation, because it facilitates the reading of written Hebrew, restricts the possibilities of error in word identification, and brings order into the variety of attempts to make the reading of Hebrew easier.

The system of the Language Council, which already has a marked influence upon the usage of the general public (in periodicals and in the daily press), should also guide teachers in the schools. Practical experience in their use will show within a reasonable period of time whether these rules require improvements, and in which respects, and it will be the task of a special committee to take care of this.

This resolution, cautiously phrased in order to be acceptable to academicians who saw in the pointed spelling the ideal solution for the problem yet stated quite unambiguously three points that formed the focus of recent discussion:

1. The consonant spelling underlying the pointing system must remain the grammatical spelling; hence, the suggestion of a "combined" pointed-full spelling is unacceptable.
2. The alternative to fully pointed spelling is not some system of partial pointing, but full spelling.
3. The insertion of the additional *v* and *y* in full spelling cannot be left to the discretion of the individual user (as had been advocated

in the discussions) but must be regulated, and the rules taught in schools.

On April 4, 1968, a double meeting of the plenum was held to carry out the decision announced in spring 1967 to try to decide the spelling question by voting on the various proposals. Although the two new systems were proposed by individual members and although the assembly was asked to take into consideration the proposal of the 1967 committee, it was clear throughout the discussion that the issue was between those who agreed to an established full spelling and those who opposed it. At this point, there also developed an opposition between those who believed that a regulation of the unpointed spelling was an immediate necessity and members who advocated waiting for the development of alternative suggestions or for perfection and revision of the full spelling. The final vote was taken in two stages: (1) whether a full spelling should be recognized side by side with the pointed grammatical spelling ("two spellings"); and (2) on the resolution to establish the 1948 spelling as the binding set of rules. In each case, thirteen voted favorably and five against, without abstentions. By this vote, the 1948 spelling became the official policy of the Academy. In a subsequent meeting the proposal to establish a special committee for observing the working of these rules in practice and for suggesting improvements in due course was separately voted on and confirmed.

The Directorate of the Academy appointed a committee of members to determine the exact manner in which the decision should be communicated to the Minister of Education and Culture and to determine what means should be adopted to make it known to the public. The work of this committee was later completed by the Directorate. On July 9, 1968, the full text of the resolution was communicated to the Minister with a request for his signature and for publication in the *Official Gazette*. The Acting President and one of the principal scientific secretaries went to see the Minister in order to explain the implications of the Academy's decision. Other meetings were held with leading officials of the Ministry in order to discuss the introduction of the new rules into school teaching. The official speaker of the Academy made contacts with journalists, and a number of newspapers carried articles that explained the decision. It was also planned to issue a booklet with the rules, phrased in a more popular way than in the booklet issued by the Language Council in 1949, but this was put off until after the official confirmation of the decision by the Minister; and in subsequent publicity work, reprints of the 1949 booklet, with its type worn by frequent reprinting, were used.

There is no doubt that many of the members who voted for the resolution were moved by concern for the good name and continued influence of the institution to which they had devoted so much of their time and energy. This concern was stated by several participants in the discussion. It was felt that the image of the Academy was becoming established as being a body unable to guide the nation on the very issues for the sake of which it had been created; and that even a set of rules that did not satisfy them was better than not having any rules at all. The opposition to all solutions suggested hitherto had convinced themselves that any consistent proposal would be doomed to fail. In any event it was proved that the existing spelling—simply by the fact that it existed even if its use was restricted—was able to rally a clear majority.

Some, however, were also guided by the belief that the root of the Academy's inability to arrive at agreement was because of the lack of a common basis of discussion and that, once the issue were decided, basically in favor of the adoption of a regulated unpointed full spelling, it would become easier to introduce agreed improvements into this spelling.

NEW DEVELOPMENTS

Without any connection with the Academy's deliberations, a new development had taken place. A group of people in Jerusalem and Tel Aviv formed a "Movement for an Unambiguous Hebrew Spelling." They were headed by an official from the Foreign Office and included several leading journalists and some writers. Their first written proclamation was handed to the Language Academy, with a request to pass it on to its members, on April 3, 1968. In it a demand was put forward that either the Academy should proceed forthwith to a complete solution of the spelling difficulties, or, if it did not, the government should appoint another body to do so. The present spelling, the proclamation stated, "causes perpetual insecurity in linguistic matters, endangers our psychological balance, and constitutes an obstacle to cultural, social, and economic progress. It also is a stumbling-block in the absorption of immigrants and in our ties with the Jewish people in other parts of the world. There exists a danger to the very existence and cultural level of the Hebrew language, in that it might in future not be fitted to serve as an exact tool for thought and artistic creativeness." The government, it demanded, should expend the necessary sums for getting an army of experts to work: "the people of Israel are worth 100 million pounds to teach them to read and write." The result must be a law enforcing a spelling that could be easily read. Only for religious books and, perhaps, for poetry, the pointing and the grammatical spelling might be retained.

As requested by its authors, this proclamation was on April 4 placed in front of every member of the Academy who had turned up for the meeting. The discussion took place under the impression of thinly veiled threats and attacks against the Academy. It is doubtful whether any member was moved by this event to change his opinion, but the incident produced a heavy atmosphere of having failed in the Academy's purpose. The Academy's endeavors to get its decision fairly reported in the press coincided with a well-run publicity campaign of the Movement for an Unambiguous Spelling, in which the Academy was berated for having done nothing, after twenty years of deliberations, except "to reconfirm the present position, in other words, to do nothing, and to give its blessing to a situation in which the two spelling systems, grammatical-pointed and unpointed-full spelling, continued to compete, neither of which answered the needs of our time." The government was asked not to confirm the Academy's decision but to pass a law that, within a certain time, an adequate spelling must be introduced. The Academy was to be given a limited time for deliberations, in full collaborations with a body of "sociologists, psychologists, graphic artists, printing technicians, journalists, publishers, and theatre people." If it failed to come up with a perfect proposal, the government was to entrust the task to a specially convened body of experts. In some of its pronouncements, the Movement raised the specter of romanized Hebrew, which would surely come if the Hebrew script were not reformed in time.

At the same time, one of Israel's linguists began a press campaign for a romanized spelling. Meetings and discussions as well as radio programs tended to become debates between advocates of a vague but extreme movement for spelling reform and the partisans of the more extreme step of romanization. Between these two extremes, the voice of the Academy's representatives was much too moderate to be audible. A certain turn for the better came, when, after a rather unsuccessful congress, the Movement began to seek contacts with the Academy in late September and its leaders allowed themselves to be convinced that the Academy had taken a step forward in establishing binding rules for spelling, thereby creating a basis from which by gradual further changes an unambiguous spelling system might be reached. In October a delegation of the Movement actually appeared before the Minister of Education and Culture and urged him to make the Academy's decision law. On some occasions after that, members of the Academy appeared in public debates with members of the Movement, in which both sides agreed in urging the acceptance of the Academy's rules by the public, with the Movement only differing in insisting on a more rapid rate of change in the future.

At the time of writing, February 1969, it is too early to say whether the intensive public discussion and the large amount of space given to the matter in the daily press have produced a change of public climate, in which the Academy's rules will be greeted as at least a partial solution and in which there will be a pressure for proceeding with further reforms in the direction of developing the full spelling. So far, the Movement has not grown beyond its original circle of members; nor has there been a tendency for writers independent either of the Academy or the Movement for an Unambiguous Spelling to enter into serious public discussion of the problems. The Minister of Education and Culture has not yet counter-signed the Academy's resolution to make it law. A question asked in the Israeli parliament concerning the "illegal" use of combined spelling (pointed full spelling) in the immigrant's weekly, financed by the Ministry of Education and Culture, did not elicit a statement on the government's intentions with regard to the spelling reform. The matter is thus still under deliberation.

About the hope that newspapers would take up the new spelling voluntarily, there are no signs of this as yet. Nor has the Academy embarked so far on an intensive campaign to obtain such voluntary adherence. Thus no facts are available to show what response could be obtained.

DISCUSSION

Two factors contribute to the success of vocabulary planning. First, such planning meets a real need and serves the immediate purposes of well-defined groups in the country. Since these groups need a standardized technical vocabulary, they are generally willing to take the normative side of the activity into the bargain. Only few among the professional customers have strong views on language matters: most of them are apt to view the members of the terminology committees with the respect of one expert for another expert and to accept their judgment in linguistic questions. Second, vocabulary comes in small units, and its digestion by the social organisms that it affects takes place with very minor upheavals. Objections are always to specific terms only, and the unwillingness to accept one or two terms out of what is generally a list of hundreds is possible without visibly upsetting the process as a whole.

As against this, a spelling reform affects all at once the entire web of communication. It cannot be introduced gradually but requires an immediate willingness to change habits. In many cases, it also requires an outlay of money in new type or in the adaptation of typewriters, and especially in reprinting school-books and, in the case of far-reaching reforms, reprinting large numbers of books in common use. The class that has to bear the brunt of the reform is not that of technical experts indifferent to linguistic niceties but educators, writers and journalists, and proofreaders and printing-room supervisors, people who are most closely tied up with the working of the previous spelling system and probably emotionally attached to it through the long process of having gotten skilled in handling it. One might almost surmise that the more complicated the spelling, the greater the unwillingness of its successful operators to abandon what cost them so much trouble to acquire and, in some cultures, what contributed so much to their status. It is also these people who are best qualified, and most inclined, to see the unavoidable flaws in the new spelling. On the other hand, they will often be temperamentally disinclined to visualize the need for compromise that is responsible for some of those flaws. Discussions on the Hebrew spelling reform have often amazed the present writer by instances of writers and scholars, with deep attachment to linguistic tradition, insisting on absurdly far-reaching and over-logical reforms involving a recasting of the grammar.

The difference between the planning of vocabulary and of spelling exists in a similar form within the planning body itself. The requirements of vocabulary planning and the need to have a body with authority lead to a policy of staffing the planning body with leading scholars, writers, poets, and outstanding educators, generally with people above the age of forty, who have made a success of their occupations. Such people have proved on occasion to be allergic even to vocabulary innovations and over-sensitive to literary and esthetic associations of words. They are, of course, all highly skilled in the use of the existing spelling, strongly aware of its historical roots, and personally unaffected by its difficulties. They may even have learned to turn these difficulties to their advantage, such as playing intentionally on the vagueness, or exploiting spurious graphic similarities. They can see all the flaws, and their whole training has conditioned them to insist on truth and consistency and to reject compromise, to the extent of unwillingness even to bow to the outcome of votes. This leads to a form of discussion in which, instead of having a growing consent, there is an increasing sharpening of positions. Unused to the give-and-take policy-making, many of those present react as if they took part in a scientific discussion, in which the facts emerging in the argument serve mainly to provide further refinement and solidity to their own theory.

Another result of the social characteristics of Academy members is the low rate of attendance at plenary meetings. Members have many other calls on their time; some spend sabbaticals abroad or attend conferences; and the high average age means that a percentage is always unable to attend because of illness. The need to have vocabulary committees in different towns and the wish to associate all universities mean that many members have to travel to attend the meetings that take place at two-monthly intervals. The average attendance is eighteen to twenty-five, but with strong variations in individual composition. Thus any progress towards compromise at one plenary meeting is often nullified by the different personal composition of the next. The consistent and fruitful work of the committees is in strong contrast to the climate in which their proposals are subsequently debated in the plenary sessions. The committee members have on various occasions given expression to their feelings of frustration because of this difference (though it needed such experiences to bring it home to them).

In the case of the Hebrew Language Academy, we have something in the nature of a control-experiment. During the same year that the spelling was debated, the Academy has also been engaged in a large-scale program of laying down rules for the inflection of nouns. The cause for this is that, with regard to many nouns, the original sources of the language provide alternative formations and inflections and that the intensive creation of new nouns has set many new problems of this kind. The Permanent Committee for Grammar of the Academy (the same body that constituted the 1962 committee for spelling) has been working since before 1953 on a complete regulation of all possible forms of nouns, and its proposals were presented chapter by chapter to the plenum. The decisions often involved giving up linguistic habits cherished by the educated historical connections and the like and dealt, like the spelling, with matters of direct concern to every speaker. The discussions were often drawn out, and members were inclined to insist tenaciously on their opinion so that others felt these discussions to be unbearably dull. However, as the subject-matter was divided into small sections and as there was no need at any point to insist on the bearing of any decision on the structure of Hebrew as a whole (which only the professional linguists among the members were trained to do anyway), it was possible to finish point after point, chapter after chapter and, today, a large part of the work has been done. The new rules are now being taught in the schools, and there has been no marked opposition—on the contrary, the general attitude is one of relief that an official decision exists on these knotty points.

It can thus be argued that the feature that makes spelling reforms so much more arduous to agree on than other areas of language planning is its systematic character. Instances can be produced of successful and easy spelling reforms that concerned only details, as, for instance, the German abolition of *th* for /t/ about 1900, or the short-interval spelling revisions of Holland and Norway. This consideration was, as we pointed out, in the minds of some of the members responsible for the decisions that were finally taken. There is something attractive about the idea of accomplishing a large-scale spelling reform in easy stages at, say, five- or ten-year intervals so that each step does not have a systematic character and does not change too much the accustomed look of the printed page. Since, in such a procedure, texts written in the last-stage spelling would still be fully intelligible to those taught the spelling in its new stage, this would obviate mass reprinting of books. It may be assumed that widely read books would in any event be reprinted during a ten-year period and that books for which no one saw any need to reprint during twenty years were likely to be read only by specialists who would be trained to understand older spellings. Those responsible for the reform would be able to take full advantage of experience and scientific follow-up studies, as well as in printing techniques and linguistics. As against this, there are at least two snags, however small. A change in spelling costs organizational effort and money, and the gradual change is likely to be considerably more costly to the national economy than would one large change. Carrying out a revolution over a number of decades presupposes a sense of planning and continuity of purpose such as can scarcely be expected from a body composed mainly of middle-aged and elderly scholars and literary men.

The Hebrew Language Academy did, over the last few years, a great deal to improve its communications with the general public. It employs a speaker whose task it is to seek out opportunities for publicizing the Academy's decisions in the press, the radio, and elsewhere and who reacts to the appearance of terms in the press that conflict with those established by the Academy. A well-printed regular news-sheet, made specially to be exhibited on walls of schools, offices, and factories, discusses groups of terms and gives grammatical information. It appears, however, that these devices are not suitable for winning the public for a large systematic change such as a new spelling. In this, the Academy is so far dependent on government approval and the hope that the Ministry will be quick and efficient in enforcing the change upon the schools; and, for the rest, it has been relying upon the daily press. The latter, of course will carry this item only as long as it has news value, and that is just not long enough to make any impression on the public. In fact, without the fortuitous appearance of the "Movement for an Unambiguous Hebrew Spelling," the reform decision might have passed almost unnoticed.

In the discussions following immediately after the meeting in which the reform was voted, it became clear to the members of the Directorate that no one really knew how such a spelling reform was to be put into practice. There is great uncertainty regarding such questions as how much time should be allowed before the date on which the new spelling would become obligatory; what should be done about school children (should they be made to change suddenly, or should they be allowed to finish elementary school with the spelling they had already learnt?); who should be made to pay for the extra letters printers would need?

It would be most important for countries envisaging spelling reform that some research should be undertaken by an international body to review the procedures by which recent spelling reforms were effected in a number of countries, both developed and developing, if possible with some critical evaluation and legal and sociological comment. Such guidance would save psychological errors, omissions, and unnecessary expense.

6. LANGUAGE-PLANNING PROCESSES AND THE LANGUAGE-POLICY SURVEY IN THE PHILIPPINES

BONIFACIO P. SIBAYAN
Language Study Center, Philippine Normal College, Manila

INTRODUCTION

A commission that examined the achievements of the public school system after twenty-five years of education in English claimed in 1925:

. . . there is little or no tendency toward building up a common language through a fusion of all or several of the dialects.[1]

Fifteen years later, the following was said on the same subject by Hayden (1942):

. . . in a little more than four years by an orderly, rational process the Philippine Commonwealth has laid the foundations for the establishment of a native national language. From the administrative and scholarly standpoint this is a surprising achievement. Even more remarkable are the facts that one of the Philippine languages was selected as the basis of the national language without acrimonious struggle and that this decision has been popularly accepted without serious protest by the other linguistic groups in the Islands (p. 585).

Hayden generously says that it took less than four years for the Filipinos to build the foundations of a national language. It is more accurate to say, however, that it took more than five years. This covers the period from February 8, 1935, when the Constitution was adopted, which provided that steps should be taken by the National Assembly for the development of a national language up to June 7, 1940, when a law was passed declaring the national language to be an official language on July 4, 1946.[2]

Furthermore, the same commission (Monroe, 1925) commented as follows on the use of the Philippine languages (dialects): " . . . the introduction of the dialects as the language of instruction would be a divisive influence" (p. 26).

In 1957, the policy determining body of the Republic of the Philippines, the Board of National Education (1958), decided:

> The Board adopts as a policy the use of the native language as the medium of instruction in Grades I and II in all public and private schools and urges the school authorities to take practical steps towards its implementation (p. 18).

It is understandable why the recognition of the value of the local languages in the life of the people took a much longer time to develop. The vernaculars do not have the urgency that a national language demands in the affairs of the nation. Even now, after more than a decade of their use in the schools, their value is still being questioned in some quarters. In fact, the vernacular is still not used in many exclusive private schools.[3]

On the other hand, the national language was seriously being considered as the language of instruction in the elementary and secondary schools by 1967. A Committee on Curriculum of the Board of National Education proposed that Pilipino be used as the medium of instruction.

This proposal, however, did not seem very popular.[4] The wisdom of a sudden change in the language of instruction to Pilipino from the vernaculars (in Grades 1 and 2) and from English (in Grades 3 through high school) was questioned by many responsible educators. It was obvious that important changes in policy were inspired by nationalistic tendencies and not by objective data. This situation created the need for a study. The Language Study Center of the Philippine Normal College proposed that a language-policy survey be undertaken as a basis for making policy decisions and as a baseline for evaluating the results of any change in language policy. This proposal was presented to the Board of National Education, which endorsed it in March 1968.

I shall confine my discussion only to the events in the postwar years since the processes that led to the adoption of the national language have been discussed in detail in several works.[5]

BEFORE THE SURVEY: YEARS OF FERMENT AND DEBATE

I list below the events that I shall discuss in some detail:

1948–54: the Iloilo experiment on the use of the vernacular as the language of instruction;[6]

1950–68: the coming of age in the Philippines of linguistics and second-language teaching;

June 3, 1955: the establishment of the Board of National Education, which determines educational policy matters in the Philippines;

July 1957: the start of the use of vernaculars as languages of instruction in the first two grades;

1960–66: two more experiments in Iloilo and Rizal;

1967–68: the word-war—the Congress investigates the procedures and ways of developing the national language; purists versus anti-purists; the use of conversational Pilipino in place of "pure Tagalog" by *Taliba*; orthography and *Katas;*

1967: proposal for the use of Pilipino as the language of instruction.

Experiment on the Use of Vernaculars: 1948–54

The use of vernaculars as media of instruction in the elementary school was tried in Iloilo in 1948–54. The experiment grew out of many factors and desires, the most important of which, according to Dr. Jose V. Aguilar, was the need to improve the life of the average Filipino citizen through the community school. It was thought that, with the use of the vernacular, both parent and child would benefit because what is learned in school could be discussed with the parent and because what is happening in the community could be discussed in school. The experiment proved the superiority of the vernacular as the language of instruction in the initial stage of education, in terms of what the child should learn, and in his social growth. By 1956–57, twenty-two school divisions were given permission to use the vernaculars.[7]

Establishment of the Board of National Education

Up until 1954, there had been no single body charged with determining language policy. The goal of the development of a national language was set by the Constitution, and its details were elaborated by legislative acts, the President of the Philippines, and the Institute of National Language.[8]

In June 1955, an Act of Congress created the Board of National Education. The Board is authorized "to formulate general education objectives and policies, co-ordinate offerings, activities and functions of all educational institutions in the country with a view to carrying out the provisions of the constitution and to accomplishing an integrated, well-rounded nationalistic and democracy-inspired educational system in the Philippines."[9]

One of the most difficult problems that confronted the members of the Board of National Education had been the conflicting views regarding the use and function, in the schools, of the vernaculars, the national language, Pilipino,[10] English, and Spanish. In 1957, however, after almost two years of study and discussion, the Board issued the Revised Educational Program, which provided the use of the vernaculars as languages of instruction. The Secretary of Education thereafter directed that both public and private schools were to take practical steps in the use of the vernaculars in the first two grades. Pilipino was to be taught as a subject from Grade 1 through college (undergraduate degree), while English was to be taught informally in the first two grades and used as the language of instruction from Grade 3 through college.[11] Such has been the language system till now.

Linguistics and Second-Language Teaching: 1950–69

In 1949, the teaching of English as a second language was introduced to the Philippines by Clifford H. Prator, who was on a Fulbright lectureship at the time. He summarized his impressions, experiences, and recommendations in his monograph, *Language Teaching in the Philippines*. Prator's work was mainly responsible in starting a movement that not only affected the teaching of English but also stimulated a host of other interests as follows: keener attention to Philippine vernaculars; the use of linguistics in language teaching; the study of linguistics as a subject; the establishment of academic programs in applied linguistics mostly on the graduate level; the writing of materials on language teaching, with the use of linguistic findings; the education of teachers, supervisors, and administrators in linguistics and language teaching; and the establishment of centers for the study of language, such as the Language Study Center of the Philippine Normal College, in 1962.

It was also during this period that the need for teaching materials was felt. The first prototype teachers' guide in the teaching of English as a second language was written in 1956–58 in the Bureau of Public Schools.[12] This guide was to be revised later by the Philippine Center for Language Study (PCLS), which was established under the auspices of the University of California, Los Angeles (UCLA), at the request of the Department of Education and with funds from the Rockefeller Foundation.

The UCLA-PCLS program was significant to the movement because it assisted (1) in the training and education in the United States of more than a hundred teachers, supervisors, and administrators; (2) in the production of models of teaching manuals and materials, including materials on the teaching of Pilipino as a second language in non-Tagalog-speaking areas; (3) in the introduction of courses in second-language teaching at the Philippine Normal College; and (4) in conducting experiments on the use of English, Pilipino, and the vernaculars.

Interest in linguistics and language teaching has also led to added concern in allied fields such as psycholinguistics, sociolinguistics, and social psychology. The increasing number of academic institutions offering courses in linguistics and language teaching and the support of thirty scholarships in this field by the Department of Education at the Language Study Center are among the more important developments towards language-planning processes to date.

Two Experiments: Rizal and Iloilo II, 1960–66

Two large-scale experiments (Davis, 1967) were conducted jointly by the Philippine Center for Language Study and the Bureau of Public Schools in 1960–66. One was the Rizal experiment, which involved thirty teachers and 1,490 pupils in thirty schools for six years. This study showed (1) that it is advisable to introduce reading in English in Grade 1 (in the fourth month), instead of in Grade 2 as advocated by a number of authorities in the field of second-language teaching; and (2) that, of the three schemes in the use of English and the vernacular in the first six years of school, *a*) the pupils taught in an all-English curriculum in Grades 1 to 6 produced the best results; *b*) those taught in the vernacular for four years and then in English in Grades 5 and 6 were the next best; and *c*) the pupils taught in the prevailing scheme of two years in the vernacular and English in Grades 3 through 6 came out the poorest.

Apparently, the results of this study have not been considered seriously by those who are in a position to make curriculum changes. I remember that when the results were coming in, a series of ten meetings were conducted to discuss the results with Fredrick Davis, consultant to the experiment. Some of the most highly placed persons in the Department of Education attended the conferences. There was a great deal of dismay over the fact that the English curriculum proved most effective. The discussions also brought out the disparity in the three systems: the teachers in the English curriculum were better trained and the materials were better prepared.

The other experiment, the Iloilo II study, justified the use of the vernacular and the simultaneous teaching of two second languages, English and Pilipino, in non-Tagalog-speaking provinces. Again, the experiment proved the value of adequately trained teachers, carefully prepared materials, and excellent supervision. This study disproved the notion that the teaching or use of three languages simultaneously would confuse the child.

The Word-War of Pilipino: 1967–68

A speech delivered on the floor of the House of Representatives by Congressman Aguedo F. Agbayani,[13] chairman of the Committee on Education and member of the Board of National Education, virtually started the word-war on Pilipino. Congressman Agbayani accused the Institute of National Language of failure to develop a national language in the thirty years of its existence. He also called the attention of the nation to two important problems in the development of a national language; namely, the borrowing of words and the spelling of these borrowed words in Pilipino. The word-war that followed was to be a war in two senses: the fact that the word output from the congressional investigation on the evolvement of Pilipino and those that appeared in print in the newspapers and magazines by people from all walks of life was tremendous; and the fact that the debate concentrated on what words to borrow and how to spell them.[14]

Congressman Agbayani mentioned the "communication gap" or the "crisis of understanding" between the government and the people. He attributed this problem to a number of causes: the use of difficult language called "officialese" in communicating ideas; the use of English by mass media; and, worst of all, the use of "pure" Tagalog by newspapers. He cited the *Taliba* as an exception. *Taliba* is the largest national language newspaper in Manila, which started to use "conversational or colloquial Filipino"—simple Tagalog, which has borrowings from English and Spanish.[15]

The *Taliba* style was to be discussed by newspaper editors and columnists and commented on by many people in the letters-to-the-editor columns. It was evident that the majority were in favor of the anti-purists' brand of Pilipino, the *Taliba* style.

In response to Agbayani's speech, the House voted unanimously "to re-examine the procedures being followed by the government in evolving a national language understood by all Filipinos."[16] The congressional hearings that followed were conducted by committees on education and national language and brought forth the "purists" and the "anti-purists." The anti-purists (whom I prefer to call popularizers), led by Geruncio Lacuesta, a lawyer and publisher of a magazine called *Katas,* were most active in the hearings.

Lacuesta used to be of the same school of thought as most of those in the Institute of National Language until he started deviating from the twenty-letter *abakada* and began advocating the spelling of borrowed words the way they are spelled in the lending languages. This practice must have prompted the director of the Institute to recommend that *Katas* be excluded from the approved reading list of the Bureau of Public Schools. (With government money, the public schools can subscribe to newspapers and magazines or buy books that are on the list approved by the Bureau.) Lacuesta has since been on the warpath. He lobbied for the passage of a bill calling for the abolition of the Institute and the creation of an *Academia ng Wikang Filipino.* The bill did not prosper in Congress.[17]

The language debate subsided by the middle-half of 1967. In July 1968, the language problem was again being debated in the papers. Congressman Agbayani wrote an article, "A Realistic Approach to the Language Problem," in which he summarized the results of the congressional hearings a year earlier. He concluded by saying:

All controversial questions on the national language, except the question on the alphabet, have already been settled by law. The "combatants" in the language "war" must, therefore, lay down their arms. They and we must utilize our efforts and energies for the accelerated implementation of the decisions we have already made, which are embodied in the law . . . .[18]

It is not clear to this writer why Congressman Agbayani thinks that only the alphabet remains controversial.

A Proposal for the Use of Pilipino

The Committee on Curriculum of the Board of National Education sub-

mitted a modified and less ambitious version of their original recommendation for the use of Pilipino. The members recommended that Pilipino
be used only in the first four grades of school. Because their plans were
set back by one year, they now want to start in 1970–71 instead of 1969–
70. It is not known when the Board will start considering the recommendation. Congressman Agbayani has publicly stated that the status quo
should be maintained pending results of the Philippine Normal College
studies (meaning the Language Policy Survey).

THE LANGUAGE POLICY SURVEY

Background of the Survey

As stated earlier, the Committee on Curriculum of the Board of National
Education proposed that Pilipino be used as the language of instruction
starting in the school year 1969–70. Pilipino was to be used in the first
year of school and then extended one grade every year thereafter so that,
by the school year 1972–73, all primary grades would be taught in
Pilipino, with English as a subject. By 1973–74, Pilipino was to be the
medium of instruction in Grade 5 and extended one grade every year to
the fourth year of high school in social studies, history, health, civics, and
government. Science, mathematics, and allied subjects were to be taught
in English.

The proposal also included a crash program, calling for the preparation of textbooks and teaching materials from January to March, the
training of key teachers from April to June, and the training of all teachers
from July to September 1968. The period to June 1969 was to be devoted
to the printing of textbooks and teaching materials. The training of
teachers at the district, municipal, and *barrio* levels was also to take place
during this period. By July 1969, Pilipino was to be used in Grade 1 in
all subjects in all schools.

It was obvious from the proposal that the proponents disregarded
the realities of textbook and teaching-materials production. They were
unaware, moreover, of the length of time and difficulty involved in training teachers. Even more serious an oversight was the fact that the committee did not take into account the opinions and attitudes of the people
who were to be involved in the change.

The proposal met considerable opposition. The outcry from a group
of educators literally forced the committee to call for hearings on the
proposal. At this point, the Committee on Curriculum was constrained

to withdraw its recommendation, and it created an *ad hoc* committee to study the matter further.

It became clear from the discussions that such a radical shift in the language of instruction in the schools should take into consideration what the people thought about the proposal. This gave the staff of the Language Study Center the idea of conducting a language-policy survey.

Although there had been a number of surveys (Monroe, 1925, pp. 24–28; Swanson, 1960, pp. 93–111) involving the schools in the Philippines, partly on language, there was never a large-scale survey in depth on the people's attitudes towards language.

Scope

The survey was intended to gather data to answer the following general questions:

1. Attitudes towards language[19]
   a) What language do people prefer or expect their educational system to use?
   b) What connection do people see between language and occupational or social advancement?
   c) What language or languages do people actually use in their daily communication?
2. Data on the educational system
   a) What languages are actually being used in the schools as the media of instruction or as auxiliary media of instruction? What is the competence of the teachers in these languages?
   b) What study materials are available to the students? In what languages are these written, by whom, and where were they printed?
   c) What subjects are best taught in what languages?
3. Data on mass communication media
   a) What languages are used in mass communication media?
   b) What facilities are available for mass information, and how effective are they?
4. Data on the status of six of the major languages
   a) How standardized are the six major languages?

The Staff

At the start of the survey, the staff consisted of the senior staff of the

Language Study Center with Dr. Fe T. Otanes, acting director and linguist, as staff leader.[20]

Data-collecting Instruments

Six data-collecting instruments (five questionnaires and fifty-item word lists) were developed for the survey. The questionnaires were divided into the following populations: householder, teacher, publisher, radio station, and adolescents. The word lists were for Bikol, Cebuano, Hiligaynon, Ilocano, Tagalog (Pilipino), and Waray.

Of the questionnaires, the householder questionnaire is the most extensive and important. It consists of two parts: four pages to yield general information on biography, economy (type of dwelling furniture, etc.), and the like, and some questions that are asked if the respondent does not qualify for further interview; twenty pages to yield information on the respondent's and his family's language background, his opinions and preferences on language use, his attitudes on variations in language, his knowledge and preferences of language in the schools, and more detailed information on his economic and social standing.

The teacher questionnaire consists of two parts: seven pages are used to record information on the actual work of the interviewee, his background and competence, the languages he actually uses in teaching, and the languages he favors or discourages for teaching certain subjects; six pages are used for gathering information on textbooks, supplementary materials, periodicals, reference books, teacher-prepared materials, and radio or television (or both) programs used in teaching various subjects. The quantity, date of publication (for books and periodicals), source (radio or television), the frequency of use, and the language used are recorded.

The publisher questionnaire has two parts: the first part yields information on the type of publishing business, the kind of materials produced, and the length of time the firm has been in operation; the second part is used to record information on printing facilities and capabilities.

The radio station questionnaire consists of eight pages for recording facilities and programs and for recording how widespread these programs are.

The adolescents questionnaire was aimed at collecting information on language background, language skills, language preferences, language uses, attitudes towards languages; and information on their educational and social background.

Interview Areas

The Philippines was divided into 21 regions, consisting of approximately 12 communities to each region except Manila, which was divided into 23 communities. A total of 259 communities were surveyed. The communities were selected for each region with the assistance of the director of the Bureau of Census and Statistics and on the basis of how well these communities reflected the demographic characteristics of the region. Except for Manila and the capitals of the provinces, most of the communities were smaller population centers (*barrios*).

Respondents

An average of 4 householders from the *poblacions* [21] and 3 from each of the *barrios* were interviewed, giving a total of 2,376 householders.

Selection of householders was based on their proximity to important landmarks in the town, the type of house they lived in, the length of residence (at least five years or five of the last eight years), their age (less than fifty years old), and on the fact that they must have children who have had some schooling or who are of preschool age.

An interviewee was rejected if he did not meet the above criteria; if any member of his family was a school teacher in the elementary or secondary schools; or if a relative of his had been interviewed in the same *barrio*.

Teachers were interviewed in at least one public and one private elementary school where the children of most of the householder-interviewees study. In elementary schools, teachers in Grades 1, 3, and 5 (or 4) were interviewed. In places where there was only a private high school and no private elementary school, first-year teachers were interviewed. A total of 2,342 teachers were interviewed.

A total of 1,577 adolescents, between the ages of twelve and eighteen, a total of 130 radio and television-station owners, and 194 publishers and printers were also interviewed.

Interviewers: Selection, Training, and Compensation

Twenty-three interviewers or field-workers (twelve males and eleven females), all graduates with either an A.B. or a B.S. in Commerce, were selected. Teachers were not employed.[22] The field-workers were given fifteen days of training beginning in April 1968. Thirteen days were spent according to a daily schedule that covered the following: phonetics, consisting mainly of training in notating the word lists; interview techniques; word-elicitation techniques; study of the various questionnaires, including translation of the questions into the language (dialect) of the interview. Two days were spent for practice-interviews in Manila and the suburbs.

Data Collection

The survey was officially started on May 17, 1968. The field-workers tried interviewing in the Manila region before they were sent out to their respective regions. Interviewers were assigned to their native regions. A standard procedure was followed by the interviewer upon arrival in a community: he was to register with the police department and then call on the mayor and the superintendent of schools to whom he was to present several letters of introduction and a copy of a letter on the nature of his work, which had been sent earlier to the mayor. Interviewers were allotted ten days to finish the task in each community. Interviews were recorded in English. All householders started by answering the first general portion of the questionnaire, and, if acceptable, according to the criteria for further interviewing, they answered the rest of the questions. Those who are native speakers of one of the six languages in the word lists were requested to give responses to these. In addition to native speakers of Tagalog, non-native speakers who claimed to speak the language fluently were asked to respond. In cases where not one of the householders was a native speaker of any of the six languages in the word lists, schoolteachers were asked instead. Word lists were also collected from adolescents. The number of word lists collected are shown in Table 1, according to language and respondent.

In addition to data gathered through the questionnaires, each interviewer completed a community data information sheet. A daily record was also kept.

Supervision

To insure the correctness of data, three supervisors were assigned to work with all interviewers. Follow-up work was conducted by the supervisors, especially during the first phase of the survey. Names and addresses of respondents were taken from the questionnaires, and then a sample of respondents were contacted and asked whether they were actually interviewed. Spot checks were also made without the knowledge of the interviewers. One interviewer was released because he did not satisfy the

Table 1: Word Lists Collected and Tabulated by Language and Respondent

Language	Householder	Teacher	Adolescent	Total
Bicolano	164	0	144	308
Cebuano	413	19	281	713
Hiligaynon	216	18	185	419
Ilocano	353	18	195	566
Tagalog	726	72	522	1,320
Waray	143	0	71	214
Total	2,015	127	1,398	3,540

standards of the job. The supervisors also took charge of all field arrangements.

All interviewers returned to Manila at least twice during the six-month period. During the first week of October, a regional conference was held in Cebu City.

The development of instruments, training of interviewers, and actual gathering of data from all over the islands took approximately eight months.

Data-processing and Analysis

Coding for computer analysis was started in November and is now still going on. All data are coded and punched to cover later unpredictable needs. The questions to be answered first and for which appropriate computer programs are being written are the following:

1. What is the attitude of the people as a whole and by regions towards the vernacular, Pilipino, and English as the language of instruction in the primary, intermediate, and secondary schools?
2. Which language is best suited for which subjects in the schools?
3. Which languages are needed for success in certain occupations?
4. Are parents aware of the languages being used to teach their children?
5. Why do people want their children to speak Pilipino, English, or the vernacular?

6. What form of Pilipino is most acceptable?
7. What are the language preferences of Pilipinos for speaking, reading, listening, and writing?
8. Is instruction in English a reason strong enough for sending a child to a private school?
9. Is Tagalog a different language from Pilipino?
10. Who should determine the language of instruction in schools?

Initial Findings

Partial data on 221 respondents (130 householders and 91 teachers) in Manila and the suburbs was analyzed to offer some preliminary findings.

Languages for contact and reading. The favored language used in speaking to relatives (contacts) is Tagalog, while the favored language of contact in writing is English. It is interesting that a number of people who report such "major" languages as Bikol, Pampango, and Ilocano as their first language do not use these languages as language of contact with relations, at least for the first three contacts listed.[23] It is possible that many of these people use either English or Tagalog now. This would seem to confirm the view that non-Tagalog-speaking Filipinos who migrate to Manila would sooner or later have minimum use of their ethnic language.

Regarding reading, most Manila respondents report that they have read in Tagalog and in English (which is to be expected) because most publications are in these two languages. More people report reading in Tagalog than in English, which seems contrary to a common belief that there are more people who read in English because of the reputedly large circulation of newspapers and magazines in English.

Language spoken best. Tagalog was reported as the language spoken best by 158 out of 221 respondents. Ilocano was reported by 7, and other languages by fewer people.

Languages needed for success in occupations. What language or combination of languages is felt to be needed for success in certain occupations? One who knows only Pilipino would succeed as carpenter, farmer, fisherman, housewife, and seller (market). A knowledge of Pilipino and English is considered necessary for success as clerk, physician, electrician, lawyer, mayor, mid-wife, policeman, postman, priest, secretary, and seller (big stores). One who knows only Spanish or only a non-Tagalog Philippine language would not succeed in any of the sixteen occupations listed. On the other hand, the combination of Pilipino, English, and Spanish would mean success for lawyers, priests, and physicians. This would seem to show the influence of Spanish on the learned professions. The only occupation where one might succeed if one knew only English is that of clerk. This may be attributed to the fact that the main language of the government is English.

While almost a third of the respondents think that a combination of Pilipino and English would be needed for success in carpentry, not one respondent thinks that a combination of Pilipino and Spanish would be needed. Success is practically assured in all the occupations if one knows a combination of Pilipino and English. And if one were to choose only one language for success, it would be Pilipino.[24]

ACKNOWLEDGMENT

The Language Policy Survey is a project of the Language Study Center of the Philippine Normal College, Manila. It was endorsed by the Board of National Education and was conducted with the cooperation of officials from the Department of Education and local governments in the areas surveyed. It is financed, in part, by grants from the Ford Foundation and the Asia Foundation.

I wish to express my sincere thanks to the following friends and colleagues: Fe T. Otanes, Robert C. Gardner, and Benjamin M. Pascual, of the Language Study Center; and Edilberto Dagot, of the Reading Center, for their assistance as well as for their comments and critical reading of an earlier draft of this paper; Attorney Cipriano Saga, secretary of the Board of National Education, for making available to me transcribed stenographic notes of the proceedings and other documents of the Board of National Education; Aurora L. Sore for assistance in checking data; Restituto Cena, Alfonso Santiago, and Ellen Papa for typing various versions of the paper; and to Emma F. Bernabe for criticizing and editing the manuscript.

NOTES

1. Monroe (1925, p. 24). This is popularly known in the Philippines as the *Monroe Survey Report.*
2. Commonwealth Act No. 570, June 7, 1946. English, Spanish, and Pilipino are official languages. Pilipino is the national language.
3. Two reasons why private schools are allowed to use English instead of the vernaculars in the first two grades are: (1) the main purpose of the use of the vernacular is to assure the child's literacy if he should drop out,

though most of the children in private schools do not drop out; and (2) parents may exercise the right to choose the education they should give their children. (Private communication, Dr. Narciso Albarracin, director of Private Schools.)

4. Maximo Ramos, president of the Philippine Association for Language Teaching, wrote on the subject: "You're not supposed to know, but a plan now close to launching stage is in the works to make Tagalog (Pilipino) the teaching medium for all but two or three subjects in the public schools .... By design or otherwise, only a handful of people in this supposedly open society are in on the scheme ...." Maximo Ramos, Pilipino or Bust, *Philippines Free Press*, 6 July 1969, p. 4 ff.

5. For the most complete account, see Frei (1959). For a shorter account, see Hayden (1950, chapter 24).

6. For evaluative reports on the experiment, see Bureau of Public Schools, Manila: *Bulletin*, nos. 9, 12, 14, 16, series 1953; no. 6, series 1954; and no. 9, series 1955. For an interpretative account of the experiment, see Ramos, Aguilar, and Sibayan (1967).

7. Venancio Trinidad, former director of the Bureau of Public Schools, before the Board of National Education, April 24, 1956. Stenographic notes of the proceedings of the Board of National Education.

8. Republic Act No. 1124, June 16, 1954. The Board was composed of fifteen members: the Secretary of Education; the Chairman of the Committee on Education in the House of Representatives; the Chairman of the Committee on Education of the Senate; the Director of Public Schools; the Director of the Bureau of Private Schools; the President of the University of the Philippines; the Chairman of UNESCO, Philippines; a representative of labor; a representative of industry and management; a representative of agriculture; a representative of the Catholic Education Association of the Philippines; a representative of Mohammedan and other cultural minority groups; a representative of the Association of Christian Schools and Colleges (Protestant); a representative of the Philippine Association of Colleges and Universities; and a representative of the teaching profession. The present membership as provided in the 1965 law consists of the Secretary of Education and seven members.

9. Republic Act No. 4372, June 19, 1965.

10. The term, *"Pilipino,"* was officially adopted to refer to the national language beginning August 13, 1959. See Department Order No. 7, series 1959, Department of Education, Manila. The spelling of Pilipino with a *"P"* has not been accepted by a number of Filipinos.

11. See Department Order No. 1, series 1957, Department of Education, Manila. Enclosed also in Circular No. 3, series 1957, Bureau of Public Schools, Manila.

12. By Bonifacio P. Sibayan and Fe Manza. For complete series, see *Teacher's Guide in Teaching English in Grade I, Memorandum*, nos. 111, 153, series 1957; nos. 32, 58, 81, 95, 136, series 1958. Manila: Bureau of Public Schools.

13. See Aguedo F. Agbayani, Development and Evolution of Our National Language, *Manila Times*, 10 March 1967.
14. This controversy on spelling proves Haugen's (1966) contention that in LP the written form of language, rather than speech, is primary: "... in the study of LP we shall have to ... consider writing primary and speech secondary" (p. 53).
15. After the switch from "pure" Tagalog to "conversational Filipino," the daily circulation of the paper rose from 19,000 (January 1967) to 30,000 in a month's time. On June 30, 1969, the audited circulation (after return of unsold copies) was 77,096, and in January 1969, two years later, the average daily circulation had gone up to 122,853. This is an indication of how readable the conversational Filipino style had become.
16. See *Manila Times*, 7 March 1967, p. 1.
17. House Bill No. 11367.
18. *Manila Times*, 28 September, 30 September 1968.
19. A small attempt at an attitude survey was made in 1965 by me. See Bonifacio P. Sibayan, Implementation of Language Policy, *in* Ramos, Aguilar, and Sibayan (1967).
20. Other senior staff members were: Dr. Richard Tucker, psycholinguist; Dr. Tommy R. Anderson, linguist; Mr. Jack Wigfield, language archives supervisor; Professor Benjamin M. Pascual, English professor and lawyer; and Miss Aurora L. Sore, field supervisor. Dr. Robert C. Gardner, social psychologist and computer expert, joined the staff in the later half of August 1968. I joined the staff upon my return to Manila in the later part of September 1968. Anderson and Tucker terminated their connection with the Center in the middle of December 1968. The staff presently analyzing the data consists of Fe T. Otanes, Robert C. Gardner, Jack Wigfield, Aurora L. Sore, Edilberto P. Dagot, Don M. Taylor, and myself.
21. The *poblacion* is the center of a municipality where the seat of government is located, in contrast to the *barrio*, which is outside the *poblacion*.
22. The interviewers were paid ₱300 a month plus ₱14 per diem while in the field (₱3.90=U.S. $1.00). An instructor who has an M.A. in a state college such as the Philippine Normal College earns ₱306 a month as starting salary.
23. Respondents were asked to name family relations not living in their community with whom they maintained contact. The questionnaire allowed for as many as seven family relations (contacts). Only the first three contacts were analyzed.
24. Pilipino is used here to mean Tagalog. In the questionnaire, the term, "Pilipino," was used. Only one respondent specifically listed Tagalog as a language needed for success in the occupations.

REFERENCES

Board of National Education. 1958. *General Education Policies*. Quezon City: Phoenix Press.

Bright, William, ed. 1966. *Sociolinguistics. Proceedings of the* UCLA *Sociolinguistics Conference, 1964.* Janua Linguarum, Series Maior, 20. The Hague: Mouton.

Davis, Fredrick B. 1967. *Philippine Language Teaching Experiments.* Quezon City: Phoenix Press.

Frei, Ernest J. 1959. *The Historical Development of the Philippine National Language.* Manila: Bureau of Printing.

Haugen, Einar. 1966. Linguistics and Language Planning. *In* Bright, 50–71.

Hayden, Joseph R. 1942 (reissue 1950). *The Philippines: A Study in National Development.* New York: Macmillan.

Monroe, Paul, chairman. 1925. *Survey of the Educational System of the Philippines.* Manila: Bureau of Printing.

Prator, Clifford H. 1950. *Language Teaching in the Philippines.* Manila: United States Educational Foundation in the Philippines.

Ramos, Maximo; Aguilar, Jose V.; and Sibayan, Bonifacio P. 1967. *The Determination and Implementation of Language Policy.* Philippine Center for Language Study, no. 2. Quezon City: Alemar-Phoenix.

Swanson, J. Chester, staff leader. 1960. *Survey of the Public Schools of the Philippines–1960.* Manila: Carmelo and Bauermann.

7. SOME FACTORS INFLUENCING LANGUAGE POLICIES IN EASTERN AFRICA

WILFRED H. WHITELEY
School of Oriental and African Studies, University of London

INTRODUCTION

Since their assumption of independence in the early sixties, the three East African countries have attracted attention by their differences rather than by their similarities, and nowhere is this more striking than in their attitudes towards, and formulations of, language policy. It is true that they all shared a colonial experience of a British pattern, more or less modified by their differing status—Kenya being a Crown Colony, Uganda a Protectorate; and Tanganyika a Mandated territory—but this tended merely to conceal, and not to destroy, factors of a historical and demographic nature, which at different times and in different degrees affected language policies in whole or in part. These factors have become increasingly important since independence, and in this paper I should like to consider the current policies in Tanzania and Kenya in terms of the interaction between certain "primary" historico-demographic factors and successive generations of policy makers, whether they have enunciated their policies in formal or informal terms. It is unfortunately impossible within the scope of this paper to consider the equally divergent situation in Uganda, but the situation will be referred to in passing.[1]

In the historical context of the latter part of the nineteenth century, it is patent that the areas over which the Germans and British assumed control were linguistically heterogenous, supporting populations that were multilingual to varying degrees. The mere fact of enclosing them within arbitrarily defined boundaries and administering them as single states, largely through expatriate officers, was certain to add a new dimension to their multilingualism. Henceforth, these countries would be linguistically tri-focal, using a non-African world language, an African lingua franca, and a localized African language in specific, well-defined social settings, which would, over time, invest these languages with particular values, themselves capable of exploitation for various purposes. I have discussed in a recent monograph[2] the pre-colonial historical factors that influenced the early administrators in their language policies; here I would like to draw attention to some of the demographic factors that seem to have influenced policy-making and to have modified the balance between the elements in the tri-focal situation.

In default of detailed and accurate figures from the earlier period, I am using those from the most recent censuses.[3] Although they are clearly of little use for making absolute statements, the situations they indicate for tribal distribution, over-all densities of population, and patterns of linguistic homogeneity within administrative districts are probably fair in relative terms. Finally, all the censuses use ethnic rather than linguistic units, but for the purposes of this paper I shall assume them to be synonymous.

THE PRE-INDEPENDENCE PERIOD

Tanzania

Tanzania covers a land area of roughly 340,000 square miles, with an average density of 25.4 persons a square mile, ranging from a regional minimum of 13.5 in the Western Region to 57.5 in the Lake Region, where nearly 25 per cent of the country's population lives. More than half the population of 8.5 million (1957) was accounted for on a little more than a sixth of the total land area. Densities in excess of 100 were restricted to the Lake Region and to one or two highland pockets (e.g., Kilimanjaro, Rungwe, Meru, and Makonde Plateau).

For the early administrators, one of the most important problems was the large number of ethnic-linguistic units, many of comparably small size. By 1957 the ten largest units accounted for only 42.7 per cent of the total population, while nearly two-thirds of the languages numbered between ten to a hundred thousand speakers only. One result of this was that when administrative districts were set up by the British, they commonly comprised two or more language units. Of the fifty-two districts listed in the 1957 census, only in 21 per cent did the dominant language unit constitute 75 per cent or more of the population in that district. In 33 per cent of the cases, it constituted between 50 to 74 per cent of the population; and in 46 per cent, it constituted between 17 to 49 per cent. This type of situation, where the units were numerically small, clearly favored the use of Swahili for administrative purposes. There were isolated occasions during the later years of the Colonial period when separatist movements, with concomitant language loyalties, sought to split districts along ethnic lines, but these proved to be abortive. A striking contrast is afforded by the case of South Nyanza in Kenya, which split into Gusii (Bantu) and Luo (Nilotic) components during the late fifties, but here the numbers involved were strikingly larger.

Another factor favoring Swahili was the absence of any large kingdoms or states around which language loyalties might coalesce. The Sukuma, who, with the closely related Nyamwezi, were probably several times as numerous as any other people (see Table 1), never formed a focus for such loyalties and were, in any case, badly placed geographically in relation to the capital. The Hehe, a people who might well have provided such a focus, had been militarily crushed by the Germans earlier. Other peoples who were important numerically (e.g., Makonde and Chagga) formed neither politically centralized nor decentralized states.

A third factor that needs to be taken into consideration was the extent to which Islamization had already been effected by the pre-colonial trading caravans and settlements. With its coastal provenance, Swahili was very closely linked with Islam, its lexicon, for example, being enriched by many hundreds of items associated with Islamic institutions. This fact was largely responsible for the early reaction against the language in Uganda, where there had been no such process of assimilation and where Islam was in immediate competition with Christian missions. By 1957, 30 per cent of Tanganyika's population claimed to be Muslims, and, among such important inland groups as the Sambaa, Rangi, Luguru, and Pogoro, Muslims constituted a large majority of the population.

Finally, Swahili is a Bantu language in a country in which 94 per cent of the population speak Bantu languages; it is closely related to several of those spoken along the littoral and behind it.

These may be regarded as the primary factors that led to the initial adoption of Swahili as the language of administration and as an important language within the educational system, first by the Germans and later by the British. Its use in such settings further contributed to its spread and development. A contribution was also made here by the formally constituted, policy-implementing body known as the East African Inter-Territorial Language (Swahili) Committee, which was set up in 1930 and which did a great deal towards developing and standardizing the language. A whole paper could be written about its activities,[4] which

Table 1: Selected Data on Tanzania's Fifteen Largest Ethnic-Linguistic Units (1957)

Ethnic-Linguistic Units	Language classification	Percentage of total population	Percentage of homogeneity in districts in which they dominate	Population density	Position in territorial density scale	Religion				Region	Education*		
						Protestant	Roman Catholic	Muslim	Other		Primary	Middle	Total
Sukuma (Kwimba)	B	12.6	96.5	130.5	5	3.5	7.2	1.2	87.9	Lake	10.6	3.9	14.5
(Maswa)		—	95.5	32.7									
Nyamwezi	B	4.2	58.8	39.2		2.8	6.1	26.0	62.9	Western	6.6	0.9	7.5
Makonde (Newala)	B	3.9	93.6	104.1	7	0.3	0.2	95.6	1.5	Southern	16.9	1.9	18.8
Haya	B	3.8	84.2	61.8		10.3	43.4	14.2	30.5	Lake	10.6	3.9	14.5
Chagga	B	3.7	85.9	179.5	2	2.3	71.8	2.0	23.8	Northern	17.0	6.0	23.0
Gogo (Dodoma and Manyoni)	B	3.4	77.2	22.0		8.0	5.6	4.0	82.2	Central	4.8	0.8	5.6
(Mpwapwa)		—	39.8	25.2									
Ha (Kasulu)	B	3.3	90.4	46.0		4.2	15.0	21.1	58.5	Western	6.6	0.9	7.5
Hehe	B	2.9	77.9	17.8		4.0	14.9	13.0	67.5	S. Highlands	11.5	1.6	13.1
Nyakyusa	B	2.5	68.9	142.4	4	23.8	3.6	.5	72.0	S. Highlands	11.5	1.6	13.1
Luguru	B	2.3	66.7	35.4		—	89.4	9.1	1.3	Eastern	12.6	2.2	14.8
Bena	B	2.2	56.5	30.4		53.4	6.7	3.8	36.8	S. Highlands	11.5	1.6	13.1
Turu	B	2.2	53.0	39.2		1.6	6.4	7.4	84.1	Central	4.8	0.8	5.6
Sambaa	B	2.2	60.5	74.3		17.7	1.1	65.1	15.6	Tanga	19.6	4.3	23.9
Zaramo	B	2.1	64.3	47.3		0.1	—	99.3	0.2	Eastern	12.6	2.2	14.8
Iramba	B	2.0	—	—		8.5	1.4	20.8	60.8	Central	4.8	0.8	5.6

extended throughout the colonial period until its absorption into the Institute of Swahili Research at the University College, Dar es Salaam in 1964.

With the passage of time, however, as a small number of local Tanganyikans became educated and aspired to responsibility in various fields of public life, the importance of Swahili became overshadowed by that of English,[5] the language of the Colonial power, from whom independence was to be extracted. English enabled a member of the educated elite to state his case in the international arena; Swahili restricted one to the local "*baraza*." English symbolized power; Swahili connoted dependence. This reaction was, essentially, a function of the educational system and of the role that education and the "educated man" played in public life. English was the medium of instruction, except in the early stages of primary education; and the lack of attention to Swahili appeared to be commensurate with its lack of status for educated persons. The equation of proficiency in English with education is still deeply held, though the present egalitarian policies are designed to change this.

Opposition to Swahili came also from some of the churches. Proselytization could only be really effective, it was argued, if carried out in the "mother tongue."[6] In some parts of the country where mission work went back without a break to the latter part of the nineteenth century, a relatively high degree of Christianization occurred (see Table 1), and in three areas in particular, Haya, Nyakyusa, and Chagga there developed— or were nourished—quite powerful, overt loyalties to the local language both as evidenced and reinforced by a religious and even secular literature (e.g., newspapers and readers). These areas had certain features in common: all were border areas; all occupied fertile parts of the country which, when exploited, yielded considerable wealth, especially through coffee; and all supported a high density of population. They were all numerically important, and their districts were all linguistically homogeneous to a high degree (see Table 1). It is interesting to speculate why other areas, which might have been expected to develop similar loyalties, did not in fact do so. They shared some, but not all, of the features listed above; the question which ones were critical is difficult to answer. The Makonde occupy relatively infertile country and are almost totally Muslim—there is a positive correlation between missions and education generally. Neither the Gogo nor the Ha possesses easily exploitable natural resources, though both they and the Sukuma exhibited covert loyalty to their own languages associated with such factors as the size of area that they occupy, poor and infrequent communication with agents of administration, low incidence of towns, and poor educational facilities.

The increase in the importance of English for certain sectors of the community should not be allowed to obscure the fact that, for other sectors, the importance of Swahili probably continued to grow during the forties and fifties, though the evidence for this is not easy to obtain. Certainly, there were numerous Swahili newspapers, though the majority were controlled by the government; Swahili "pop" music flourished; and there was an increasing body of reading material produced by such bodies as the East African Literature Bureau. Furthermore, in the middle fifties, the Society for the Preservation and Development of Swahili was started both in Tanga and at the University College in Makerere.

In general, however, the tri-focal nature of language behavior was differentially stressed by the administration, education, and missions. The former demonstrated the usefulness of Swahili; education provided the incentives for learning English; the missions emphasized the emotional associations of the "mother tongue." Only in certain spheres did practice become formalized into overt policy (e.g., the courts, higher education, the councils, etc.). In general, usage reflected convenience rather than compliance to a policy formally made.

With the founding of TANU in 1954, Swahili started to play a new and increasingly important role. The party used the language as a means of political communication, and, when this was seen to be effective, it began to stress its role in the political unification of the country. If the actual negotiations for independence were carried on in English, that they could have taken place when they did was due in no small measure to the role of Swahili in creating a united front. Thus, at the achievement of independence, Swahili had already acquired the status of a "party" or "national" language.

Kenya

In sharp contrast to Tanzania, Kenya has a relatively small number of ethnic-linguistic units. Furthermore, these units are not only larger, but they also represent more equally the various language families (see Table 2). Seventy-five per cent of the population is accounted for by the seven largest groups, six Bantu and one Nilotic; of these, the Kikuyu-Meru-Kamba cluster comprises almost half. The country presents a striking series of contrasts: the arid plains that comprise more than three-quarters

Table 2: Classification of Languages of Kenya and Tanzania by
Ethnic-linguistic Units

Language Groups	Tanzania		Kenya	
	Number of Units	% of Population	Number of Units	% of Population
Bantu	102	94	13	65
Highland Nilotic				
River-Lake, e.g., Luo	1	1	1	15
Highland, e.g., Kipsigis*	3	0.5	8	11
Plains, e.g., Masai	3	1.5	5	5
Eastern Cushitic				
Eastern, e.g., Somali			4‡	4
Southern, e.g., Iraqw	4	2		
Other				
Click†	1	0.3		
Mbugu		0.1		
Total	114	99.4	31	100

*I am here following the terminology of J.E.G. Sutton (1968) in his The Settlement of East Africa, *in* B.A. Ogot and J.A. Kieran, eds. *Zamani: A Survey of East African History,* (Longmans) pp. 69-99.
†No reference is made in the census to the Handza, a second Click-speaking group.
‡The two 'Eastern Cushitic' (?) languages Waata and Dahalo are not included in the census.

of the land area (*c.* 220,000 square miles) support only a tenth of the population, while nearly three-quarters of the 8.5 million (1962) population live in the well-watered highlands on either side of the Rift Valley —the Kikuyu-Kamba to the east; the Gusii, the Luyia, and the Nilotic Luo to the west, with densities in excess of 300 persons to the square mile in most places and in excess of 1,000 in parts of the Western and Central Provinces. Between these blocks and along their periphery were substantial areas of land that were alienated to European settlement creating a linguistically dehomogenized buffer zone. As a function of the numerical size of the linguistic units, many of the administrative districts were extremely homogeneous linguistically: the dominant language group constituting 75 per cent or more of the population in 63 per cent of the districts—only in 10 per cent of cases did it constitute less than 50 per cent.

While the over-all linguistic diversity encouraged the use of Swahili as a language of administration, the size of several of the linguistic units

Table 3: Selected Data on Kenya's Fifteen Largest Ethnic-Linguistic Units (1962)

Ethnic-Linguistics Units	Language classification	Percentage of total population	Percentage of homogeneity in districts in which they dominate	Population density	Position in territorial density scale	Religion				Education*		
						Protestant	Roman Catholic	Muslim	Other	1-4	5-8	Total
Kikuyu (Fort Hall)	B	19.8	99+	626	3	50.2	21.6		28.2	23.4	26.7	50.1
(Kiambu)			98	1103	1	40.4	17.5	0.5	41.6	25.8	32.5	58.3
Luo (C. Nyanza)	N1/r	13.8	86	355	6	47.7	34.7	0.8	16.9	17.6	15.6	33.2
Luyia (N. Nyanza)	B	13.1	92	545	4	56.4	30.0	3.8	9.8	22.0	19.5	41.5
Kamba (Machakos)	B	11.2	99	121	2	50.4	10.8	0.2	38.6	20.8	14.5	35.3
Gusii	B	6.5	99	686	9	38.3	31.3	0.2	30.2	22.3	19.9	42.2
Meru	B	5.8	92	225		23.1	14.3	1.0	61.6	16.4	15.4	31.8
Mijikenda (Kilifi)	B	5.2	95	53		9.8	4.3	4.7	81.2	9.3	5.1	14.4
Kipsigis	Nh	4.1	74	203	11	29.8	26.5	0.4	43.3	24.4	14.8	39.2
Somali (Wajir)	C	3.2	100	5.6								
Turkana	Np	2.2	100	6.8								
Nandi	Nh	-2	90	197		27.3	22.9	0.3	49.4	17.9	19.4	37.3
Masai (Kajiado)	Np	-2	79	8.5		27.7	0.4	1.5	70.4	3.3	4.7	8.0
Pokot	Nh	-2	90	32		5.6	1.6	0.2	92.6	5.5	5.3	10.8
Tugen	Nh	-2	79	34		28.5	5.5	0.3	65.7	13.4	10.7	24.1
Elgeyo	Nh	-2	57	223	10	23.2	14.3	0.7	61.7	12.4	10.3	22.7

*Percentage distribution of males aged 15 and over reporting up to 8 years of schooling.

also encouraged the use of local languages and, indeed, in the Colonial period as a whole, both administrative and educational policy vacillated between the two,[7] a fact that provided another argument in favor of an increased use of English.

The position of Swahili was complicated by the fact that, although the northern Kenya coast was the center of Swahili's rich literary tradition, this tradition never moved away from the coast; up-country Kenya was never exposed to the Islamization that was so marked in Tanzania. Between 1948–62, the number of people claiming to be Muslims fell from 4.7 to 3 per cent.[8] As a result, sharp divergencies occur between the conservative varieties of the language found on the coast and those up-country varieties, which developed, for example, around the use of the language in administration, on European farms, and in the rapidly growing urban areas. Swahili also had to contend with attitudes ranging from indifference to hostility from many Nilotic speakers, from the Bantu groups like the Kikuyu and the Gusii, and from some Colonial civil servants. On the other hand, in certain national institutions (e.g., the army, police, railway, etc.), no solution other than the use of Swahili was possible so that, among groups like the Nilotic Kipsigis or Turkana that had a long tradition of police or army service, the use of the language is widely distributed among adult males. Furthermore, from the late thirties until 1952, the headquarters of the East African Inter-Territorial Language (Swahili) Committee were in Nairobi, and, although much of their work was directed towards the standardization of the language as used in schools, there is little doubt that the availability of reading material in a standardized form of the language did much to strengthen its position more generally.

As in Tanzania, it was the missions—and to a much lesser degree the primary schools—that provided the focus for interest and work in the local languages. They produced orthographies, grammars, and dictionaries, together with a fair amount of religious reading material. During the later years of the Colonial period, there were numerous newspapers in local languages, and the output of secular reading materials was given a marked impetus after 1948, by the setting up of the East African Literature Bureau. During the fifties, in particular, there was a large number of local Language Committees,[9] which, though concentrating, often inconclusively, on providing standard orthographies for their languages, did serve as important foci for local sentiment. Their activities, however, were often stultified by the equivocal nature of educational policy, which not only alternately encouraged and discouraged the use of local languages in the primary schools but also provided no on-going incentives for anything beyond the most elementary exercises. Only English, it seemed, could serve as a respectable language for educated adults.

Again, as in Tanzania, English was the medium of instruction, except in the lower forms of the primary schools; and, after 1948, efforts were increasingly made to lower both the point at which English was taught and the point at which English became the medium of instruction. Its status as a world language guaranteed its prestige amongst the educated and among those aspiring to such distinction, but its position was further enhanced by the lack of any clear alternative for the country as a whole. Following such reports as that of the Royal Commission[10] in the mid-fifties, there was a sharp cutback in the teaching of Swahili.

To sum up, language behavior in Kenya was marked by the same tri-focal character as in Tanzania, but with sharply differing emphasis. Administrative convenience and linguistic diversity favored the use of Swahili, but there was uneven popular support for the language; the size of the most important linguistic units engendered local sentiment towards language, and this was reinforced by the missions who commanded a much greater following than in Tanzania. Educational policy increasingly favored the use of English, and the language was more widely used at a much lower level than in Tanzania. This situation favored the non-formulation of any policy that might imbue any one language with a "national" image, and, as independence approached, the sensitivity of the two main political parties to any question concerning language suggested that the whole question of national unity might be at issue here.

THE POST-INDEPENDENCE PERIOD

Tanzania

The United Republic of Tanzania has taken what, in the light of previous events, seems a logical step, by adopting Swahili as the "national" language.[11] It is not always clear what Tanzanians mean by the term. One thing is clear, however, that, amongst its many meanings, that of "the language to be used on national occasions and whenever the image of the nation is on display" is very important. This does not mean, however, that Tanzanians are no longer tri-focal in their language behavior, but rather that there has been some reallocation of the settings in which specific languages are held to be appropriate. This reallocation has largely been at the expense of English in favor of Swahili and has taken place especially in those settings most likely to catch the public eye (e.g., street signs, coinage, public notices, etc.), but it has also resulted in Swahili being used in the national assembly, town councils, party meetings, the lower courts, and the like. Efforts have also been made to extend the use of Swahili into the civil service. English remains the medium of instruction in post-primary education, in the high court, as the language of technical discourse, and in anything that is most clearly associated with upward mobility.

It seems to me important to stress the informal and ideological aspect of this policy, as opposed to the technological aspects by which it is implemented. The policy should not be construed as ". . . the decisions of formally constituted organizations with respect to . . . the functional allocation of codes within a speech community . . .";[12] nor as a set of principles that necessarily require rigorous implementation, but rather as an ideological imperative, inducing a state of mind towards the language as one of the behavioral corollaries of the national ethos. Much use is made of generalized exhortations to use Swahili, on such grounds as "it is an African language," "it played a crucial role in our struggle for independence," "it is shameful to use the language of the Colonialists and neo-Colonialists," or "it is the language of the people (Wananchi)." There can be no doubt that such methods have contributed to a considerable extension in the use of the language, especially when taken in conjunction with current policies—markedly anti-elitist in character—which aim at harnessing the resources of the nation as a whole for nation-building.[13] On the other hand, those settings in which an increase in use is most conspicuous are precisely those settings that are most easily influenced by generalized exhortations and most easily implementable—e.g., public notices, meetings, and the like. What goes on out of public earshot is difficult to establish and increasingly inaccessible, as public pronouncements about appropriate linguistic behavior become more strongly worded.

To say this, however, is not to imply that no implementation has taken place. In 1964, the position of Promoter of Swahili, within the Ministry of Community Development and National Culture, was created. The promoter's task was not only to coordinate the work of local Swahili societies—where such existed—but also to disseminate to the public at large the results of any relevant research work. Two years later, the Inter-Ministry Committee was set up charged with the specific tasks of preparing lists of technical terms for use within the civil service. Finally, in 1967, following the amalgamation of the Ministry of Community Development and Culture with the Ministry of Education, the National Swahili Council was formed. Amongst its functions were listed "promoting the development and usage of the Swahili language," encouraging the "achievement of high standards" in its use, and acting as consultant over technical matters. No detailed report of the work of any of these bodies has yet been undertaken, and, indeed, it is not a field in which there is likely to be any enthusiasm for such a study.

Within the educational system, much work has gone into the revision and planning of syllabuses; the preparation of teaching materials, especially for the primary schools; and refresher courses for teachers. Swahili is now the language of instruction throughout the primary school (seven years), and there is a compulsory examination in the language before the student can start his secondary course. Courses in the language were introduced into the bachelor's program in 1964, and Swahili will be available as a full subject—with some courses taught in the language —from 1969. All this has involved some formal implementation of policy, the work devolving on bodies like the Swahili Panel, of the Institute of Education at the University College, and the Inspector of Swahili, within the Ministry of National Education. The Institute of Swahili Research at the University College was responsible for the first two Primary School Swahili Workshops held in 1965–66.

Much less formal are the activities of bodies like the national posts' association (UKUTA)—*Usanifu wa Kiswahili na Ushairi Tanzania*— which attempts to raise the level of interest in traditional poetry and in other cultural forms (e.g., plays). It is said that there are similar groups in factories, schools, and the like and that they occur right across the country.

To conclude, the mandate on Tanzanians to use Swahili as a national language is clear; the degree to which detailed implementation is being affected or effective is less clear.

Kenya

The Republic of Kenya made no pronouncement about "national" languages, and understandably so. Precedence, officially stated, for English would be liable to evoke charges of neo-Colonialism; similar precedence for Swahili would lead to strong reactions from the powerful groups on either side of the Rift Valley; precedence for one of these languages, Luo or Kikuyu, would provoke vigorous reactions from the others. Further-more, any investigation, however impartial, that established as a fact that a particular language was being given precedence and drew attention to that fact would be most unwelcome; national unity is far too precious a commodity to be risked by releasing conflicting language loyalties and all that they symbolize. On the other hand, there has been a growing feeling for some time that official recognition should be given to Swahili, and a motion was recently approved in the national assembly calling on the government to declare Swahili, as well as English, an official language for use not only in offices but also in Parliament.[14] This has now been followed by a pledge by the President that Swahili should be the country's "national language."[15] No indication has so far been made regarding how these decisions will be carried out.

That language behavior is tri-focal is tacitly accepted. In the home and amongst speakers from a single unit, the local language is used; at work, English or Swahili is used, depending upon such factors as the nature of the work, its geographical location, the educational level of the speakers, their age and sex, and the number and composition of the listeners. On public occasions, any language may be used depending on the above factors and on such other factors as the purpose of the function. In some institutions (e.g., the army, the police, the provincial administra-tion, the press, etc.), Swahili or English is characteristic; in others (e.g., the civil service, Parliament, business, and the high court), English is characteristic. Finally, in broadcasting (English, Swahili, Gujarati, and twelve local languages), in the Information Services Broadsheets (Eng-lish, Swahili, and six to eight local languages), and in education, all three receive attention to differing degrees and at varying points in the system. English is taught as a subject and is the medium of instruction throughout post-primary education and from the outset of education where the "New Primary Approach" is being practiced. This approach, worked out orig-inally for English, is also being applied in some areas to local languages; and reading materials in fourteen languages have recently been published. Swahili is taught as a subject where teachers are available up to the Cam-bridge School Certificate (twelve years of schooling) and in one school even up to the Advanced Level (two further years).[16] The acute shortage of Swahili teachers now is, in part, a result of the earlier decision to cut back the teaching of Swahili referred to above.

Not only, therefore, does the situation vary from institution to in-stitution, but there are also considerable variations within institutions.

Consider the provincial administration. The country is divided into seven provinces. Between the provincial headquarters and the central government, all official correspondence is in English; this is also true for such correspondence between provincial and district officers and between the latter and their subdistricts. Correspondence between district officers and location officers (chiefs and subchiefs, etc.) may be in Swahili or English. Verbal communication between the administration generally and those it administers is likely to be in Swahili, while that between members of the administration is likely to be in the local language or English, particularly if they happen to be members of different linguistic units. Yet, although members of the administration may address meetings in Swahili throughout the country, the impact of the language on the audience varies enormously. In areas of high linguistic homogeneity (e.g., Luo and Kisii), members of the audience are liable to translate the speaker's words into the local language as he goes along (if he doesn't use an interpreter), and the meeting is certainly discussed afterwards in that language. In areas of lower linguistic homogeneity (e.g., Kitale and the settlement areas generally), the impact of Swahili is liable to be such that the meeting can be discussed in Swahili. In attempting to assess the role of the respective languages in such settings, we need to know much more about the frequency with which specific choices are made, rather than be content with accounts of the settings in which they are made. For this, intensive studies of small groups are called for. The key factors here are education and ethnicity. In areas where a high proportion of the population has received primary education, English may well take over the role of Swahili. By the same token, in areas where members of the administration, local government, and other social services are "local" people (e.g., in the Central Province) Kikuyu, a local language, may take over the role of Swahili. If one were to look into the future, education and localization may be singled out as two critical factors. If the educationist's claim that functional literacy in English can be achieved by the end of primary school is validated, then we might expect English to assume an increasing importance at increasingly lower levels. If members of government services become increasingly "local" people, then local languages may also increase their importance. Thus one might expect that, in areas of low linguistic homogeneity (e.g., urban areas such as the Rift Valley Province), Swahili and English would assume greatest importance, while in areas of high linguistic homogeneity (e.g., Luo, Kikuyu, Gusii, and Kamba), local languages and English would assume such importance, the balance depending on the levels of education and localization effected.

Interestingly enough, the over-all situation is being influenced in this direction by migration—both rural-rural and rural-urban.[17] From areas that have a high population density, especially the Kikuyu Central Province, people are moving out into the farming areas formerly occupied by Europeans as shopkeepers (this is likely to increase with the exodus of Asian shopkeepers), taxidrivers, clerks, and also as farmers. The Rift Valley Province is a conspicuous example, an area of low population density and of low linguistic homogeneity. Ironically, therefore, while Central Province is itself a center of heightened language loyalties, it is, by its over-spill, creating a situation elsewhere in which Swahili is the obvious means of communication, at least in the short run. The movement from other high-density areas—including Luo, Luyia—to the towns creates a similar situation. Although in 1962, only 5.2 per cent of the population was classified as urban, 63 per cent of this was located in the Rift Valley and the associated Highlands; and Nairobi itself (with a population of over 250,000) accounted for 46 per cent of the total. But the increase in the urban population since the previous census (1948) of 6.3 per cent per annum suggests that not only will the urban areas be of increasing importance themselves, but they will also be investing Swahili and English with similar importance.

CONCLUSION

The policies of these two neighboring countries, Tanzania and Kenya, represent two rather diverse solutions to the language problems of multilingual states. Tanzania's choice of Swahili as the national language, however logical in historico-demographic terms, represented first a gesture of independence from colonialism and an affirmation of the role that the language had played in Tanzania's achievement of independence. In the period following the Arusha Declaration (1967), Swahili's position has been strengthened by association with the anti-elitist character of educational policy and of Tanzanian socialism generally. Its use has contributed to the development of institutions that serve popular needs and interests and has helped to create widespread "instrumental" attachment to the system (Kelman, paper 2, this volume). On the other hand, its close and explicit association with the party's political ideology means that its "charter" is liable to revision by the party as new political objectives are formulated.[18] Furthermore, as the achievement of independence recedes into the past, Swahili's role in it may well cease to serve as validation for its continuing preeminence in society so that greater attention will need to be given to the problems of carrying out the policy technologically; that is to say, in providing for its use over an ever increasing range of technical fields and as a medium of instruction progressively further up the educational system.

In Kenya, language policy is not associated with the choice of a particular language as integral to a political ideology. The historico-demographic situation has contributed to a recognition that each of the languages in the tri-focal situation has an important part to play in the national life, thus implicitly recognizing the divisive possibilities of language stressed by Kelman (paper 2, this volume). At the same time, as particular languages become characteristic of particular social settings, they are likely to become invested with particular social status, which is liable to reinforce divisiveness. Tanzania is, in one sense, no less tri-focal than Kenya, but she has chosen to place her emphasis differently; by having Swahili linked with her political ideology, Tanzania makes it possible for the language to act as a continuing force for unity. Kenya, by stressing the importance of the tri-focal division of language behavior has not been able to utilize any one language as a unifying force but must continually reckon with their divisive potentialities. Both countries, however, are faced all the time with the need to reconcile the competing claims of modernity and authenticity.[19] At any given moment, political decisions may appear to favor the one rather than the other, and it is in the light of the need for periodic shifts in emphasis that any policy should be judged.

ACKNOWLEDGMENT

I am grateful to Mr. Clifford Lutton of the Survey of Language Use and Language Teaching in Eastern Africa and to Mr. T. P. Gorman of the University College, Nairobi, for commenting on an earlier draft of this paper.

NOTES

1. See in this connection Clive Criper, Linguistic Complexity in Uganda (paper presented to the Ninth International Seminar of the International African Institute on *The Social Implications of Multilingualism*).
2. Wilfred H. Whiteley, *Swahili: The Rise of a National Language* (Methuen, 1969).
3. *African Census Report (1957)* (Dar es Salaam: Government Printer,

1963). *Kenya Population Census 1962*, vol. 3 (African Population Statistics Division, Ministry of Economic Planning and Development, Nairobi, 1966). W. T. W. Morgan and N. Manfred Shaffer, *Population of Kenya: Density and Distribution* (O.U.P., 1966).

4. Whiteley, *op. cit.*, chapter 5.

5. Ali A. Mazrui, Some Sociopolitical Functions of English Literature in Africa, *in* J. A. Fishman, C. A. Ferguson, and J. Das Gupta, eds., *Language Problems in Developing Nations* (Wiley, 1968), pp. 185–197.

6. See in this connection Marcia Wright, Swahili Language Policy 1890–1940, *Swahili* 35, no. 1 (1965): 40–49.

7. T. P. Gorman, Bilingualism in the Educational System of Kenya, *Comparative Education* 4, no. 3 (1968): 213–219.

8. This figure would probably be raised somewhat if figures had been obtainable for the Northern Province.

9. Mr. P. A. N. Itebete of the Kenya Institute of Administration is currently making a study of the development of Luyia, in which the local language committee played a major part. Luyia represents an attempt to standardize a group of seventeen Bantu dialects; the history of this experiment and the reactions it evoked constitute a fascinating case study in language planning on a small scale.

10. *Report of the E. A. Royal Commission, 1953–55* (HMSO, Cmd. 9475, 1955).

11. See Whiteley, *op. cit.*, chapter 6. For further details see M. H. Abdulaziz, Tanzania National Language Policy and the Rise of Swahili Political Culture *in* Wilfred H. Whiteley, ed., *The Social Implications of Multilingualism* (in press); also, Lyndon Harries, Language Policy in Tanzania, *Africa* 39, no. 3 (1969): 275–280.

12. *Research Outline for Comparative Studies of Language Planning*, p. 1. This volume. Paper 17.

13. There is a more detailed discussion of this point in Walter Rodney, Education and Tanzanian Socialism, *in* Idrian N. Resnick, ed., *Tanzania: Revolution by Education* (Longmans, 1968), pp. 71–84, and in the review article of this book by Ahmed Mohiddin in *Mawazo* 1, no. 4 (1968): 84–85.

14. *East African Standard*, 8 June 1969.

15. *The Daily Nation*, 9 January 1969.

16. Some account of the general situation and of the problems of initiating the study of Swahili at this level is given in J. D. Wanjala Welime, Problems of Teaching Swahili at Advanced Level in the Experience of the Friends' School, Kamusinga, (paper presented to the First Regional Conference of Language and Linguistics held in Dar es Salaam, December 1968).

17. For a more detailed discussion of migration, see S. H. Minde, *Land and Population Movements in Kenya* (Heinnemann, 1968), part 3.

18. The essentially political role of a language policy is well illustrated by Macnamara (paper 4, this volume) for the Irish Republic, and the cor-

relation of periodic resurgence of interest in language policies with particular political situations is documented for Turkey by Gallagher (paper 8, this volume).

19. This is discussed in much greater detail in J. A. Fishman, National Languages and Languages of Wider Communication in the Developing Nations, *in* W. H. Whiteley, ed., *The Social Implications of Multilingualism* (in press). See also introduction to this volume.

8. LANGUAGE REFORM
AND SOCIAL MODERNIZATION IN TURKEY

CHARLES F. GALLAGHER
American Universities Field Staff, New York and Honolulu

In the domain of social modernization as well as in the specific problems of language development, which form an integral part of the total pattern, contemporary Turkey offers an example to modernizing nations in the non-Western world that merits considerable attention.[1] Some of the features that make the Turkish experience highly distinctive as a whole are: the complexities of social development expressed not only within an individual culture but also as part of a movement from one civilization to another; the depth in time span over which the experience has taken place and the fundamental nature of many pattern changes; the long interaction of imposed or directed change with periodic bursts of spontaneous transformation; and, finally, the relationship that is intricate, but not always antipodal, between self-expression via nationalist particularism, on the one hand, and fulfillment through participation in a more universalist community, on the other, with both elements in the national personality given impetus by a historical and continuing preoccupation not merely with verbal prestige and pride but more with effective power.[2]

The basic differences between Turkey and the majority of developing, newly independent nations today—differences which may be more instructive than comparisons of the similarities often found among newer nations that have often gone through much the same process of colonization and decolonization—can be put in more concrete form within the framework of the interrelated fundamentals outlined above.

During the latter centuries of the Ottoman Empire, between roughly 1650 and 1850, Turkish contact with European civilization was marked by at least two outstanding characteristics. One was that the Ottomans were the first non-Westerners to become aware, belatedly and at first dimly after their major defeats in the seventeenth century, of the growing material and technical capabilities of Europe. The second was that the Ottoman Empire—until the final breakdown in the latter half of the nineteenth century—was considered as a foe and a dangerous rival but as an equal and a participant in the European and international power system. This would be true only in the case of Japan at a later date, but it marks Ottoman history with a different stamp from that given to Iran, India, China, and the rest of the European-colonized world. Ottoman favor was on occasion curried, and the Sultan was even invited in 1798 to join the coalition of European allies in opposing French revolutionary expansion. In a word, the Ottomans were at almost all times active protagonists of European and later global history, not merely its objects.[3] This long-standing psychological condition of granted equality has been of the utmost importance in the formation of modern Turkish attitudes and reactions in every aspect of social and cultural change induced by more recent contact with the West.

Equally important is an understanding of the profundities involved in the full-scale rearrangement of Turkish social, cultural, and religious life in this century—an event equivalent in magnitude to a civilizational passage rite. As Bernard Lewis has noted, a major Turkish credential is that this is not the first time they have set out to reshape their national ethos in such dramatic fashion.[4] And, just as their absorption into early and medieval Islamic civilization was mirrored by the introduction of an extensive Arabic and Persian vocabulary, phraseology, and even syntactical turns, so also is the contemporary manifestation of deep social change reflected, in part, by the adoption of a large and growing body of new words and phrases—both borrowed and home-grown—and, concomitantly, by the rejection of much that had already been assimilated from Islamic civilization.

Like the process of shedding an old skin and growing accustomed to the new layer, the effort to form a community on the basis of being primarily Turkish and only incidentally Muslim, as well as of being European rather than Middle Eastern, requires going through an unsettling and sensitive period. For the past half century the Turks have been asking themselves what an authentic Turkish identity should be and, in language, what the real and proper tongue of modern Turks should be. Even before this period of stress, during much of the nineteenth century, the Ottoman Turks were taking steps along a transitional road, each one of which was instrumental in changing the face of Turkish culture and in helping to develop a national language. From the traditionally unquestioning Islamic

Ottomanism, they moved through multicommunitarian pan-Ottomanism, the incipient national sentiments of the Young Ottomans in the nineteenth century and the Young Turks in the early twentieth century, and brushes with pan-Turkish "Turanism" to the dominant ethic of territorial "Anatolian Turkism," as espoused by the Republic after 1923.

In language development, the role of Atatürk personally was unquestionably the most decisive. Nevertheless, the interlinkage of planned and unplanned change that had begun as early as the 1830's and the 1840's and that had involved the first translators of the *tercüme odǝsı*, the secretaries in embassies abroad, the reformist writers of the Tanzimat period (1839–76), the desire of Young Turk government leaders after 1908 that their policies should be more widely understood, and the influence of army officers and the changes effected under the pressure of military needs in World War I—all these were vital preconditions to the far-reaching reforms that began in 1928. They illustrate the various phases of recent Turkish history by the contributions each made to the building up of a simple Turkish (*sade türkçe*) that would, it was hoped, lead to a pure Turkish (*öz türkçe*), which is still being tortuously created even today in a movement synchronic with the processes of detraditionalization, de-Arabization, de-Persification, secularization, and modernization.[5]

OTTOMAN LANGUAGE REFORM UNTIL 1918

Although an interest in European technical, and especially military, vocabulary was apparent as early as the eighteenth century, when the first translations of Western works were made during the period 1729–42 and again when printing presses were once more allowed to operate after 1784, it was only in the second quarter of the nineteenth century that the Ottomans began to realize that their language was insufficient to the task of keeping up with European advances. *Osmanlıca*, the official written language of the empire, was a synthetic amalgam of Arabic, Persian, and Turkish, with grammatical and syntactical features of each. As a literary language it was unintelligible to the peasantry, even to the ordinary townsman, and inaccessible without prolonged special study. It was contrasted with disdain to the crude Turkish (*kaba türkçe*) of the illiterate masses. In sum, it was the language of a religion, Islam; of its culture and its Caliphate; and of the Ottoman political institution, which had been the defender of the faith since the fifteenth century.

Concern about the future of *osmanlıca* arose as new administrative, legal, educational, and military terms entered the Ottoman world in the nineteenth century. Some of these were translated with terms formed by analogy with earlier borrowings from Arabic or Persian, but increasingly as time went on it was felt that these were wanting as sources for expressing contemporary and popular ideas. The problems attendant on the translation of such words as liberty, justice, nation, nationalism, *et al* are well known with respect to both Arabic and Turkish in the nineteenth century.[6] By the 1860's, political writers like Ziya Paşa and Namık Kemal had grasped the idea that Ottoman linguistic obscurantism was a barrier to the political reform and increased freedom they were seeking; hence, they called for the simplification of the language and the elimination of unnecessary borrowings from Arabic and Persian. Within a short time, between about 1880 and 1900, Ottoman lexicography gradually started to reflect this new attitude by incorporating more native words, by eliminating rare Arabo-Persian terms, and by modifying spelling in the direction of greater phonetic logic. The simultaneous beginning of the emancipation of Ottoman poetry towards the end of the century, which directed rhyme towards the sound—and not the visual—effect, opened the doors of the literary tongue to the language of popular expression. Furthermore, reformers began to interest themselves in the Turkish—or even other Turkic languages—elements in *osmanlıca*. In 1874, Suleyman Paşa wrote a grammar, *Sarf-ı Türkî*, in which he proposed that the national language be called Turkish and not Ottoman. Others, such as the lexicographer Şemseddin Sami and Necib Asim, stressed the Turkicness of western (Anatolian) Turkish for motives laced with pan-Turkish nationalism, a theme that was to become more evident in a later period.

For almost half a century, moderate language reform of this kind continued, taking halting steps towards standardizing the language and reducing the gap between the written *osmanlıca* and the spoken *Türkçe*, but not without opposition—opposition that crystallized around the end of the century with the rise of the *Servet-i Fünun* literary school. This group of writers and poets sought to preserve Ottoman Turkish as an entity distinct from the spoken language; they emphasized the difference between the beauty of Arabic and Persian compounds and the mundane quality of Turkish speech. The *Servet-i Fünun* had its heyday from about 1895 to 1905, but the movement ultimately failed. Its demise and the onward movement of language reform were hastened by two forces: the growing influence of the press and the rise of Turkish nationalism that culminated in the Young Turk Revolution of 1908. The eagerness of the Young Turk directorate, in its first years in power, that political consciousness be stimulated and the general enthusiasm with which the revolution was greeted led to a rapid expansion of journalistic activity and a considerable simplification of expression. During the same period, a group of writers and journalists in Salonika, known as the *Genç Kalemler* (Young Pens) and formed under the intellectual leadership of the most famous Turkish nationalist thinker of the times, Ziya Gök Alp, pressed for continuing change of a moderate nature, eschewing the ideas of both the conservatives and the neo-Turkish purists who wanted to eliminate all traces of Arabic and Persian.[7] Their attitudes seem timid today, given the evolution of society and language since 1928, but they were a useful stimulus at a time that was ripe for steady, limited reform. Official government organs used the so-called new language (*yeni lisan*); Parliament hesitantly adopted it; and, with the coming of World War I, change became more rapid. A telegraphic style was invented, a script of modified Arabic letters was conceived by the Minister of War—although not successfully propagated—and propaganda was increasingly addressed to Turkish soldiers and civilians in simple, everyday language.

By the end of the war in 1918, what has been termed the "Ottoman mandarin style" was completely moribund. To replace it, there was coming into being a flexible, living language arising in good part from the spoken language of the educated classes of Istanbul and the larger cities. Although this language still had a large foreign vocabulary scarcely understood by the uneducated and although this language was still written in an alien and difficult script and was in no sense a truly national, standardized vehicle of communication, the accomplishment between 1850 and 1920 had been considerable. In the desperate, hectic era of defeat, redressment, and refocusing of national purpose between 1918 and 1923, the multirooted *osmanlıca* was dying, along with the multilingual empire whose tongue it had been for five centuries.

LANGUAGE REFORM UNDER THE REPUBLIC

The scope of language change in Turkey since the establishment of the Republic in 1923 is best seen by considering the broad canvas of the past five decades. For a Turkish schoolboy today, it is virtually impossible—even apart from the problem of script—to read anything written before World War I without special aids. In general it is difficult to understand the documents and formal speeches of the early republican period without a gloss—even the famous *Nutuk*, the reasonably modernized thirty-six hour discourse of Mustafa Kemal (Atatürk) to the Republican People's

Party Congress in 1927. And although the Constitution of the First Republic (1923–60), originally written in 1924 and later superseded by a
"purer" Turkish version in 1945, was subsequently reinstated in its original version, this was done to preserve its flavor of authenticity for the
time of its writing; but no one pretends that its language is other than
archaic. Finally, beginning with the issue of the first Ottoman-Turkish
pocket glossary (*Osmanlıcadan-Türkçeye Cep Kılavuzu*) in 1935 and
continuing down to the more extensive current dictionaries, the Turks
have felt a need unshared by any other people: to offer translations and
explanations in the contemporary national language of the historical national language as it existed in the first two decades of this century.[8]

Specific changes of a planned nature since 1928 may be divided
into two main areas concerning script and vocabulary, the latter including
problems of purging, new formations, and borrowings. Unplanned change
concerns, in the main, borrowing of words and phrases and the evolution
of language style. Of the planned changes, the substitution of the Latin
alphabet for Arabic letters is without question the cardinal event, one
which in itself would merit the name of "language revolution" (*dil devrimi*) given to the ensemble of changes. Use of the Latin alphabet had
been discussed as far back as 1878, and, given the incompatibility of
Turkish phonetics with Arabic orthography, there was much merit in the
step. But broader political and cultural questions played a part. For one
thing, the Soviet Union had changed the script of Turkic-speaking peoples
in its territory to Roman letters shortly before the Turkish decision, although it later revised this in favor of the use of the Cyrillic alphabet. The
move to the Latin alphabet seemed to some Turks to be a way of retaining ties with their linguistic brethren from Azerbaijan to Central Asia.
Much more important, however, was Atatürk's desire to cut the new
Turkey off from what he held was the dead weight of the Islamic past and
his view that the new script should be thought of as a logical part of the
corpus of secularist measures taken in the first years of the Republic. The
objective was facilitated by the fact that in 1927 only about 10 per cent
of the population was literate and even fewer felt personally concerned
with perpetuating the Perso-Arabic literary heritage of Ottoman civilization. Nonetheless, there was opposition on religious grounds.

Looking back, it is remarkable that the feat was accomplished so
rapidly, so thoroughly, and with so little overt resistance. The new letters
were first taught in November 1928; Arabic writing was abolished from
the beginning of 1929; and Arabic and Persian were no longer taught as

foreign languages from September of 1929. In a relaxation from the severity of the early reforms, in recent years the Ministry of Education has published romanized versions of the large body of Ottoman and other Middle Eastern literature, but the critical step that was taken in 1928 marked the educational life of all subsequent generations and did more than any other single undertaking to transform Turkey by cutting it off from the rest of the Middle East, by turning it in upon itself, and in channeling its intellectual contacts in the direction of the West. It is striking to compare Turkey with the case of Iran, where many similar social and cultural reforms were carried out excepting script revision, and to consider the influences of this one act on all later social evolution.

Once romanization was well under way, Atatürk personally turned to broader language questions. In 1932, at his suggestion, the Turkish Linguistic Society (*Türk Dili Tetkik Cemiyeti*, later restyled in its own new Turkish the *Türk Dil Kurumu*) was formed. It was originally conceived of as an accompaniment to the Society for the Study of Turkish History established the previous year; both organizations and the activities that they pursued, during the 1930's in particular, did much to strengthen the spirit of parochial Turkish nationalism.

Although this paper is not an account of the history of the Turkish Linguistic Society (TDK), its role and the emotions aroused by its concept of that role in the development of modern Turkish deserve some comment. There were three essential tasks laid down by the central Committee, elected at the first Turkish Language Congress in 1932: to collect Turkish words from the popular language and from old Turkish texts; to define the principles of word formation and to create words from Turkish roots; and to encourage the use of true Turkish words in replacement of foreign words used in the written language. With the first objective, there has never been any quarrel, but the other two tasks and the intermittent zeal with which they were approached have often stirred controversy and opposition.

Like most enthusiastic reform movements, the efforts of the TDK have waxed and waned in progressively longer undulations over the years. The zealousness of the first years was supported by all the authority of the state, but because the work was carried out in many instances by volunteers and local amateurs, the initial results threatened to lead to linguistic anarchy. Through the use of the mass media and party institutions, public suggestions were invited for alternatives to Arabic and Persian terms; teachers were asked to examine lists of substitutes; and in 1934 there was published the first *Collection of Turkish Equivalents for Otto-man Words* (*Osmanlıcadan-Türkçeye Söz Karşılıklrı Tarama Dergisi*), which was not a dictionary but a listing of some 30,000 equivalents for more than 7,000 "foreign" words in Ottoman Turkish. Although the evident confusion led to a temporary quiescence, excess in one or another domain was the mark of the decade. In 1935 a less radically oriented Ottoman-Turkish glossary, known as the *Kılavuz*, was prepared; although it allowed numbers of Arabic and Persian terms to be retained, these were justified by noting that ". . . a number of words which are now used in our language and which until now were thought to have been taken from foreign languages had originally passed from Turkish into those languages."[9] Neo-nationalist history and neo-nationalist language theory went hand in hand in 1935 and 1936. The historians discovered that most of the accomplishments of antiquity were the works of Turks or of peoples influenced by early Turkish culture, while the linguists evolved the "Sun Language Theory," according to which Turkish was the mother tongue of the world. The practical advantages of this view are clear, making it no longer imperative to weed out commonly used foreign terms because, in effect, all words were originally Turkish. It has even been suggested that the idea was put forward deliberately to restrain the extremist reformers, and it did have that effect for several years. The period from 1936 to about 1941 was marked by a slackening of effort and a relative tolerance extended to well-established, classical words. Of greater importance, however, was the fact that these were also the years when the first comprehensive lists of Turkish terms in mathematics and the exact sciences were prepared, tested by scholarly commissions, and introduced (1939) into official textbooks.

A return to language-reform activism was evident during World War II. It seems to have gone along with a general feeling of isolation and insecurity in troubled times, with the Germans on the Greek islands, only a few miles from Turkish shores, and the British poised on the southern frontiers of Anatolia in Syria and Iraq. The sentiment was expressed in the capital levy applied with notorious unfairness to indigenous minority groups in 1942 (*varlık vergisi*) and in various measures designed to reinforce the scope of early reforms, especially those dealing with religion. In a larger sense, in the face of the first major external threat since the Allied and Greek interventions after World War I, a need was felt to resist again in the same way as before: by becoming more Turkish, more chauvinist, and less cosmopolitan and ecumenical.

Nonetheless, the severe nature of the Turkification changes that were proposed by the TDK in 1942 brought strong and open criticism, particularly from academicians, many of whom had been involved on their own in working out solutions to terminological problems. Basically, university faculty favored greater internationalization in scientific and learned terminology, both to insure accuracy of translation and to preserve ties between Turkey and the advanced countries, while the TDK insisted on a more national terminology. Although the TDK, beginning in 1948, has published long lists of technical terms in the scientific, technical, and legal fields, which are incorporated in its most recent dictionary (*Türkçe Sözlük*, 3rd edition, 1959) and guide to orthography (*Yeni İmlâ Kılavuzu*, revised second printing, 1966), the struggle continues and is far from settled.

With the coming to power of the opposition Democrat party in 1950, the political history of Turkey changed decisively, away from the *dirigiste* one-party state in the direction of greater individual freedom. Externally, the period since then has been marked by an increasingly intimate Turkish association with the affairs of the European and Atlantic worlds. The social corollaries of this political evolution have brought a more balanced view of the early, often drastic reforms. A new attitude has arisen, not free from sharp controversy, about the nature of the secular state and the place of religion in it. There has grown up a tendency to resist official interference in matters of private concern, and a revival of interest has taken place in the whole of Turkey's past, both pre-Islamic and Islamic. Corresponding developments can be seen in the field of language, some of the outstanding characteristics being: a long-range drift towards compromise and coexistence among several alternatives that involves a kind of standardization of its own; a lessening of governmental guidance in language matters; a revivalist tendency with respect to some cultural and religious terms and phrases; and growing sophistication and internationalization of some segments of the vocabulary.

In line with the trend towards private—but more professional—initiative, the TDK had its semi-official status removed and lost its government subsidy, while a wide range of moderate scholars was elected to the Executive Committee. On the whole, it can be said that since 1950 the TDK has worked in a more sober and scholarly way. It has tried to continue the simplification and modernization of the language, without undue nationalist fervor, suggesting and counseling more often without than with success. The TDK now lacks the authority to impose decisions, and it is looked upon by many Turks as an exotic group of specialists whose endeavors and pronouncements have little relation to their own problems or those of the nation today.

THE LANGUAGE SITUATION TODAY

It is probably too early to make a definite assessment of the whole body of changes in modern Turkish, if only because the language is still being standardized. Many Turks will insist today that there are still several separate Turkish languages—for the press, for official discourse and communication, in literature, and in the speech of educated persons compared to that of peasants and villagers. But this phenomenon of different registers, which is true in all languages to some extent, is perhaps exaggerated by the Turks. Certainly, compared to the vast differences between the various forms of Turkish as they existed fifty years ago, a remarkable degree of language coherence has been reached very quickly, and Turkish is far ahead of its Middle Eastern neighbors in this respect. The nation possesses essentially one language, the grammar of which is solidly established. The radio and television, the textbooks used by the more than 80 per cent of school-age children now receiving instruction, and the two-year compulsory military service for all young men that has the tradition that the army teaches and educates as well—all are vital factors reinforcing the linguistic jell. Moreover, although important residual splits exist between the speech of the city and country, there are now fewer speech differences linked to class, something which again reflects the social evolution in the direction of egalitarianism so marked since the establishment of the Republic.

On the whole, despite excesses and occasionally ridiculous pomposities, the language reformers have had considerable success in their major aims, and they have contributed much to modern Turkish. In a general way, it might be said that they have been the active godfathers of today's national language, by conducting research into its history and background; by classifying, ordering, and publishing lists of specialized, technical terminology; by stimulating interest and even controversy among writers and intellectuals about language questions; and by having had in recent years the grace to step somewhat aside and allow the genius of the language community to develop more on its own.

More specifically, one profound influence of the TDK innovations has been in the emphasis put upon the widespread use of affixes of all kinds in forming new words.[10] The regular Turkish plural *lar/ler* has become generalized for almost all words where, formerly, Arabic broken plurals or sound plurals were used. It is never incorrect to use the regular Turkish plural; in fact, to do so is more "modern," and the survival of broken plurals marks one's speech as obsolescent or suggests to some the shadow of Islamic reaction. Another example of the simplification and nationalization favored by the TDK of a similar nature is the attaching of fixed Turkish suffixes to Arabic or Persian words, such as *tarafsız* for *bi taraf* (neutral); *imkânlı* (from Arabic-Turkish *imkân* [possibility] for *mümkün* (possible); and similarly with other adjectives derived from Arabic participles in *mü-*, *ehemmiyetli* for *mühim* (important); *iltizamcı* for *mültezim* (tax farmer). Thus, today we have standard Turkish forms such as: *fayda* (use, advantage); *faydacı* (utilitarian); *faydacılık* (utilitarianism); *faydalı* (useful, advantageous); *faydasız* (useless); *faydasızlık* (uselessness)—all using suffixes of long standing in spoken Turkish but which were looked down upon in Ottoman times, where *imkânsız* (impossible) would have been rendered with the Arabic turn of phrase *gayrimümkün*.

But a very large number of neologist-affixes have been coined in recent decades, and a good many of these have taken root. Among the prefixes, we find *son-* (last) in *sonek* (suffix); *üst-* (upper, above) in *üsteğmen* (first lieutenant) and *üstinsan* (superman); *alt-* (under, below) in *alteğmen* (second lieutenant) and *alttaraf* (continuation, sequel); and many others that are even more exotic, such as *öngörmek* (foresee) from *ön-* (ahead, front) plus *görmek* (see). More important as tools of the reformers have been the newly coined suffixes, some of them derived from other members of the Turkic language family, like Kazan and Chaghatay Turkish, or even from Mongol. The Chaghaty *-ey* has given the new common words *kuzey* (north) and *güney* (south), which are displacing the older, Arabic-derived terms. *Doğu* and *şark*, "east," appear to be running neck and neck, although *Orta Doğu*, for "Middle East"—as in *Orta Doğu Teknik Üniversitesi*—is quite common. (A suggestion has been made that *doğu* and *batı* be used in the geographical sense of "east" and "west," while *şark* and *garb* are reserved for the "Orient" and "Occident".) Likewise, the Mongol *-tay* has produced *kurultay* (congress, the annual meeting of the TDK being given this name), and the Kazan *-ev* has given the widely accepted *söylev* (speech), among other new coinages.

Some other successful suffixes are calques on the order of al/el, sal/ sel, as in *siyasal* (political), actually an innovation of the nineteenth century Tanzimat period for the Arabic-Turkish *siyasî*, by analogy with *sosiyal*, and today *tarihsel* (historical) for the Arabic-Turkish *tarihî*. *Ta-rihsel* has not displaced *tarihî* but is gaining ground; *tarihsellik*, however, occurs for "historicness," which may result in *tarihsel* being fixed as "historic" and not "historical," another example of the potential of new suffixes. Likewise, *-men,* in a double recall brings back an early Turkish suffix *-man* in *kocaman* (huge) and *şişman* (fat) as well as suggesting the English 'man, men,' in such new formations as *öğretmen* (teacher), *okutman* (lector), and *yazman* (secretary), the last contending with *sekreter*. The principle of calques is one that has appealed to the reformers in many instances, among the best known being *okul* (school, cf. French *école*) and *genel* (general), both of which have true Turkish roots.

Regarding European loan words, which have been entering Turkish in large numbers since the last century, the future is not completely clear, but there are some indications. Despite the re-Turkification of some earlier borrowings (but many fewer than was the case with Arabic and Persian borrowings), as with *demiryolu* for *şimendifer* (train, from French *chemin de fer*), European terms are flooding into Turkish today. As Charles Issawi has noted, a study of short stories and newspaper articles indicated that in Turkish the " . . . incidence of European words is three times as high as Persian and about ten times as high as in Arabic . . . . One is struck by the multitude of French words for which Arabic equivalents have been coined."[11] Heyd concurs in this estimate.[12]

Geoffrey Lewis, discussing the reform movement in general, notes that:

. . . even its critics nowadays find it hard to express themselves without using some of the neologisms, at least if they want to appeal to a mass audience. . . . But danger to the purity of Turkish threatens from the opposite quarter, in the form of an inundation of English and French words . . . .[13]

Heyd, writing in 1954, had already deplored this trend:

Modern Turkish appears to repeat what its reformers consider an unfortunate development of the time when the Turks accepted Islamic civilization. Instead of framing words for Western objects and concepts out of its native word-material, it adopts European terms in ever increasing numbers.[14]

My findings in a cursory survey this spring showed that the invasion has been progressing rapidly. A check of the listing, in the 1966 Ankara telephone book, of headings for the classified pages—comprising essentially concrete and usually modern everyday objects—showed that, of 947 words used in the titles, 267 or 28.2 per cent were modern European loan words.[15] If repetitions had been eliminated, it is very likely that the percentage would be even higher. It is naturally in the areas of modern-style consumption as well as in science that one would expect to find the most numerous borrowings, and this is indeed the case. Even the TDK gave its blessing to the adoption of European scientific terms for use in higher education on the occasion of its 1949 Congress, announcing that " . . . scientific and technical terms used in common by the advanced nations may be accepted according to a definite system."[16] Thus, one finds at a basic level such terms as *bioloji, speleoloji, telgraf, telefon, televizyon, teleskop, fotoğraf, galveniz, kompresör, elektrik, dinamo, eleman,* and a host of similar terms; while at the other end of the technical spectrum, the most abstruse medical and scientific terminology has been adopted almost wholesale.[17]

It has been noted that some students of Turkish are alarmed by the influx of European words into the modern language. G. Lewis has written explicitly on this subject:

The most depressing feature of the modern Turkish linguistic landscape is the vast mass of unnecessary borrowings from French and, to a lesser extent, English. Where no "genuine Turkish" word was available, it was understandable that the Westernizers should exchange Arabic for European words . . . . But it is impossible to justify the sort of snobbery that can put up a notice reading *Izmir Enternasyonal Fuari (cf. French foire) Enformasyon Burosu* or can engage on a campaign for the *eradikasyon* of malaria. Although there are perfectly good Turkish words for "horse-race" and "winner," the Turkish punter will go to the *konkuripik* in the hope of becoming a *ganyan.*[18]

G. Lewis may underestimate the strength of the Turkish drive regarding "Westernization," keeping in mind the proper distinction that Issawi makes " . . . between Westernization and Modernization."[19] This would appear to be true of at least the elite of the country—and in that term today there should be included several million educated, literate, urban dwellers. This elite has doggedly pursued two goals since the establishment of the Republic. One is to become a more purely Turkish national group within a geographical area called "Turkey" and to find and establish an identity that, it was felt, had been lost by being smothered under the universalist blanket of Islam and by being laden with the burden of providing leadership for the Islamic community. The other has been to be accepted as an equal in all facets of contemporary life by the economically and socially advanced societies of the West, much as the Ottomans had been accepted, albeit as dangerous foes, throughout most of the history of their relations with the West. At all times in their past, from the earliest days of conversion to Islam down to the most recent period of relations with Europe, the Turks have been exponents of the dictum that counsels joining those who cannot be beaten; and the Turkish elite of our times has viewed "joining" as a total process of societal change.[20]

It is within this framework that planned language change in contemporary Turkey should be considered. The changes effected have been not only revolutionary in scope, but they have also paralleled the fundamental societal change under way in political, economic, and social fields. The direction of language planning has complemented the macrocosm of Turkish social modernization, as can be seen in the terms used to describe the republican state: it is, above all else, secular (*lâik*) in its renunciation of a script and so much of a vocabulary linked to religious values; it is populist (*halkçı*) in its pressure for the elimination of diglossia; it is nationalist (*milliyetçi*) in its efforts to remove foreign borrowings and coin indigenous equivalents, and it has been statist (*devletçi*) in impetus and direction.

The felicitous congruence of language-planning goals and other objectives of societal change may be counterbalanced in the Turkish case, however, by tensions generated within the domain of what might be termed societo-cultural change; i.e., societal change involving a fundamental rearrangement of values with the displacement of pre-existing local values and the acceptance of items imported from other civilizations within a short period. The polarities of nationalism and cosmopolitan solidarity may not inevitably be antithetical, but the pursuance of the two-fold effort mentioned above, in which increased participation in the life of the West is sought at the same time that attempts are being made to strengthen the sense of identity in specifically national terms is beset with difficulties. These difficulties are reflected in part also in the fact that unplanned language change has tended towards cosmopolitanism, often excessively so, despite the efforts at restraint on the part of the planners.

It might be granted that the Turks are better equipped to try than most peoples. The record of their passage through civilizations and the high degree of adaptability shown so far are indexes to suggest optimism, especially when compared with the deep resistance of the Arabs to accepting anything from the West outside the rather narrow area of material technology or when contrasted with the disparity found in contemporary Iran between the considerable movement in socioeconomic development in recent years and the relatively closed spirit of smugness about more cultural matters, including the domain of language change and borrowing. The insistence of the Arabs on maintaining their identity, bound up as it is in a special relationship with Islam, is well reflected in the vicissitudes of Arabic today in language planning and reform. The comparatively modest effort of the Persians likewise stems partially from similar feelings of a special link with the whole of the Iranian cultural continuum and a consequent uneasiness at the thought of any drastic break with it. In contrast, Turkish concern with the realities of power allowed the Turks to accept traditional Middle Eastern civilization wholeheartedly and to participate in it fully—although more receptively than creatively on the whole—as long as that civilization appeared dominant and vital and while it offered an effective means to express the energies of a people who have been distinguished from the earliest times by their practicality.

For the modernizing Turkish elite, the realities of power in this century have been expressed by Europe and the West. Even if doubts have arisen in most recent years about the political (and to a lesser extent the social) stamina of Western civilization, nevertheless, the economic, scientific, and technological superiority of the West have, if anything, increased the preference of the elite for a continuing adaptation and integration. Indeed, while the Turks have been rediscovering themselves with considerable pride and success, they have become deeply involved with Europe since 1945, in ways that are having a profound influence on the whole spectrum of their social evolution.

Turkey is a member of the most important European and Atlantic organizations, including the Council of Europe, the Organization for Economic Cooperation and Development, and the North Atlantic Treaty Organization, and it is an associate member of the European Economic Community with the right—granted only to Greece and Turkey as "European" associates—to full membership in the EEC eventually. More than 200,000 Turkish workers are employed in Europe, and their periodic or definitive return to the homeland has a social influence at least equal to the economic value of their remittances from abroad. Moreover, the more advanced regions of Turkey are painfully but steadily becoming a European-type mass consumption society. Although OECD figures place per capita income in Turkey at the bottom of the twenty-two nation group, with about $320 a year (in 1968), the income of some eight million urban inhabitants is about $500 a year, and the level of city dwellers in the largest and most advanced cities, like Istanbul, Izmir, and

Ankara, comes close to $800 a year. Even more important than figures, however, is the fact that the urban life-style that is being forged slowly through the tenuous socioeconomic integration with Europe—whose cultural values were taken as a distant standard during the past half-century—has a Balkan or Mediterranean color to it, which is quite distinct from what is found in the rest of the Muslim Middle East. This is reflected in diverse ways, but what is perhaps most relevant culturally is the quantity of European literature found in translation, often in paperback, and the spread of Western or Western-inspired theater, music, ballet, and the fine arts in the larger cities.

CONCLUSION

The long history of language reform in Ottoman and Republican Turkey offers some valuable matters for consideration by all societies. Among them are (1) the successful use made of the need to focus on an imaginary scapegoat—in the Turkish case, the Arabo-Persian contribution to the language; (2) the role of the military as a catalyst in preliminary language modernization, from the first beginnings at the end of the eighteenth century on up to 1918; (3) the determined application of the concept of *tabula rasa* after 1918, by which defeat was turned into a form of victory; (4) the skillful reversal of popular contemporary theses about colonialism, by which it was held that it was those under Ottoman rule (i.e., the colonized) who had impeded the natural advance of the ruling group towards self-awareness and progress; and, of perhaps the greatest importance today and for the future, (5) the role of the elite and the tension between elite-will and popular recalcitrance.

If one of the critical questions in language planning is "who decides what and how," in the Turkish case, we have clear-cut answers richly documented. More pertinent to the continuing sociolinguistic problems of Turkey is the other crucial question of "who accepts what and why"; here the answers are more elusive. Republican Turkey is a much more homogeneous country today than the Ottoman State in every respect, ethnically, socially, and economically. But the reduction in ethnic hostility and class antagonisms has not been accompanied by a similar lowering in the intensity of value conflicts between men whose outlook is *grosso modo* "modern"[21] and those whose world-view is still essentially traditional, or at best transitional or quasi-modern. The fault lines run between, on the one hand, a sophisticated and largely secular but not necessarily a religious, urban group and, on the other hand, the more traditional artisans and shopkeepers, the petty bourgeoisie in the medium and smaller towns, and, at one extreme, the mass of the peasantry in a country still about 50 per cent illiterate. The value-split cuts across class and politics, particularly among the more articulate groups. Thus one may find Marxists and supporters of the left-wing Turkish Labor Party, whose world-view is quite similar to that of Kemalist intellectuals or business-men who favor the Justice Party. The designations normally used for political and social differentiation, like "conservative" and "liberal," are meaningless in most cases as an indicator of how the individual perceives his society until it is known whether he is basically "modern" or not. And the touchstone of modernity in Turkey, as in Islamic society as a whole and even more generally, turns on the matter of the attitude of the citizen towards the secular state.

If, as has been remarked, language is close to the heart of the culture but functions as an autonomous part of it, it is natural that it should mirror the problems, conflicts, and value-differences of a society with some faithfulness. This is true in Turkey today, where much may be known about the fundamental outlook of a man by the language he uses. His vocabulary may give him away before the content of his utterances has been digested. To take an example from one of the borrowings mentioned above, the word "international" can be expressed in four ways. The traditional, Arabic-derived term is *beynelmilel,* an Arabic pronoun put together with the broken plural form of the Turkified form of the Arabic noun *millet* (people, nation), all of which create an air of fusty and elegant literarism-cum-piety. Another widely accepted, neo-traditional Turkish coinage is *milletlerarası,* where the preceding noun has been given indigenous suffixes to express the same concept of "between nations." A more recent and national invention of the language planners is *uluslararası,* where the Turkish noun *ulus* has replaced the Arabo-Turkish *millet,* found now in textbooks and government publications as well as being given broad usage. Finally, a popular modern word found in much advertising and throughout the mass media is *enternasyonal.* In the process of listening to this example and many similar ones of multiple choice, one learns much about who has accepted which of the alternatives. The struggle for primacy among such words and expressions is a view in miniature of the still bitterly contested struggle for the cultural and social future of Turkey.

NOTES

1. The best over-all work on the modernization of Turkey is Bernard Lewis, *The Emergence of Modern Turkey* (2nd ed.; London, 1968). In addition to this excellent general study, specific problems are treated in the following works: Şerif Mardin, *The Genesis of Young Ottoman Thought: A Study in the Modernization of Turkish Political Ideas* (Princeton, 1962); Niyazi Berkes, *The Development of Secularism in Turkey* (Montreal, 1964); Richard D. Robinson, *The First Turkish Republic: A Case Study in National Development* (Cambridge, Mass., 1963); Dankwart A. Rustow, Turkey: The Modernity of Tradition, *in* Lucian W. Pye and S. Verba, eds., *Political Culture and Political Development* (Princeton, 1965); and Daniel Lerner, *The Passing of Traditional Society* (Glencoe, 1958).

2. Turkey thus does not easily fit into any one of the three categories or "clusters" proposed by Fishman in Joshua A. Fishman, National Languages and Languages of Wider Communication in the Developing Nations (paper given at the Regional Conference on Language and Linguistics, Dar es Salaam, Tanzania, 1968), although it comes somewhat closer to "Cluster B" than to any other. One of the basic problems is whether contemporary Turkey should be regarded all in all as a developing country or as a non-Western nation or both.

3. For an interesting comparison of the problems of modernization and how they have been handled by Turkey and Japan, without any reference to language or language reform in either case, however, see the collective work of a group of scholars in Robert E. Ward and Dankwart A. Rustow, eds., *Political Modernization in Japan and Turkey* (Princeton, 1964).

4. Lewis, *op. cit.*, p. 479.

5. The standard work is Uriel Heyd, *Language Reform in Modern Turkey* (Jerusalem, 1954). In Turkish, see Agâh Sırrı Levend, *Türk Dilinde Gelişme ve Sadeleşme Safhaları* (Ankara, 1949); Türk Dil Kurumu, *Türkiyede Dil Devrimi* (Ankara, 1951); Ö. Aksoy, *Atatürk ve Dil Devrimi* (Ankara, 1963); the accounts of the Linguistic Congresses, *Türk Dil Kurultayi* (held from 1933 through 1966); and the periodical *Belleten* published by the TDK.

6. On Arabic, see Franz Rosenthal, *The Muslim Concept of Freedom* (Leiden, 1960); and Charles F. Gallagher, Language, Culture, and Ideology: The Arab World, *in* K. H. Silvert, ed., *Expectant Peoples: Nationalism and Development* (New York, 1963); for Turkish, see Lewis, *op. cit.*, pp. 323–361.

7. On the life and work of Ziya Gök Alp, see Uriel Heyd, *The Foundations of Turkish Nationalism* (London, 1950); and N. Berkes, trans. and ed., *Turkish Nationalism and Western Civilization: Selected Essays of Ziya Gök Alp* (London, 1959).

8. In the Japanese case, explanatory aids are required only for pre-Meiji material and not in all cases. Despite the moderate language reform after

World War II and the reduction of characters, almost all material since 1868 can be read without undue difficulty. The only possible exception that comes to mind would be Communist China and the problems of the current generation in reading late Manchu and early Republican literature written in *wen-li* earlier in this century.

9. Heyd, *op. cit.*, p. 33.
10. On word formation in general in Turkish, including both standard affixes and remarks on the new endings, see Geoffrey Lewis, *Turkish Grammar* (London, 1967), chapter 14, pp. 220–237.
11. Charles Issawi, European Loan-Words in Contemporary Arabic Writing: A Case Study in Modernization, *Middle Eastern Studies* (Spring, 1967), p. 127.
12. Heyd, *op. cit.*, p. 80.
13. Lewis, *op. cit.*, p. xxi.
14. Heyd, *op. cit.*, p. 80.
15. By way of example, among them were the following under the letter *A* (plurals have been suppressed): *agans, abajur, ambalajci, akümülâtör, arkeoloji enstitü, asansor, avize,* and *avokat.* Under *B: banka, bar, baro* (legal Bar), *berber, beton, bijüteri, bira fabrika, bisiklet ve motosiklet, bisküvit, borsa, briket, brülör, büfe,* and *büro makina.*
16. Türk Dil Kurultayi VI, p. 146, cited in Heyd, *op. cit.,* p. 84.
17. A good example of intermixed modern technical terminology is seen in the following advertisement for an ıbм systems analyst, placed in the newspaper *Cumhuriyet,* 23 February 1969 (European loan-words are italic):

ıbм Programcısı Ariyor

ıbм 1401 *sistemi programlarında* sps, rpg veya *autocoder* lisanlarından asgari bir tanesine vakıf, benzeri bir *sistemde* asgari üç senelik is tecrübesi bulunan bir *programcı* ve *sistem analisti* aranmaktadır. Ingilizce bilenler tercih edilecektir, Ücret, yapılacak *test* sonucunda tecrübe ve liyakata göre tâyin edilecektir. Adayların, is tecrübelerini ve talep ettikleri ücreti havi bir dilekce ve bir adet *fotoğraf* ile: Mensucat *Santral,* Domirhane Caddesi 126, Istanbul *Programcı, adresine* müracaatları rica olunur.

18. Geoffrey Lewis, *Turkey* (3rd rev. ed.; London, 1965).
19. Issawi, *op. cit.,* p. 130.
20. For a definition and discussion of societal change, see Edward A. Tiryakian, A Model of Societal Change and its Lead Indicators, *in* Samuel Z. Klausner, ed., *The Study of Total Societies* (New York, 1967).
21. The definition of "modern" and "modernization" used here posits modernization as a total, continuing, and relative process that reveals new aspects or levels of problems after, and as the result of inputs of new segments of information into a society and its reaction to them. Modernity is thus both a relative state and one that is inherently unstable, in effect receding as we advance towards it. For further discussion of this

view of modernization, see Cyril Black, *Modernization* (Princeton, 1966); Robert N. Bellah, ed., *Religion and Progress in Modern Asia* (New York, 1965); and Charles F. Gallagher, *Lessons from the Modernization of Japan, Part I: Ecumenism, Pragmatism, and Ideology (CFG–1–'68)*, American Universities Field Staff Reports, East Asia Series, vol. 15, no. 2 (October 1968).

9. SOME PLANNING PROCESSES IN THE DEVELOPMENT OF THE INDONESIAN-MALAY LANGUAGE

S. TAKDIR ALISJAHBANA
Rector, National University, Djakarta

INTRODUCTION TO LANGUAGE PLANNING

Our age is an age of planning. Planning manifests itself not only in the huge, all-comprehensive five- or ten-year plans of the totalitarian states but also in every commercial enterprise. It has even penetrated into the most intimate aspects of life such as the much-discussed family planning.

Belief in planning has its roots in the current conviction that man is able to mold not only his individual behavior but also the patterns of society and culture. It is in this sense a phenomenon typical of our time when man has become so confident of his own capacity to take his future into his own hands. This belief contrasts sharply to bygone eras when man believed in and entrusted his destiny to an all-powerful God.

It should be clear, however, that real planning—the determination of a particular course of action to achieve a specified goal—is only possible and effective within certain boundaries. It is only feasible where the planner and later the executor of the plan have real power to manipulate the behavior of the people whom they include in their planning. If the plan is to have some chance at success, it must consider certain psychological, social, and cultural prerequisites.

Since language is one of the most widespread and most essential of all the activities of man, it is clear that planning in this field will be very difficult, if not impossible. Thus, we should only speak of language planning in a very limited sense and for a very special goal. Nobody should think of planning for all the language behavior of all the members of a nation. Such rigid regimentation would also mean the end of man as a thinking and free being.

This is the reason why, in my efforts at language planning (or, as I usually call it, language engineering), I have concentrated mainly on the language of the schools. It is the school-language that really lends itself to planning and regulation. Planners may hope to control effectively the kinds of textbooks and the kinds of teacher training. In the classroom, originality and the freedom of the language of the individual student can be controlled. I am convinced that standard English, French, German, and other standard languages are mainly the products of compulsory education.[1]

SPREAD AND CHOICE OF THE MALAY LANGUAGE

If we consider the development of the Indonesian and Malay languages, it is clear that the decision to make them the national and official languages of two countries was purely the result of historical and social processes, with its many political and sociological conflicts. Malay had been the lingua franca of the area for over a millenium: the topography of Indonesia and Malaysia determined the emergence of some 250 separate but related languages, but the development of trade, political, and cultural contacts evoked the necessity of a lingua franca.

The rise of Malay in this area seems a natural outcome of these variables. Geographically, Malay was favored because it was used on both sides of the Straits of Malacca. Second, the fact that this area for centuries had been the political center of Southeast Asia, while Sriwijaya, Malacca, and Acheh were great centers of trade, only accentuated the already favorable position of Malay in this area. Third, it was the Malays who, from the earliest times seafarers, populated the coastal areas of Sumatra, Borneo, and other islands. Again, it has also been suggested that the simplicity of the Malay language when compared to the sociolinguistic complexities of the Javanese language enhanced its use as a lingua franca. Later colonizers (the Portuguese, the Dutch, the English, and the Japanese) had to recognize the fact that Malay was the only language that could be used to reach the large majority, which, in turn served—though unintentionally—to help the spread of the Malay language. Religious missionaries (both Islamic and Christian) also had to recognize this fact and helped as well in the spreading of Malay. Finally, it seems that Malay speakers are more tolerant than most native speakers towards foreign "abuse" of their language by non-native speakers.

Early Indonesian nationalists recognized the need for unity among the ideals and actions of the various national movements to combat the strongly centralized Dutch government. Thus, the Oath of the Indonesian Youth of October 28, 1928 called for one fatherland, one nation, and one language. With this oath, not only was the goal of the Indonesian nationalist movement formulated but also the Malay lingua franca was chosen as the future national and official language of an independent Indonesian nation. The consecration of this ideal took place in 1945.

This formulation of the linguistic goal of the Independence movement was still a long way from what we earlier termed a plan; namely, a predetermined course of action. At this time, the goal was no more than an ideal, with strong motivating force. In 1933, a literary and linguistic magazine *Pudjangga Baru* ("The New Writer") was founded and served as a rallying place for those committed to this ideal.

Nearer to the formulation of a plan was the First Congress of the Indonesian Language in Solo in 1938, convened at the initiative of the editors of *Pudjangga Baru*. Present at the congress were journalists, politicians, linguists, and literary figures. To a degree, this congress can be considered as a planning conference whose goal was to implement the Oath of the Youth of 1928. The Congress resolved that it was necessary (1) to create a faculty of language and letters; (2) to establish a standardized grammar and orthography; (3) to write a comprehensive dictionary; and (4) to create a modern terminology. But since there was no government behind the Congress and the *Pudjangga Baru* or an organization with sufficient money and experts, such decisions were little more than the expression of a desire to see an improvement in the Indonesian language. And, indeed, nothing further happened to this desire until the Japanese occupation during World War II.

PLANNING EFFORTS DURING THE JAPANESE OCCUPATION

Although it was clear from the outset that the Japanese view on the language problem in Indonesia was quite different from that of the Indonesian national movement (i.e., the Japanese wanted to make Japanese the official language of Indonesia as they had in Formosa and in Korea), the exigencies of war forced the Japanese occupation forces to carry out the Indonesian national goals for their language. Almost immediately, the Dutch language was forbidden. All legal pronouncements for Indonesians took place in the Indonesian language, and Indonesian became the sole medium of instruction in the schools.

Since Indonesian high-school and university instruction during the Dutch colonial regime was given almost entirely in Dutch, naturally, there were neither enough competent teachers in Indonesian nor the

necessary textbooks and reading materials. To produce high-school textbooks, a translation committee was created (within the Balai Pustaka—
the government publishing house) whose task was to translate Dutch
textbooks into Indonesian. It was soon clear to this committee that, before
a translation could be completed, an equivalent Indonesian term must be
created. Thus, these translators and other interested persons organized
meetings to discuss and codify the new terms. The new terminology was
published in the *Pandji Pustaka*, a magazine of the Balai Pustaka. This
lack of terminology was felt not only by the schools but also by the Japanese war administration. After some hesitation, the Japanese authorities
established an Indonesian Language Committee, whose task was to standardize the language and to provide it with the necessary modern vocabulary for administrative, educational, and other purposes. The committee
had some thirty members, including, among others, Sukarno and Hatta.

This committee decided in its first meeting that the work should be
divided into three sections: (1) the coining of a modern terminology for
science and technology; (2) the writing of a modern grammar; and (3)
the selection of daily words to be incorporated into the standard language.
Of the three tasks, it turned out that the first was both the most urgent
and the most comprehensive task.

Modern Terminology

To expedite its work, the terminology committee urged offices and institutions to send in a list of terms either in use by them or needed by
them. In the Language Office, these terms were put on cards with one or
more tentative Indonesian equivalents. On one set of cards were given
those terms defined within a special subject such as botany, physics,
economics, and mathematics. On another larger set of cards were pooled
together all of the terms of the various special areas. For example, it was
easy to see that the term, "function," was used in many different fields.
Knowledge of these various meanings and contexts is necessary for the
efficient coordination of a term in its various fields of usage.

The terms were then submitted to a meeting of a subsection on a
special subject. The results of this meeting were sent on to a larger meeting on terminology. No less a person than Vice-President Hatta himself
served as chairman of this meeting. In the meeting of this larger section,
the representatives of other subsections had the opportunity to compare
the terms with their own and to express their criticism. As a result of

these deliberations, some changes were often made in the list. Later, this list of terms was again discussed in the plenary session of the three sections: terminology, grammar, and daily words. The decision of the plenary session was final. These terms were then published in the official Government Gazette. The lists were also published by the Language Office and distributed to the public.

Some guidelines for the coining of modern terms were established. The order of preference for terms was as follows: Indonesian words, if possible; if not, then Asian words; and if not, then, international terms. Luckily, these guidelines were never literally applied. In most cases, the decision regarding a new term depended on the composition of the members present at a particular meeting. Those of Javanese origin usually preferred Sanskrit or old Javanese words. For the Javanese, these words carry high prestige since they belong to the thinking and feeling of the mystico-feudal sphere of the Old Javanese culture. The Moslem group had a tendency to prefer words of Arabic origin. A third group preferred international terms. I myself preferred the third choice since it united Indonesia with the world of science and technology.[2]

Although one might expect that the use of Sanskrit and Arabic might have furthered Indonesia's unification with countries where these languages were spoken, such was not the case because there has never been any serious efforts to get in touch with Indian or Arabic scholars to coordinate language-planning efforts. Indeed, the choice of terms from such languages without consultation further isolated Indonesia.

The systematic coining of these new terms can indeed be considered as the execution of a planned process. In the quick transition from the Dutch to the Indonesian language during the Japanese occupation, everybody not only felt the need for the codification of the new terms but also was eager to contribute to that task. Since the scientific, technological, and other modern concepts were already available and easily assessible in the existing modern languages, the process of the codification of modern Indonesian terms could proceed steadily without too great difficulties.

Modern Grammar

The task of writing a standard modern grammar posed a more difficult problem. First of all, it was necessary to decide just what the Indonesian language was and what it should be. First, the Indonesian language was defined as a modern language comparable to Dutch or English, based sociologically on the lingua franca and linguistically on the Malay language. The next step was more difficult. While the job of the modern linguist usually consists of describing the rules of grammar of a group of people, the task of the Indonesian language planners in writing such a grammar was indeed a creative one. It was necessary not only to examine the existing Indonesian-language varieties but also to decide what the new standard language would be.

In deciding on a standard modern language, the planners faced many problems. It was necessary to find, first of all, the best samples of Indonesian, as defined above, upon which to base the new grammar. The best examples of Indonesian were thought to be in the writing of those persons who had a command of the rules of the Old Malay Language and who, at the same time, had a good modern education. The examples were taken from the written language of such persons as H. A. Salim, Sanusi Pane, Hatta, Dajoh, and Imam Supardi. It was felt that the standard grammar should be a normative grammar, which reflected the most disciplined, sophisticated, and polished modern language.[3]

The problem was not impossible because standardization had in fact already begun. Charles van Ophuysen had already written an acceptable Malay grammar and created an efficient orthography. In addition, other forces helped. During the Dutch period, the Balai Pustaka was founded (1911), and Malay was systematically taught in the primary schools and in the teacher-training colleges.

In many instances, the rules of the traditional Malay language could be accepted without modification since the Indonesian language is indeed a continuation of Malay. However, because the Indonesian language has been continuously under the influence of the local languages as well as that of Dutch and English, differences in the use of affixes, syntax, word-formation, and word usage did become apparent.

The problem was how to cope with these differences. If the grammarians leaned too heavily on the traditional Malay language, the resulting grammar would have been a traditional Malay grammar, which would not only be awkward for modern needs but also appear strange in one way or another to modern users of Indonesian. If the grammarians, however, were too eager to accept influences from other local languages, then the grammar would not appear consistent. Additionally, if one were too liberal in the acceptance of forms deriving from modern languages, there was the possibility that the language would lose a great deal of its Malay or Malayo-Polynesian character. It would be difficult, moreover, to arrive at a consistent set of rules.

Thus the task of the grammar-writer was a very responsible, delicate, and complex one. It was unavoidable that his task, to a certain extent, was a creative one. Just as the creation of a new modern constitution in Asian countries served as a source of a new system of modern laws, so the creation of a normative grammar set forth rules for language behavior within the official sphere of the new states.

In addition to a thorough command of the modern language at all levels of usage, the grammarian must also have a liberal mind so that he is able to understand the multifarious tendencies, possibilities, and tensions posed by the special situation of the rapid change of the language. At the same time, he should be aware that a well-formulated and a well-integrated language should achieve a balance between old potentialities and the exigencies of the new realities.[4]

Since I had the task of writing such a grammar at that time, I studied both the morphology and syntax of Malay as well as those of the other languages of Indonesia. In those cases where the use of an affix was ambivalent, I chose the rule that was supported by the other Indonesian languages so that the new rule became more acceptable for the whole of Indonesia.

The grammar was never submitted to the Language Committee because, by the time I had some work to submit, the Japanese occupation had ended and the Language Office was closed. However, it received approval through usage. I taught the rules of this grammar in the senior high school and at the Indonesian University in Djakarta. My work was finally published in 1948 and has now gone through some thirty-seven editions. It is called *Tatabahasa Baru Bahasa Indonesia*.

Daily Words

Still another procedure was followed by the section concerned with words of daily use. The task of this section was to determine which, among the thousands of new words used in the newspapers, books, speeches, and other materials, could readily be incorporated into Indonesian. The need for this committee was apparent because of the common belief that Malay was confined to those words listed only in van Ophuysen's work or in other dictionaries.

It goes without saying that the task of this section was much less important and urgent than that of the other two sections. More of a problem was the writing of an up-to-date dictionary. This task was done by W. J. S. Poerwadarminta in his excellent *Kamus Umum Bahasa Indonesia*.

After the Indonesian Independence, the work of the Language Committee was continued by the Lembaga Bahasa dan Budaja (Institute of Language and Culture), which was affiliated with the University of Indonesia. The new institute emphasized further codification of modern terms. The current successor to this institute is the Lembaga Bahasa dan Kesusastraan (Institute of Language and Literature). Unfortunately, this body is understaffed, has a negligible budget, and does not have the authority to effect its decisions. An indication of the last point is the great resistance the new spelling, proposed a few years ago, met with.

FINAL COMMENTS ON LANGUAGE PLANNING

Before closing this paper, may I add a few words about the meaning of authority in language planning. Since language can be the possession of every member of society, not all planning is in the hands of the government. Besides the Ministry of Education, which is responsible for the language of the schools, and the Ministry of Information, which also influences language, there are less organized sources of change. During Sukarno's regime, the army had a great deal of influence in the coining of new terms and words of daily usage. Indeed, Sukarno himself introduced new words and slogans in almost every one of his speeches. Poerwadarminta's dictionary was more the result of his personal love and dedication to the language than of governmental efforts. The direction of human behavior is not always controllable. During the revolutionary years, the Minister of Education rejected my grammar on account of my political views; yet the teachers of the high schools prescribed it for their students. A more recent example of unexpected and unplanned-for results is the controversy around the new Indonesian-Malay spelling.

In spite of the planning or lack thereof, it can be said that today the Indonesian language is already an efficient medium of instruction and communication in our modern life.[5] The task that still lies ahead is the publication of enough books and magazines to stimulate the necessary basis for modern thought and progress. If this need for more textbooks in Indonesian is not fulfilled as quickly as possible, the switch to Indonesian will prove to be a detriment to the progress of Indonesia. That is, modern information and thought must be made available to language users.

NOTES

1. In addition to writing a grammar of the Indonesian language, I also prepared a four-volume collection of Indonesian short stories and essays on modern topics for high-school students. The language used in this collection, *Pelangi* (Rainbow), was annotated according to my ideas of modern Indonesian grammar. In addition, at that time, I published a monthly magazine entitled *Pembina Bahasa Indonesia* (The Builder of the Indonesian Language) to help teachers answer their grammatical and terminological dilemmas in the language. At the university level I trained my students in the translation of rather difficult English texts into modern Indonesian. At the Second Congress of the Indonesian Language in Medan in 1954, there was a controversy between the teachers and the journalists. The former reproached the latter for their carelessness and their anarchistic attitude towards the language. I advised the former that there was no use in attempting to correct the latter, especially since the latter claimed that they were the true bearers of modern Indonesian. I suggested that the teachers had better concentrate on the language of the coming generation of journalists who were still their pupils in the schools.

2. See my paper, The Modernization of the Languages of Asia in Historical and Socio-Cultural Perspectives, to be published soon in *The Modernization of the Languages of Asia* (Kuala Lumpur, Malaysia).

3. Another choice of material is, of course, possible. For the last several years, I have been engaged in research pertaining to language usage in the Malaysian newspapers and magazines, in the Malaysian parliament, in the Malaysian radio and television, and in the textbooks of the Malaysian secondary schools. The research includes a word count to ascertain the necessary level for standardization as well as a study of the usage of Malay affixes.

4. See my paper, The Writing of a Grammar for a Modern Asian Language, to be published soon in *The Modernization of the Languages of Asia* (Kuala Lumpur, Malaysia).

5. For a more comprehensive discussion of the development of the Indonesian and Malay languages, see my article, Language Policy, Language Engineering, and Literacy in Indonesia and Malaysia, to be published soon in *Current Trends in Linguistics*, vol. 8.

10. THE DEVELOPMENT OF BENGALI SINCE THE ESTABLISHMENT OF PAKISTAN

MUHAMMAD ABDUL HAI
Deceased, formerly of the University of Dacca

Bengali has about ninety-five million speakers, of whom about sixty-two million live in East Pakistan and thirty-two million in West Bengal and Tripura in India. Bengali belongs to the Aryan group of Indo-European; its structural pattern, however, shows a striking resemblance to the Dravidian languages of Southern India.

Bengali's literary history is divided into three periods: Old (A.D. 800–1200); Middle (A.D. 1201–1800); and Modern. The Modern period begins with the establishment of the Fort William College in 1800 in Calcutta by English missionaries, whose purpose was to teach Bengali to English administrators.

In the 1840's, Persian was replaced by English in administration and education. Western ideas poured in through English literature, history, and philosophy, resulting in the growth and development of modern Bengali literature in all fields, particularly in poetry (e.g., Rabindranath Tagore). During the British rule, the vernaculars developed mostly along literary lines. Since these languages had very limited use in the nation's administration and education, they did not develop as languages of modern thought and learning. The underlying idea was that the British might go but that the English language would remain. Ultimately, the British did leave in 1947. When they left, our education was firmly geared to English, as was the administration.

In the wake of Independence, the demand for adoption of the vernaculars at all levels of education and administration became popular. A supporting factor was that the medium of instruction used for most

---

NOTE: A full version of this paper will appear in S. Takdir Alisjahbana, ed., *The Modernization of the Languages of Asia* (Kuala Lumpur, in press).

students was already Bengali up to the time of matriculation, or the examination for the secondary-school certificate. In Pakistan, the question of which language was to be used as the medium of instruction was finally settled and accepted, after a bitter State-language controversy, in the 1956 Constitution, which stated that both Bengali and Urdu should be the State languages of Pakistan and that the former should be the sole language of education and administration in East Pakistan.

A Bengali Academy was established in 1957, at the Provincial Headquarters at Dacca, "to promote the culture and development of Bengali language and literature in East Pakistan." To fulfill this objective, the academy was equipped with six departments: research, translation, compilation, publication and sales, cultural, and library. Immediately after the Ayub Government came into power in 1958, it set up a large number of commissions to introduce reforms. One such commission, while emphasizing the teaching of English, recommended its gradual replacement by our national languages—Bengali in the East and Urdu in the West—as media of instruction at all levels of education.

In pursuance of the recommendations of the Commission on National Education, the Central Board for the Development of Bengali was established in Dacca in 1962 with the following aims and objects: (1) to develop Bengali language and literature; (2) to remove deficiencies in Bengali, particularly in the field of natural and social sciences as well as in technological subjects so that Bengali could become the medium of instruction at a higher level; (3) to coordinate the work of other organizations engaged in promoting literary and scientific work in Bengali.

Bengali prose has an effective history of only a century and a half. In general it lacks terseness, precision, and economy of words that are characteristic of scientific prose. What the Bengali language lacks in its scientific, technical, and administrative vocabulary and in its precise and exact expression of abstruse, complex, and complicated ideas; and what it has suffered from its, perhaps, excessive emotionalism and softness and also from its lack of scientific literature—these shortcomings the Bengali Academy and the Central Board for the Development of Bengali have been at work to remove. The Department of Bengali at the University of Dacca has also participated in this work.

The Academy has done the following:

1. It has collected nearly fifty thousand folklore tales. These have been catalogued by subject and are being edited for publication.

2. It has compiled and published a dialect dictionary (about eighty thousand words), edited by Dr. Md. Shahidullah.
3. It has translated approximately 180 books on different subjects.
4. It has published in 1964 a comprehensive scientific study by me of the phonological features of Bengali entitled *Dhani Vijnan O Bangla Dhani Tattawa.*
5. It has compiled an encyclopedia of Islam in Bengali, based on Lydens' shorter encyclopedia. (I may also mention here the larger Bengali encyclopedia under preparation by the Dacca branch of Franklin Book Programs, Inc., of U.S.A.).
6. It has compiled a list of administrative terms, now being examined by a government committee.

The Central Board for the Development of Bengali has done the following:

1. It has carried out planned programs to prepare and publish books for introducing Bengali as a medium of instruction in B.A. and B.Sc. Pass and Honors courses.
2. It has engaged itself in trying to solve the theoretical and mechanical problems of printing in Bengali.
3. It has decided to improve the existing unsatisfactory Bengali typewriter. Mr. Munier Choudhury (Department of Bengali, University of Dacca) has proposed a keyboard in his *An Illustrated Brochure on Bengali Typewriters.* However, the Optima Company (East Germany) was unable to release the typewriter for sale in East Pakistan by 1969.
4. It has completed the first phase of the Bengali renderings of technical terms of different science and art subjects. The work covers 21 subjects (11 sciences and 10 arts) out of which lexica on 7 subjects (4 sciences and 3 arts) have already been published. Most of the international terms have been kept intact; others are being rendered with the help of Sanskrit, Bengali, and Perso-Arabic roots and endings.

We in the Department of Bengali at the University of Dacca have concentrated on research into the language and literature and also on training personnel for governmental departments, educational institutions, and other organizations. The department publishes under my editorship a bi-annual research journal known as *Sahitya Patrika* (The Journal of Letters). The government of Pakistan and the Central Board for the Development of Bengali subsidize recurring expenses on publication of our research notes and this journal.

According to the present Constitution, the government of Pakistan would set up a committee around 1970 to review the progress of our two national languages—Bengali and Urdu—and fix a date by which the change-over from English would be possible.

A General Approach to Language Planning

11. TOWARDS A THEORY
OF LANGUAGE PLANNING

BJÖRN H. JERNUDD
Department of Linguistics, Monash University
JYOTIRINDRA DAS GUPTA
Department of Political Science, University of California, Berkeley

THE CONCEPT OF PLANNING

Planning[1] refers to the utilization of resources in a consciously controlled manner. Social planning is an example of decision-making behavior normally attributed to intelligent individual action for problem-solving. The complexity of social planning can be understood if one specifies the empirical referent of such planning in actual behaviors and within the limits of political possibility.

Social planning at high levels of enlargement ("macro" levels) involves the construction of an over-all design of organized action that is considered necessary for economic utilization of resources and that is directed by a formally constituted authority. It consists of a structure of coordinated programs, and the latter in their turn consist of a set of coordinated projects (Hagen, 1963, p. 19).

The Process of Planning

In this paper, planning is considered at the level of national society.[2] Here planning can be understood with reference to national planning for the whole economy, education, population, or any other specified social sector or combination of sectors. The popularity of "economic" planning has been such that many other social sectors are being increasingly brought within the scope of planned direction.

"Economic" planning usually comprises only a limited set of national resources; namely, easily monetized (pecuniary) resources like labor, buildings, machines, or reserves of raw materials in nature. However, leisure, theater activity, and libraries (reading) are also resources that are subject to economizing. Increase (pecuniary) in the gross national product (GNP), as it is commonly understood, is but one measure[3] of the growth of some of a nation's resources. We could also employ measures of cultural activity, which might be used together with "traditional" measures of success of economizing or planning. Language is in this respect also a resource and can be taken into account in planning.

In a national community, the role of conscious superordination of the major interdependent social sectors belongs to the political authority. Other metaplanning factors like the nature of the social system, the cultural values, the tradition of the community, and the like impinge on national planning. Given the importance of the metaplanning factors in determining and constraining a plan, one can still theoretically construct boundaries for a planning process. The lines of closure will become clearer as one looks at concrete processes of planning.

The broadest authorization for planning is obtained from the politicians. A body of experts is then specifically delegated the task of preparing a plan. In preparing this, the experts ideally estimate existing resources and forecast potential utilization of such resources in terms of developmental targets. Once targets are agreed upon, a strategy of action is elaborated. These are authorized by the legislature and are implemented by the organizational set-up, authorized in its turn by the planning executive. The implementation of the tasks may be evaluated periodically by the planners. In these ideal processes, a planning agency is charged with the over-all guidance. The nature of guidance varies depending on the responsibility given to the agency in each particular case.

The process of planning stated so far in ideal and general terms seems to fit well with abstract intentions of "economic," demographic, and educational planning at the national level. There could be a comparable process of language planning for national communities, although existing cases may fall short of abstract ideals. The notion of language planning has attracted some attention in recent times, though the existing literature is not very clear about the nature of planning involved in such cases.

LANGUAGE AS A RESOURCE

The logic of language planning is dictated by the recognition of language as a societal resource. The importance of this resource is due to the communicational and identific values attached by the community to one or more languages.

A simple example on the level of the individual is the case of a person who would at some given occasion be willing to pay for knowing a certain language. Regretting that he did not take time off last year (thus fore-saking an income then) to enroll in a language course (to invest in language knowledge), he engages a paid translator instead (which means that he must consume less of something else now). On a national level of language planning, we are taking an aggregate view about language decisions both on the individual level as well as the successively higher levels.

Language planning can proceed by identifying the concrete areas of society that demand planned action regarding language resources. In carving out this area of relevance, the values and ideas of technical experts will be matched against those of the representatives of the community. Similarly, an optimal design of a plan would require the coordinated attention of political, educational, economic, and linguistic authorities. It is important to recognize the relations of interdependency among the above authorities because, otherwise, the social rationale of language planning may become subordinated to a predominantly normative linguistic rationale, or hidden by method.

QUEST FOR THE IDEAL

Contemporary treatment of language planning does not seem to be sufficiently sensitized to the complexity of the social rationale of language planning in practice. Existing definitions of language planning are more in the nature of normative linguistic definitions.

Haugen's (1966b) definition of language planning as "the evaluation of linguistic change" (p. 52) is too open-ended. It may suggest a reluctance to include scope for deliberate creation of a new set of linguistic elements, though the exposition of the definition does provide for the possibility of norm creation. In fact, the emphasis on norm creation and absolutes of evaluation are carried to the extent of conceding an almost total freedom to the planner to incorporate his preference patterns in planning so that only a subordinate role is granted to the preferences of society members through their political representatives.

Our understanding of planning allows for problems to be consciously recognized sometimes first among the planners, rather than by a political authority. Such awareness and faculty of problem-identification can be a major contribution by professional planners, in reply to a vaguely or only generally articulated demand for action in the community. This freedom of theirs to act must, however, be constrained both by political consultation and by the practicality of the task. Haugen (1966b), instead, advocates the use of absolute knowledge to cope with "convictions and rationalizations concerning speech and writing, against which the planner may turn out to be powerless, unless he can turn them to account for his own purposes" (p. 60). To the extent that he seeks to clarify social beliefs that contradict social goals, the planner's attempts to persuade community representatives may be in the best interest of his political superiors and, therefore, within the terms of reference of planning. However, attempting to influence the contents of planning beyond such clarification is not. The latter might result if planning is identified with abstract linguistic thought alone.

Language planning in this latter conception ceases to be the reflection of a composite urge articulated in the national community. Instead it is identified with an expert enterprise motivated by abstract ideals of a selected, albeit deeply concerned, group of linguists. Tauli's definition of language planning suggests this kind of enterprise.

Since "it is a well-known fact that language lags behind thought" (Tauli, 1968, p. 14), partly because of the fact that "the ethnic languages were not constructed methodically according to plan," there is, in his opinion, a clearly motivated case for developing a "science which methodically investigates the ends, principles and tactics of language planning" (Ibid., p. 27). Tauli disapproves of existing languages and of the irrationality of their patterns of emergence; and he proposes to improve on their present, in his opinion, unsatisfactory state.

We do not define language planning in this manner. We agree, however, with the desirability of approaching language problems in their social reality, with scientific methods and with a desire to acquire knowledge that may help mankind to improve communication.

The emphasis on enumeration of abstract ideals reveals a misconception of the activity involved in planning language for a community; the quest for golden rules of language development indicates a propensity for a utopian linguistic solution oblivious of the preferred compromise appropriate to the needs of the community. Our definition of language planning excludes search for universal linguistic "means" to achieve "results," like "clarity," "economy" (e.g., that "the number of linguistic units must be the least possible," etc.), "aesthetic form," and "elasticity" (Tauli, 1968, pp. 30–42).

Our understanding of planning implies that the decision-makers choose a satisfactory, or even optimal, course of action but within limits of given amounts of resources and only in order to reach the goals that have been approved by the political authority. They aspire to find effective solutions to their planning tasks.

Criteria of Choice

Haugen (1966b) proposes three criteria for language decisions; namely, "efficiency," "adequacy," and "acceptability" (pp. 60–64). (1) "Efficiency" is postulated as a criterion that is to be applied independently of the two others. It refers to the specification and application of a set of linguistic rules.[4] (2) "Adequacy" refers to the "degree of precision" of linguistic forms in conveying information. (3) "Acceptability" is the "sociological component of evaluation."

In our definition, the "efficiency," or effectivity, of a decision cannot be determined without a knowledge of the particular values that the decision makers allow "adequacy" and "acceptability variables" to assume. "Adequacy" is itself subject to evaluation. It is a catch-all for linguistic elements expressing the symbol- and signal-, as well as symptom-function, of language (Bühler, 1934); and it therefore necessarily forms the substance of any language problem. "Acceptability" poses the social constraints on the use of proposed, adequate, linguistic forms. It may very well be that a linguistically adequate theory (e.g., if judged by metalinguistic theory) cannot be implemented because, for example, of "acceptability-obstacles" in the speech community. Such obstacles may, however, be overcome at a cost of time and energy; as a result, however, it may not be a very effective solution.

An alternative for solving a language problem is effective, in our definition of the term, when it is expected to accomplish what we want it to accomplish. When making a prognosis, planners take into account the "acceptability" of possible alternatives. The alternatives are formulated because a linguistic phenomenon is felt to be less "adequate." (See figure 1.)

Planning versus Happening

Haugen's (1966a) important and unique study of a language-conflict situation does not demonstrate the existence of orderly planning (not even as a superstructure for the complex social events that may result) but a social movement without unifying control; in Haugen's own words: "Little by little a linguistic avalanche has been set in motion, an avalanche which is still sliding and which no one quite knows how to stop, even though many would be happy to do so" (Ibid., p. 1). He convincingly

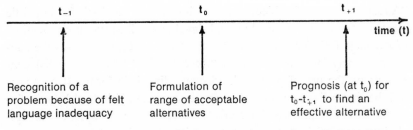

Figure 1: Recognition, formulation, and choice of alternatives in time.

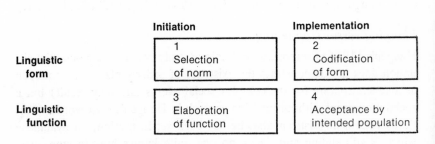

Figure 2: Haugen's scheme of language decision-making.

shows the absence of planning from "language planning" (cf. Steblin-Kamenskij, 1968).

From this empirical study, Haugen develops an analytical scheme (of two dimensions and four categories) of language problem-solving.

This scheme can be made to apply to decisions on a national level as well as on an individual level. It is likely that any language decision is less effective if it fails to take into account aspects of all four categories, either by implication or by choice. (See figure 2).

A decision on selection of norm for a community is likely to be irrational unless consideration is given to the functional capacity of the norm, to the need for accompanying linguistic guides, and to the probabilities of acceptance. Similarly, vocabulary extension is hardly meaningful unless consideration is given to rules of the language (norm) for which it is intended, as well as to the mode of presentation to the community and to the probabilities of acceptance in the speech community.

Square (category) *4* presupposes either equare *1, 1-2,* or *1-3*. Square *3* or *2* implies *1* but not necessarily *2* or *3*. (See figure 2).

In a national administration, decisions are taken on different political and administrative internal levels. It is likely that empirical studies will demonstrate that there is a relation within such an administration between the level of a language decision and its content. Selection of norm would be a political, thus top-node, decision, whereas decisions to produce acceptance, for example, of a set of terms in a given subpopulation would concern a particular lower-level administrative unit. (See figure 3).

Deliberate government planning will have to coordinate, politically and administratively, a hierarchy of experts, officials, and laymen, all differing in the importance they attach to the above categories.[5]

The Context of Planning

Even the more empirical accounts of national language planning merely cite certain cases of planning assignment.[6] Very little is elaborated on the formulation of this assignment or the nature of the administration charged with the responsibility of implementation.

No valid discussion of the problems of interdependency and coordination of language in relation to other relevant sectors of social planning can proceed because of this gap of knowledge.

Decisions on language usage in education,[7] for example, may give an impression of being an exception to this statement. However, only rarely are available educational resources taken into consideration. Educationally motivated language problems, such as problems of vernacular or second-language medium of instruction, are often solved only in ideal terms; i.e., by learning experiments and not by simultaneous assessment of the capacity of teachers and the like.[8]

Experimentation may provide answers such that more subject matter is learned with one pattern of language use than another; if that outcome is translated into a recommendation for the whole school system without calculations about teacher training, material production, and the like that need to be weighed against the value of the effect of an increase in knowledge of subject matter, it leads to unsound decisions.

The use of native languages in education provides another example. In teaching a group of pupils a certain amount of subject matter, it is probably so that in most cases (if not all) instruction by means of their mother tongue is superior to instruction in a second language. The introduction of a non-native language would lower the achievement in subject matter. In order to decide on an amount of second-language teaching, it is necessary to assign, therefore, a value to the effects of educating pupils to know this second language. In this simplified case, the right mix of native and second-language teaching and use has been found when a further unit reduction in the knowledge of subject matter would cost the same as

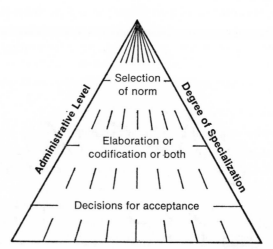

Figure 3: Relation between content and level of language decisions in the national administration.

the benefit of a further unit increase in the knowledge of a second language.

Unless educational authorities have been given nationally relevant criteria of valuation of language knowledge, not only may an official (national, etc., as the case may be) language—if non-native—be taught in insufficient amounts as a result of such lack of coordination; but there will also be other consequences, in the long run, which will result in a lowering of intensity of use and a lowering of communicative efficiency because of the necessity of translating or because of language obstacles to labor mobility.

To avoid such unwanted effects, government activities can be coordinated with regard to national goals, by rules concerning liaison between departments, specification of measures for valuation, or problem-solving techniques, etc.[9] The content and extent of such coordination will depend on the kind of language problem.

A TYPOLOGY OF LANGUAGE PROBLEMS

Ferguson (1968) and Neustupný (1968b) have suggested schemes of classification of language problems. While Ferguson takes a functional approach and separates three components of language development, namely, graphization, standardization, and modernization, Neustupný emphasizes the linguistic objects of development. According to him, there are communication problems of two kinds, verbal and non-verbal. Verbal problems are subdivided into language-code and language-speech problems. We will attempt to interpret and combine these two schemes.[10]

Language problems can be classified at least by motivation and by language characteristics, in the latter case specifying at least whether they require code change in addition to evaluation of code output (i.e., of speech).[11]

Motivations for Language Problems

Ferguson's terms (standardization, modernization, and graphization) can be seen as intermediate goals for the development of language in society. These auxiliary concepts summarize sets of ultimate goals that are attained by means of solutions characterized by features of standardization, modernization, and graphization, respectively.

Standardization as an intermediate goal may itself be motivated by modernization. It is not language-specific but directed towards language in one of its applications.

We may interpret Ferguson's (1968) definition of standardization—namely, the process of acceptance of one variety of a language throughout the speech community as a supradialectal norm (p. 31)—as a special case of standardization resulting from successive applications of such effort. It is obvious that standardization of language means benefits by uniformation, but it is also obvious that the optimal point of no further gain may be sociolinguistically complex.

This understanding of standardization makes it possible to apply the concept also, for example, to cases of orthographical and terminological supranational standardization, raising issues of coordination beyond any single standard language.[12]

Social emphasis on written language makes standardization relatively easier and may explain the greater saliency of written-language problems, such as orthography and vocabulary in "literate" domains of usage.[13]

Standardization efforts can be directed both towards a speech variety in its entirety (establishing this variety as a supradialectal norm) and towards aspects of a variety (e.g., terminological standardization). It is likely that as a result other, perhaps competing, language features and varieties are eliminated or that linguistic convergence of remaining—now subordinated—socio- and regional dialects takes place.[14] As standardization is repeatedly applied to language, the speech community acquires a "language system"[15] displaying successively less (and presumably more efficient) linguistic differentiation.

Figure 4 shows the basic relations between modernization, standardization, and language. Modernization creates demands for language

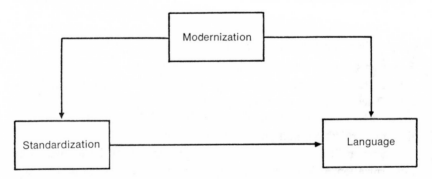

Figure 4: Fundamental relations between
modernization, standardization, and language.

change and demands for standardization, which may be directed also towards language. The kind and intensity of relation will change as society develops.

Orthographical reform and change of written discourse may also be functions of modernization. Orthographies are reviewed successively during development of modern society.[16] We will treat graphization as a class of language problems (objects).

Linguistic Classification of Problems

Using a rough linguistic scheme, demands for language change are directed towards (1) speech variety, (2) discourse, (3) pronunciation, (4) orthography, and (5) morphology, including vocabulary.

1. The very salient and recurring problem of choice of the entire speech variety for national or other functions may obviously motivate efforts at making the variety distinct and may, therefore, involve all other linguistic components. Otherwise, there would seem to be little need for an entire variety to be changed, except, of course, by development of its components (which will often result in differentiation of this original variety into further professional and social varieties).

2. Demands on discourse may involve—e.g., in journalism, literary prose, or poetry—code change as well as speech change.[17]

3. Phonetic demands are documented in their phonological, phonic, and usage aspects.[18]

4. Orthographic innovation is fundamentally a speech problem. This is so because orthography is primarily motivated by phonological and morphological rules, in the case of alphabetic or syllabic script; or by derivations, in the case of logographic scripts.[19]

5. Vocabulary demands have the greatest saliency in the literature on language problems. These demands can be met by subjecting to evaluation either new derivations from existing—or new but possible—lexical entries or derivations after changes in the code.[20] In either case, we note that the derived vocabulary items, as other linguistic elements above, must be evaluated in speech. In fact, vocabulary can often be found without other than the intuitive use of rules of a given language. The important point is that, given a set of code rules, there are practically inexhaustible possibilities of generating language.[21]

TOWARDS A THEORY OF LANGUAGE PLANNING

Language Problems for Planning

The study of language planning requires an identification of major language problems facing a national community. Such an identification should be informed by the basic premises of national development. It will be our task to show how increasing awareness of situational imperatives, generated by developmental needs of the national community, may lead to possibilities of influencing language by a conscious choice.

A Critical Decision: Spread of Language Products

We claim that the most important function in any prospective language-planning effort is to judge spread-alternatives for suggested linguistic solutions. Spread refers to effects in square *3* of Figure 5 as a result of actions in square *2*.

When there is economy in uniformity, the important factor in planning would be to judge standardization-alternatives (a type of spread-decision). In Figure 5, standardization-alternatives (*2a*) are based on the hypothesis that resulting effects (in *4a*) are especially beneficial, in which case, obviously, the relation between *2a* and *3a* is critical.

Our spread-hypothesis implies (1) that planners attempt to find such alternatives that would make *2* have a considerable effect on *3*; and (2) that planners attempt to detail forecasting so that uncertainty about effects of *2* on *3* is reduced. They try to find, in other words, the best alternative for coordinating subsets of people into recognizing the existence of, or accepting the specific use of, certain language products. The valuation of effects in *4* requires a clarification of goals (i.e., desired consequences) as well as scales of valuation (criteria) and techniques for measuring consequences.

Goals of Language Planning

Goals are desired consequences for the future—e.g., easier international communication with less misunderstandings for certain transactions. Classes of goals can be expressed on a high level of abstraction in aggregate economic terms;[22] namely, (1) allocation of resources (raising the standard of living, GNP, etc.); (2) distribution (equality of participation,

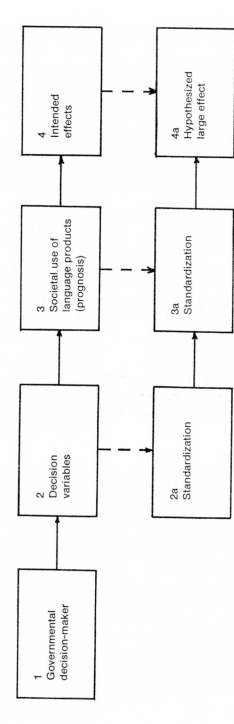

Figure 5: Language planning on a national level.

etc.); and (3) stabilization (developing national consciousness for unity, etc.).

Knowing the differential returns during specified periods of time from allocation of resources to areas of geographic concentration[23] and to groups of people already possessing skills, etc., it is immediately clear that there is a conflict between allocational and distributional goals; neither one can be pursued without affecting the other.

Some language problems, such as the matter of creating a lesser number of language systems in a nation, may be motivated from the point of view of factors from all the above sets of goals:

1. Communications are more effective if there is a certain degree of linguistic homogeneity; this means quicker and more reliable exchange of messages that leads to higher production, both directly and as a consequence of the freeing of resources from previous translating for use elsewhere now, etc.
2. True equality of social participation appears possible only if people understand each other.
3. It is perhaps beneficial for political loyalty and order to have a unifying language symbol.

In this abstract case we note, however, that short-term decisions may cause temporary effects that are counter to the aggregate and longer-term goals for which these decisions were intended. It may be necessary, for example, to reinforce or expand the usage of an unproductive group's language which action may then reduce returns from the economy for some time; and also to induce other language groups to oppose the imposition of that language, upsetting domestic stability as a result. Short-term decisions are often taken on lower administrative levels and are continuously necessary; they are, in principle, caused and circumscribed by less frequent decisions on higher levels.

Another aspect of goal pursuit, the translation of macrogoals into particular goals, can be obtained by looking at vocabulary problems. On a national level, one benefit from such vocabulary standardization as the issuing of particular word lists and insistence on their use, seems to be derived from national consolidation goals. The problem dominating vocabulary decisions in such a case would seem to be the matter of selecting and enforcing a supradialectal norm that can provide a rule system, interpreting whatever individual derivations are produced and also a norm of nativization of foreign roots. The norm then sets the boundaries within which other language development activities can be carried out—e.g., the vocabulary development.

Despite inherent conflict, short-term or longer, between the enumerated classes of goals, it should be possible to find a reasonably efficient path during development towards higher values on all three classes of goals. Approximations of observed diachronic patterning of language change during modernization must not be assumed as an efficient over-all course of action. The question always remains whether the interplay of variables as it actually happened was optimal. The pursuit of an optimal policy requires an explicit understanding of language development in the context of societal development.[24]

Motivation of Public Planning

Since there may be no commensurability between, on the one hand, the benefits that accrue to an individual as a return on his attempts at increasing his communicative capacity by language change and, on the other hand, the benefits that accrue to society from his actions, it is motivated that the public assumes the burden of cost, thus, directing it to be shared by all citizens.[25]

This is not always so. Professional societies (e.g., professional engineers, chemists, etc.) may decide on nomenclatures, in which case it is likely that the benefits of such uniformity and creation accrue primarily to this group, by an increase in the efficiency of interaction taking place among themselves. Terminologies, document standards, and the like are very often manufactured and accepted by voluntary organizations of people with direct vested interests, often also internationally. In the case of highly specialized speech rules, such as developing orthographies for computer use, it may even be necessary for outsiders to purchase the information to get access to its use.

In case of larger benefits to society than to individuals from particular language decisions, it would be motivated, and often necessary, that society makes the decision and pays for it. An individual may not on his own take into account consequences that he would find attractive if he were acting on behalf of a larger group. There are externalities arising from language change that justify language planning beyond the frames of calculation of individuals. It may not make much difference to an individual's career which foreign language he chooses to learn, but, from a

social point of view, transfer of knowledge, production of teaching materials, and the like are greatly alleviated if the choice is restricted and
tied to, for example, expectations regarding major partners of trade and
the accompanying extent of communicative need. A role of government
in this case may be to stimulate language choice by inducement.[26]

Organization of Public Planning

One controversial question of planning is the extent and mode of public
organizational involvement: in such cases, (1) can a government rely on
competitive mechanisms (the interaction of private decision makers)
within broader public policies? and (2) can it exercise a greater measure
of control over certain activities? Such questions of organization are subject to political preference and circumstance, and, from an observer's or
adviser's point of view, such questions constrain the selection of alternatives in finding solutions to language problems in a given nation.

An example of relative non-involvement of government action is
provided by the sales incentives of textbook writers and publishers if they
use governmentally approved terminology (or rules for terminological
derivation) and therefore have their texts approved for school use—with
large and recurring orders as a result. Preparation of textbooks by governmentally appointed writers and publishing companies would obviously
present different incentives and administrative routines.

Creation and unification of vocabulary, for example, could be left to
individuals and professional groups, in a free play of competitive forces,
provided there is an agreement on the general principles of vocabulary
admissibility (e.g., criteria of "nativity," etc.). This latter agreement could
be induced by active government policy. Empirical studies[27] suggest that
broadcasters, journalists, and writers create and disseminate vocabulary
with far greater success than government agencies. These professions enhance their living by engaging, for example, in vocabulary extension.
Spread effects in the "market" disseminate the particular vocabulary with
greater effectiveness than a public agency, which could then concentrate
on stimulating vocabulary creation and on obtaining agreement on deri-
vational or adjustment principles for admissibility.

This example also demonstrates that our assessment of government
involvement should depend not so much on smaller differences in timing
of achieving uniformity or on the introduction of particular vocabulary
but more on the explicit understanding of which kind of goals that the

government allows to dominate their decisions, for example, particular listed vocabulary goals or the conformity of vocabulary with a supranorm for reasons of national unity.

SUMMARY

This paper outlines an approach to language planning as decision-making. We do not define planning as an idealistic and exclusively linguistic activity but as a political and administrative activity for solving language problems in society. Public planning, that is, orderly decision-making about language on a national level, is motivated by public effects of some language problems and by the social context. We maintain that language is subject to planning because it is a resource that is and can be valued. Aspects of language code and language use can be changed to better correspond to the goals of society.

ACKNOWLEDGMENT

This paper was made possible by the generosity of the Ford Foundation and the Institute of Advanced Projects (East-West Center, Honolulu), where the authors spent their 1968–69 academic year. Drafts of this paper have profited from suggestions for improvement by Drs. Thomas Thorburn, Jiří Neustupný, and Joan Rubin and Mr. David Holden.

NOTES

1. Planning is used in a wide variety of meanings. A selective reference to some categories of use of this concept may be in order. In the first place, one may refer to a continuous functional distinction between structurally rationalizing planning and developmental planning. The former refers to planning aimed at maintenance and at controlled growth of given resources, while the latter points to the rapid growth of new resources. It is this latter kind that has attracted considerable attention because of its appropriateness for the underdeveloped world (Lewis, 1966, p. 13 ff.). In the second place, some people distinguish types of planning in terms of the envisaged scale of comprehensiveness. It is here that the distinction between partial and total planning becomes apparent. In the third place, another criterion of distinction may be obtained by examining the degree of concentration of control over planning. In this connection, it is appropriate to make the distinction between monocentric and polycentric planning. (On variations of monocentric planning, see Tinbergen, 1964, and Porwit, 1967. For polycentric planning, see Bićanić, 1967, especially p. 87 ff.) The nature of the decision-making environment in which a plan operates yields a further differentiating criterion. Some, for example,

distinguish plans based on monistic decision systems from those that operate in a pluralistic decision system. (For an earlier version of this kind of distinction, see Mannheim, 1950, chapters 5, 6, and 12.) For a recent exposition of the same, see Deutsch, (1964, pp. 46–74). Our characterization of planning is primarily based on notions from Thorburn (1966 and 1968; also paper 13, this volume).

2. Neustupný (1968a) makes a distinction between a "policy approach" and a "cultivation approach" to language problem-solving ("language treatment"). Planning as defined here is rather a reflection of his policy approach.

3. A *productivity* measure, based only on quantifiable consequences. We use the term "effectivity" when referring either to productivity or efficiency. An *efficiency* measure considers both pecuniary and non-pecuniary consequences (cf. Jernudd, paper 14, this volume).

4. There are undoubtedly possibilities of specifying a number of linguistic *"ceteris paribus"* principles to guide the formulation of alternatives. Given an explanatorily adequate theory of language (which we do not have as yet), it would seem possible to manipulate rules that are language specific, for example, in the direction of greater generality (cf. the preliminary statement on "epirules" in Bailey, 1969, p. 100).

5. Tauli's (1968) theoretical treatise even explicitly rejects the participation of government in matters of language (p. 153). His views are neatly explained by his idealism.

6. One of the better lists is contained in Noss's (1967) book on language policy and higher education (pp. 39–41, 77–79, 93–94, 111–114, 125–126, 137–142, 161–163, 178–179, 197–200).

7. Cf. Rubin (paper 12, this volume) for further discussion of language problems in education.

8. Cf. Sibayan (1967, pp. 178, 183–189). Also, Jernudd (1968, p. 181, n17).

9. Cf. suboptimization (Jernudd, paper 14, this volume).

10. Cf. also Rabin (paper 15, this volume).

11. Metalinguistic research, as performed by scientific linguists, deals with code alone, since no attention is devoted to the function of code. We may regard this effort as perhaps the most important language problem of all. Evaluation of code without considering speech is only possible in the sense that we may gradually approximate the true mechanical model of language.

12. Cf. Bergman (1968, pp. 210–211) and Asmah (1967).

13. Cf. also Haugen (1966b, pp. 53–55).

14. Cf. Gumperz (1966 and 1967).

15. For this term, see Neustupný (1965, p. 86). In this article, he uses the equivalent "language block."

16. Cf. Bergman (1968, pp. 156, 185) and Tauli (1968, pp. 135–144).

17. For a typology of discourse, cf. Hausenblas (1964).

18. Cf. Sibayan (1966), Aguilar (1967, pp. 50–52), or Prator (1968).

19. Orthography may itself motivate phonetic demands. Orthography decisions may result in changes in the phonological component eventually and in strong feelings of written-language primacy; but spelling pronunciations are nevertheless pronunciations. When "reforming zeal" goes beyond phonological constraints, generalizing on the basis of typeme similarities rather than on the basis of the relationships between the phonological rules and the typeme system, "efforts fail, at least in part because the beliefs do not correspond to the realities of the written-spoken relationship" (Ferguson, 1968, p. 30). Cf. Vachek (1962) for a discussion of interaction between written and spoken languages.

20. Not one category in Noss's (1967, pp. 62–63) classification belongs to the latter type. Of the classes of procedures for creating Turkish substitutes for deleted foreign-marked lexical entries and rules, there are no instances of code restructuring, according to Heyd (1954, pp. 88–92), except perhaps the changes in semantic specifications of the lexicon.

21. For an interesting practical example of systematic use of this insight for suggesting family names, cf. Bergman's (1968, p. 217) reference to *Svensk namnbok* (appearing occasionally since 1920).

22. Cf. Amonoo (1963, p. 80) and Neustupný (1968b, p. 292) for application to language. For a general discussion of macroeconomic goals, cf. Musgrave (1959, chapter 1).

23. For a geographical example, cf. Jernudd (1968, p. 178).

24. This necessity is explained in Neustupný (1968b).

25. Cf. Musgrave (1959, chapter 1).

26. On inducement and subsidy, cf. Lewis (1949).

27. Cf. Noss (1967, pp. 141–142).

REFERENCES

Aguilar, Jose V. 1967. The Determination of Language Policy: The Role of Research. *In* Ramos, Aguilar, and Sibayan.

Amonoo, R. F. 1963. Problems of Ghanaian *Lingue Franche*. *In* Spencer.

Asmah binti Haji Omar. 1967. Towards the Unification of Bahasa Melayu and Bahasa Indonesia. *Tenggara*, 1: 112–115.

Bailey, Charles-James N. 1969. The Integration of Linguistic Theory: Internal Reconstruction and the Comparative Method in Descriptive Linguistics. *Working Papers in Linguistics*, 2. Department of Linguistics, University of Hawaii, 85–122.

Bergman, Gösta. 1968. *Kortfattad Svensk Språkhistoria*. Stockholm: Prisma.

Bićanić, Rudolf. 1967. *Problems of Planning, East and West*. The Hague: Mouton.

Bright, William, ed. 1966. *Sociolinguistics. Proceedings of the UCLA Sociolinguistics Conference, 1964*. Janua Linguarum, Series Maior, 20. The Hague: Mouton.

Bühler, Karl. 1934. *Sprachtheorie*. Jena.

Deutsch, Karl. 1964. Communication Theory and Political Integration. *In* Jacob and Toscano, 143–178.

Ferguson, Charles A. 1968. Language Development. *In* Fishman, Ferguson, and Das Gupta, 27–35.

Fishman, Joshua A.; Ferguson, Charles A.; and Das Gupta, Jyotirindra, eds. 1968. *Language Problems of Developing Nations.* New York: John Wiley and Sons.

Gumperz, John J. 1966. On the Ethnology of Linguistic Change. *In* Bright, 27–49.

———. 1967. On the Linguistic Markers of Bilingual Communication. *Journal of Social Issues,* 23: 2: 48–57.

Hagen, Everett E. 1963. *Planning Economic Development.* Homewood, Ill.: Irwin.

Haugen, Einar, 1966a. *Language Conflict and Language Planning: The Case of Modern Norwegian.* Cambridge: Harvard University Press.

———. 1966b. Linguistics and Language Planning. *In* Bright, 50–71.

Hausenblas, K. 1964. On the Characterization and Classification of Discourses. *Travaux Linguistiques de Prague,* 1: 67–83.

Heyd, Uriel. 1954. *Language Reform in Modern Turkey.* Oriental Notes and Studies, 5. Jerusalem: Israel Oriental Society.

Jacob, Philip E. and Toscano, James V., eds. 1964. *The Integration of Political Communication.* Philadelphia: J. B. Lippincott.

Jernudd, Björn H. 1968. Linguistic Integration and National Development: A Case Study of the Jebel Marra Area, Sudan. *In* Fishman, Ferguson, and Das Gupta, 167–181.

———. This volume. Notes on Economic Analysis for Solving Language Problems. Paper 14.

Lewis, William A. 1949. *The Principles of Economic Planning.* London: D. Dobson.

———. 1966. *Development Planning.* New York: Harper and Row.

Mannheim, Karl. 1950. *Fredom, Power, and Democratic Planning.* London: Oxford University Press.

Musgrave, Richard A. 1959. *The Theory of Public Finance.* New York: McGraw-Hill.

Neustupný, Jiří V. 1965. First Steps Towards the Conception of "Oriental Languages". *Archiv Orientální,* 33: 83–92.

———. 1968a. Language Problems of National Development. Paper presented at the *Symposium on Current Frontiers in Linguistic Anthropology,* held at the 8th International Congress of Anthropology and Ethnological Sciences, Tokyo and Kyoto, September 3–10. Mimeo.

———. 1968b. Some General Aspects of "Language" Problems and "Language" Policy in Developing Societies. *In* Fishman, Ferguson, and Das Gupta, 285–294.

Noss, Richard. 1967. *Language Policy and Higher Education.* Higher Education and Development in South-East Asia, 3:2. Paris: UNESCO and the International Association of Universities.

Porwit, Krzysztof. 1967. *Central Planning: Evaluation of Variants.* London: Pergamon Press.

Prator, Clifford H. 1968. The British Heresy in TESL. *In* Fishman, Ferguson, and Das Gupta, 459–476.

Rabin, Chaim. This volume. A Tentative Classification of Language Planning Aims. Paper 15.

Ramos, Maximo; Aguilar, Jose V.; and Sibayan, Bonifacio P. 1967. *The Determination and Implementation of Language Policy.* Quezon City: Alemar-Phoenix.

Rubin, Joan. This volume. Evaluation and Language Planning. Paper 12.

Sibayan, Bonifacio P. 1966. Should We Teach Filipinos to Speak Like Americans? *Philippine Journal of Education,* April, 736–738.

———. 1967. The Implementation of Language Policy. *In* Ramos, Aguilar, and Sibayan.

Spencer, John, ed. 1963. *Language in Africa.* Cambridge: Cambridge University Press.

Steblin-Kamenskij, M. I. 1968. Is Planning of Language-Development Possible? (In Russian). *Voprosy Jazykoznanija,* 3: 47–56.

Tauli, Valter. 1968. *Introduction to a Theory of Language Planning.* Acta Universitatis Upsaliensis, Studia Philologiae Scandinavicae Upsaliensia, 6. Uppsala: Almquist & Wiksell.

Thorburn, Thomas. 1966. *Företagsekonomi.* Lund: Studentlitteratur.

———. 1968. *Kompendium i Förvaltningsekonomi.* Stockholm School of Economics. Mimeo.

———. This volume. Cost-Benefit Analysis in Language Planning. Paper 13.

Tinbergen, Jan. 1964. *Central Planning.* New Haven: Yale University Press.

Vachek, Josef. 1962. On the Interplay of External and Internal Factors in the Development of Language. *Lingua,* 11: 433–448.

12. EVALUATION AND LANGUAGE PLANNING

JOAN RUBIN
Department of Anthropology, Tulane University

INTRODUCTION

Any approach to evaluation and language planning at this point must remain fairly academic and theoretical because of the dearth of data on the actual processes that characterize language-planning evaluation within a specific setting. There is relatively little information about the actual criteria used or about the weighing of alternatives. Within the process of language planning, evaluation appears to have been the least frequently used technique.[1]

It should come as no particular surprise that little information is available on language planning and evaluation. First of all, formal evaluation per se is a relatively new and evolving field; the techniques of evaluation and of studying evaluation are only at a beginning stage. Secondly, the process of language planning, while one of the most frequent areas of decision-making in new nations, has not been approached in a systematic way. That is, alternatives have often not been identified, or, if they have, they have not been considered in a systematic way. My hope is that this discussion will encourage language planners and their supporters to improve their work by consciously focusing on the alternatives that are available to them.

PLANNING

Definition of Planning, Especially Language Planning

The concept of planning has been the subject of considerable literature. The definition of planning has ranged from one specifying an activity that includes the broadest kind of human problem-solving or decision-making to a more limited one specifying an activity that is initiated and supported by some formal body. The more limited definition (of what is still very complex activity) views planning as an activity whereby goals are established, means are selected, and outcomes predicted in a systematic and explicit manner.

It is only recently that *language planning* has been isolated as a type of planning (Ray, 1961; Haugen, 1966; Ramos, 1967; Tauli, 1968; Fishman, Das Gupta, et al. 1968; Fishman, Ferguson, et al., 1968; Jernudd and Das Gupta, paper 11, this volume). Language planning focuses upon the solutions to language problems[2] through decisions about alternative goals, means, and outcomes to solve these problems. The emphasis that Jernudd and Das Gupta place upon language as a resource promotes our consideration of how language, too, might be subjected to planning.

Work of the Planner and the Language Planner

Fact-Finding. Before beginning the actual planning, a planner[3] must have a certain amount of information about the situation in which the plan is to be effected. Thus, the planner must investigate the existing setting to ascertain what the problems are, as viewed both by persons who will execute the plan and by persons who will be the targets of the plan. It is important for him to know what constraints, tendencies, and rationales the existing social, cultural, political, and economic parameters offer.[4] It is also important for him to assess or to estimate the structural direction of each of these parameters. If these parameters are not isolated and taken into consideration by the planner, he is likely to find it difficult—if not impossible—to carry out his plans. At the very least, the planner should be aware of the tools with which he is working so that he can effect the proper changes with the least effort.

In seeking clues about the direction and rate of change, the fact-finding personnel should, of course, use whatever general knowledge that is available about the change process. They should, however, be sure to test these hypotheses within the specific population in which the plan is to be implemented. For example, it appears that some populations within a society are more susceptible to change than others. Thus, younger, urban men who are economically motivated or perhaps motivatable would seem to be more likely to change. If this "truth" is validated within a particular society, it might be of some help to planners in specifying target populations within which certain strategies would be more likely to receive acceptance.[5]

It is important to emphasize that, within the initial fact-finding period, the language planner goes through the same sort of considerations as any other planner. Although the problem to which language planning addresses itself may be first and foremost a linguistic or sociolinguistic one, the process of planning solutions to these problems involves the social, cultural, economic, political, and educational dynamics of a society. Planning should take account of many such structural features as the cultural and linguistic direction of change, the type of urbanization, the kinds of elites, and the economic level of the area.

Planning (goals, strategies, and outcomes). The second stage of planning is the "actual planning." The planner will formulate plans based on his knowledge of the constraints. At this point, the planner will establish goals, select the means (strategies), and predict the outcome.

Linguistic goals seem to be of two kinds: either the choice and spread of a particular variety within certain sectors of the population; or the standardization or elaboration, or both, of a particular variety for particular purposes.

In planning for the former goal, many international congresses dealing with problems of language teaching have tried to isolate universal answers to questions of how, when, and where a language can most efficiently be taught. Such information, however, must be considered as only one kind of information to be used in establishing strategies for language teaching. In the planning process, knowledge about second-language learning and its universal qualities can be useful, but this information must always be considered within the local situation to establish its importance. It might be true, for example, that children learn a second language best between the ages of four and twelve.[6] Still, the establishing of the most appropriate time to begin a language within this period in a particular country will depend on available resources and on the goals that language teaching is attempting to satisfy. Planners may decide that other goals have higher priority; that, even though the cost may be greater, language teaching is best delayed to a later period.

An overemphasis on universal strategies in language teaching may divert the planner's attention from certain relevant factors. Perren and Holloway (1965) point out this discrepancy:

Looking oddly old-fashioned among the clamour for more and better language teaching to more and more children are traditionally controversial questions such as: the "right" age at which to begin language-learning; the "correct" number of hours per week to be devoted to language-learning; or the "best" method by which all languages should be taught. *Answers to such questions cannot be final, are not indeed possible, except in relation to the full environmental circumstances of each country, each school, each teacher, and each class.* [italics mine] Probably the questions are the wrong ones, for language is learned rather than taught, and it is never effectively learned in isolation from its use—whether it be put to the limited use of passing examinations or the necessary and valuable task of individual and social communication (p. 21).

Indeed, it may be misleading to see more in common between the teaching of English in Ghana and the teaching of English in Malaya than there is between the teaching of Malay and English in Malaya. Is the common factor the language to be taught or the child to be taught? Is it the purposes for which languages are taught or the countries where they are taught; or, for that matter, the kind of teacher who teaches them? (p. 21).

Implementation.   After the plan is made, the planner may be involved in the implementation of the plan. Here he will be concerned with communicating the need and reasons for following the plan. He will need to persuade the plan's executants to act upon the plans and also to help in mobilizing the cooperation of all those persons upon whom the successful implementation of the plans depends.

Feedback.   Finally, the planner must see whether the plan has in fact worked. He must assess whether the actual outcome matches his predicted outcome; and if not, why not. He must know this to modify his strategies in order to match the predicted outcome. It may be that there will be some need to reestablish goals or to select other means after the plan has been operationalized. Thus, once the three stages listed above have been completed—fact-finding, planning, and implementation—the planner checks to see if the plan is working; if it is not, it may be necessary for him to go through the three stages again. In fact, it can be predicted that some revision of all three will be an essential part of any planning activity.

It is important to emphasize that planning must be seen as a continuous process. All of the decisions of the planner will need to be reviewed regularly because the goals of the decision-makers are in a state of continuous change, because the means and their assessment are always changing, and because the environment is constantly changing. Moreover, any given plan is subject to change because the policy makers themselves may also change.

EVALUATION

Definition

In the formal activity defined as planning whereby goals are established, means selected, and outcomes predicted, information is needed to enable planners to make choices among alternatives. Evaluation thus defined emphasizes the isolation of criteria to be used in making decisions and requires the specification of the values that are meaningful in the making of choices (Guba and Stufflebeam, 1968). It has been suggested that evaluation be seen as a process through which information might be provided to help determine which kinds of decisions seem to be the best of several alternatives.[7]

Work of the Evaluator; Examples from Language Planning

In the aforementioned four stages of planning—fact-finding, planning, implementation, and feedback—evaluation seems to be most important in providing information about the variables in the following three stages: fact-finding, planning, and feedback.

Fact-finding. In the fact-finding stage, an evaluator can help the planner identify his needs and isolate his problems; he can also help him isolate the important parameters (social, cultural, and the like) that will be relevant to the establishing of his goals, strategies, and predicted outcomes.

When the language planner has some sort of standardization as his goal, Ray (1963, p. 17) suggests that we should first study linguistic innovations within a particular language. He suggests further that we consider the relative compatibilities and incompatibilities of proposed changes with accepted custom. He proposes that "Instead of considering all change to be equally likely, equally costly, equally far-reaching or equally unbalancing," we distinguish between changes, some of which might well be unequal in these and other respects. Ray also points out that to be promptly accepted, linguistic and cultural change must be consistent with the existing structures, a point that has been stressed over and over again in the anthropological and linguistic literature.

A more complicated example of the need to know the environment and to take it into account before deciding on a plan comes from the study by Macnamara (1966), which suggests that part of the reason for the poor linguistic attainments of Irish students, which he found, may be the fact that there are few opportunities or little motivation to learn Irish. "The incentives put forward for learning Irish are cultural and political only, and they do not appear to inspire any sense of urgency in the majority of the Irish people" (p. 135). Macnamara seems to be suggesting to the planners that if they really want to promote the learning of Irish, they must be aware of two facts: (1) that the existing cultural environment would need to be changed to promote Irish, although this would be a difficult task that seems to go against the direction of current culture change; and (2) that if those who carry out the plan really want to promote Irish, they must provide better incentives.[8]

Another example of a study of the environment in which a need was felt for planned sociolinguistic changes is found in the Canadian volume *A Preliminary Report of the Royal Commission on Bilingualism and Biculturalism.* The information in this report has been compiled according to their relevancy to a language problem, irrespective of the comparing or weighing of the alternatives presented. Alarmed by the crisis that developed in the Province of Quebec in the early sixties, a commission was appointed by the Governor General to examine the causes of the crisis. The commission travelled throughout Canada to ascertain, through public meetings and interviews with representatives of business, education, journalism, urban and rural organizations, and provincial premiers, just what the two major language groups thought of each other and under what new conditions they would be prepared to live together. It elicited the people's suggested solutions to language problems found in the army, schools, transportation, and communication facilities. In addition, a series of research projects on many aspects of the language problem was carried out during the course of three years.[9] In this study, we find a noteworthy attempt to isolate problems and to identify alternative solutions. Two things remain unspecified, however: (1) How the policy makers can, should, or did weigh the attitudes and solutions that emerged? How much attention can, should, or did the government pay to each of the opposing views? (2) What use has been or will be made of the report, which is simply an evaluatory document specifying information that might be used as the basis for decisions? Probably, this document served two functions: (1) it probably pacified some of the French by pointing to the government's concern; and (2) it probably also heightened the awareness of some citizens of the country's language problems.

Planning. In the planning stage, there are many ways in which the evaluator can be of help. *First of all,* he can help the planner identify and construct alternative goals, strategies, and proposed outcomes. In the existing literature on codification and elaboration, several general goals for this process have been suggested. Some of these are: (1) to modernize the language or to make it available for modern purposes (Deutsch, 1953; Das Gupta and Gumperz, 1968); (2) to enhance development, democracy, foreign relations, and unity (Neustupný, 1968); and (3) to represent the national essence. It should be evident that these goals are not all consistent with each other; thus, if the planner had several of these as goals, one of the evaluator's functions might be to study whether the planner's several goals of language codification and elaboration were mutually compatible.

Planners who wish to promote a national language may face the dilemma of mediating between the individual's good and the society's good. The question educators raise is how to balance the demands for a healthy development of an individual with the requirements of the society for the development of a properly socialized individual who can contribute to the growth of that society. The volume by UNESCO entitled *The Use of Vernacular Languages in Education* and many others (for example: *International Seminar on Bilingualism in Education,* 1965; UNESCO, *African Languages and English in Education,* 1953) have pointed out that it is in the best interest of an individual to be educated in his native language. Many advantages have been spelled out—individual ease and speed of expression, greater self-esteem, greater independence of thought, greater creativity, greater speed in learning subject matter, firmer grasp of subject matter, longer retention of subject matter, and the like (Aucamp, 1926; Prator, 1950; Rubin, 1968; and others). However, Bull's review of the volume by UNESCO points to the need to examine other goals, especially the need for a balanced view:

> What is best for the child psychologically and pedagogically may not be what is best for the adult socially, economically or politically and, what is even more significant, may not be best or even possible for the society, which, through its collective efforts, provides the individual with the advantages he cannot personally attain (p. 528).

Thus, the dilemma of educators often is how much weight to give to each of these languages at each stage of education. The questions that must be resolved as a result of this conflict of goals are: (1) at what stage should the medium of instruction be the vernacular, if at all? and (2) at what stage should the national language become the medium of instruction?[10] The weight given these two goals will depend in part on the uses envisaged for the national language, but it will also depend on the local setting and the strategies required to implement any decision (required changes in quantity and quality of existing resources).

Second, the evaluator can help the planner formulate or identify criteria (measures and values) through which to judge (weigh) the effect of pursuing different goals, employing various strategies, and preferring certain outcomes.[11] In identifying these criteria, the evaluator may serve to call the attention of the planner to the need to include some empirical findings in the establishing of goals, strategies, and outcomes.

Two recent studies that evaluate language-teaching methods illustrate how evaluators may shed some light on the costs or effectiveness of certain strategies, either during the planning stage or during the feed-back stage. Of the two studies, the one by Macnamara (1966) focused on the costs of second-language learning, while the one by Davis (1967) focused on the alternatives that might be used in teaching the second language. Macnamara seems to appeal to policy makers to consider educational goals along with political and cultural ones; Davis assumes that the goal of second-language learning is given and is concerned only with the most efficient strategies.

In his research, Macnamara had two main objectives: "(i) to discover the effect on arithmetical attainment of teaching arithmetic through the medium of Irish to children from English-speaking homes; (ii) to discover the effect of the entire programme for reviving Irish in national schools on the level of English attainment" (p. 6). His major conclusions were:

1. Native speakers of English in Ireland who have spent 42 per cent of their school time learning Irish do not achieve the same standard in written English as British children who have not learned a second language . . . .
2. Neither do they achieve the same standard in written Irish as native speakers of Irish . . . .
3. Further, the English attainments of native-speakers of Irish fall behind those of native-speakers of English both in Ireland (13

months of English age) and in Britain (30 months of English age).

4. Teaching arithmetic in Irish to native English-speakers is associated with retardation in problem, but not mechanical, arithmetic (p. 136).

Through his research, Macnamara has demonstrated that it may cost something to learn a second language—time, ability in one's mother language, and some reduction in subject proficiency for at least a period of time. He suggests to the planners that they might want to reconsider their educational policies. Macnamara himself seems to feel that the attempt to revive Irish in Ireland is a futile and expensive effort in the light of today's reality. "For many of these children, the adult world, in Ireland or in England, will be an English-speaking one; and they appear to be ill-equipped indeed for life in it" (p. 138). Starting with this value criterion, Macnamara seems to suggest that the cost of learning Irish as a subject and through the Irish medium is very high indeed. He chides the present movement for teaching primary-school subjects through the medium of the second language because it has not considered the educational costs but has emphasized other considerations more. "The movement owes its origin to political, commercial and cultural incentives rather than to the findings of educational research" (p. 136). As an educator, Macnamara would like to emphasize school achievement more; it is clear, however, that other Irish decision-makers are emphasizing other values—such as political and commercial ones.[12] If, however, the politicians feel that a second language is needed for unity, for national mobilization, or for wider communication, the cost might still be considered worthwhile, and the necessary incentives and opportunities might better be included as part of the strategies used.

Starting with the opposite assumption that learning a second language (particularly English) is necessary in the Philippines, Davis focused on an evaluation of the most efficient strategies to achieve a goal of sufficient proficiency in English in order to learn subject matter through English. The purpose of the Rizal Experiment was: "(1) to determine how much time should be allowed for aural-oral activities in English in the lower primary grades (Grades 1 and 2) before formal reading is introduced: and (2) to find out the relative effectiveness of introducing English as the medium of instruction at three different points in the elementary grades" (p. 3). "The purpose of the Iloilo second-language experiment was to test the assumption (in the words of the Swanson Survey) that 'many problems and difficulties arise in initial language instruction when three different languages are presented' and that, therefore, by delaying the introduction of one language [in non-Tagalog regions], it should be possible to do a more thorough job on each of them" (p. 3).

Among the major conclusions from these experiments are:

1. Proficiency in English is directly related to the number of years in which it is used as the medium of classroom instruction (p. 81).
2. The average level of literacy in Tagalog is not closely related to the number of years in which it has been used as a medium of classroom instruction (p. 82).
3. Subject-matter achievement of pupils at the end of Grade 4 tended to be the highest on the English version [of tests] among pupils who had used it [English] as the medium of instruction in Grades 1–4, highest on the Filipino version among pupils who had used English as the medium in Grades 1–4. At the end of Grade 6, the group that used English as the medium of instruction in Grades 1–6, displayed, on the whole, the highest level of achievement, whether the tests were given in English, in Tagalog, or bilingually (p. 83).
4. The major conclusion to be drawn . . . is that the achievement of pupils at the end of Grade 3 in social studies, health and science, and arithmetic was not appreciably affected by the scheme of second-language study in Grades 1 and 2 (p. 8).

These conclusions drawn by Davis suggest that certain strategies should be promoted, provided that English is to continue at the highest level of education and that educators expect everyone to attain this level. It is certainly clear from the results indicated in 1 and 3 that more time should be spent learning English, even if the costs are considerable.[13]

Both of these documents are extremely important examples of evaluation criteria isolated within the local setting. What remains unstated is the weight that these studies were given by their respective Ministries of Education.

Third, evaluation criteria may help the planner establish an order of priority for alternative goals, strategies, and predicted outcomes. *Finally*, the evaluator may help investigate the logical consistencies[14] of strategies with goals, of strategies with predicted outcomes, and goals with predicted outcomes. He may seek a system of weights to be assigned to alternative strategies in relation to a particular goal and to different goals. The complexities that are involved in these operations are discussed in Appendixes B and C.

A document exemplifying the role of the evaluator in establishing logical relations between goals, strategies, and outcomes is that by Noss (1967). In this report, he examines the problems inherent in implementing language policy in higher education in several Southeast Asian countries. For each country, he considers the national language policies as given and proceeds to analyze the ways in which these policies have been implemented within the framework of higher education.[15]

Noss' document is especially important (1) because Noss identifies inconsistencies between goals and strategies within each country; (2) because he attempts to isolate some of the universal cost factors in implementing policies; and (3) because he attempts to show how some solutions are more costly, given certain situations.

In the following, Noss (1967) exemplifies the need to weigh and compare costs of alternative strategies relative to particular goals and desired outcomes:

1. When unfamiliar languages are to be taught by means of language courses only, the language instruction should be delayed as long as possible, being given just before the objective for which they are designed (e.g., general instruction in a new medium) comes into play. This takes maximum advantage of both the attrition rate and the compression factor.
2. Native speakers of unfamiliar languages, if in short supply, are best utilized in language-teaching activities, including direct instruction, supervision, teacher training and text preparation, rather than as teachers of other subjects in the language medium.

[Items 3, 4, and 5 are omitted here.]

6. The relatively high cost of higher education in any language medium makes the selection of specialists, texts, language of instruction and examination very much a matter of individual cases. Apparent economies achieved by applying the conclusions listed above to the university situation may be more than offset by inferior results. The only generalization possible is that, wherever both basic texts and staff capable of teaching in the medium used in secondary schools are available, instruction will be cheaper in that medium, for the simple reason that more students will be able to understand the subject matter (pp. 68–69).

A second example of the importance of specifying the relationship between goals and strategies is given in a recent article by the linguist Abraham Demoz in the *Ethiopian Herald*. Abraham underlines for his readers the problems inherent in the implementation of language policy and the need for clarity in assessing alternative strategies (see Appendix A). Abraham does not quarrel with the governmental goal of making Amharic the language of the school system but rather points to the need to coordinate the existing conditions in order to achieve outcomes that would be acceptable.

A third example of the role of the evaluator in relating goals to strategies is that of the second volume of the Canadian Bilingual and Bicultural Commission. The intent of the commissioners here was to review the data that had been collected for, and by, them and to suggest the necessary action required at each level of government, including the transformation of the language regime in the federal capital. Although the second volume reviews the background data in making its policy recommendations, it seems to fall short of being a good plan because it does not take into account the existing values of the provinces for which it is making recommendations. It is my suspicion that the commission's suggestion, for this reason, will not be accepted by a number of the provinces. I also think it unlikely that the guiding principle of the commission—the greatest equality with the least impracticality—will be accepted even by some of the provinces.

Implementation.   Evaluation would not seem to provide much information in the process of implementation. Data collected during this process on effectiveness of strategies would be relevant in the feed-back stage.

Feedback.   In the feed-back stage, the evaluator can help the planner formulate *a*) criteria to judge the actual outcome and *b*) criteria to compare the actual outcome with the predicted outcome. He can help formulate criteria to judge the usefulness of alternative strategies and suggest ways to modify the existing strategies.

In assessing the outcome of specific strategies, he can help establish what the projected outcome is, what the perceived outcome is, what the actual outcome is, and what weights are given to each. These may all influence subsequent policy and strategy decisions.

As an example of the assessment process, we can look to that made by Walker (1965) for the Cherokee literacy program. In assessing the success of the program, Walker takes into account many local variables: why the Cherokee learn to read; Sequoyah's writing system; Cherokee learning patterns; the role of education in the lives of all concerned; the nature of the learning and teaching process. Walker underlines the need to consider the local situation in selecting a strategy and the point that no absolute strategies could be established to predict the conditions under which such a literacy program might be accepted.

Criteria for Good Evaluation

Providing information for decision-making is therefore an important function within the planning process. However, Guba and Stufflebeam (1968) wisely call our attention to the fact that not only must this information meet the criteria that are ordinarily required of information— namely, scientific criteria (internal and external validity, reliability, and objectivity)—but, since the information is to be used in the planning process, it must also meet criteria of practical utility. Guba and Stufflebeam isolate seven more criteria that any evaluation must meet: *relevance* to the decisions being made; *significance* for the decisions being made; *scope* relative to the decisions being made; *credibility* by the decision-maker; *timeliness* relative to the decisions being made; *pervasiveness* relative to the decision-maker; and *efficiency* relative to the collection of information.

Advantages of Evaluation

Formal evaluation techniques described thus far can contribute greatly to the planning process because they help to isolate and assess alternative goals, strategies, and predicted outcomes that can or should be taken into the process of planning. The evaluator can help decide the weight to be assigned to the alternatives held by the policy makers (at different levels of administration), to those held by the executants of the policy, and to those held by the targets of the policy. He can attempt to find the logical inconsistencies between strategies and goals, strategies and predicted outcomes, and goals and predicted outcomes. Some noteworthy values of evaluation are that it enables one to keep track of changes (feedback) and that, through clarification of goals, strategies, and outcomes, the possibility emerges of weighing alternatives and of seeing the relationships between different levels of operation.

LIMITATIONS OF EVALUATION ACTIVITIES

Limitations

Although planning in more "modern" societies seems to require an evaluation of a more systematic, rigorous, and objective kind, it remains an open question which aspects of planning would most profit from extensive evaluation. In general, it appears that there are limitations to the amount and kind of evaluation that can or should be built into any planning process. The evaluation literature shows some of these limitations.

Political limitations. Suggestions regarding limitations are available from the fields of business-administration, economics, and political planning (Cyert and March, 1963; and Braybrooke and Lindblom, 1963). One suggestion is that formal evaluation may not always be welcome because policy makers may not want to—and perhaps should not—face all the inconsistencies in their policies at one time.[16] The process of planning usually involves several participants who try to establish their own goals as important; thus, planning may involve a coalition of participants *who may not want to reveal their values at any one point in time.*

There might be circumstances, however, in which the evaluator's isolation of inconsistencies would be welcomed. If there is one major policy maker who wants to eliminate resistance to his policies or if the policy makers meet an impasse in agreeing on strategies or outcomes, then the evaluator may be asked to help to coordinate. As coordinator, he could try to get individuals whose goals are at variance to come to some sort of agreement, by pointing out their differences.

Uncertainty of environment. Another limitation that is suggested is that it is well-nigh impossible to predict all of the environment, plus the fact that the environment is always subject to change. Within any program for change, there is always a high degree of uncertainty. If required, deeper investigation of the environment can be built into succeeding plans, particularly if the change is important enough and if lack of knowledge of the environment is deleterious enough.

To account for the changing environment and, when necessary, to incorporate this change into the plan, evaluation may begin with a list of combinatorial elements, together with the limitations on their combinations; but it must always permit imaginative anticipations of, and persistent searches for, new elements and new combinations (Ray, 1963, pp. 14–15).

Importance of decisions.   Guba and Stufflebeam (1968) raise the question: For which type of goals is evaluation most useful? Following Braybrooke and Lindblom (1963), they suggest that there are different kinds of changes that a planner might want to bring about, be they small or large changes. Small changes are those that are not considered controversial; large changes are those that are so considered. As yet, however, we know little about which type of goal can most effectively be planned for and when evaluation can be useful.

Type of evaluation techniques.   Another consideration in evaluation is the need to establish criteria for selecting from among existing evaluation techniques those techniques that are best fitted for a particular evaluation task,[17] taking into account both cost and information gained. Although the experimental process might seem the most valid and reliable procedure to evaluate alternative strategies, it is the most tedious; and some evaluators (e.g., Stufflebeam, 1968a) have pointed out that this technique is useful only when one is considering or evaluating the final outcome. For decision-making, planners and implementers cannot wait for the final outcome—they must make decisions and inplement them on a continuous basis.[18] Furthermore, Prator, in the introduction to Davis' *Philippine Language Teaching Experiments*, observed that the experiments conducted in the Philippines by Davis are both time-consuming and expensive. He suggests that less costly ways need to be found to experiment on the problems of language teaching.[19]

Intellectual limitations.   Cyert and March (1963) and Braybrooke and Lindblom (1963) point out that any organization (or set of planners) is limited in its ability to assemble, to store, and to utilize information. This difficulty may eventually be overcome to some extent if there are machine programs to compare either goals and criteria or strategies and criteria. It is unlikely, however, that such programs will ever completely solve the problem because many of the relevant criteria are not quantified or quantifiable and, therefore, cannot be programmed easily.

Difficulties of relating behavioral outcomes to particular strategies. Since planning (and language planning) is carried out usually over a fairly long period of time and can be seen to be part and parcel of other social changes (Lewis, 1968; Fishman, 1966), it is difficult to establish causal relationships between strategies and outcomes. For example, an increase in the number of persons who speak a particular language in an area may not be the result of the efforts made to implement a plan but may rather be the result of a migration of rural speakers to urban areas; or, perhaps, the result of an increase in the birth rate of a particular language group. An increase in newspaper circulation may be owing to the availability of more money to buy newspapers or to an increase in literacy, rather than to an increase in the number of speakers or users.

Incorporation of non-measurable criteria. One of the continuous problems of evaluation is the knowledge that many variables, while not currently subject to quantification, are as important—if not more important —as those that are. How to assess these non-measurable variables and how to incorporate them into the evaluation are problems yet to be solved.

Universal versus specific criteria for evaluation. Another continual problem is the importance of having universal criteria for evaluating strategies and outcomes. Although evaluation would be simpler if such universal criteria did exist, one major point of this paper is that such criteria must always be considered as modified by factors operating within the local setting.

In language planning, there is considerable literature about the evaluation criteria to be used for codification and elaboration. There are suggestions ranging from universal criteria to be used for this task (Tauli, 1968; Ray, 1963; Garvin, 1964b) to a description and discussion of what criteria were or could be used for a specific language (Heyd, 1954, for Turkey; Haugen, 1966, for Norway; Gonsalo del Rosario, 1968, for Southeast Asia). Of all the above writers, Ray (1963) is most aware of the need to mediate between absolute criteria (linguistic efficiency, linguistic rationality, and linguistic commonalty) and the application of these in specific contexts. Jernudd and Das Gupta (paper 11, this volume) question whether any such universal can be defined except within the local context. They suggest that such terms as "efficiency" cannot be defined without a knowledge of the particular values that decision-makers allow other criteria, such as "adequacy" and "acceptability," to assume within a local setting.

An example of the need to take account of the environment when considering language-teaching strategies comes from Philippine language planning. Although there is considerable evidence that learning through the first language is the most effective, other environmental factors may modify this learning process. In a recent report on *The* UCLA-*Philippine Language Program 1957–1966*, Bowen underlines this point:

> On the face of it a reasonable assumption is that, other things being equal, pupils will learn faster and more effectively if they study in their own language than if they have to first learn and then study in a foreign language. *But other things aren't equal*. Besides the vested interests pulling one way or another, there are different status judgments for the two languages, particularly in the educational tradition; there are vastly different resources available to teach and study in the two languages; there is an almost system-wide inability to take advantage of the inherent superiority of native-language instruction, since time-honored curricula are based on the need to teach in a foreign tongue; there is the probable lower quality of what textbook materials are available in local languages. Furthermore, almost all textbooks in Philippine vernaculars are derived books—few indeed represent original work, and translations tend to suffer unless the translator is as much an artist as the original author (p. 26). (italic mine)

Other. Braybrooke and Lindblom (1963) list several reasons that make ideal evaluation impossible. Among those not listed above are: (1) the costliness of analysis; (2) the analyst's need for strategic sequences to guide analysis and evaluation; and (3) the diversity of forms in which policy problems actually arise (p. 113).

EMERGENT OR CONTINUAL EVALUATION

Definition

As a result of the limitations that I have isolated above, evaluation must have certain characteristics to be useful. The evaluation process must be conceived as a continuing one that is constantly providing new and relevant information that is to be incorporated into planning. It should provide a technique both for continuous and systematic assessment of variables as well as for unpredicted *ad hoc* information that emerges as time goes on.

Advantages

  a) In societies where opinion may not be adequately formed or
      where people may not be aware of or able to verbalize their
      needs, the planner may have to rely in the beginning on very
      inadequate information about feelings in different sectors. As
      the plan begins to be implemented, however, these feelings or
      opinions may emerge. Then, if the feed-back process, especially
      during implementation, assesses the reception that the plan is
      receiving, the planner may be encouraged to change his strategies
      to improve attitudes and motivations of the target population or
      to change his goals to be more consistent with the problems that
      emerge as the plan is implemented.

  b) Planners may use the feedback obtained from some of the target
      population to convince the rest of the population of the value
      of a policy. That is, if the plan succeeds and the planners ad-
      vertise this success, they may find greater confidence in future
      programs (Griessman, 1969, p. 17).

  c) It is clear that continual evaluation with built-in feedback allows
      more flexibility in goals and strategies.

SUMMARY AND CONCLUSIONS

In this paper, I have attempted to demonstrate two points: first, that
evaluation can shed light on and improve language planning; and second,
that the evaluation used thus far in language planning has been lacking
in many ways. By illustrating both of these points in this paper, I hope
that future language planners will become conscious of their own valuation
criteria and will seek to examine these in a more systematic manner.

   The review of language planning and evaluation has shown to date
that:

1. Language planning and evaluation have often been neither specific nor systematic enough to be useful. Exceptions include the
   works of Macnamara and Davis, which isolate information that
   could be used in language planning.
2. Most evaluation criteria are formulated as universal truths rather
   than as particulars within the contexts of the country's goals and
   the logical relationships involved. Some exceptions have been
   indicated in this paper.

3. Little use has been made of formal feed-back techniques.
4. Most specifications of the variables to be used in evaluation of strategies and outcomes have been lists and did not include specification of the priorities for strategies, goals, and projected outcomes.
5. It is usually not clear what effect—if any—the documents examined had on the establishment of policies and strategies and on the assessment of proposed outcomes.

Although none of the documents examined here adequately illustrate the importance that evaluation might have within language planning, they do indicate that such a process might help improve the understanding of the role of language planning within national development. The need now is for more field investigations to ascertain just what criteria (measures and values) are being used in decision-making and what further sorts of information might be of use in decision-making within language planning.

ACKNOWLEDGMENT

I wrote this paper while I was a senior fellow at the Institute of Advanced Projects, East-West Center, University of Hawaii. The preparation of this paper was made possible by the cooperation of the staff of the Institute of Advanced Projects and by a grant from the Ford Foundation.

I am indebted to Tom Owens, of the Hawaii Curriculum Center, who introduced me to the current uses of the term "evaluation" and the relevant literature within the educational framework and who made me aware of the complexities involved in formal evaluation; any errors in understanding remain mine alone. A major revision of the paper resulted from the excellent criticism John Macnamara gave it; for the criticism and for the kind way in which he made his critique, he is due my profound gratitude. I thank Joshua Fishman, Björn Jernudd, and Wilma Oksendahl for their editorial criticisms; and in particular, Björn Jernudd, who introduced me to some of the literature on planning and business administration.

NOTES

1. Alisjahbana (1965) and Tauli (1968, pp. 15–17) point to the negative attitude in linguistic circles towards all problems of evaluation. Ray (1963) does attempt to establish some criteria for language standardization. Both address themselves to evaluation criteria for the codification and elaboration stages of language planning. Noss (1967) specifies some criteria for evaluation of the implementation alternatives for solving language problems within the university setting in Southeast Asia.

2. The list of problems that might be solved by language planning is probably extensive, and there are many examples in the literature. Haugen (1966) lists the following: the establishment of the norms of good writing and speaking, the adequacy of the language as an expression of the people who use it, and the sharpening of language as a tool for creative and scientific thinking. Dil (1968) offers another list of problems among which are the following: lack of understanding among various language communities, choice of medium in schools, translation of literary works, language in which to exchange scientific information and knowledge, restrictions on the use of language in certain societies. Neustupný (1968b) discusses the study of language problems from the point of view of various national concerns. The volume, *Language Problems of Developing Nations,* contains articles that discuss language problems in specific countries.

3. Bićanić (1967) describes the process of planning in the following way:

> In every planning action, there may be said to be four different functions and correspondingly four kinds of actors or organs of planning: (1) preparation of the plan; (2) decision-making in planning; (3) execution of plans; (4) control of planning activity (p. 47).

Each of these may be further subdivided. Bićanić borrows from management science to do so:

> *Preparation of plans*: Theory of need determination; assessment of wants and needs, means and ends, and turning them into planning resources and planning requirements. Model building in planning by choosing the determinants, the equations, the sets and exploring the values that make the plan consistent. Theory of data-processing and collecting.
> *Decision*: Theory of choice, fixing objectives and instruments, assigning the actors their role, selecting alternatives, evaluating them, and deciding on a solution.
> *Implementation of plans*: Theory of persuasion—how to make executants of the plans act and implement the plans; mobilizing actors in participation, getting approval for implementation. Theory of communication; formulating, splitting, addressing targets to actors; concretization and detailization of the plans; application of the specific language of communications in planning.
> *Control*: Theory of testing; measuring aims against deeds; resources and requirements in plans against the attainment of targets; procedure and evaluation of testing, communication results; closing the cycle of information by building controlled results into new plans (Footnote pp. 47–48).

4. The planner must also be aware of the goals of other policy makers as part of the background within which his policies will be implemented.
5. Some other suggestions regarding how to use existing culture-change data came from Bachi (1956) and Fishman (1966). Looking at the census data of Israel, Bachi notes that younger, native-born males of higher education use Hebrew more. From this information, we can examine needs and motivations and propose future strategies. In his 1966 volume, Fishman offers three "semi-universals" about language maintenance. He examines language maintenance in relation to the exclusiveness of group membership, to the degree of urbaneness, and to the prestige of the language (pp. 442–445).
6. Considerable bibliography exists on this problem. Verbeke (1966), however, points to the fact that there is really no agreement about when second-language learning should begin. The reason for the age range given here is: the age range is after that period in which children are said to have gotten the basics of their first language but still within that period in which a native-like competence-skill is said to be attainable in a second language (Lenneberg, 1967).
7. Guba and Stufflebeam (1968) call our attention to the fact that there are many ways to define the term "evaluation." They isolate three that are commonly used but contain certain disadvantages. The definition used in this paper avoids these disadvantages.

1. Evaluation is measurement. This definition has the advantage of stressing the importance of reliability, validity, and objectivity, but it has the disadvantage of ignoring the judgmental aspect of evaluation and tends to eliminate as unimportant variables for which instruments were not readily available.
2. Evaluation is a process for determining the congruence of performance and objectives. The advantage cited is that the process encourages feedback. Disadvantages are that it focuses upon outcomes and does not lend itself to correction during the process, that it does not require the specification of criteria, and that it overemphasizes behavioral objectives.
3. Evaluation is equated with the judgmental process. The disadvantage cited is that this definition ignores the process of arriving at information; that is, it ignores objectivity and validity. It has the advantage of quick response (pp. 8–11).

8. Some of the Irish policy makers seem to have recognized the need to implement this second observation because the government subsequently employed a motivational research group to make recommendations to the government for the promotion of Irish.
9. The list of research reports is organized under the following headings: the Official Languages; the Work World; Government and Private En-

terprise; Education; Other Cultural Groups; Arts and Letters; the Mass Media; the Federal Capital; Governmental Institutions; Voluntary Associations; Other Studies: Constitutional Problems, Linguistic Questions, Attitude Surveys, Foreign Comparisons, Immigration (Canada, 1967).

10. The whole situation is infinitely more complicated when the planners wish to implement both a national language and a Language of Wider Communication.

11. The process of isolating these goals, strategies, and outcomes can become quite complex, particularly if consideration is given both to the fact that the plan is often considered in relation to other governmental plans and may be in competition with these as well as to the fact that, within the planning, there may be competing policies.

12. In 1926, Aucamp lamented that, in the discussion about which language was to be accorded the central position in the education of the pupil and how long that position was to be maintained, the decision had very seldom been arrived at from a purely educational point of view. She noted that, instead, the problem had been left either to solve itself or to the mercy of irrelevant local circumstance. In many cases, the problem had been solved under pressure of available educational institutions or through lack of funds. Often the decision had been made on purely political grounds, through the numerical strength of an overwhelming majority or under the influence of an all-powerful minority. Although one can commend Aucamp for pointing to the necessity of considering the pedagogical position and for bringing it to the attention of decision-makers, it seems naive of her to assume that all other considerations are unimportant even in the realm of education.

13. The results (2) and (4) seem strange, at least intuitively, since the range of vocabulary in reading would appear to depend on the amount and kind of exposure to a language.

14. In the recent volumes of *Asian Drama*, Myrdal abstracts "valuations" that are implicit in the statements of policy makers and points to those aspects of the culture that are inconsistent with these valuations and that must be modified if the goals specified are to be achieved.

15. In order to analyze the implementation process, he examines the instruments of policy (such as the ministries of education, public relations organizations, communications media, educational planning boards, educational research organizations, teacher-training institutions, materials development centers, translation services, national-language development agencies, foreign and international assistance and cultural organizations), the language-teaching resources, the objectives of language courses, the ethnic groups, and their objectives. He also considers the effects of language policy on non-language subjects.

16. Enloe (1967) points to the awareness of Malaysian leaders that certain values should not be brought into juxtaposition because this would heighten existing conflicts.

17. Stufflebeam (1968a) lists 11 different kinds of evaluational techniques

that are used to assign values to alternatives: market research, cost-benefit analysis, experimental design, objective testing, operational analysis, operations research, program-evaluation and review technique, program-planning and budgeting system, quality control, and systems analysis. These, he says, are differentiated by: (1) the decision situations that they serve; (2) the settings within which decisions are made; (3) the kinds of tools and techniques used; (4) the level of precision in collecting information and in analytical modes; and (5) the methodological skills of those who conduct evaluations and who are served by the evaluations (p. 20).

18. Some of the difficulties mentioned by Stufflebeam (1968a) about using the experimental technique are:

> *First, the application of experimental design to evaluation problems conflicts with the principle that evaluation should facilitate the continual improvement of a program.* Experimental design prevents rather than promotes changes in the treatment because treatments cannot be altered in process if the data about differences between treatments are to be unequivocal . . . .
> [passage left out]
> *A second flaw in the experimental design type of evaluation is that it is useful for making decisions after a project has run full cycle but almost useless as a device for making decisions during planning and implementation of a project.*
> At best, experimental design evaluation reflects *post hoc* on whether a project did what it was supposed to do . . . .
> [passage left out]
> *Guba has pointed out a third problem with the experimental design type of evaluation; it is well suited to the antiseptic conditions of the laboratory but not the septic conditions of the classroom* (pp. 13–16).

19. Two documents (Macnamara, 1966; Davis, 1967) that describe investigations conducted specifically to ascertain the value of different language-teaching strategies within a local setting illustrate how time-consuming and expensive experiments on language teaching can be.

The Davis volume reports in detail some of the expenses involved. Two experiments are described. One of them, the Iloilo second-language experiment, took place over a period of three years (1961–64) and involved about 200 personnel (superintendents, assistant superintendents, deans of the Iloilo normal school, division supervisors, school principals, teachers of experimental classes, and test administrators). Over 900 students were tested in the course of the three-year period. Preparations included locating the experimental groups, preparing guides and textbooks, training and supervision of teachers of experimental classes, administration and scoring of tests, and data-processing. For the second experiment described in that volume, even more extensive personnel were involved over a longer period of time. The number of personnel was approximately 400 and included superintendents, assistant superintendents, division supervisors, district supervisors, principals, teachers of experimental classes, test administrators, and curriculum writers. Preparations similar to the Iloilo experiment were made. In this expriment, some 1,500 students were sampled.

Although the Macnamara investigation took less time and involved fewer personnel and students, similar detail was required for the preparation of the investigation, the control of variables, and the analysis of data.

APPENDIX A: EXCERPTS FROM AN ARTICLE
by Abraham Demoz in the Ethiopian Herald, *January 19, 1969*

For Ethiopia, we can divide the linguistic problem into two major parts: First, what relative roles must be played by English and Amharic and, second, what kind of participation—if any—should be given to the other Ethiopian languages.

English now fulfills in Ethiopia the role of a second official language in various areas . . . The Ministry of Education has recently replaced English by Amharic as a medium of instruction in elementary schools up to and including the VI grade. This trend is very likely to continue. In the not-too-distant future English may be replaced by Amharic in the secondary schools as well. It is not too early yet to speak of replacing English as a medium of instruction at the university level.

The problems that such a step has created and will continue to create are many and obvious.

Some attempts have been made to produce the necessary teaching materials in Amharic. These are beset by untold difficulties due to the *lack of properly trained manpower to do the task adequately.* The attempts so far have been translations of textbooks written for schools in advanced countries with some rather lame attempts at adaptation to local conditions. This is compounded by the rather difficult problem of the *inadequacy of the Amharic vocabulary,* especially for science subjects.

Although English continues to be taught as a subject from Grade III on, yet the fact that it does not come into full use until the Grade VII has meant that the *level of English acquired by students by the time they finish elementary school is so poor that their ability to follow secondary-school instruction in English is thereby very seriously impaired* . . . .
[section left out]

Clearly then, [sic] the solution for the problem of inadequate English at the secondary level is to make Amharic the medium of instruction there too. This means, of course, that *the set of problems enumerated above will be taken one step higher up the education ladder* and present themselves again in some cases with even greater intensity, at the secondary level.

That is the problem of producing teaching materials in Amharic at the secondary-school level is an even more forbidding task than that of producing these materials for elementary schools. To this is added the necessity of having an all-Ethiopian staff at the secondary-school level if the teaching medium is Amharic. *What with the present rate of teacher drop-out and the extremely slow rate of teacher production for the secondary schools, this may prove to be a practically insurmountable problem. The net result of this may be the employment of unqualified people to teach in the secondary schools simply because they can teach in Amharic.*

At the same time, the level of English acquired by students at the end of their secondary schools will be so low that it may be well-nigh impossible to carry on with English as the medium of instruction at the university level.

The same cycle of problems would then repeat themselves at the university level, only in a more intense fashion than before. It is not easy to say whether or how one can cut such a vicious circle (p. 6). [italics mine]

APPENDIX B:
SOME VARIABLES SUGGESTED IN THE LITERATURE

Some of the variables suggested in the literature (Spencer, 1963, pp. 130–135; Prator, 1964, pp. 67–80; Noss, 1967, chapters 2–4) that might be measured and balanced to assess efficient *strategies* to implement a policy to promote the national language are:

1. The teachers and teacher trainers
   a) Their knowledge of the language and language-teaching techniques:
       (1) Their knowledge of the language to be taught either as subject or as medium of instruction (both the vernacular and the national language)
       (2) Their knowledge of language-teaching techniques

b) Their motivation to teach the assignment, which may be based on:

   (1) Their perception of the useful function of change (in this case to use the national language where LWC or vernacular was used)

   (2) The type and strength of sanctions employed in introducing and maintaining change

   (3) Their positive attitudes toward the change object (the national language); the users of the change object; and the change agent (principal, planners, inspectors, and others)

c) The opportunities to acquire:

   (1) Better language-teaching techniques

   (2) The knowledge of the language[1]

d) The amount of time it takes to acquire the two opportunities mentioned above

2. Students

a) The knowledge of language to be taught as subject or as medium of instruction

b) Motivation to learn, which may be based on:

   (1) Their perception of the useful function of change[2]

   (2) The type and strength of sanctions employed in introducing and maintaining change

   (3) Their positive attitudes toward the change object; users of the change object; and the change agent (teacher)

c) The opportunities to acquire knowledge of language:

   (1) Within school, but outside classroom

   (2) From peers

   (3) From family

   (4) From communication media

d) The amount of time it takes to acquire knowledge of language for use as subject

e) The assessment of differential knowledge, motivation, and opportunities among different populations (this was mentioned earlier as important in programming different strategies)

3. Materials

(For teaching of national language, for teaching of subject in

national language, for training teachers to teach the national language and subject matter in the national language)
Quality and quantity available or projected of:
  a) Textbooks, curriculum plans
  b) Examination materials
  c) Library facilities
  d) Personnel to write *a*) and *b*)
  e) Time it takes to prepare *a*), *b*), and *d*) against existing materials
4. School organization
  a) Relation of language of instruction at each level to projected usage
  b) Length of pupils' duration in school to the language-learning task and to the national and modernization goals
  c) Number of vernacular languages to be used in the education system (Cost of multiplying vernacular versus the cost of motivating and training teachers in a national language)
5. Methodology
  a) Knowledge of the relationship between the vernaculars and the national language and the difficulties of shifting from one to the other
  b) Knowledge of and availability of alternative approaches to language teaching (possibilities of differential use of teachers, students, and materials to achieve language-learning task)
6. Feed-back facilities
  a) Types available (inspectors, evaluators, opinion analysts, and others)

In aiding the isolation and assessment of strategies within language planning, evaluation may assume extensive proportions. Goals are often more specific; the strategies are often multiple (and even *more* culturally specific); and the projected, perceived, and actual outcomes can be almost infinite. The task is both more complex and more susceptible to quantification than to evaluation of the goals within language planning.

The implementation of language planning is often viewed as occurring within specific sectors of the population—the educational, the military, the industrial, the judicial, the communication, and the transportation sectors. Planning is often executed with one or another of these areas that is held as the target. The area of education is perhaps the one that has most frequently received this sort of attention.

While the list of variables to be considered in evaluating alternative strategies is extensive, fortunately, not all of them are salient in any one situation at any one time. If the planner's goals are clear, then the necessity for looking at the existing resources is urgent. Formal evaluation may promote a more realistic assessment of the proper sequence of strategies to be followed.

A case in point is the author's 1968 description of the inefficient teaching of Spanish in the Paraguayan situation, where if local educators would recognize the fact that their students are not bilingual and that they have little opportunity to hear Spanish, they would probably change their teaching methods from that of translation-repetition to one emphasizing the teaching of Spanish as a second language.

Some suggestions in the literature offer useful ways to measure the value of the language. In their study of the Irish language, the Ernest Dichter International Institute for Motivational Research asked: "If you had to learn language X as a second language, how much would you be willing to pay to do so." In a recent survey of language in the Philippines, The Language Study Center, Philippine Normal College, asked several questions that might be indicative of motivational strength such as: Would a person need to know Language X to be successful in the following occupation in your community? Further measures need to be developed to test motivational strength in learning the second language.

NOTES

1. Noss (1967, chapter 1) suggests that there are three elements that must be present in positive degree for an individual to learn a language whether it be his first or second: aptitude, motivation, and opportunity. He suggests that, of the three, opportunity is the most manipulable at the moment, although further research may eventually provide us with the means of increasing individual and group motivation. He suggests that we do not know the mathematical relationship between these three factors partly because both motivation and opportunity are difficult, if not impossible, to measure now.

2. Several writers (Mackey, 1962; Epstein, 1968) have suggested that learning a second language requires a very different motivation from that of learning a first.

It seems obvious that the motivation for acquiring the first language is more compelling than the motivation for learning a second. For once the vital purposes of communication have been achieved, the reasons for repeating the effort in another language are less urgent (Mackey, 1962, p. 67).

Unlike skills in a vernacular, a person must ordinarily be highly motivated to acquire skills in a second language; he may have to be persistently aware of its potential benefits to master it (Epstein, 1968, p. 366).

APPENDIX C: THE ASSESSMENT OF OUTCOMES

While the establishment of relevant variables and the weights to assign them in assessing language-planning strategies (within the educational sector) is complex, it may be even more difficult to establish, assess, and predict the outcomes. The difficulty in assessing outcomes arises partly because different persons have different expectations of what the outcomes should be (policy makers, administrators of the Ministry of Education, teacher trainers, teachers, students, inspectors, parents, and textbook writers, and others); and partly because it is difficult to establish a causal relation between strategy and outcome. In education, it is difficult to determine what has been learned and which variables have been effective in producing learning. Many factors are known to influence the learning process such as: opportunities for use of the language, attitudes towards the language by outsiders, and anticipated value of the language in future life plans. Such factors obscure the influence of language policies.

In assessing the outcome of specific strategies, we need to establish what the projected outcome is, what the perceived outcome is, what the actual outcome is, and what weights should be given to each. These may all influence further policy and strategy decisions.

There are many kinds of outcomes that might be considered of importance within the framework of the policy decision to promote the national language through the school system. The weight to be given to these can only be specified within the setting of local values and within the projected time schedule for achieving each of them. In addition, there is a need to assess the effect of one outcome on others. The relationship between goals and outcomes is often not made clear.

There are many outcomes that could result from strategies aimed at promoting the national language within the educational system. An examination could consider changes in the existing resources (teachers, teacher trainers, inspectors, textbook writers, materials, methods, and school organization) to see what qualitative and quantitative changes had occurred. Measures that might be used are:

1. For teachers
    a) Number and ability of teachers who had had training in the national language either as a subject or as a medium of instruction
    b) Number and ability of teachers who had had training in language-teaching techniques
    c) Changes in motivation to teach the language or through the language
    d) Changes in attitude towards the national language, users of the national language, and change agent
    e) Changes in opportunities to acquire language-teaching techniques or knowledge of the language
2. For materials
    a) Number and quality of books (written, printed, distributed) for use in education
    b) Changes in quantity and quality of producers of material
3. For pupils
    a) Number and ability of those who had had training in the national language either as a subject or as a medium of instruction. Many measures might be used to demonstrate effectiveness: number who passed a school year, number who passed a language examination, and number who became literate. (All of these measures are dependent on many other factors than just language ability and knowledge.)
    b) Changes in motivation to learn in or through the language
    c) Changes in attitude towards the national language, users of the national language, and change agent
    d) Changes in opportunities to acquire knowledge of the language
    e) Changes in uses made of the national language
    f) Changes in second-language ability relative to other variables: subject-matter achievement and I.Q. development

Other measures for changes in resources exist, or they could be created.

Finally, outcomes could be evaluated in terms of the following: the extent to which they promote non-linguistic goals; the extent to which they increase mobilization; the extent to which they promote national integration as a result of language-teaching strategies.

BIBLIOGRAPHY

Alisjahbana, S. Takdir. 1965. New National Languages: A Problem Modern Linguistics Has Failed to Solve. *Lingua*, 15: 515–530.

Anderson, C. A. and Bowman, M. J. 1968. Theoretical Considerations in Educational Planning. *In* M. Blaug, ed. *Economics of Education 1*. Modern Economics Series. Baltimore: Penguin Books.

Aucamp, Anra J. 1926. *Bilingual Education and Nationalism: with Special Reference to South Africa*. Pretoria: J. L. Van Schaik.

Bachi, R. 1956. A Statistical Analysis of the Revival of Hebrew in Israel. *Scripta Hierosolymitana*, 3: 178–247.

Bićanić, Rudolf. 1967. *Problems of Planning: East and West*. The Hague: Mouton.

Bowen, J. Donald. 1968. The UCLA-Philippine Language Program 1957–1966. Unpublished paper, Department of English, UCLA.

Braybrooke, David and Lindblom, Charles E. 1963. *A Strategy of Decision: Policy Evaluation as a Social Process*. Glencoe: Free Press.

Bull, William. 1964. The Use of Vernacular Languages in Fundamental Education. *In* Dell Hymes, ed. *Language in Culture and Society*. New York: Harper and Row, 527–533.

Burns, Donald. 1953. Social and Political Implication in the Choice of an Orthography. UNESCO. *Fundamental and Adult Education*, (April) 5: 2.

Canada. Royal Commission on Bilingualism and Biculturalism. 1965. *A Preliminary Report*. Ottawa: The Queen's Printer.

———. 1967. *General Introduction, Book I: The Official Languages*. Ottawa: The Queen's Printer.

———. 1968. *Book II: Education*. Ottawa: The Queen's Printer.

The Canadian National Commission for UNESCO. 1967. *International Seminar on the Description and Measurement of Bilingualism*. Université de Moncton, June 6–14. Preprint.

Carroll, John B. 1967. *The Foreign Language Attainments of Language Majors in the Senior Year: A Survey Conducted in U.S. Colleges and Universities*. Laboratory for Research in Instruction, Graduate School of Education. Cambridge: Harvard University.

Cyert, Richard M. and March, J. G. 1963. *A Behavioral Theory of the Firm*. Englewood Cliffs: Prentice-Hall.

Dakin, Julian; Tiffen, Brian; and Widdowson, H. G. 1968. *Language in Education*. London: Oxford University Press.

Although it is not common to attach a bibliography to an article, I have done so because the newness of the topic may interest readers to wonder about related references. Many of the materials, although not referred to in the text, have influenced my views and I wish to acknowledge as many of these sources as possible.

Das Gupta, Jyotirindra and Gumperz, John. 1968. Language, Communication and Control in North India. *In* Fishman, Ferguson, and Das Gupta, 151–166.

Davis, Frederick B. 1967. *Philippine Language-Teaching Experiments.* Philippine Center for Language Study, no. 5. Quezon City: Alemar-Phoenix.

Del Rosario, Gonsalo. 1968. A Modernization-Standardization Plan for the Austronesian-derived National Languages of Southeast Asia. *Asian Studies,* 6: 1: 1–18.

Deutsch, Karl W. 1953. *Nationalism and Social Communication.* Cambridge, Mass.: MIT Press.

Dil, Anwar. 1968. The Language Factor in Emerging Nations. Unpublished doctoral dissertation, Department of Education, Indiana University.

Enloe, Cynthia. 1967. Language Politics in Malaysia. Unpublished doctoral dissertation, Department of Political Science, University of California, Berkeley.

Ernest Dichter International Institute for Motivational Research. 1968. *A Motivational Research Study for the Greater Use of the Irish Language,* 2 vols. New York: Croton-on-Hudson.

Epstein, Erwin H. 1967. National Identity and the Language Issue in Puerto Rico. *Comparative Education Review,* II: 2: 133–143.

———. 1968. Social Change and Learning English in Puerto Rico. *In* Kazamias and Epstein.

Fishman, Joshua A.; Nahirny, Vladimir C.; Hofman, John E.; and Hayden, Robert G. 1966. *Language Loyalty in the United States.* The Hague: Mouton.

Fishman, Joshua A.; Das Gupta, Jyotirindra; Jernudd, Björn; and Rubin, Joan. 1968. Research Outline for Comparative Studies of Language Planning. Paper 17, this volume.

Fishman, Joshua A.; Ferguson, Charles A.; and Das Gupta, Jyotirindra, eds. 1968. *Language Problems of Developing Nations.* New York: John Wiley and Sons.

Frei, Ernest H. 1947. Tagalog as the Philippine National Language: The Inception and Development of the Idea of a National Language, Final Choice of Tagalog, and the History and Character of Its Grammatical Treatment and Promotion. Unpublished doctoral dissertation, Hartford Seminary Foundation.

Garvin, Paul L. 1964a. *A Prague School Reader on Esthetics, Literary Structure, and Style.* Washington, D.C.: Georgetown University Institute of Language and Linguistics.

———. 1964b. The Standard Language Problem—Concepts and Methods. *In* Dell Hymes, ed. *Language in Culture and Society.* New York: Harper and Row, 521–526. Reprinted from *Anthropological Linguistics,* (1959) 1: 3: 28–31.

Griessman, Eugene. 1969. An Approach to Evaluating Comprehensive Social Projects. *Educational Technology,* February: 16–19.

Gorman, T. P. 1968. Bilingualism in the Educational System of Kenya. *Comparative Education,* (June) 4: 3.

Guba, Egon G. 1968. Evaluation and Change in Education. Prepared for Elk Grove Training and Development Center, May 16. National Institute for Study of Educational Change. Bloomington, Indiana University.

Guba, Egon G. and Stufflebeam, Daniel L. 1968. Evaluation: The Process of Stimulating, Aiding, and Abetting Insightful Action. An address delivered at the *Second National Symposium for Professors of Educational Research,* November 21.

Haugen, Einar. 1959. Planning for a Standard Language in Modern Norway. *Anthropological Linguistics,* 1: 3: 8–21.

———. 1965. Linguistics and Language Planning. *In* William Bright, ed. *Sociolinguistics. Proceedings of the UCLA Sociolinguistics Conference, 1964.* Janua Linguarum Series Maior, 20. The Hague: Mouton, 50–71.

———. 1966. *Language Conflict and Language Planning: The Case of Modern Norwegian.* Cambridge: Harvard University Press.

Heyd, Uriel. 1954. *Language Reform in Modern Turkey.* Oriental Notes and Studies, 5. Jerusalem: Israel Oriental Society.

Hutasoit, Marnixius and Prator, Clifford H. 1965. A Study of the "New Primary Approach" in the Schools of Kenya. An unpublished paper based on the study (February–March, 1965) requested by the Ministry of Education and supported by Ford Foundation.

India. Ministry of Education. 1956. *Programme for the Development and Propagation of Hindi.* Agra: Republic of India.

———. 1966. *Report of the Education Commission 1964–1966 on Education and National Development.* New Delhi: Government of India Press.

India. Ministry of Education and Scientific Research. 1957. *Bulletin on the Progress of Hindi in the States (up to October 31, 1956).* New Delhi: Republic of India.

India. Official Language Commission. 1957. *Report, 1956.* New Delhi: Government of India Press.

India. Parliament. Committee on Official Language. 1959. *Report.* New Delhi: Government of India Press.

International Seminar on Bilingualism in Education, Aberstwyth, 1960. 1965. *Report.* London: H. M. Stationery Office.

Ireland. Commission on the Restoration of the Irish Language. 1965. *The Restoration of the Irish Language.* Dublin: Stationery Office.

———. 1966. *White Paper on the Restoration of the Irish Language: Progress Report for the Period Ended March 31, 1966.* Dublin: Stationery Office.

———. 1968. *White Paper on the Restoration of the Irish Language: Progress Report for the Period Ended March 31, 1968.* Dublin: Stationery Office.

Jernudd, Björn and Das Gupta, Jyotirindra. This volume. Towards a Theory of Language Planning. Paper 11.

Kazamias, Andreas M. and Epstein, Erwin H., eds. 1968. *Schools in Transition: Essays in Comparative Education.* Boston: Allyn and Bacon.

Krathwohl, David R. and Bloom, Benjamin S. 1964. *Taxonomy of Educational Objectives. Handbook II: Affective Domain.* New York: D. McKay.

Lenneberg, Eric H. 1967. *Biological Foundations of Language.* New York: John Wiley and Sons.

Le Page, Robert. 1964. *The National Language Problem: Linguistic Problems of Newly Independent States.* London: Oxford University Press.

Lewis, E. Glyn. n.d. Bilingualism and Language Policy in the Soviet Union. Unpublished manuscript.

———. 1964. Conditions Affecting the "Reception" of an Official (Second/Foreign) Language. *In* Scientific Council for Africa, 83–103.

Lieberson, Stanley. 1967. How Can We Describe and Measure the Incidence and Distribution of Bilingualism? *In* The Canadian National Commission for UNESCO.

Macnamara, John. 1966. *Bilingualism and Primary Education: A Study of Irish Experience.* Edinburgh: Edinburgh University Press.

———. 1967a. The Effects of Instruction in a Weaker Language. *Journal of Social Issues,* 23: 2: 121–135.

———. 1967b. How Can One Measure the Extent of a Person's Bilingual Proficiency? *In* The Canadian National Commission for UNESCO.

Mackey, William F. 1962. The Description of Bilingualism. *Canadian Journal of Linguistics,* 7: 51–85.

Malherbe, Ernest G. 1946. *The Bilingual School: A Survey of Bilingualism amongst Pupils and Teachers in South African Schools.* London: Longmans.

Myrdal, Gunnar. 1958. *Value in Social Theory.* New York: Harper and Row.

———. 1962. The Theoretical Assumptions of Social Planning. *In* World Congress of Sociology, *Transactions of the Fourth World Congress of Sociology.* Milan and Stresa, September 8–5, 1959. London: International Sociological Association, 155–167.

———. 1968. *Asian Drama,* 3 vols. New York: Pantheon.

Neustupný, Jiří V. 1968a. Language Problems of National Development. Paper presented at the *Symposium on Current Frontiers in Linguistic Anthropology* held at the 8th International Congress of Anthropological and Ethnological Sciences, Tokyo and Kyoto, September 3–10. Mimeo.

———. 1968b. Some General Aspects of "Language" Problems and "Language" Policy in Developing Societies. *In* Fishman, Ferguson, and Das Gupta, 285–294.

Noss, Richard. 1967. *Language Policy and Higher Education.* Higher Education and Development in Southeast Asia, 3: 2. Paris: UNESCO and the International Association of Universities.

Organization for Economic Cooperation and Development. (OECD). 1967. *Social Objectives in Educational Planning.* Paris: OECD.

Ornstein, Jacob. 1959. Soviet Language Policy: Theory and Practice. *Slavic and East European Journal,* 17 (new series): 3: 1–24.

Owens, Thomas R. 1968. The Role of Evaluation Specialists in Title I and Title III Elementary and Secondary Education Act Projects. Unpublished doctoral dissertation, College of Education, Ohio State University.

Perren, George E. and Holloway, Michael F. 1965. *Language and Communication in the Commonwealth.* London: H. M. Stationery Office.

Pietrzyk, Alfred. 1965. Problems in Language Planning: The Case of Hindi. *In* B. N. Varma, ed. *Contemporary India.* London: Asia Publishing House, 247–270.

Prator, Clifford H. 1950. *Language Teaching in the Philippines: A Report.* Manila: United States Educational Foundation.

———. 1964. Educational Problems Involved in the Teaching of English as a Second Language. *In* Scientific Council for Africa, 65–81.

———. 1967. Language Policy in the Primary Schools of Kenya. *In* B. W. Robinett, ed. *On Teaching English to Speakers of Other Languages,* Series 3. Washington, D.C.: TESOL, 27–35.

Ramos, Maximo; Aguilar, Jose V.; and Sibayan, Bonifacio P. 1967. *The Determination and Implementation of Language Policy.* Philippine Center for Language Study, no. 2. Quezon City: Alemar-Phoenix.

Ray, Punya S. 1961. Language Planning. *Quest,* 31: 32–39.

———. 1963. *Language Standardization, Studies in Prescriptive Linguistics.* Janua Linguarum, Series Minor, 29. The Hague: Mouton.

Rubin, Joan. 1968. Language and Education in Paraguay. *In* Fishman, Ferguson, and Das Gupta, 477–488.

Scientific Council for Africa. 1964. *Symposium on Multilingualism. Second Meeting of the Inter-African Committee on Linguistics.* Brazzaville, July 16–21, 1962. Louvain: Commonwealth Conference for the Teaching of English as a Second Language.

Socrates, Jose B. 1964. The Language Problem in the Public Schools of the Philippines. Unpublished doctoral dissertation, Department of Education. University of Chicago.

Spencer, John, ed. 1963. *Language in Africa.* Cambridge: Cambridge University Press.

Stufflebeam, Daniel L. 1968a. Evaluation as Enlightenment for Decision Making. Columbus, Ohio, Evaluation Center, College of Education, Ohio State University, January 19.

———. 1968b. Toward a Science of Educational Evaluation. *Educational Technology,* July: 5–12.

Tauli, Valter. 1968. *Introduction to a Theory of Language Planning.* Acta Universitatis Upsaliensis, Studia Philologiae Scandinavicae Upsaliensia, 6. Uppsala: University of Uppsala.

UNESCO. 1953. *The Use of Vernacular Languages in Education.* Monographs on Fundamental Education, 8. Paris: UNESCO.

UNESCO, Educational Clearing House. 1953. *African Languages and English in Education.* A report of a meeting of experts on the Use in Education of African Languages in Relation to English, Where English Is the

Accepted Second Language, held at Jos, Nigeria, November, 1952. Educational Studies and Documents, 11. Paris: UNESCO.

Urbanization and Standard Language. 1959. A symposium presented at the 1958 Meetings of the American Anthropological Association. Department of Anthropology, Indiana University. In *Anthropological Linguistics,* (March) 1: 3.

Vachek, Josef. 1962. On the Interplay of External and Internal Factors in the Development of Language. *Lingua,* 11: 433–448.

Verbeke, Ronald. 1966. Language Vehiculaires de l'Enseignement en Afrique Noire. Problematique du Choix et Implications Pedagogiques. *International Review of Education,* 12:4: 450–466.

Walker, Willard. 1965. An Experiment in Programmed Cross-Cultural Education: The Import of the Cherokee Primer for the Cherokee Community and for the Behavioral Sciences. *Tahlequah,* March.

Weber, Rose-Marie. 1967. Preschool Maya-Spanish Bilingualism in a Yucatecan Village, *Anthropological Linguistics,* May 9: 5.

Wright, Charles R. 1968. *Evaluation Research.* International Encyclopedia of the Social Sciences, 5. Macmillan and Free Press.

Wurm, Stephen A. 1968. Papua-New Guinea Nationhood: The Problems of a National Language. *In* Fishman, Ferguson, and Das Gupta, 345–363.

———. In press. Language Policy, Language Engineering and Literacy in New Guinea and Australia. *In* T. A. Sebeok, ed. *Current Trends in Linguistics.* The Hague: Mouton.

13. COST-BENEFIT ANALYSIS IN LANGUAGE PLANNING

THOMAS THORBURN
Stockholm School of Economics

WHAT IS LANGUAGE PLANNING?

As an economist, specializing in microeconomics of public administration, I lack specialist knowledge of language planning. On the other hand, I am aware of cost-benefit analyses applied to other fields of public decision-making. It appears to me that the methodology of evaluating public decisions that have long-range effects will be similar for regulation of floods, fluoridization of drinking-water, care of criminals, community planning, and language planning. This is the reason why I hope to be able to put forth some comments of interest.

Description, Relationship, and Planning

Those who study language as a social phenomenon do so in order to increase human knowledge. This, however, is hardly their ultimate goal. They probably hope to contribute to better language planning in the future.

There are several steps in scientific work. The first step is *description,* which is the method used when fairly little is known about a subject. In studying language, a scientist may, for example, try to find out: What goals do people have? What alternatives do they contemplate? What are people's attitudes?

A somewhat more sophisticated step is the one where the scientist tries to find *relationships.* What relationships, for example, exist between attitudes towards language and people living in the countryside, on the one hand, and in the cities, on the other? What relationships exist between pronunciation and people living in various parts of the country? Relationships may sometimes be found to exhibit general rules. If so, the relationship is of more interest than a description of the facts in a special case; and it may then be used as a device for forecasting.

A third step in scientific study is *planning*. It occurs when one tries to apply the amalgamated knowledge of language to change the language behavior of a group of people. This paper concerns only this type of (applied) scientific work.

Definition of Planning

Planning is used not only in connection with language but also in all types of public administration. Planning implies a conscious choice between alternative ways of solving a problem—a choice that is made on the basis of a conscious effort to predict the consequences of the proposed alternatives. Planning thus always includes several alternatives and a forecast of future consequences. Like all forecasting, planning therefore must include uncertainty. The longer the time-horizon in the planning, the greater, as a rule, is the degree of uncertainty. To judge consequences fifty years ahead is usually more difficult than to judge consequences ten years ahead. If the time-horizon is extremely long, uncertainty may grow to such proportions that conscious planning may become impossible. As a rule, therefore, one must limit the time-horizon in all planning.

Planning is oriented towards a problem. Planning is an aid to politicians in solving a problem. The first step in planning, therefore, is to define the problem. A problem in language planning may concern an adoption of a new language; a change in vocabulary; or a change in writing, spelling, or pronunciation in a language.

Language Planning

In this paper, I will restrict myself to the problem of the adoption of a whole language. The character of the planning discussed here can be further specified; it will be subject to the aims of the planning. For planning may aim at changing language usage in different ways: it may aim at a language *a*) that shall become the sole language; *b*) that shall always be used in parity with another language; or *c*) that shall be allowed to be used by those who want to.

The alternatives in the planning can be further specified.

    I. Geographical Area
        A. Language as a means of communication among the inhabitants of the country

      1. To be used over the whole country
      2. To be used in one region only
   B. Language as a means of communication between the inhabitants of the country and the inhabitants of other countries
II. Media
   A. Written communication
      1. In all official publications
      2. In literature
      3. In public education
      4. In newspapers
      5. In handwriting
   B. Oral communication
      1. In communication with public authorities
      2. In radio and TV
      3. In everyday communication

The kind of planning discussed in this paper will refer to policy decisions in the above-mentioned respects. Language planning, however, may also involve various levels. On a national level, it may concern the adoption of a language or not. Afterwards, a number of subdecisions have to be made on the lower levels, where the primary decision is implemented. There are alternative ways of reaching a long-range goal; and here, again, language planning may involve adult education or ordinary school education. Various types of rewards or social pressures may also be contemplated in order to stimulate the inhabitants to accept the language policy chosen. In this paper, I shall restrict myself to a discussion of language planning on a national level where the problem is the adoption of a language.

In sum: I shall discuss language planning as a conscious choice on a national level between alternative languages intended for defined geographical areas and media as well as for an intended degree of dominance. This planning shall be founded on a systematic forecast of consequences of alternatives.

OUTLINE OF COST-BENEFIT ANALYSIS

When a problem is stated and some likely alternative solutions have been proposed, calculation can start. One wants to compare consequences of proposed alternatives, which is the object of cost-benefit analysis. The calculation aims at giving a true picture of the probable consequences—not at bringing about or supporting a decision that has already been made.

Frame for Calculation

An ordinary economic calculation for a firm starts with the cost of wages, materials, and the like, which is compared later with the prices received when the products are sold. In such a calculation, it is comparatively simple to state what the input and output are, as well as what they are worth in monetary terms. For the calculation takes place within an easily distinguishable frame around the firm—a frame that is formed by the time and place of the change of legal ownership, pertaining to the input and output of the firm, and by the prices. This gives the ordinary calculation a narrow but distinct frame.

A cost-benefit calculation in public administration differs considerably from the above pattern. The frame of the calculation is much wider and more diffuse, the essential reason being that the output of large public projects, such as road-building, flood-regulation, and hospital-building, are not paid for at a fixed price at a fixed time. Instead, the output affects the economy of a society through a chain of consequences taking place over a long period of time. For example, medical care results in cures of various degrees. The time it takes to cure and the degree of cure will influence the number of working days in production later. That is an economic effect. The degree of cure will also influence the degree of sickness in the future and, hence, the cost of medical care to society.

The main problem in cost-benefit calculation is to decide which one of these endless chains of consequences is to be included—and which not—in the calculations. An appropriate analogy here, with reference to time and consequences in public administration, might be the consequences that arise when a stone is thrown into water. Circles appear that become wider and wider. If one were to try to describe these consequences, there would be no clear boundary at which to stop.

Cost-benefit analysis in language planning is, in principle, an attempt to state the difference in consequences between two exactly defined alternatives in language planning. In this paper, I shall discuss the problem of adopting a whole language. The method put forward, however, may be used for solving other types of language problems as well. It is not possible, however, to make a cost-benefit analysis of language planning in general. Moreover, the calculation must be limited to essential consequences, the implication being that one has to start with a preliminary frame. Consequences outside that frame are consciously omitted. One aspect of that frame is the time-horizon chosen; another is a point to be determined in the chain of consequences.

Identification, Quantification, and Evaluation of Consequences

The basic idea behind the cost-benefit calculation is that the language behavior of groups of people is a national resource in the same way as technical skill or number of workers. Language is an instrument to achieve certain results and is, therefore, to be looked upon as a resource. The calculation implies that one tries systematically to identify, quantify, and evaluate all essential consequences that would arise if one were to choose planning alternative A instead of planning alternative B (zero-alternative). Each of these three steps usually offers considerable difficulties. More consequences can be quantified than evaluated; this means that the monetary calculation within the cost-benefit analysis is incomplete. The long-range character of a cost-benefit analysis, moreover, brings with it an increasing degree of uncertainty in the forecast. Consequently, a cost-benefit calculation can be more suitable as a supporting analysis than as a sufficient basis for the final decision. It is thus evident that a cost-benefit analysis is not intended to be a complete and absolutely reliable foundation for language planning. There are many consequences that are extremely difficult to identify, quantify, and evaluate; they must, nevertheless, be taken into account in any final political decision. A cost-benefit calculation ought to assemble all relevant scientific knowledge pertaining to the problem in question (description and relations), which ought to be presented to the politicians in an impartial and clear way. How to weigh the advantages and disadvantages and to judge the uncertainties is up to the politician. In my opinion, such a cost-benefit analysis can be extremely valuable in language planning.

OUTLINE FOR A COST-BENEFIT CALCULATION IN LANGUAGE PLANNING

To make cost-benefit calculation more concrete, an outline of such a calculation is given below. Lack of knowledge about sociolinguistic factors compels me to restrict my discussion to principles. If the calculation had referred to a real problem in a specific country, the author would have had to interview a number of linguists for expert knowledge. In that case, the figure that now contains 11 squares, might have included not 11, but perhaps 111, identified consequences.

Alternatives

Main-Alternative. Adopting a (Western) Language of Wider Communication (LWC) as means of communication among inhabitants in a developing country of the type called "Multi-modal Nations."[1] The language is adopted for written communication in all official publications and shall be used in parity with other languages.

Zero-Alternative. Adopting one of the national languages (NL) within the country as means of communication among the inhabitants in the country. The language is adopted for written communication in all official publications and shall be used singularly in the region of the country where the NL is the mother tongue of the inhabitants and in parity with other languages in the rest of the country.

The cost-benefit calculation aims at identifying, quantifying, and evaluating the differences in consequences that may be expected if one decides to choose the main-alternative instead of the zero-alternative. The consequences for inclusion are those that are judged to be essential from an economic, social, or cultural point of view. The time-horizon shall be long, but it shall stop before the point where the uncertainty appears to make any forecast meaningless. In the following outline, a time-horizon of twenty-five years has been chosen. A cost-benefit calculation of such a length, for example, may be carried out in three parts. The first part should cover the expected consequences during the first five years. The second part can refer to the consequences during the tenth year and be looked upon as representative of the sixth year through the fifteenth year. The third part, then would refer to the twentieth year and represent the sixteenth year through the twenty-fifth year. The total cost-benefit analysis will be arrived at by having the three parts brought together.

Analysis

The comments below pertain to the outline for cost-benefit analysis that is shown in Figure 1; each numbered comment corresponds to a numbered block in the figure.

> *1.* If a country chooses an LWC instead of the NL, one consequence will be that the teaching of the LWC must be arranged for. This will cost the nation money, which amount may be calculated on the basis of a forecast of teacher-hours and a

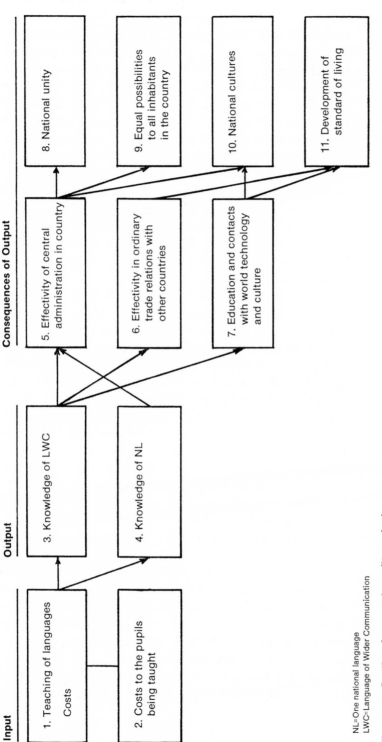

Input

1. Teaching of languages
   Costs

2. Costs to the pupils being taught

Output

3. Knowledge of LWC

4. Knowledge of NL

Consequences of Output

5. Effectivity of central administration in country

6. Effectivity in ordinary trade relations with other countries

7. Education and contacts with world technology and culture

8. National unity

9. Equal possibilities to all inhabitants in the country

10. National cultures

11. Development of standard of living

NL=One national language
LWC=Language of Wider Communication

Figure 1: Outline for cost-benefit analysis.

forecast of their salaries. One must remember, of course, that a certain amount of teaching of an LWC is required also in the zero-alternative (NL is the main language). The inhabitants of the country have to communicate with inhabitants in other countries even in that case. The cost to be included in the cost-benefit calculation shall refer to the increase, not the total volume, of the teaching of the LWC. If one chooses an LWC as the main language, a certain amount of the teaching of the NL must be retained, which is still the mother tongue of one of the regions of the country. The extent of the teaching of the NL in other parts of the country will diminish. This reduction in the teaching of the NL may be quantified in teacher-hours and evaluated in monetary terms. It appears that the net difference between the two alternatives of teaching language can be calculated in monetary terms.

2. Education takes time for the pupils. They study instead of being producers, thus, postponing production. It appears possible to forecast the value of this time in hours. It one wants to evaluate those hours in monetary terms, an average price an hour has to be applied. Such a price will be an uncertain estimate, but it is a possible technique that can be used. Similar rough price estimates have been used in other cost-benefit calculations.

3. Knowledge of an LWC is what is accomplished, and this knowledge can be quantified; a forecast of the number of people who will know the LWC can be specified in such terms as age and sex as well as quality. The knowledge of an LWC, however, is not to be evaluated directly in the calculation. The value of the knowledge of the LWC manifests itself through the items shown under the heading, *Consequences of Output.*

4. Knowledge of an NL is dealt with in the same way as knowledge of an LWC.

5. The effect on the central administration of the difference in knowledge of the LWC and the NL may be quantitatively measured by forecasting the number of civil servants as well as inhabitants generally, who will be unable to understand fully the contents of official publications and decrees. They may need interpreters, which will be a further charge on national resources; they may possibly decrease the effectivity of central administration; or they may never grasp the contents. Similar

quantifications may be made about communication in the opposite direction. The loss or gain in time to the inhabitants in their communication with the authorities might be measured in hours; and, perhaps, it may even be evaluated in monetary terms. The frequency of misunderstanding might be judged. Through investigations along these lines, it appears possible to get a general idea of the consequence of the effectivity of central administration of choosing an LWC instead of an NL. An evaluation in monetary terms appears unrealistic.

6. The difference in the knowledge of languages will obviously influence trade with other countries. It seems possible to forecast in two alternative ways the additional cost for foreign trade that may be expected; but it seems more difficult to grasp the effect on the size and type of foreign trade.

7. The difference in the knowledge of languages will influence the educational conditions within a country, the possibilities to study in foreign countries, and the cultural contacts with foreign countries. Such consequences of the choice of language may be forecast to some extent.

8. The effect on national unity of the choice of language can partly be anticipated. The consequences, however, may be different during the first years when compared with the last years of the twenty-five-year period.

9. Persons belonging to different language groups within the country may meet unequal chances for advancement within the central administration. If a NL is chosen as the main language, those who have this NL as their mother tongue may advance more rapidly than they would have advanced if an LWC were chosen as the main language. This inequality can hardly be evaluated in monetary terms.

10. The choice of language will influence the development of national cultures. In this case, an evaluation in monetary terms also appears impossible.

11. A forecast appears possible of the influences the choice of language have on the development of the standard of living, although the degree of uncertainty will be great.

The discussion above shows that a cost-benefit analysis of the choice of language will probably result in monetary values for blocks *1, 2, 5, 6,* and *11*; and that the degree of uncertainty will be great for blocks *5, 6,* and *11*. An evaluation in monetary terms is probably not possible for blocks *7, 8, 9,* and *10*. The probable direction of consequences, however, can be stated. Some further quantifications may also be possible. A cost-benefit analysis concerning the choice of language alternatives thus results in (1) net difference in money, (2) quantifications of further differences, and (3) vague indications of other consequences. If such an analysis is used by politicians to support a final decision, I believe that cost-benefit analysis in language planning may prove itself valuable.

NOTE

1. Joshua A. Fishman, National Languages and Languages of Wider Communication in Developing Nations (paper presented at the Regional Conference on Languages and Linguistics, Dar es Salaam, Tanzania, 1968).

14. NOTES ON ECONOMIC ANALYSIS FOR SOLVING LANGUAGE PROBLEMS

BJÖRN H. JERNUDD
Department of Linguistics, Monash University

This paper attempts to show how economic analysis can be used (1) to find informed solutions to language problems and (2) to guide the study of planned language change for description and problem-solving.

DECISION IS CHOICE

A characteristic of an economic viewpoint is the concept of opportunity, or alternative. "Opportunity cost" expresses the loss of opportunity by doing one thing rather than another—by selecting one course of action at the expense of another.

One of the implications of this concept for the economic study of decision-making is the fact that perhaps no one can be observed to act in an optimal manner always: there is constantly a need for the researcher or decision-maker-actor to explore *what else* could have been, or can be, done. The actor cannot just consider one way of doing his thing, and the researcher or scientist-adviser cannot confine his study to a description of actual, occurring behaviors. We require generalization and generation of alternatives beyond a particular *ex post* list of events or the local currently and immediately available list of possibilities.

New knowledge must be sought out. A reasonable first step for the decision-maker would be to consult others for more information. This search for new knowledge could continue until uncertainty about possible future events had been reduced to a very small amount. A school, for example, may reach its objectives more efficiently by employing teaching techniques unknown to its teachers at that particular moment of time. Knowledge of present behavior *and* reduction of uncertainty in expectations about the future are necessary to arrive at alternatives or to estimate and weigh together consequences of alternatives. The opportunity concept demonstrates the insufficiency of descriptive data alone.

Reasonably effective conscious planning-ahead also requires that we know *how to use* increased knowledge of relevancy for our problem-solving. Cost-benefit analysis is one method of using pertinent information to aid in decision-making. The choice of an alternative, a decision, is a valuation of which alternative is better than any other.

For societal decisions, this is the politician's job. Scientists can assist them in performing this job—better according to scientists' values—by bringing more knowledge to bear on real-life decisions, both about the decision-making process per se and its objects.

A Generalized Cost-Benefit Model

We can conveniently view the decision-making processes in terms of a generalized *cost-benefit* (c/b) *model*.

Consequences: costs and benefits on the margin. Any problem demands an interpretation within the limits of a frame of time and space in order to check uncertainty and to make the formulation and weighing of alternatives possible. A calculation for purposes of valuation implies: (1) identification, (2) quantification, and (3) valuation of all essential consequences of the alternatives under consideration within the given frame of calculation. A study of the effectiveness of language change should ideally find, quantify, and make commensurable all y's (y_{1-n}) which are the consequences to society of a change in the expression

$$f \text{ (marginal language change)} = y_{1-n}.$$

A meaningful solution is only possible if we relate all consequences (y_{1-n}) to the preferences (values) of some specified group of people, such as, a nation, an enterprise, etc. This group of people will perceive some of the consequences as *costs*, other consequences as *benefits*. Some consequences are *intangible*, some *tangible*. Intangible consequences defy quantification. This implies that cost-benefit analysis (if seen particularly in the context of considerable time depth of horizon chosen and, therefore, of high uncertainty) is supportive rather than definitive, for the problem. Cost-benefit analysis has its greatest value in identifying problems and in clarifying consequences—rather than the value of the solving of a problem by weighing consequences together.

Cost-benefit analysis, like most economic analysis, is essentially *marginally* oriented. The cost-benefit differentials between alternatives, not average or total values of consequences, are included in the analytical apparatus.

Decision processes can be classified into the following components:

1. Recognition of a problem
2. Specification (or intuitive acceptance) of goals and accompanying specification of available alternatives (which implies clarification of available instruments and awareness of constraints)[1]
3. Choice of problem-solving model (in a technical sense, e.g., investment techniques, simulation techniques, etc.)
4. The concrete numerical calculation of the consequences of selected alternatives
5. Cost-benefit valuation by linking costs and benefits
6. Problem-solving by decision hopefully meaning a step towards effective action in terms of the decision-maker's goals.

Productivity versus efficiency. In our model, we take *productive* to express the relation between costs and benefits within a given frame of calculation to the extent that it can be quantitatively measured by a *unit* measure. We take *efficient* to express the relation between *all* costs and benefits, even though they may only be identifiable, not quantifiable. A productive solution is therefore not necessarily efficient. Decisions based on productivity-indications alone can be delegated to subordinates more easily than decisions aiming at efficiency. Productivity-decisions are *suboptimizations* by will. It is clear that suboptimization leads to efficient decisions only by chance, if judged against higher-level goals (See figure 1).

Cost-benefit valuation. The cost-benefit valuation (item 5 above) can be performed in various ways. Figure 1 illustrates the following possibilities of combining costs and benefits:

1. *1* and *6*: is impossible, since the relation is non-quantifiable.
2. *3* and *4*: is profit maximization.
3. *2* and *4*: is benefit maximization.
4. *3* and *5*: is cost minimization.
   a) by identical benefits
   b) by minimization per unit of benefit
   c) by minimization per weighted index of benefits

5. *2* and *5*: cost minimization or benefits maximization
    a) by quantity benefit per unit of cost
    b) by standards (references) of profitability or technical productivity

Strictly speaking, only items 2, 3, and 4 are cost-benefit procedures, since they alone involve pecuniary productivity-measures or profit-measures. Item 5 is a technical productivity-measure. It appears that, in language planning, the usually wide-ranging intangible benefits within a societal frame of calculation make some cost-benefit valuation procedures particularly feasible, namely, cost minimization (item 4) and standards specifications or comparisons (item 5). To the extent, however, that the administrators have found it more feasible to prescribe productivity-criteria (i.e., to consciously *suboptimize* by not attempting optimal efficiency) for subordinates' decision-making, it would appear

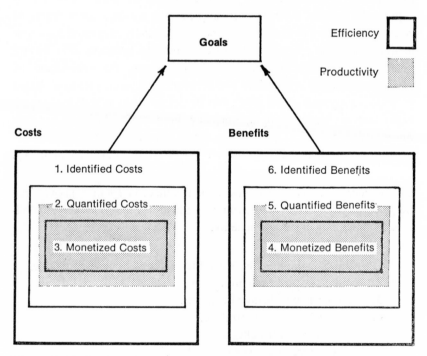

Figure 1: Evaluation of consequences (after Thorburn).

that the remaining cost-benefit alternatives become increasingly useful, both as analytical tools and for specifications of problem-solving criteria at various administrative levels.

The problem of reaching efficient and not only productive decisions may often have to be solved by "residual" techniques: a quantification is made according to the productivity-technique above. Then the decision maker estimates efficiency in terms of the resulting cost-benefit gap: a cost gap (i.e., a negative gap) measures how much the decision maker at least would have to be willing to pay to go ahead with this alternative.

Difficulties of the Application of Cost-Benefit Analysis

Many benefits of language change are difficult to locate and identify, partly because they are *intangible* or because they effect individuals' performance with considerable *time lag* between learning and use. Feelings, for example, factors of "sentimental" nationalism, are intangible in contrast to matter- or time-consuming consequences. Time lag makes identification of factors difficult for two reasons: one is the increased uncertainty in forecasting; the other is the increased possibility that other factors can interfere after a decision has been made.

Difficulties of ascertaining the benefits of education, literacy, and the like in any precise manner are well-known. This difficulty of defining all factors, benefits or costs, has led to misunderstandings of the possibilities of economic analysis. A frequent error in judging economic analysis is to divide the universe into economic and non-economic factors and to assign the study of the former to the economist (who may sometimes accept it!).

Breton (1964), for instance, found only negative "economic" effects resulting from "nationalistic" acts (presumably, therefore, also being led to give advice against nationalism). The transfer of pecuniary benefits from one group of society to another allegedly led to "economic" inefficiencies; that is, to losses in terms of utilizing the nation's resources. He failed, in my opinion, to understand the intangible goals: goals that value this transfer higher than they value the particular so-called economic loss, shared not only by those in power but also by a majority of the population (even other ethnic groups!).

Because intangibles are difficult to handle, many authors suggest methods that avoid them. In order to reduce uncertainty in forecasting and interference from unanticipated factors and difficulties of measuring intangibles, we may, on the one hand, (1) choose to concentrate on individual or smaller-group decisions on language; (2) decide to deal only with problems that are well defined in time and space so that we can ignore intangibles without serious error; and (3) select techniques that concentrate on cost differentials rather than on both benefit and cost, since costs are usually easier to specify.

On the other hand, we may choose to take intangibles into account. A frequently stressed device of analysis, and likewise of analytically motivated advice, is to point out that only a particular and listed set of factors has been taken into account and to stress that other factors are unknown or unmanageable but must be considered by the decision-maker himself before he decides what to do. The possibilities of effective language decision-making would seem to be considerably broadened by such clarification of analytical methods.

Frame for Analysis

The ultimate decision or valuation must, if we want it to be efficient, always take into account all consequences in time and space of intended action. This does not mean that we follow consequences into eternity. We know such a claim on analysis to be false, because we do not usually wish to consider consequences beyond, for example, a certain time-horizon; nor are we able to do so. Uncertainty increases with (1) time and (2) new consequences. When uncertainty grows too great, it becomes meaningless to try to follow further consequences. This means that our analytical sight should be limited by the decision maker's time-sight and by a cut-off point in space, as well as by his resources, etc. We must, in short, have a *frame* for analysis.

Governmental frame.   The most inclusive point of view is the government's. Techniques of cost-benefit analysis were developed primarily to cope with governmental (and governmental subunits') problems of decision-making,[2] particularly, investment. This cost-benefit approach is in principle a transfer of business management methods to the government sphere, exploring, necessarily, differences of government management from private management.

An important difference is evidently the role of elected representatives of the people, which is to have public-administration decision-units not act on grounds of personal-success goals alone but in accordance with public policy.

Many language decisions are essentially a public matter, as we have shown elsewhere,[3] but not at the exclusion of private decisions. The extent to which public and private initiatives interact to influence benefits and costs of language change (e.g., through associations) needs to be ascertained.

Theoretical relation between government language decisions and benefits. In order for an official language decision to be of benefit to a nation, people would have to feel uniformly solidary with such a decision. This means that only the government (if representative) would have the rights to enforce or would act to reap all benefits of such a decision. Although people can be excluded, for example, from the rights of appearing in courts if they speak only languages other than the official language, this would lead to absurdities of equality before the law. Likewise, the official language decision would hardly benefit the society unless most people apply it in appropriate situations. It is motivated, therefore, that the government is given responsibility for such decisions and their implementation. Large time lags and uncertainty regarding benefits also motivate public, rather than private, decision-making. In order for many decisions on language use to be effective, they usually require considerable public (governmental) encouragement. Government decision-making is characterized by its societal inclusiveness, involving large time lags between input and output, considerable numbers of people, etc. The frame of analysis (and calculation) will therefore be rather diffuse, or it will incorporate high uncertainty.

Non-governmental frame. It may be more rewarding to begin the economic study of language decisions by looking at associational or private language decisions, *given* government policy or changes in policy.

Individuals have opportunities of choosing languages in school or of paying for additional language teaching later. Their choice is presumably governed to a considerable extent by income expectations and by their valuation of the timing of benefits. If they did not learn now, then they would be able to work and earn an income (or enjoy leisure)—which during learning is postponed but perhaps becomes increased later, even in terms of present value. The individual may also take intangibles into explicit account, for example, family or religious tradition requiring an extra language skill. The scale and, therefore, frame of such a study is in any case much more manageable than aggregate, national approaches.

Other examples of individual frames of analysis and decision are: *a textbook writer* who may seek to maximize his income or professional status but can do so only if he uses officially authorized terminologies. Teacher usage or school usage (in cases of non-prescription of texts by central authorities) must be promoted to maximize sales. If teachers are negative to term-innovation, the writer may as a result decide to avoid certain of the official nomenclatures. A *government employee* may, on the other hand, measure his success in department status, perhaps, caused by rigorous adherence to official policy and would, therefore, not exercise modesty in employing nomenclatures, even though it may decrease his communicative efficiency, at least in the short-run. *Companies* may require the employment of personnel categories according to language knowledge for tasks that require some where there are personnel who have specified language skill. Knowledge of decisions regarding recruitment or in-service training and expected benefits would offer important insights of value for branch or sector aggregations. Similarly, decisions concerning specific nomenclatures, document standards, memo routines, etc., present themselves as the language objects of study. Another important question in the *company* frame of reference is to find what alternative organizations have emerged to cope with ethnic multiplicity or features of language development.

RESEARCH EMPHASIS ON "MICRO" LEVELS

Blaug (1966) gives ample support to a disaggregated and "micro" level approach in his article, "Literacy and Economic Development":

... it is at the level of the individual firm and at this level alone that one can come to grips with the impact of literacy on productivity. It is all very well to talk about literacy contributing to a favorable climate for economic development via its spillover benefits. In view of the fact that literacy programs take time and that much else is happening in a growing economy, the global approach to literacy research yields little beyond vague generalizations. What is needed now is hard data on the output, earnings, aptitude, and achievement of literate as opposed to illiterate workers.

Blaug (1967) also pleads that what educational researchers need is not so much past data as present data about lower-level decision-makers and decision-consequences. We also need information not so much about the results of past complex interaction of components of decision-making systems but the knowledge of the characteristics of the system itself:

This point has obvious implications for the future development of statistical data collection implying a shift from purely empirical observations of gross numbers to individual data systems incorporating evidence about the attitudinal determinants of the demand for education.

Such a systems approach will, in my opinion, necessarily clarify past experience also. A systems study gives prominence to quantifications of interrelationships in time and space between changes in government policy and public decisions, on the one hand, and resulting changes of individual decisions, on the other.

We know that the succession of levels (e.g., government, education ministry, school district, school teacher) leads to administrative and therefore economically relevant problems that themselves need evaluation and trial on each level. The government may wish to maximize the gross national product, but this is hardly the concern of the school inspector who has been assigned certain tasks that, I hope, may operate towards the GPN increase, if they have been wisely chosen. The teacher measures examination knowledge of pupils, and again the Minister may hope that this suboptimization is (see, *Productivity versus efficiency*, p. 265) reasonably efficient in terms of his GNP goals. A successful administration subdues contradictive goals of successive subordinate levels and reinforces supporting goals.

Our lack of data and knowledge of microcomponents and their relationships and our lack of knowledge of how to aggregate such relations into larger and more complex system models point to a research emphasis on microlevels. We need to observe at least that uncertainties in relationships between various, perhaps hierarchically ordered, administrative levels motivate care in analysis and decision-making: by aggregating knowns and not unknowns.

Regarding language planning, we have opted for going even a step closer to the source of new knowledge by studying first the effectivity of educational and planning institutions, measuring learners' performance resulting from institutional activities only in "graduation" marks, attitudes, and expectations.[4]

ECONOMIC THEORY AND LANGUAGE PROBLEMS

The above "build-up" study technique proceeding from detailed studies by generalizations into aggregates can profitably be guided by economic hypotheses of some degree of specificity. Certain gross relationships may be approached on largely quasi-logical grounds. We may (1) employ theories of aggregates (macrotheories) from other fields of economics to provide us with hypotheses about classes of microrelationships for subsequent investigation or (2) proceed to correlate linguistic and other aggregate entities directly, knowing that the outcome needs substantial theoretical validation.

Sociolinguistic Macrotheory

An example of the latter approach is found in Fishman (1968b). He claims an apparently strong correlation between economic growth and a sociolinguistic trend from heterogeneous (several languages) to homogeneous (few languages) language situations, as a concomitant of modernization.

Economic theory may offer an explanation of this correlation. It seems natural that a nation aspiring for efficient use of resources and for self-definition would attempt to rationalize its linguistic resources in order to eliminate such heterogeneity that hinders communication and identification. It is obvious that translations (duplications of personnel or addition of personnel, of print, limited labor, and professional mobility, etc.) are inefficient from the point of view of production as compared with their absence. When an economy is being strongly integrated by division of labor, specialization, and the like into modern structures of production, the pressure on "translations" is increased, and it becomes proportionately all the more desirable to have it eliminated because of increased scarcity of resources. Only certain kinds of political group-problems (e.g., ethnically or religiously based) that are given linguistic expression seem to pull in opposite directions. This latter pull would presumably remain only as long as such linguistic differences correlate with obstacles of access to desired roles in society.

Tendencies towards centralization and agglomeration are strong in developing countries, and this also leads to a certain amount of elimination of linguistic heterogeneity (or an interpretation into political circumstance of factual difference) (Deutsch, 1953).

I also feel that a given state (homogeneous or not) of development (as we may choose to define it) is not the most immediate problem that seeks an explanation. Rather, *alternative paths towards certain developmental states* should be the object of study because of the promise of profits from the application of resulting insights.[5] We can, as I hope the above discussion shows, readily discover and appreciate the importance of some general macroeffects, for example, of language and foreign relations and internal unity; of domestic or international communication, for societal well-being; and of identific goals for emotional or cultural satis-faction. We can prescribe (predict) in our theory that, were the one kind of effect to dominate national decisions, then such and such a language should ideally (would) be monolingually used—but such is not reality! We might introduce some further refinement by employing sociolinguistic notions of repertoire and functional differentiation: if those persons com-municating for purposes of foreign relations are provided with a spe-cialized group of translators, then monolingualism can still prevail for internal communication and the expense of continuing the necessary bilingualism kept at a minimum. We know, however, that such situations do not exist. We are again brought to microquestions that need to be answered.

Macroeconomics and Language

Macroeconomic generalizations about modernization can fruitfully be used as a source of hypotheses for sociolinguistic theory. Kuznets (1966) relies on relatively detailed data in support of his generalizations. Al-though little or no language data is available, it is possible to deduce some hypothetical linguistic relations to guide further research.

The following discussion is based on Kuznets (1966, pp. 490–502):

1. *With high rates of increase in per capita product, there is a sub-stantial rate of population growth. This creates increasing pres-sures on natural resources, relative to the size of successive generations, and leads to wide differentials in rates of natural increase among various economic and social groups* (pp. 490–491).

   It does not seem unreasonable to expect that people pos-sessing language skills who are in demand in economic growth sectors will be comparatively favored over people without these skills. The latter may require a greater share of educational re-sources or temporary privileges to off-set their linguistic inability; if they are unsuccessful in their demands, they will be held back in economic advancement (although, by their own effort, they would be likely to attempt acquiring the key language unless constrained by circumstance or lack of insight or both; or, al-ternatively, to increase their political pressure for compensation, etc.).

   Population growth per se will alter the relative strength of speech varieties. Migration particularly may have substantial effects (via a second generation), as Deutsch (1953) has discussed extensively.

2. *Quality increase rather than quantity increase will successively account for a greater share of the rise in per capita product, by greater effectivity of production brought about by increases in useful knowledge and better institutional arrangements* (p. 491).

There will be demands on language as an instrument in bringing about such quality increase, in training, communications, etc. It is likely that a per capita expansion of knowledge of speech variation is necessary.

3. *There are rapid shifts in the industrial structure of product and, therefore, rapid shifts of shares of labor, coupled with expansion of foreign trade and of changes in the international division of labor* (p. 493).

This obviously means (1) that language must allow for such shift, by extent of individual knowledge of language features, by availability of vocabulary and speech patterns; and also (2) that, for international trade, languages of wider communication (LWC) must be sufficiently known. There must be routines for translating, and communication networks must be established.

Language loyalties and educational patterns determine how the nation adjusts to some of these demands. Nations that have clearly monolingual non-LWC language solutions and multiethnic states and areas that have an already strong LWC solution will obviously take different paths towards meeting these demands.[6]

4. *High interindustry, interstatus, and interoccupational mobility of the labor force is a characteristic of modern economic growth* (p. 494).

Language knowledge is obviously a constraint on mobility, but language is also under demand pressure for this very fact. It is probable that an efficient solution (towards which state we would expect developing nations to move) is to have a single language system.[7] Such unification would be slowed down, by lingering ethnic dominance in sectors of economic activity, and modified, by the LWC demand above.

5. *The sequential spread of modern economic growth rather than simultaneous emergence meant inequalities in the rate of aggre-*

*gate growth even among the countries that eventually became
(what we now consider) developed* (p. 500).

This fact (colonialism, of course, is another) explains, at
least partly, the hegemony of certain "world languages" as
models, for example, of vocabulary development but, above all,
as LWC's.

The non-linguistic magnitudes enumerated above seem relatively
well known. But the language magnitudes remain hypothetical. Thus,
Kuznets' generalizations are possible because of a considerable data bank,
whereas we lack as yet support for equivalent sets of language propositions.

ACKNOWLEDGMENT

This paper was written while I participated in a project on language problems of developing nations as a Senior Fellow at the Institute of Advanced
Projects, East-West Center, Horolulu. A Ford Foundation grant supported
the project.

The presentation of cost-benefit analysis relies in all essentials on personal
communications and publications (1964 and 1968; also, paper 13, this volume)
by Thomas Thorburn, professor at the Stockholm School of Economics. I
also gratefully acknowledge Professor Thorburn's and Professor Neustupný's
suggestions for improving this paper.

NOTES

1. Goals are classes of alternatives. The formulation of alternatives expresses the decision maker's goals, by making explicit what he believes
   is going to happen as a result of his alternative decisions.
2. This is particularly apparent in Prest and Turvey (1965).
3. Cf. Jernudd and Das Gupta (paper 11, this volume).
4. Cf. the research proposal by Fishman, Das Gupta, Jernudd, and Rubin
   (1968).
5. This follows from our insistence that description of events needs to be
   put to use by a decision-theory. Decisions require formulation of alternatives; paths, not states, express these alternatives. Cf. also Marschak
   (1965):

   . . . people do not always follow logical rules unless they make an effort ("stop
   to think"). Indeed, logic is not psychology. The data available to linguistic
   politicians in particular . . . , for checking and re-checking their tastes and
   beliefs, are, I fear, quite rough. Yet the present attempt to sketch a relation

between their task and the logic of policies in general may help to understand the debate and debaters of dictionaries and grammars.

6. Cf. Fishman (1968a).
7. Cf. Ferguson (1968) and Neustupný (1965). Neustupný employs the term "language block" for our "language system."

REFERENCES

Blaug, M. 1966. Literacy and Economic Development. *The School Review*, 74: 4: 393–418.
————. 1967. Educational Planning: Review Article. *Minerva*, 6: 1: 43–47.
Breton, A. 1964. The Economics of Nationalism. *Journal of Political Economy*, 12: 4: 376–386.
Deutsch, Karl. 1953. *Nationalism and Social Communication*. Cambridge, Mass.: MIT Press.
Ferguson, Charles A. 1968. Language Development. *In* Fishman, Ferguson, and Das Gupta, 27–35.
Fishman, Joshua A. 1968a. National Languages and Languages of Wider Communication in the Developing Nations. Paper presented at the Regional Conference on Language and Linguistics, Dar es Salaam, Tanzania.
————. 1968b. Some Contrasts Between Linguistically Homogeneous and Linguistically Heterogeneous Polities. *In* Fishman, Ferguson, and Das Gupta, 53–68.
Fishman, Joshua A.; Das Gupta, Jyotirindra; Jernudd, Björn H.; and Rubin, Joan. 1968. Language Planning Processes in Developing Countries. Research Proposal.
Fishman, Joshua A.; Ferguson, Charles A.; and Das Gupta, Jyotirindra, eds. 1968. *Language Problems of Developing Nations*. New York: John Wiley and Sons.
Jernudd, Björn H. and Das Gupta, Jyotirindra. This volume. Towards a Theory of Language Planning. Paper 11.
Kuznets, Simon. 1966. *Modern Economic Growth: Rate, Structure, and Spread*. New Haven and London: Yale University Press.
Marschak, J. 1965. Economics of Language. *Behavioral Science*, 10: 135–140.
Neustupný, Jiří V. 1965. First Steps Towards the Conception of "Oriental Languages." *Archiv Orientální*, 33: 83–92.
Prest, Alan R. and Turvey, R. 1965. Cost-Benefit Analysis: A Survey. *Economic Journal*, 75: 300: 683–735.
Thorburn, Thomas. 1966. *Företagsekonomi*. Lund: Studentlitteratur.
————. 1968. *Kompendium i Förvaltningsekonomi*. Stockholm School of Economics. Mimeo.
————. This volume. Cost-Benefit Analysis in Language Planning. Paper 13.

15. A TENTATIVE CLASSIFICATION OF LANGUAGE-PLANNING AIMS

CHAIM RABIN
Hebrew University, Jerusalem

EXTRA-LINGUISTIC AIMS

Concerning the use of a given language block or relative extent of usage of competing language blocks

A. Horizontal

Change in area of use

1. Geographical (country, province, etc.)
2. Communal (with mixed populations)

B. Vertical

Change in social use

1. Between classes
2. Between town and country, settled and nomads, etc.
3. In specific uses (e.g., literary *vs.* spoken, or religious *vs.* vernacular use)

C. Diachronic

This type of aim is often radical

1. Revival of a "dead" language
2. Use of a written language for speaking or of a spoken language for writing (see B3 above)
3. Creation of a new language block
4. Killing, or allowing to die, an existing language

Extra-linguistic aims would appear to concern primarily sociologists and political scientists. Existing literature treats these aims as typical instances of language planning. Their implementation often involves teaching a language to large numbers of people. Therefore this kind of planning tends to shade off into educational planning. There obviously is a case here for a study to evaluate how the above kinds of extra-linguistic decisions and decisions on methods and scope of language teaching affect each other.

SEMI-LINGUISTIC AIMS

A. Writing
   1. To change the writing system (e.g., from logographic to alphabetic script, from diacritic to linear representation of vowels)
   2. To change features of the writing system (e.g., introduction of capitals; new single graphs instead of digraphs; abolition of special initial or final graphs; abolition of word-divider, as in Ethiopia)
   3. A change in ductus (e.g., cyrillic *vs.* roman in Yugoslavia, gothic *vs.* roman for German, improvements of graph distinctiveness)
   4. Para-orthographical change (e.g., punctuation, standards of transliteration)
B. Spelling
   1. Systematization and unification
   2. Simplification
   3. Phonemization (especially of etymological spelling)
   4. Word-boundary spelling changes (e.g., dividing prepositions, articles, and the like from nouns, abolition of *sandhi* spelling)
C. Pronunciation
   Unification of regional or social allophones and the like that are not affecting the distribution or number of phonemes
D. Restrictions in Speaking
   1. Use of politeness forms (e.g., the Swedish campaign for using the "tu"-pronoun *du* rather than polite circumlocutions)
   2. Language taboos

Semi-linguistic aims represent the most frequent type of planned language change. Yet it seems very difficult to decide to which discipline this study could belong. Strong sociological and psychological factors seem to be involved, although mostly linguists do the research. This situation seems to call for a new type of specialist.

A problem of classification is whether aims concerning lexical borrowing *vs.* new creation for vocabulary enlargement and other forms of interlanguage or intralanguage purism should not properly come under this heading? See for the present A3, p. 279.

LINGUISTIC AIMS

A. Vocabulary
   1. Vocabulary enlargement
      a) Systematic decisions (generative processes)
      b) Practical planning (vocabulary items)
   2. Vocabulary standardization
      a) Technical vocabulary
      b) Non-technical vocabulary (neologisms, archaisms)
      c) Dialectal
   3. Sociosemantics (decisions on sources of vocabulary enlargement)
      a) Foreign *vs.* native
      b) Borrowing from older forms of the same language
      c) Borrowing from regional dialects
      d) Adaptation from closely related languages
      e) Admissibility of vulgarisms and slang
B. Structure
   1. Phonology
   2. Morphology (see, however, A1 above)
   3. Syntax
C. Style
   1. Traditional *vs.* europeanized style (specified according to domain of language use)
   2. "High" style *vs.* simple straightforward writing
   3. Should National Prestige Literatures (e.g., the Hebrew Bible, Ramayana, Homer, Chaucer) be read in the original form, in modernized spelling, or in translation?

This section is the province of the normative linguist, in collaboration with the literary practitioner. The study of language planning, however, should show what qualifications may be required from a normative linguist, as opposed to a descriptive linguist.

16. INSTRUMENTALISM IN LANGUAGE PLANNING

EINAR HAUGEN
Department of Germanic Languages and Literature, Harvard University

Two interesting attempts have recently been made to establish theories of language planning (LP) or language standardization (LS), which are here used in roughly identical meanings. One is by the Indian scholar Punya Sloka Ray (1963); the other is by the Estonian scholar Valter Tauli (1968). Ray wrote his book in the United States; Tauli, in Sweden. Both are deeply concerned with past and current problems in the standardization of their respective native languages. Both wish to project these problems into a larger framework that will provide a model for research and development in the field.

The two books are very different in style and focus, and the authors' backgrounds could hardly be more different than they are. Ray's book is more philosophical and provocative; Tauli's, more learned and cautious. They agree, however, in their appraisal of the basic problem of LP: that the heart of any program in this field is the evaluation of competing linguistic forms. Ray grants that LS is prescription rather than description and "value-neutrality is therefore openly abandoned" (p. 15). He then argues that "value-neutrality is not a necessary characteristic of all science" and that a scientific view is quite compatible with "relativity of assumptions." Tauli similarly opens with a call for "language evaluation," which he justifies in terms of the theory of value (p. 9). He grants that this theory is non-unique; his book is the presentation of his own "ideal norms" in language (pp. 27–28). Once certain postulates are established however, he believes that an objective evaluation is possible; e.g., if shortness of words is agreed to be an ideal, there will be no problem in establishing a criterion of length, whether in terms of phonemes, syllables, morphemes, or whatever.

The basic postulate to which both writers appeal is essentially the same: language is an instrument, a tool of communication. It will be the purpose of this paper to examine more closely the implications of this postulate, which I shall call the hypothesis of *instrumentalism*. Their statements of this hypothesis are so similar that one might almost suspect the second author of having derived it from the first, were it not that Tauli's manuscript was largely completed before Ray's was published. While Tauli includes Ray's book in his bibliography, he makes only the scantest reference to it in his text. It seems clear that their agreement is largely due to a common purpose—and a common prejudice.

Ray makes the point on page 11 by drawing an analogy between a standardized tool ("cheaper to acquire and maintain, more dependable in performance, and in each specimen more like one another") and a standardized language, which is similarly superior to a non-standardized one with respect to efficiency, rationality, and commonality. "A language is from this point of view only an instrument of communication, not a symbol of revelation, only a means, not an end."

Tauli states the same view in his opening sentence, defining a language as "a system of signs, the main purpose of which is communication." "It must be borne in mind that language is an instrument, a means, never an end." "Since language is an instrument, it follows that a language can be evaluated, altered, corrected, regulated, and improved, and new languages can be created at will" (p. 9).

The analogy of language to a tool is commonplace enough and even somewhat banal. One need go no further than the American College Dictionary to find under the entry "tool subject" that this is "a branch of learning taught to enable students to perform specific or useful tasks, and not for its own sake, as grammar, spelling, calculation(!)" As ordinarily taught, this may indeed be true of grammar and spelling; these are the chief instruments for inculcating the standard language in its written form, which is also the chief target of LP in most countries. It is less cogent, however, to apply the analogy to language itself, and especially to press from it the conclusions presented above by Ray and Tauli. They are saying, in effect, that language is available for manipulation by its user, not merely to accomplish its normal purpose, as a hammer is used to pound nails, but as an external object that can be trimmed or repaired or extended so that it will have a different appearance or structure and either accomplish its normal purpose more effectively or some additional purpose not previously envisaged.

It will be my contention that in saying this they are reifying one aspect of language, and not necessarily the most important. Words like "tool" or "instrument" have their literal meaning in reference to objects external to man, forming extensions of his physical capacity and technologically subject to variation and reshaping for greater adequacy. In their metaphorical or transferred meaning they are merely synonyms for "means" or "agency," and it remains to be demonstrated that language possesses these other properties of man's tools.

Tauli cites a goodly number of references from the linguistic literature to support his argument, even contending that the instrumental hypothesis "is the general view among linguists, language philosophers, psychologists, sociologists, ethnologists, etc., of various schools" (p. 9). When one checks on these references (p. 173), it is apparent, however, that many of them are too casual to support his far-reaching conclusions. Thus Martinet (*Word*, 1954, 10: 74) is referring in passing only to the problem of how one can best characterize a given language as "the communication medium of a certain community." Katz (1966, p. 176) views language as "an instrument of communication of thoughts and ideas," but identifies it also as "a highly complex system of rules" and makes no assumptions about the possibility of changing these. Lenneberg (*Language*, 1953, 29: 467) is discussing the "differences in the ease and facility for the expression of certain things among various languages" and doubts that we are able to decide whether this difference in ease is "attributable to the properties of a given language qua vehicle of communication or to the cultural development of the speakers." Hjelmslev refers to language as an "instrument" in his *Prolegomena* (1953, p. 1) but only as one aspect of its nature, and he goes on to say: "Language is no external accompaniment—it lies deep in the mind of man, a wealth of memories inherited by the individual and the tribe," etc. These four examples from Tauli's list should be enough to indicate that when linguists refer to language as an instrument, they are not describing its essential nature, only its purpose. "Instrument" or "tool" is merely a metaphor that is synonymous with "means" and contrasted with "end" or "purpose."

One famous linguist not cited by Tauli in this connection is Sapir, who made frequent use of this metaphor. In his *Language* (1921), he referred to language as a "method of communicating ideas, emotions, and desires" (p. 7), "an instrument capable of running a gamut of psychic uses" (p. 13), "an instrument originally put to uses lower than the conceptual plane" (p. 14), and "the tool of significant expression" (p. 23).

It is clear that these terms are little more than vivid writing for describing the ends of language. Bloch and Trager (1942) put it more succinctly in their well-known definition of language as "a system of arbitrary vocal symbols by means of which a social group cooperates" (p. 5). Everyone agrees that language is man's principal and peculiar means of communication, but it does not follow, as Ray and Tauli suggest, that this means that language, like a tool, is subject to being "altered, corrected, regulated, and improved" at will. The analogy to a tool falters and breaks down when we consider the nature of language itself and the method of its acquisition and storage in the human brain.

Linguists have wrestled for a long time with the problem of defining the essential nature of language. Some have stressed the behavioral, observable aspect; take, for example, Jespersen (1924): "The essence of language is human activity—activity on the part of one individual to make himself understood by another, and activity on the part of that other to understand what was in the mind of the first" (p. 2). Hermann Paul (1886) defined the true object of linguistic research as *"sämmtliche äusserungen der sprechtätigkeit an sämmtliche individuen in ihrer wechselwirkung auf einander"* (p. 22). Bloomfield (1933) also emphasized the empirically observable behavior of the speakers and their "system of speech-signals" (p. 29). He regarded this system as consisting of "speech-habits" (p. 38), a term which is echoed by his followers, for example, Hockett (1958), who describes language as "a complex system of habits" analyzable into such subsystems as grammar, phonology, morphophonemics, semantics, and phonetics (p. 137). Saussure (1916), who introduced the distinction between *langue* and *parole,* found that language (*langue*) *"existe dans la collectivité sous la forme d'une somme d'empreintes déposées dans chaque cerveau"* (p. 38). Chomsky (1965) has replicated and clarified Saussure's dichotomy by introducing the concept of competence ("the speaker-hearer's knowledge of his language"), in which Bloomfield's "habits" have been replaced by "rules," conceived of as "generative processes" (p. 4). The stress has been shifted to the internal, non-observable aspects of language, that which Sapir (1921) called the "peculiar symbolic relation . . . between all possible elements of consciousness, on the one hand, and certain selected elements localized in the auditory, motor, and other cerebral and nervous tracts, in the other" (p. 9).

However one names it, all linguists would agree that language is a highly complex system stored in the brain of each speaker, which enables him to perform intricate acts of communication. There is nothing in all this to remind us of the kind of tools that man has devised in order to extend his mastery of the environment. A hammer and a saw can do things that the bare hand cannot; similarly, a printed book or a telephone can extend the range of human speech in time and space. These are tools, and one would be hard put to it to show that language as defined above has any similarity whatever to them.

The argument turns on the question of whether it is possible to evaluate one language in comparison with another ("*A* is a better tool than *B*") or whether it is possible to evaluate one form of a language in comparison with an alternate form ("item *x* in *A* makes it a better tool than item *y*"). The evaluation of *A* as better than *B* implies a discrimination of *B*. Logically, it should lead to a policy whereby speakers of *B* are encouraged/urged/forced to learn *A*. The evaluation of *x* as better than *y* similarly requires that speakers of *A* ought to unlearn *y* and replace it with *x*. The problems involved are of a magnitude that experience shows cannot be compared with those of replacing one tool with another. If my old hammer wears out, I gladly replace it with a new one; if power saws are available and I wish to simplify and expand my sawing operations, I eagerly avail myself of the opportunity. Changes in language are neither so immediately obvious as improvements nor so easily accomplished. Neither a language as a whole nor any part of it is replaceable like a spare part in a machine; it is not to be discarded like an old coat, and it cannot be bought at the store like a new one.

A primary requirement in communication is that both parties have a code in common. Without this, understanding will either be totally absent or seriously impeded. Abstractly speaking, it makes no difference whether *A* learns *B* or *B* learns *A*: one code is as good as another. When speakers have in fact shifted language, the motivations have regularly been associated with personal advantage and self-preservation. Language *A* gives access to money, power, influence, learning, while *B* does not. Where *B* in spite of all temptations has resisted the learning of *A*, it has usually been due to a desire to maintain group identity, which is in itself a form of personal advantage (when it is not simply due to lack of access, failure of mobilization). If *A* is a standard language and *B* is a dialect related to it, their social prestige is the significant factor in promoting one over the other. In this situation it may be feasible for speakers to adopt the former item by item, leading to their evaluating item *x* and better than *y*. Is *x* therefore a "better tool" than *y*? Probably not, except in the sense that it makes the user more acceptable in the group where *A* is spoken. If the pressure is great enough, the individual will yield (assuming he is young enough and submissive enough to change rather than endure the consequences). Uniformity of code is enforced by the necessities of face-to-face communication; who shall yield when there are differences that are determined by social factors.

Is there then no room for evaluation of *A* versus *B* or *x* versus *y* other than by their social prestige? A negative answer would probably accord with the views of most serious linguists, who tend to be fatalistic and egalitarian in these matters. Tauli even accuses them of maintaining a "prescientific mystical view" when they hold that all languages are equally good and adequate (p. 23). Since the scholars he cites as evidence for this view are neither unscientific nor mystical, his charge is not too convincing. One could easily bring in others whom he does not cite, for example, Lenneberg in the passage cited above: "A basic maxim in linguistics is that anything can be expressed in any language" (*Language*, 1953, 29: 467). Greenberg (1957) has one of the fullest statements of this hypothesis: "While it may seem somewhat rash to prejudge the case, it appears that natural languages are all very much on the same level as far as efficiency is concerned. A comparative measure of efficiency which includes all relevant phonological, grammatical, and semantic aspects has never been worked out, and, in view of the complexity of each aspect and the disparity among them, it does not appear very likely that one can be developed. . . . The evolution of language as such has never been demonstrated, and the inherent equality of all languages must be maintained on present evidence" (p. 65).

Tauli calls this "a popular fallacy among linguists," "an unfounded hypothesis which has never been tested" (p. 13). As Greenberg indeed admits, it is probably untestable. It is, however, based on a number of common and testable observations. One of these is that children will learn any language that is presented to them in infancy, apparently with equal ease and at about the same time. Another is the mutual translatability of languages, which is attested by the success in translating the Bible into virtually all the idioms of the world. A third is the well-known tendency of languages to add complexity in one area when reducing it in another, for example, the substitution in many Indo-European languages of prepositions and fixed word order for disappearing case endings. Each living language appears to have achieved a form that is kept in equilibrium by the law of least effort on the part of its users.

Any attempt of language planners to alter a language in the name of some ideal principle has to take into account the process whereby language is transmitted and maintained. Infancy is the only period when children will learn freely any language to which they are exposed. But at this age they are still too young to profit from formal instruction. Any modification introduced into their language has to come from models in their environment so that one can affect them only by changing or severely restricting that environment. Playmates are known to be more important than parents in establishing their language. Beginning with school age, the child can be taught a new language, either through reading or personal contact, though already with considerable resistance. Again, the main influence will come from schoolmates rather than teachers. In adolescence and early youth, patterns may be modified upon the youth's realization that he is entering the ranks of the adult world. He may decide to replace some forms of his dialect with those of a more "cultured" language. This is virtually his last chance, for puberty has made him relatively impervious to new language teaching.

The language planner is therefore limited to the influence he can exert through the school system, especially grammar schools. He may be able to make the choosing of certain forms into an academic, cultural decision. Through this process, he may lend his choices a certain social prestige, at least in some circles. If he has plenty of time and power and is dealing with a population where many individuals are changing status, he may succeed in establishing some of his innovations. But most would-be language planners (spelling reformers, educators, grammarians, etc.) do not have this kind of support, and in any case they tend to disagree among themselves on the nature of the reforms they wish to promote; hence, the need for academies and commissions, for expert consultants in ministries of education, and for the mobilization of public opinion. In the English-speaking world, the problem has been left to private enterprise, which means the makers of dictionaries.

The ideal qualities with which our two writers wish to endow their languages could hardly be challenged, even when they are in part mutually contradictory. Ray, as we have seen, wants efficiency, rationality, and commonalty; for definitions of these, the reader is referred to his book. Tauli wants clarity, economy, and beauty; the detailed rules he sets up for these abstractions contain many interesting observations and examples.

The qualities desired are those that good writers have long cultivated in making choices among alternate modes of expressions in their own languages. Language planning goes farther, however, in proposing the extension of these rules to established patterns and proposed innovations. The writer is not free to follow these principles in order to achieve some ideal rationality or efficiency, say, by making all the strong verbs of English regular. Aside from the fact that he would occasionally be misunderstood and often misjudged, he would be violating a basic principle of communication: the historical stability of the code, which corresponds to its synchronic uniformity. Each generation wishes to be able to speak to its juniors as well as its elders. Stability is of the highest value in the written language, which in some degree speaks to eternity.

Tauli is particularly severe on the inadequacies of natural languages: it is evident, he writes, "that all languages are fatally imperfect and unsystematic, with lacunae and unnecessary elements" (p. 14). There is no doubt that, when judged by strictly logical standards, natural languages are both redundant and ambiguous. Familiarity with more than one language makes one painfully aware of the inadequacies of each. This is indeed the reason for the development of logic and mathematics: these allow one to escape from the logical imperfections of natural languages. But who would wish to replace language with mathematics in our social life? The rich diversity of human languages and dialects is part of the human condition. To iron them out so that all languages would either be uniformly logical or identical in reference is not only a work of Sisyphus, but a monstrous goal unworthy of a humanist.

To be sure, neither of our authors proposes anything so vast. They are primarily concerned to hold up before men the ideals of a more efficient and insightful use of language. It is the contention of this paper that one cannot do so by limiting oneself to an instrumental view of language, which implies that its quirks are not to be respected but call for regulation. Language is much more than an instrument; among other things, it is also an expression of personality and a sign of identity. Hjelmslev (1953), in the passage quoted earlier, went on to call language "the ultimate, indispensable sustainer of the human individual, his refuge in hours of loneliness, when the mind wrestles with existence and the conflict is resolved in the monologue of the poet and the thinker" (p. 1). These words should be pondered well before one sets forth on a program of either language planning or standardization.[1]

NOTE

1. For a more detailed consideration of Tauli's book, see the writer's review in *Language* (December, 1969). For further discussion of Ray, see Haugen (1966), which came too late for inclusion in Tauli's bibliography.

REFERENCES

Bloch, Bernard and Trager, George. 1942. *Outline of Linguistic Analysis.* Baltimore: LSA Special Publication.
Bloomfield, Leonard. 1933. *Language.* New York: Holt.
Chomsky, Noam. 1965. *Aspects of the Theory of Syntax.* Cambridge, Mass.: MIT Press.
Greenberg, Joseph H. 1957. *Essays in Linguistics.* Chicago: University of Chicago Press.
Haugen, Einar. 1966. Linguistics and Language Planning. *In* William Bright, ed. *Sociolinguistics. Proceedings of the* UCLA *Sociolinguistics Conference, 1964.* Janua Linguarum, Series Maior, 20. The Hague: Mouton, 50–71.
Hjelmslev, Louis. 1953. *Prolegomena to a Theory of Language.* Translated by Francis J. Whitfield. *Supplement to International Journal of American Linguistics,* 19: 1.
Hockett, Charles F. 1958. *A Course in Modern Linguistics.* New York: Macmillan.
Jespersen, Otto. 1924. *The Philosophy of Grammar.* London: George Allen and Unwin.
Katz, Jerrold J. 1966. *The Philosophy of Language.* New York: Harper and Row.
Paul, Hermann. 1886. *Principien der Sprachgeschichte.* 2nd ed. Halle: Niemeyer.
Ray, Punya S. 1963. *Language Standardization: Studies in Prescriptive Linguistics.* Janua Linguarum, Series minor no. 29. The Hague: Mouton.
Sapir, Edward. 1921. *Language.* New York: Harcourt, Brace.
Saussure, Ferdinand de. 1916. *Cours de Linguistique Générale.* Ed. by C. Bally, A. Sechehaye, and A. Riedlinger. Paris: Payot.
Tauli, Valter. 1968. *Introduction to a Theory of Language Planning.* Acta Universitatis Upsaliensis, Studia Philologiae Scandinavicae Upsaliensia, 6. Uppsala: University of Uppsala.

Research Strategies and a View towards the Future

17. RESEARCH OUTLINE FOR COMPARATIVE STUDIES OF LANGUAGE PLANNING

JOSHUA A. FISHMAN
Ferkauf Graduate School, Yeshiva University
JYOTIRINDRA DAS GUPTA
Department of Political Science, University of California, Berkeley
BJÖRN H. JERNUDD
Department of Linguistics, Monash University
JOAN RUBIN
Department of Anthropology, Tulane University

The following outline[1] offers topics and procedures for comparative (cross-national), interdisciplinary investigation of the process of language planning viewed as an example of planned social change. The process of language planning is regarded as having four major subdivisions: policy formulation, codification, elaboration, and implementation. Each of these is discussed below in turn and a section is appended on possibilities for economic analysis of language planning (B. Jernudd).

POLICY FORMULATION

Policy formulation deals with the decisions of formally constituted organizations with respect to either: (1) the functional allocation of codes within a speech community or (2) the characteristics of one or more codes within the code matrix (linguistic repertoire) of such a community. Most studies of policy formulation have been historical in nature and have concentrated their attention on official (i.e., governmental) bodies operating at the national (or polity) level. These emphases are certainly proper but would benefit from being complemented by on-going process data and by data pertaining to local languages not considered for nation-wide functions.

The Consensual Basis of the Policy-making Body

How is the policy-making body selected or constituted? How is its authority in the language field derived? What provision is there, if any, for the renewal of this authorization? What is the relationship between the decision-making body of language policy and other decision-making authorities (political, military, educational, etc.) at the same and at higher as well as lower levels? What are the similarities and differences between language decisions and other decisions so far as authorization is concerned? If there is more than one body for language policy-making, on what basis and concerning which tasks are they differentiated and coordinated?

The Process of Policy-making

The policy can be reviewed, preferably in conjunction with some recent important decision(s), but also in the context of the history of policy-making during the past decade or more. Language is frequently symbolic of seemingly unarguable ("primordial") loyalties; however, language policy-making may be interwoven with political or other processes that operate on the basis of bargaining, compromising, influencing, and the like.

As a result, it is important to examine the conflicting pressures *within* the language policy-making (or recommending) authority per se (be it study commission, review commission, legislative assembly, etc.) as well as the conflicts and the resolutions of conflicts *between* that authority and other authorities (economic agencies or interests, educational agencies or interests, political parties, etc.). What are the similarities and differences between the processes of language-policy decisions and the processes of other decisions at similar levels? With what other decisions do language decisions get to be tied or intermeshed?

The Interest-Basis of Language Policy

Who has what to gain and what to lose by what language-policy decisions? "Primordial" groups (e.g., language, religious, "tribal", regional, or "ethnic" organizations) can be compared with the so-called modern sector groups (e.g., occupational, political, special purpose, recreational organizations, etc.) wherever possible. Their goals, rationales, and priorities can be reviewed, particularly to clarify the relationship between language goals and other goals. The awareness and the explicitness of policy makers with respect to nation-building goals require probing since goal-differences are often kept vague to prevent discord or to permit new situations to "develop from below" before they are formalized.

The perceived absence or presence of decision-alternatives should be examined for various organized groups and bodies, and the consideration given these alternatives (reasons for considering them, reasons for abandoning them, possibility of reconsidering them) can be indicated. Predictions and evaluations of the alternatives in quantitative economic terms may be possible. Alternatives may be of interest to specialists in other planning contexts (particularly if they can be objectively evaluated), even long after decisions have already been made. The intellectual, educational, industrial-commercial, and military "establishments" are particularly worthy of study in connection with the interest-basis of language policy.

Data

Sources of data for studies of language-policy formulations are government reports and documents, organizational reports and archival materials, newspaper and journal accounts, and library resources, more generally. Considerable use should probably be made also of structured and unstructured interviews with officers and members of the decision-making bodies themselves and of the influencing (whether supportively or oppositionally), authorizing, and implementing bodies related to them. It may also be possible, given the proper auspices, to distribute a brief mail questionnaire to legislators or to agency members to obtain very brief replies to very specific questions.

In general, the policy-formulation aspect of language planning probably calls for more detailed discussion and contingency-questioning than questionnaires are likely to permit. A few knowledgeable informants can provide much of the basic information needed in order to pinpoint the process of language decision-making.

CODIFICATION AND ELABORATION

Codification and elaboration[2] refer to the two major aspects of language planning as viewed from the vantage point of technical linguistics. *Codification* deals with the normalization (standardization) of regional, social, class, or other variation in usage via the preparation of recommended (or "official") grammars, dictionaries, orthographic guides, etc. *Elaboration* deals with the need for intertranslatability with one or more *functionally diversified* languages by such means as the preparation of recommended (or "official") word lists, in particular, the substantive, professional, or technical fields.

Previous studies of language planning have concentrated on describing the "products" of language planning, the structural principles on which they are based (or which they seek to establish), and the differing views with respect to the latter among the language planners per se. Once again, these emphases are certainly proper but might well be accompanied by a number of additional concerns as well; examples are discussed below.

Auspices and Control

The auspices and control of codification and elaboration vary from place to place as well as from time to time. Not only are the source and renewal of authorization of interest here (as they were in connection with decision-making of language policy) but also the work-auspices of planning. Some planning agencies (boards, academies, bureaus, institutes) are entirely governmental; some are entirely independent of government (private, academic, party, etc.); some have multiple auspices. There is also the question of the exclusiveness of language planning, some countries or regions revealing several agencies engaged in simultaneous efforts. Where the latter occurs, it is desirable to explore the basis of the differentiation that obtains since it may be based on several factors that have implications not only for codification and elaboration but also for policy and implementation as well. Among the most common bases of differentiation between coactive agencies are: technical versus literary training of personnel, academic versus self-training of personnel, ideological-political differences between respective sources of authorization, and topical-functional differentiation of responsibilities (for example: planning for school use; planning for armed forces use; planning for radio or mass-media use).

Agency personnel. It is in connection with the review of auspices and control of language-planning agencies that the characteristics of their personnel (age, training, and project-involvement) may well be reviewed, both in connection with "normal operations" as well as in connection with special projects that are launched from time to time. Both the composition of agency personnel and the nature of interpersonal ties (within and between agencies) influence agency goals and operations, thus justifying attempts to study the informal as well as the formal operation of language agencies.

Agency Operations

The major "products," programs, and plans of planning agencies must be described, both in terms of their *content* and *purpose* (including the pedagogic and other applied products that many agencies produce in addition to their more scholarly and academic products). Some agencies set themselves primarily functional goals (e.g., that new lexical items be maximally understandable and acceptable), while others set themselves more ideological goals (e.g., internationalization, indigenization, classicization, etc.) that relate to broader cultural and even economic and political views.

The tasks that the planners undertake and the plans and programs they entertain must be described in conjunction with the materials and information available to them concerning the language situation of the area. Some planning agencies seek to obtain basic descriptive information (requiring years of painstaking research), whereas others are primarily product-oriented. Some must be concerned with graphization (orthography-planning or revision), whereas others can draw upon well established literary traditions. Some encourage translations from other languages as well as original writing in all spheres of science and literature. Some establish committees of experts in various fields to help in the creation of nomenclatures that possess "international transfer-value," whereas others are entirely self-contained in their operations. Some aim at introducing the teaching of the mother tongue for diverse literary uses, including the development of a range of styles and registers (thus involving the subsidization of a whole literature rather than merely technological writing), whereas others are oriented only towards the professions and the communication media. Some established special translation agencies or divisions whose selection of Western or other foreign works for translation may have considerable impact on student groups and other newly literate population segments, whereas others proclaim contests and offer prizes for the best translations or research reports prepared independently of the planning agencies themselves.

Financial control.   It is clearly desirable to gather information concerning the funds available to the agencies in question, the sources (and control) of these funds, the proportions such funds represent relative to the entire resources (or other appropriate superordinate budgets) of authorizers of appropriators of funds, and the funds the agencies expect or desire for future projects and activities. How are budgets formulated? Are they program- or item-budgets, long-term or short-term? How is budget control managed? Are authorized funds invariably appropriated? Spent? Long-term budgeting by language planners should be studied in comparison with long-range planning in other areas as far as possible so that meaningful contrasts will be available.

Interest-Basis

Intra- and inter-agency processes are frequently overlooked aspects of the study of language-planning agencies. As mentioned before, the agencies themselves often include factions along technical and other lines. However, even when this is not the case, other agencies provide an inevitably complex environment for language planning in view of the interests and concerns of education, commerce, industry, military, finance, and various other legislative and executive bodies in the products produced (or scheduled to be produced) by language-planning agencies. Extra-agency relations with organized clientele groups (e.g., publishers, public-school teachers, private-school teachers, printers, radio broadcasters, pop-music and pop-literature "suppliers," manufacturers and distributors of equipment related to education, and printing and office work, etc.) must also be examined since these frequently influence the products of the agencies in question. Once again, the relations with intellectual, educational, and commercial-industrial groups probably deserve greatest attention.

Languages of Wider Communication

The relationship to Languages of Wider Communication also deserves attention in language planning. Although these languages usually do not require local elaboration and codification, they may well require contrastively designed textbooks, various supplementary and graded reading materials, bilingual dictionaries, teacher training and retraining, curricular experimentation vis-à-vis methods of instruction, particularly with respect to length and sequence of instruction relative to indigenous national (and regional) languages. Since the above topics pertaining to languages of wider communication merit extensive inquiry in their own right, it would not be feasible to look into all of them in depth in a project dealing primarily with the processes of planning indigenous languages. However, it would certainly be desirable to determine the extent to which both sets of activities are coordinated regarding policy formulation and implementation. Are they conducted by separate agencies, each of which independently seeks to influence policy and implementation, or are indigenous programs and plans (not to mention "foreign" language programs) functionally interrelated at one or more points? Very similar questions should be examined with respect to planning for indigenous languages for which a regional or other non-national role is intended, including the preservation (teaching, collection) of oral traditions where no literacy planning is contemplated.

Data

The past products of language-planning agencies, records concerning their staffs and budgets, and records pertaining to the authorization of their work can all be located via library and archival research. The bulk of the information concerning the dynamics of intra-agency, interagency, and extra-agency relations must be obtained via interviews with past and present staff members of the agencies and clientele groups involved as must most information concerning current projects, programs, plans, and purposes. Questionnaire approaches to such data do not seem particularly promising in view of the fact that what seems to be needed is in-depth information from a few crucially knowledgeable people. Where conflicting information is obtained via this method, additional clarification will be called for in order to differentiate between personal and organizational biases.

IMPLEMENTATION

Implementation refers to all efforts to gain acceptance of the policies and "products" of language planning, including grammars, spellers, word lists, and school curricula for the implementation of language-policy decisions. Implementation efforts may have local impact only upon the dissemination of new language policy "products" to their respective target (or user) populations, or their impact may begin with official measures to influence the utilization of "products" or the improved implementation of policies. In either case, formal or informal feedback may be obtained or solicited from target populations (including findings of officially sponsored research) to provide makers and language planners with information about the success of their efforts.

The entire process of implementation has been least frequently studied in prior investigations of language planning. It has remained particularly unstudied in such a way that makes it impossible to compare the effectiveness of implementation in the language-policy area with the effectiveness with which other policies are implemented.

Evaluation

The general area of implementation may be expanded to include a review of the curricular research, methodological research, material-testing research, and any other approaches, formal or informal, utilized to obtain detailed or systematic information that might be of value for the evaluation of current practice or for the improvement of future policy or practice, on the part of the language-planning agency or on the part of other authorized (executive or legislative) bodies. Evaluation may also be an ingredient in basic policy formulation (see above) and beyond particular products and practices. The basic questions to pursue in connection with evaluation are: (1) Who conducts it? (2) How good is it? and (3) Who listens to it?

Target Populations

The choice of target populations of the study is a crucial consideration in overcoming the gap in our understanding of the process of language-policy implementation. Whereas implementation efforts can be reviewed "in general," that is, without any particular target populations in mind (so that language policy as such can be more fully compared with other policies), it seems decidedly preferable not to remain merely at the level of agency-centered programmatic descriptions in this connection, particularly in view of the availability of an alternative (target populations) approach. Target populations must be selected with great care since it seems clear from much other information that huge populations in developing countries long remain substantially untouched by most of the specific "products" of language planning. Among the most feasible populations to reach and among those in which some discernible impact of language planning may be expected are the following: (1) teachers and secondary-school pupils, in two areas, one agreeing in the mother tongue and one differing in the mother tongue relative to the language (or variety) undergoing planning; (2) university staff members and students, if possible also chosen from two different language areas; (3) municipal office employees, if possible also chosen from two different language areas; (4) the employees and management of two larger industrial plants. A final target population might well be more specialized, namely, a population that is quite specific to a particular recent "product" of the language-planning agency, for example, teachers of biology if a biology word list has been produced and disseminated during the past year or two.

Topics of Study in Target Populations

The following topics might well be investigated with respect to the implementation of language planning in particular target populations.

How are "products" of language planning *disseminated* to target populations? What media, alternative channels, or agencies are involved? How are dissemination decisions reached (evidence related, experience related)?

What attempts are made to *influence or convince* target populations to adopt or use the "products" of language planning? What use is made of persuasion—positive or negative sanctions (promotions-demotions, raises-penalties, subsidies, and fellowships versus their denial, etc.)? How are decisions in this respect reached? How are counter-influences discovered and handled?

What do target populations *know* about the language-planning agencies and about their major recent "products"? How is this information obtained? Which of the media, channels, and agencies utilized by the planning agency (if any) seem to be reaching the target populations?

What are the *attitudes or preferential views* of the target populations with respect to the language-planning products in question (and, more generally, with respect to official attempts to influence usage)? If possible, both direct and indirect measures of attitude should be employed, for example, Lambert's (and, more recently, Shuy's) speech-guise approaches[3] might be utilized to determine the images that target populations have of speakers using recommended language forms versus their images of speakers not using the forms that are products of recent language planning.

The extent to which target populations *actually use* the "products" (or various recommended usages) derived from language planning is difficult to ascertain through large sample methods. Nevertheless, the measures currently being developed by Cooper (e.g., frequency estimations, usage ratings, word naming, etc.)[4] may yield excellent self-report data in this very connection. Measures of written usage are not as problematic as are spoken language measures. Both can be examined, and the influence of the one upon the other can be probed.

As with *knowledge* (see above), so also in the case of *attitudes and use*: the possibility of relationships between different patterns and levels of attitude and use and different dissemination processes should be examined.

The newly selected and newly developed national language is normally but *one* of many symbols of sociocultural and political integration at a broader and more inclusive level. Other integrative symbols (national holidays, national rituals, national dress, national food, national flag, etc.)

also depend upon a favorable balance of attitudes, cognitions, and behaviors related to the attitudes, cognitions, and behaviors that are focused
upon other symbols of national integration. What evidence exists of
counter-integration? Language policy is but one instance of national
policies. How are language attitudes, cognitions, and behaviors related
to those pertaining to other national policies?

Of course, whatever public records there may be concerning the
reaction to language planning must be tapped. If there have been debates,
protests, articles, advertisements, resolutions, or meetings in conjunction
with the release or dissemination of one or more recent "products," these
too must be located, for these too are types of feedback that planners may
accept or reject.

Data

Whereas policy formulation is primarily studied through library and
archive materials and whereas codification and elaboration processes are
best studied through interview methods, the implementation of policy
lends itself to survey methodology, particularly where specific "products"
and selected target populations are concerned. In general, it must be determined whether language-planning agencies obtain feedback on such
matters, whether it is systematic or intermittent, and whether it is utilized
to guide future planning, replanning, or implementation. Nevertheless,
as in the other major subdivisions of this proposed project, a variety of
methods should be employed in order that a complete picture may be
obtained, including, for example, relatively unstructured discussions with
physicians, university professors, university students, and the like to obtain samples of their formal and informal spoken and written language for
purposes of linguistic analysis.

APPENDIX ON ECONOMIC ANALYSIS

by Björn H. Jernudd

Some Proposals

Economic analysis of language planning could concentrate on: (1) the
estimation of costs and, so far as possible, of benefits that are attributable
to goals and consequences of factual cases of language planning; (2) costs
of the processes of language planning per se; (3) a formulation of the

array of alternatives that are (were factually) available at every point in a hierarchy of successively more specific language-planning decisions (making appropriate assumptions to render this latter task manageable and meaningful); or (4) formulating recommendations or suggestions for recurring and characteristic components of language planning in general.

Need for Exploration of Alternatives

Consequences of language-planning actions should be contrasted, in either case above, with prepolicy economic situations, ideal alternatives, and predicted consequences. Although costing per se is of considerable interest (and novelty) in the language-planning field, for example, cost-benefit analysis (or other techniques) should try to move towards improving future decision-making rather than remain entirely at the level of description, namely, to facilitate forecasting in addition to clarifying aims and available techniques. Such an approach may well require more data than may have been available to, or utilized by, the language-planning agencies themselves. However, a determination of what data such agencies at least have and of what data they do in fact use is itself essential for a correct description of the decision-making processes in which they engage and a necessary prerequisite for realistic suggestions concerning future decisions.

Need for Limiting the Study Perspective

The determination of factors relevant to language planning and the establishment of their relationships to each other will be essential in arriving at suggestions for future language-planning decisions. However, a limitation of scope of decisions to be studied (e.g., those of a particular government office concerning the next five years) means a comparatively greater accuracy in determining costs involved, because of a lesser amount of uncertainty, because of a more immediate access to historical data, etc. On the other hand, as a result of such a limitation, the more distant is this object from decisions that influence national policy, which provides a frame for a large number of other behaviors. In seeking to illuminate both "macro" and "micro" decisions, it is necessary at first to discover which language variables can at all be costed in any realistic way. This work is more fruitful if the scope of both the study and the object of study, that is, the set of decisions, is limited to start with. The more manageable variables there are in any particular setting, the easier it is, also, to evaluate residual non-quantifiable variables. Similarly, selecting a shorter time perspective reduces uncertainty and gives clarity to relevant variables but, therefore, reduces the wider applicability of the findings as well.

A Note on Quantification in Terms of Money

It must be remembered that expenditures and incomes are not equivalent to costs and benefits, although expenditure data is probably most readily available. Cost-benefit analysis also requires search for other than monetized factors alone.

Cost factors like those entailed in personnel retraining, plant reorganization or relocation, obsolescence and replacement of equipment (including textbooks and other printed materials), non-promotion of students, and non-promotion or dismissal of unretrained or unretainable personnel, as well as feelings resulting from these actions or from the primary-language decisions, also require looking into. Indeed, matters such as these might well be looked into in some developing countries, in which no language planning is underway, to shed further light upon the unique cost of language planning per se, above and beyond the costs of development more generally.

The cost of codification and elaboration is an interesting but difficult problem. Productivity-measures of agencies and analyses of work routines might be attempted first to determine which codification-elaboration alternatives appear to be most effective under simplified but common assumptions; i.e., one might seek to arrive at some *standards*.

The Linking of a Decision and Successive Consequences

A crucial prerequisite for economic analysis is an understanding of (1) the ultimate consequences for an economy of any decision and the chain of interdependencies that link the origination of an action through further specification, part-decisions, and the like to such final outcome. Relations between any two links in this chain may be studied from the point of view of (1) alternatives available at each point *and* (2) effects of a change in the one link upon the other (in either direction).[5]

The most comprehensive (exhaustive) analysis would attempt to describe and valuate the complete chain of events, which in terms of language planning means the consequences of planned language change, or normation, for a society's (economy's) entire production and sentiment. It will be necessary, in a practical study (such as the proposed study), to restrict the inquiry to some relationships only. A natural option (which has also been selected in the present case) would then be to study (1) (authorization and) internal organization of language-planning agencies *and* (2) relationships between decisions of a particular language-planning agency and language behavior (use and knowledge) in some nominated target population.

Another possibility would be to define some desired ultimate consequences in terms, for example, of productivity in a given sector of the economy, and study the effects of language-planning decisions in terms of changes in productivity.

NOTES

1. An earlier version of this Research Outline was appended to a successful application for a Ford Foundation grant. The resulting research project (Language Planning Processes Project) is directed by Dr. Joshua A. Fishman and Dr. Charles A. Ferguson and is administered by Stanford University, California.
2. Cf. Einar Haugen, *Language Conflict and Language Planning: The Case of Modern Norwegian* (Cambridge, Mass.: Harvard University Press, 1966), chapter 1.
3. Cf. e.g., W. E. Lambert, A Social Psychology of Bilingualism, *Journal of Social Issues* 23, no. 2 (April 1967): 91–109.
4. Cf. Cooper's articles *in* Joshua A. Fishman, Robert Cooper, and Roxanna Ma, *Bilingualism in the Barrio* (Office of Education, 1968).
5. Cf. both paper 12 and paper 14 in this volume.

18. A VIEW TOWARDS THE FUTURE

JOAN RUBIN
Department of Anthropology, Tulane University

The papers in this book have demonstrated that language planning shares many similarities with other kinds of planning. The processes of planning (fact-finding, policy-setting, implementation, and feedback) required for language planning are essentially the same as those required for other kinds of planning. As a result of our discussions in Hawaii, it is now clearer that language planning is possible because language is, or can at least fruitfully be considered as, a resource, and as such it does get evaluated. To the extent that language is a resource, it can be subjected to alternative goals and strategies in order to exploit it. It is a known fact that people do evaluate their own and others' language. This evaluation goes on in spite of the linguists' attempt to deny the superiority of any one language for any one purpose. However, it is also clear that this evaluation relates to social values and not to inherent linguistic characteristics. (Dell Hymes, 1961, and Einar Haugen, 1962, demonstrate the importance of such evaluations in the processes of social mobility and cultural change.) Language planners must include such evaluations in the planning process if they propose to forecast successfully the outcomes of their efforts. They must seriously consider these values when they attempt to provide motivations and opportunities for change. The *motivation* for and *rationalization* of planning are often similar to that of other kinds of planning: a desire for unification (of a region, or a nation, or a religious group, or a political group, or other kinds of groups), a desire for modernization, a desire for efficiency, or a desire for democratization as well as others. The *constraints* on language planning are also similar to those of other kinds of planning. As in all planning there are limitations to the amount of planning that can or should be achieved. There will always be many unpredictable variables that set limitations on the predictability of outcomes. There will always be vested interests that run contrary to the goals of the persons charged with planning—these will also constrain the planners. Our discussions in Hawaii merely opened the door to the consideration of the possibilities and limitations of language planning.

However, since the *object* of language planning is unique—namely, language—differences must be expected. The sequences of change will be unique to the planning object. We need to explore what the nature of these differences are. Surely they will provide some considerable information to students of language change. The limitations for changing the object of planning will also be unique. Many linguists see language as basically unplannable; language planning suggests that this is not wholly the case.

In spite of these differences, language planning may serve to highlight difficulties in planning in other areas. Attempts to change language habits may serve to reveal otherwise latent conflicts in other sociopolitical realms. Many examples can be found in modern nations; most remain undocumented. What is remarkable is that often attempts to change even the spelling of a group of people can serve as such a clear barometer of other socio-political-economic problems. On the other hand, the goals of language planning may be served when they are consistent with other planning. An example might be the results of migration for economic purposes that may lead to increased knowledge of a particular variety, something that might not be achieved by the educational process alone— at least not without considerable effort and cost.

As we indicated in the preface and the introduction to this volume, while the activity of language policy-making has been going on for a long time, the process has never been made the object of intensive study. This means that there is a considerable gap between our knowledge of planning in general and that of the language-planning process in particular. There is a need to coordinate the search for the constraints on behavior that obtain in language planning. We need to explore what the sequences of attitudes and values to language variation are.[1] We need to consider under which circumstances modernization does lead to a demand for new modes of communication. We need to study the kinds of work routines of the language-planning agency as well as the regularity of changes in the saliency of its work at various stages of its own development and the development of the nation.

Language planning is currently the concern of new nations, yet one would certainly benefit from further consideration of the similarities and differences between the development of Western or Japanese language cultivation and the present language problems that these new nations face.

Many questions have been raised by this first consideration of language planning as a process: What should be the goals of language planning concerning linguistic variables? How can we measure the costs and benefits of language planning and to what extent are these measures relevant and useful for language-planning decisions? What are the social and political constraints that a language planner can expect to face in making decisions? What can standardization theory tell us about the reasonable limits of planning?

All of these and many other questions remain—as always—for future research and thoughtful consideration. We hope that future students of sociolinguistics will consider the full range of variables that are relevant to language planning and that they will produce field data to shed light on some of the problems raised in this volume. We are hopeful that the on-going Survey of Language Use and Language Teaching in Eastern Africa and the on-going Language Survey of the Philippines will soon provide valuable information to help in our knowledge of sociolinguistic attitudes and values. In addition, the on-going field study of language-planning processes in four countries directed by Fishman and Ferguson should add considerable depth to our understanding of language planning.

The study of language planning will shed light both on the nature of the process of language change and on the nature of planning as an important and current human endeavor. Although language is the subject matter, the interdisciplinary implications of the topic are considerable. Language planning is one more kind of social change, and as such it promises to reveal much about the possibilities and limitations of the "architectural" approach to change.

ACKNOWLEDGMENT

I am pleased to acknowledge the help of my co-editor, Björn Jernudd in the writing of the paper. Although I have written the paper, it represents in fact many hours of discussion and intellectual stimulation with him. I am grateful to Björn for the generous manner in which he participated in these discussions. I am also most grateful to Joshua Fishman for providing the opportunity for such discussions.

NOTE

1. Ferguson's oral presentation dealt with this problem; unfortunately, in the rush of getting this book to press we were unable to include his contribution in this volume.

REFERENCES

Haugen, Einar. 1962. *Schizoglossia and the Linguistic Norm.* Monograph Series on Languages and Linguistics, 15. Washington, D.C.: Georgetown University Press, 63–69.
Hymes, Dell. 1961. Functions of Speech: An Evolutionary Approach. *In* Fred Gruber, ed. *Anthropology and Education.* Philadelphia: University of Pennsylvania Press.

SOME INTRODUCTORY REFERENCES
PERTAINING TO LANGUAGE PLANNING

BJÖRN H. JERNUDD
Department of Linguistics, Monash University
JOAN RUBIN
Department of Anthropology, Tulane University

This annotated list serves as a first introduction for interested readers to the study of language planning. We have attempted to cover the wide range of interests subsumed under our topic; at the same time, we have tried not to expand the reading list beyond a reasonable brevity. The entries are all in English, for the sake of convenience, but we have made an occasional reference in the text to sources in other languages. Furthermore, we have only included publications that we hope are relatively easy to obtain. The first set of publications below refers to a general theory of planned language change. We thought it necessary to add concreteness to our topic by listing a very few government reports and descriptions of language-planning agencies in operation, in section 2. Section 3 refers to discussions of language problems. The entries either account for the manner in which problems were actually solved or indicate how such problems could be solved.

1. Towards a theory of language planning

Fishman, Joshua A.; Ferguson, Charles A.; and Das Gupta, Jyotirindra, eds. 1968. *Language Problems of Developing Nations*. New York: John Wiley and Sons. 521 pp.

Several of the articles isolate and illustrate language problems and language-planning problems. Neustupný calls for the development of a general theory of language problems and language policy. Other articles discuss the motivation and rationalization behind language policies. Several typologies are included which link macro-sociolinguistic characteristics to other sociopolitical and economic features; there are suggestions regarding these casual relationships.

Haugen, Einar. 1966. Linguistics and Language Planning. *In* Bright, W., ed. *Sociolinguistics. Proceedings of the* UCLA *Sociolinguistics Conference, 1964.* Janua Linguarum, Series Maior, 20. The Hague: Mouton, 50–71.

Haugen presents a systematic account of language planning. The paper is brief and to the point. It serves as an excellent introduction to the topic. His approach is based on a decision-making theory. Haugen considers problems of language planning, kinds of decision makers, alternatives of action and their limitations, criteria for evaluation, and principles of evaluation. Cf. chapter 1 in Haugen, following.

Jespersen, Otto. 1946. *Mankind, Nation and Individual from a Linguistic Point of View.* Reprint 1964. Bloomington: Indiana University Press. 199 pp.

Jespersen states initially that the individual is not always as unconscious about language change as is sometimes assumed (chapter 2). Against a background of observations on propagation and stability of language, particularly a Standard Language, he discusses the value of linguistic unification (chapters 3 and 4). He leads on to questions of correctness of speech and individual and social control of language use (chapters 5 and 6). There are, he demonstrates, a multitude of forces controlling language, one of them being the officially sponsored "Academy." A great many (European) references on language correctness are quoted throughout chapters 1–6.

Kloss, Heinz. 1967. "Abstand" Languages and "Ausbau" Languages. *Anthropological Linguistics,* 9: 7: 29–41.

Speech varieties may be judged to constitute distinctly separate languages by the application of linguistic criteria alone (*abstand* languages) or by sociological criteria (*ausbau* languages). The latter have been reshaped by deliberate action, in order to become distinct standardized tools of literary expression. "Dialectization" is the reversal of the status of an *ausbau* language. Examples of *ausbau* activity and dialectization are given, and some generalizations offered. (For further reference, cf. Kloss, H. 1952. *Die Entwicklung Neuer Germanischer Kultursprachen von 1800 bis 1950* [The Development of New Germanic Standard Languages 1800–1950]. Schriftenreihe des Goethe-Instituts, Band 1. München: Pohl. 254 pp.).

Ray, Punya Sloka. 1963. *Language Standardization; Studies in Prescriptive Linguistics.* Janua Linguarum, Series Minor, 29. The Hague: Mouton. 159 pp.

Standardization is defined in terms of "three necessary components." These are: (1) efficiency (adaptation to a special range of
expense of human resources); (2) rationality (correspondence to
knowledge); (3) commonalty (adoption in use). Part I of the book
explains the role of these components in the theory of language standardization. Ray also discusses the operation of standardization in
terms of creation and promotion of a model for imitation. Part II exemplifies his theory, mainly by graphemic problems. Part III discusses
the value of a language and aspects of prose development.

Struglia, Erasmus J. 1965. *Standards and Specifications: Information
Sources*. Detroit: Gale Research. 187 pp.

This guide to the standardization of literature and to public and
private agencies serves here as an introduction to the wider class of
standardization activities of which language standardization can be
seen as a member. Some examples of overlapping concern of standards
associations and language-planning agencies are technical terminologies
and graphic expression.

Tauli, Valter. 1968. *Introduction to a Theory of Language Planning*.
Acta Universitatis Upsaliensis. Studia Philogiae Scandinavicae
Upsaliensia, 6. Uppsala: University of Uppsala. 227 pp.

Tauli outlines a normative theory, "which methodically investigates the ends, principles, methods and tactics" of language planning.
Such planning is defined as "the methodical activity of regulating and
improving existing languages or creating new common regional, national, or international languages." In his normative task of finding a
language ideal, the author seeks an answer to the "ideal norm" and,
in turn, to morphological, syntactical, lexical, and graphemic language
problems, basing himself on principles of clarity, economy, and aes-
thetics. There is also a brief discussion of tactics and of international auxiliary languages. The book has no separate bibliography,
but the reader may, after considerable cross-paginating, profit from an
abundance of detailed reference.

2. *Government documents and language planning agencies*

Canada. Royal Commission on Bilingualism and Biculturalism.
1965. *A Preliminary Report*. Ottawa: The Queen's Printer. 211
pp.
1967. *General Introduction, Book I: The Official Languages*.
Ottawa: The Queen's Printer. 212 pp.

1968. *Book II: Education.* Ottawa: The Queen's Printer. Pp. 350.

The 1965 report describes the views of a selected section of the population on what bilingualism ought to mean in Canada within the several public spheres. Like the Irish report (see post), this one attempts to *interpret* the law regarding public language usage; unlike it, it seeks to do so by a survey of the public. The second volume examines the public sectors to see how the two official languages are, in fact, utilized and in what proportions. It outlines measures that public authorities ought to take to assure equal status to the two official languages. The volume on education considers the linguistic and cultural needs of the official language minorities and the techniques of teaching both official languages as second languages, and it makes recommendations to the national government and the provinces about how to improve the fulfilling of these needs and the teaching of these two languages.

Dewan Bahasa dan Pustaka [The Language and Literature Agency].

1967. *A General Outline of Its First Ten-Year Progress and Achievement.* Kuala Lumpur. 44 pp.

In Malaysia, the governmental language-planning agency, Dewan Bahasa dan Pustaka, plays a major role in promoting and developing the national language, Bahasa Melayu.

This pamphlet gives a historical introduction to the agency and briefly describes its main activities under the following headings: publication, translation, research, terminology, national atlas committee, junior encyclopaedia, a science encyclopaedia, the dictionary, national language courses, the library, the Dewan's monthly magazines, the national language operation room—all projects of the agency.

Cf. Heyd, following in 3a.

The role of the Turkish Linguistic Society as an agent for language change is traced throughout the book. Cf. particularly 25ff. and 44ff.

Ireland. Commission on the Restoration of the Irish Language.

1965. *The Restoration of the Irish Language.* Dublin: Stationery Office. 181 pp.

1966. *White Paper on the Restoration of the Irish Language. Progress Report for the Period Ended March 31, 1966.* Dublin: Stationery Office. 39 pp.

1968. *White Paper on the Restoration of the Irish Language.*

Progress Report for the Period Ended March 31, 1968. Dublin: Stationery Office. 45 pp.

The 1965 document states the interpretation that a specially formed commission suggests be given to Article 8 of the Constitution, which recognizes Irish as a national language. The document sets out the government's general policy on Irish and the government's views on the Commission's recommendations. The 1966 document considers the progress made by various sectors in implementing the restoration of Irish as a general medium of communication. In the 1968 document recognition is given to the fact that little formal evaluation has been made of actual language uses, processes, and behavior.

Istilah Fizik, Hisab dan Kimia [Physics, Mathematics and Chemistry Terms]. 1968. Kuala Lumpur: Dewan Bahasa dan Pustaka. 224 pp.

This volume is an example of a list of terms produced by the terminological committees of the Malaysian Language and Literature Agency.

Noss, Richard. 1967. *Language Policy and Higher Education.* Higher Education and Development in South-East Asia, 3: 2. Paris: UNESCO and The International Association of Universities. 216 pp.

In order to analyze the implementation process, Noss examines the instruments of language policy, such as: ministries of education, public relations organizations, communications media, educational planning boards, teacher-training institutions, materials development centers, translation services, national-language development agencies, foreign and international assistance, and cultural organizations.

Scientific and Technical Translating and Other Aspects of the Language Problem. 1957. Geneva: UNESCO. 282 pp.

This is a reference to national and international organizations engaged in terminological standardization.

Cf. Tauli, above in 1.

A survey of language planning agencies is found in pp. 157–160.

3. Language Problems

3a. General References

Haugen, Einar. 1966. *Language Conflict and Language Planning:*

The Case of Modern Norwegian. Cambridge: Harvard University Press. 393 pp.

This book is a unique case study of the sociopolitical history of a national language problem. Norway's problem of creating one Norwegian language has been a major political issue since late in the last century. Haugen presents the full complexity of the emergence of *riksmål* and *nynorsk* and of the strife between their respective proponents.

Heyd, Uriel. 1954. *Language Reform in Modern Turkey.* Oriental Notes and Studies, 5. Jerusalem: Israel Oriental Society. 116 pp.

Turkish language reform and development began in the middle of the last century, but its intensity increased with the introduction of Latin script under Kemal Atatürk in 1928. The introduction and first chapter gives a short history of the interest groups of the language movement in their social context, and later chapters deal with the linguistic content of reform.

Kurman, George. 1968. *The Development of Written Estonian.* Indiana University Publications: Uralic and Altaic Series, 99. Bloomington: Indiana University Press. 120 pp.

Estonian language planning is famous through the work of one of its most active participants, J. Aavik. Kurman's chronologically organized account spans from the early beginnings of deliberate language development up to the Second World War. He divides this time period into three phases: Beginnings: From the Thirteenth through the Eighteenth Century, Including the Adoption of the Old Orthography (chapter 2); 1800 to 1905, Including the Adoption of the New Orthography (chapter 3); and Reform and Normalization: 1905 to 1937 (chapter 4). Aavik belongs to this last phase. The book contains considerable linguistic detail.

3b. Speech Variety

Fishman, Joshua A., ed. 1968. *Readings in the Sociology of Language.* The Hague: Mouton. The following articles: Deutsch, Karl W. The Trend of European Nationalism—The Language Aspect, 598–606. Original in *American Political Science Review*, 1942, 36: 533–541.

—Guxman, M. M. Some General Regularities in the Formation and Development of National Languages, 766–779. Original in Guxman, M. M., ed. 1960. *Voprosy Formirovanija i*

Razvitija Nacional'nyx Jazykov [Formation and Development of National Languages]. Moscow, 295–307.

—Jakobson, R. The Beginning of National Self-Determination in Europe, 585–597. Original in *The Review of Politics,* 1945, 7: 29–42.

—Leopold, W. The Decline of German Dialects, 340–364. Original in *Word,* 1959, 15: 130–153.

Jakobson, Deutsch, and Guxman deal with national(istic) motives for language development, usually in terms of defining a vernacular speech variety for use in new functions previously expressed by a non-native variety. (Fishman, in this volume, develops our knowledge of this correlation into greater depth). Leopold's article on German speech variation focuses on individual language adjustment in response to changes (here mainly migration) in a linguistic environment. The other articles devote more attention (also with German examples) to conscious normalization and systematic propagation of language as unifying factors.

Friedrich, Paul. 1962. Language and Politics in India. *Daedalus,* 91: 3: 543–559.

Isolates some of the variables (social, demographic, linguistic, economic, logistic) that might be affecting the successful implementation of the Indian language policy. Does not indicate the extent to which the decision makers were aware of these variables or the weight they assigned them in their establishment of a language policy for India.

Macnamara, John. 1966. *Bilingualism and Primary Education.* Edinburgh: Edinburgh University Press. 173 pp.

A carefully organized investigation that provides evidence for judging the economic costs and educational attainments (which might be put in monetary terms) of teaching subject matter through a second language, in this case Irish in Ireland.

Cf. Noss, above in 2.

Noss examines the problems inherent in implementing language policy in higher education in several countries in Southeast Asia. For each country, he considers the national language policy as given—mainly concerning whole speech varieties—and then analyzes the ways in which these policies have been implemented. Particularly, Noss (1) identifies inconsistencies between goals and strategies within each country; (2) isolates some universal cost factors of implementation; and (3) shows how some solutions are more costly, given certain circumstances.

Spencer, John, ed. 1963. *Language in Africa*. Papers of the Leverhulme Conference on "Universities and the Language Problems of Tropical Africa" held at University College, Ibadan, in December, 1964. Cambridge: Cambridge University Press. 167 pp.

The working party report of this conference includes a very useful chapter entitled "Choice of a National Language: Factors and Consequences," 129–135. Contributed papers principally consider the choice of language in education and for wider communication.

UNESCO. 1953. *The Use of Vernacular Languages in Education*. Monographs on Fundamental Education, 8. Paris: UNESCO. 156 pp.

Discussion of the *universal* reasons why education should, if at all possible, be provided in the Mother Tongue. Isolates some of the relevant variables that constrain implementation of such recommendation, as well as some of the logistic problems that must be considered in the implementation process. Includes case studies indicating: (1) the value of the use of MT in education— Mexico, Philippines; (2) the difficulties of deciding on a variety for education—New Guinea; (3) the further need to develop the variety from a lexical, grammatical, or graphic point of view regardless of whether it be used in education—Indonesia, Finno-Ugric languages, Akan dialects, and Arabic dialects.

3c. Discourse

International Organization for Standardization (ISO). 1953. *International Code for the Abbreviation of Titles of Periodicals*. ISO/R4. 4 pp.

Provides rules for abbreviating in a consistent way the names of periodicals referred to in articles or other contributions, abstracts, bibliographies, etc.

Style Manual for Authors and Printers of Australian Government Publications. 1966. Canberra: Commonwealth Government Printing Office. 265 pp. *and* University of Chicago Press. 1964. *A Manual of Style*, containing typographical and other rules for authors, printers, and publishers that are recommended by the University of Chicago Press, together with specimens of type. Chicago and London: University of Chicago Press. (First published 1906). 534 pp.

The flora of style manuals is an example of the speech community's need for guidance in language use. Spelling, abbreviation, and capitalization are regulated; forms of letter-writing are presented. Brevity of style is explained. Sentence structures may be specified in some manuals, as well as usage of specific morphemes (like English *shall/will*). In the Australian manual, syntactic phenomena like sentence-linking and the use of copula are discussed. Etiquette manuals and dictionaries also belong to this class of publications on language correctness.

3d. Vocabulary

Del Rosario, Gonsalo. 1968. A Modernization-Standardization Plan for the Austronesian-derived National Languages of Southeast Asia. *Asian Studies*, 6: 1: 1–18.

Discusses three possible sources for scientific vocabulary creation: from within a language, consistency with related regional languages, or borrowing from world language. Del Rosario suggests that the first source will probably lead to faster learning of science by elementary-school children, although the second would also be acceptable to him. The third source, he suggests, should probably be limited to a very small number of scientific names; national languages should not rely heavily on the vocabulary of the Languages of Wider Communication because this impedes their function.

Garvin, Paul L. 1959. The Standard Language Problem—Concepts and Methods. *Anthropological Linguistics*, 1: 3: 28–31. Reprint 1964 *in* Dell Hymes, ed. *Language in Culture and Society*. Harper and Row, 521–526.

Suggests three sets of criteria with which to measure degree of standardization: (1) intrinsic properties of the language (flexible stability and intellectualization); (2) functions (unifying, separatist, prestige, and frame-of-reference); and (3) attitudes (language loyalty, pride and awareness of norm). The author indicates that flexible stability and intellectualization are focused largely on vocabulary and style.

Havránek, Bohuslav. 1964. The Functional Differentiation of the

Standard Language. *In* Paul L. Garvin, ed. *A Prague School Reader on Esthetics, Literary Structure, and Style.* Washington, D.C.: Georgetown University Press, 3–16. (Original in B. Havránek and M. Weingart, eds. 1932. *Spisovná čestina a jazyková kultura* [Literary Czech and the Cultivation of Language]. Prague, 41–70.)

Using a scheme of functional differentiation of a standard language, Havránek classifies vocabulary according to the relation between the lexical units and their referents (whether the relation is free, definite by convention [terms], accurate [concepts], etc). Havránek also indicates other linguistic consequences of different purposes of utterances.

Householder, Fred W. and Saporta, Sol, eds. 1962. *Problems in Lexicography. International Journal of American Linguistics,* 28: 2. The following articles:

—Barnhart, C. L. Problems of Editing Commercial Monolingual Dictionaries, 161–181.

—Tietze, Andreas. Problems of Turkish Lexicography, 263–275.

Some of the problems discussed by these two authors are the same as those facing other language planners. Both authors isolate as a problem the status of levels of usage (slang, "substandard" forms, regional vernaculars). Tietze outlines some of the social, cultural, and historical variables that impinge on a lexicographer's task (i.e., status of borrowings and new creations). Barnhart discusses other problems, such as normative spelling, pronunciation, and the treatment of cross-national usage.

Wüster, E. 1955. *A Bibliography of Monolingual Scientific and Technical Glossaries.* Paris: UNESCO.

This bibliography is essentially a catalog of lists of technical terms. Within each subject group, the glossaries are arranged in alphabetical order under the language to which they belong. It contains references to international efforts of terminological standardization and names of standardizing bodies that issue the glossaries listed. (Cf. also his *Internationale Sprachnormung in der Technik* [International Standardization of Technical Language]. Bonn. 1966.)

3e. Phonetics

Denes, Peter B. and Pinson, Elliot N. 1963. *The Speech Chain: The*

Physics and Biology of Spoken Language. Bell Telephone Laboratories. 166 pp.

The last two chapters (8 and 9) introduce the reader to some of the future improvements of communication that may result from a better understanding of speech. The use of communication machines requires human adjustment (cf. necessary discipline of writing when filling in, for example, some bank documents)—but at the same time a judgment has to be made about the relative advantage of improving the machine rather than regulating the speaker. We all know what the telephone does to us!

Morag, Shelomo. 1959. Planned and Unplanned Development in Modern Hebrew. *Lingua*, 8: 3: 247–263.

Describes planned versus unplanned development in Modern Hebrew of aspects of phonology, morphology, and vocabulary. Phonology—here the problem of "correct" or standard pronunciation—is found to be the least responsive to planning, despite vigorous discussion.

Prator, Clifford H. 1968. The British Heresy in TESL. *In* J. A. Fishman; C. A. Ferguson; and J. Das Gupta, eds. *Language Problems of Developing Nations.* New York: John Wiley and Sons, 459–476.

Prator discusses second-language varieties of English and their legitimacy as instructional models. His examples are phonological.

3f. Writing

Berry, Jack. 1968. The Making of Alphabets. *In* Joshua A. Fishman, ed. *Readings in the Sociology of Language.* The Hague: Mouton, 737–753.

Berry recognizes that "the problems of alphabet-making are problems of conflicting principles, aims, and needs." Among the principles operative and often in conflict in the process to which the author points are: linguistic, psychological, pedagogical, and typographical.

DeFrancis, John F. 1950. *Nationalism and Language Reform in China.* Princeton: Princeton University Press. 306 pp.

Discusses the history of interest in, and promotion of, an alphabetic script for Chinese from both the linguistic as well as the social point of view. Considers the relation between: attitudes toward social change and attitudes toward linguistic reform; goals of nationalist movements and acceptance of script reform; desire for universal literacy; willingness to pay for reform and acceptance of script reform.

Fasold, Ralph W. 1969. Orthography in Reading Materials for Black English Speaking Children. *In* Joan C. Baratz and Roger W. Shuy, eds. *Teaching Black Children to Read.* Washington, D.C.: Center for Applied Linguistics, 68–91.

Black English is a societal language problem in the United States of considerable concern to the government. Some of the reasons for the lack of success in implementing "proper" English usage in Black communities are high-lighted in Fasold's article. Drawing from advances in linguistic theory, he suggests that a change in spelling is necessary to teach reading without undue wastage. His suggestion reads: "the alphabetic symbols represent segments which are fully specified in accordance with the redundancy conditions on the structure of English morphemes, but not for any features determined by the phonological rules proper." This view is based on Chomsky and Halle's treatment of *The Sound Pattern of English*, 1968, and opposes a phoneme basis for spelling design.

Garvin, Paul L. 1954. Literacy as a Problem in Language and Culture. *In* Hugo J. Miller, ed. *Report on the Fifth Annual Round Table Meeting on Linguistics and Language Teaching.* Washington, D.C.: Georgetown University Press, 117–129.

Recognizes some of the sociopolitical factors that constrain the construction of and acceptance of an adequate orthography for a standard language. Suggests that the devising of an acceptable spelling system is not purely a linguistic matter but must "be tempered by a consideration of cultural attitudes, traditions, and even prejudices . . . ."

Sjoberg, Andrée F. 1966. Socio-Cultural and Linguistic Factors in the Development of Writing Systems for Preliterate Peoples. *In* William Bright, ed. *Sociolinguistics. Proceedings of the UCLA Sociolinguistics Conference, 1964.* Janua Linguarum, Series Maior, 20. The Hague: Mouton, 260–276.

Suggests some of the sociocultural variables that affect the creation and implementation of orthographies. Among these are: the orientation of the group to the larger society (whether the region, the nation, or a former colonial power) and its writing system, the history of writing systems in the area, and the extent to which the writing system must cover several divergent dialects.

Smalley, William. *et. al.* 1964. *Orthography Studies. Articles on New Writing Systems.* United Bible Societies, London. Amsterdam: North-Holland Publishing. 173 pp.

The articles consider procedures and problems of providing orthographies for hitherto unwritten languages. The articles by Smalley and Nida contain general discussions about linguistic and sociopolitical factors that must be weighed together before providing a new writing system. The phonemic principle is given as the prime linguistic criterion for a new system, but other possibilities, such as morphophonemic and syllabic spellings, are taken into account as well. Cultural and technological conditions often limit the range of choice of spellings. Other articles review cases of orthography development.

INDEX

abbreviations, for titles of periodicals, 318

"Abstand" Languages and "Ausbau" Languages (Kloss), 312

Academia ng Wikang Filipino, 129

Academy for the Hebrew Language, 100, 102–4, 107–8; low rate of attendance at plenary meetings, 119; 1962 Committee for spelling, 108–10, 119; 1964 Committee for spelling, 110–11; 1967 Committee for spelling, 111–12, 114

Academy for the Hebrew Language. Permanent Committee for Grammar, 119

Acheh, 180

administration, and choice of a national language, 260–61

adolescents: and language change, 287; questionnaire, 132

advertising, 79, 175

affixes: in Indonesian languages, 184–85; in the Turkish language, 168–69

Africa, 9; censuses in, 142; colonies in, 7, 13, 141, 143; Jews from, 95; language policies in, 141–42, 318

African Languages and English in Education (UNESCO), 223

Agbayani, A. F., 128–29

agencies, 296–97, 301, 303, 305, 308, 313, 315; extra-agency relations, 298; factions, 296, 298; financial control of, 297; government, 210–11, 269, 296, 313; operations, 296–97; personnel, 296

Aguilar, Jose V., 125

aims. *See* goals

Akan dialects, 318

Alderson, W. and Halbert, M. H., xvii

Aligarh movement, 61 *n*

Alisjahbana, S. Takdir, xiv, xv, xvii, xxi

alphabets, 164, 321–22

alternatives, and planning, 199, 222–24, 255–65, 294–95, 303–5, 307, 312

Amárach (Irish periodical), 82

America, 21; black revolution in, 36; colonies in, 7; Jews from, 95; Negroes in, 40; language problems in, 322

American College Dictionary, 282

American Commission on Conditions in Ireland, 87 *n*

Amharic, 228, 240–41

Anatolian Turkish, 162

"Anatolian Turkism," 161

Andhra Pradesh, 59

Anglo-Irish literary movement, 66